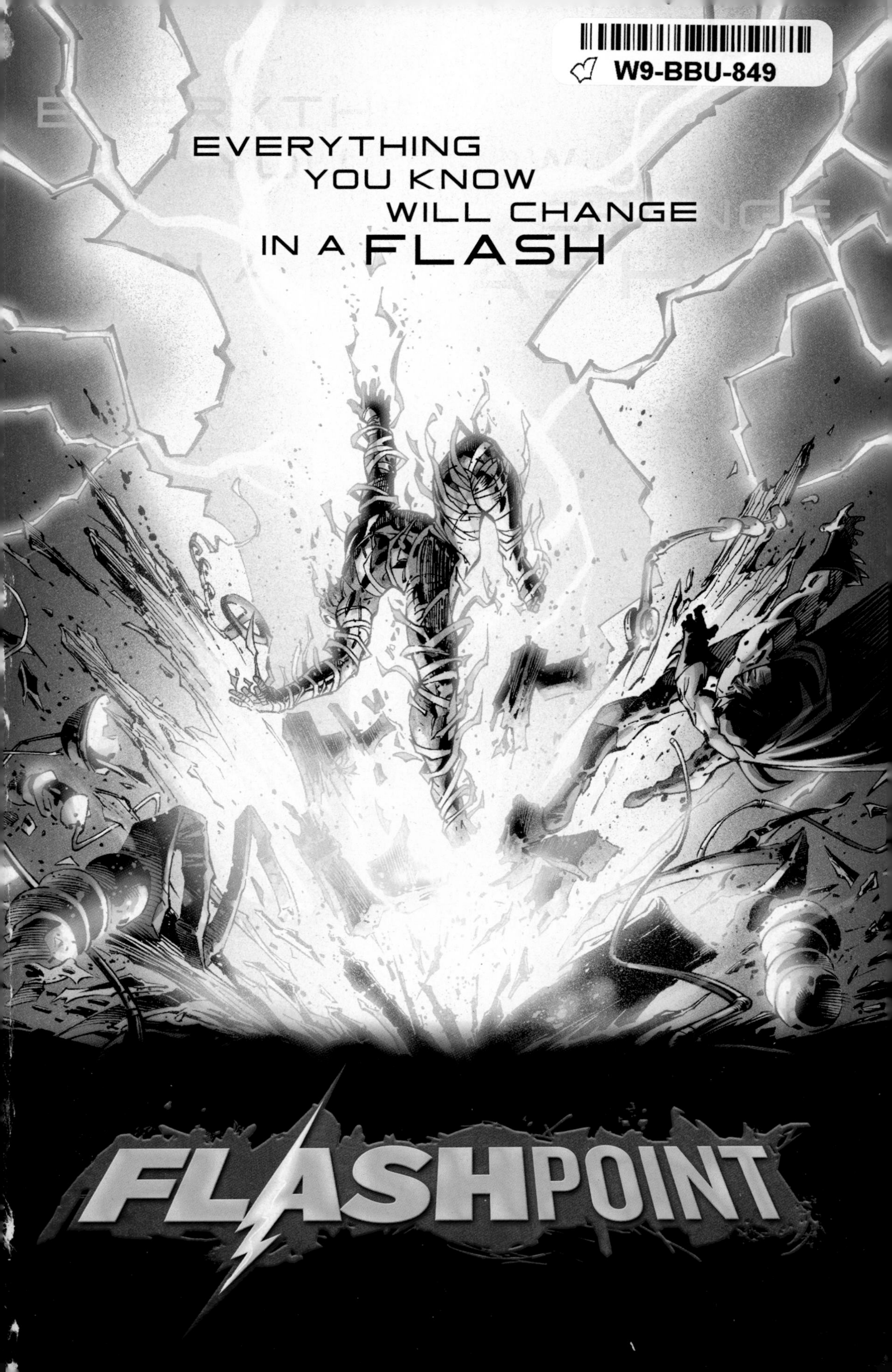
EVERYTHING
YOU KNOW
WILL CHANGE
IN A FLASH
FLASHPOINT

GEOFF JOHNS
WRITER

ANDY KUBERT
PENCILLER

SANDRA HOPE
JESSE DELPERDANG
INKERS

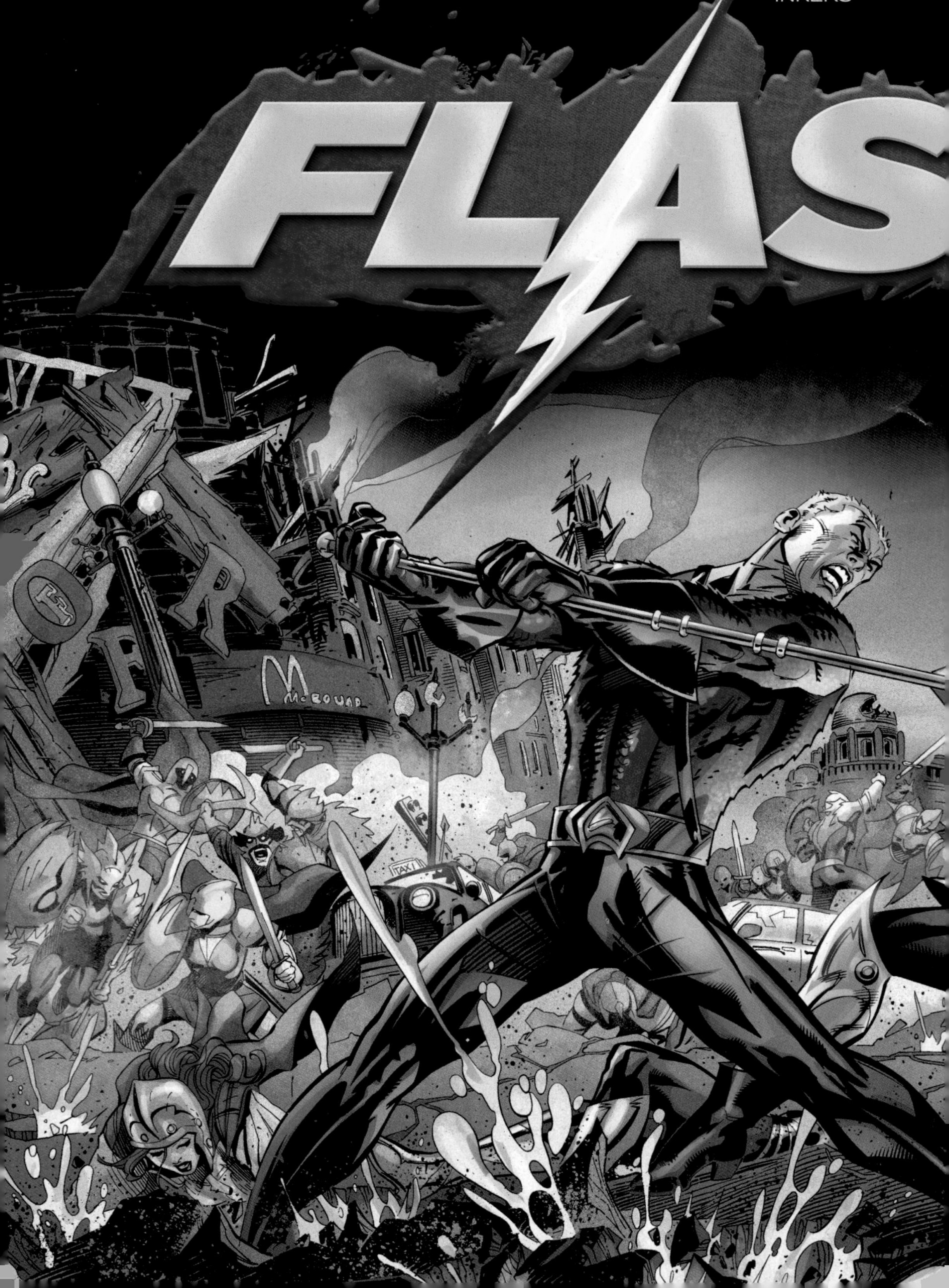
FLAS
TAXI

ALEX SINCLAIR
COLORIST

NICK J. NAPOLITANO
LETTERER

KUBERT, HOPE & SINCLAIR
ORIGINAL SERIES AND COLLECTION COVERS

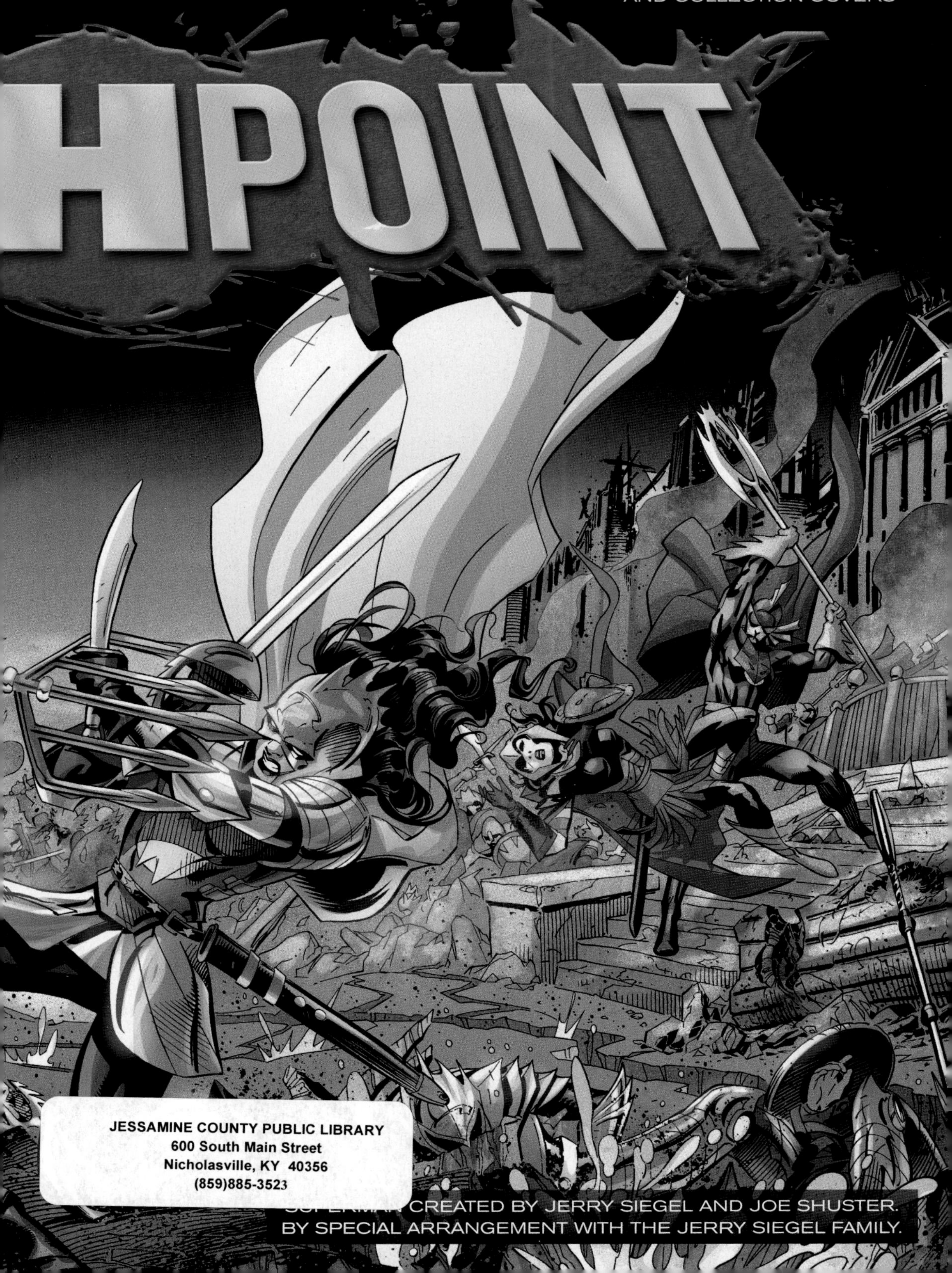
HPOINT

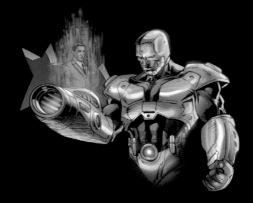

EDDIE BERGANZA
Editor – Original Series

REX OGLE
ADAM SCHLAGMAN
Associate Editors – Original Series

KATE STEWART
Assistant Editor – Original Series

JEB WOODARD
Group Editor – Collected Editions

STEVE COOK
Design Director – Books

BRAINCHILD STUDIOS/NYC
Publication Design

BOB HARRAS
Senior VP – Editor-in-Chief, DC Comics

PAT McCALLUM
Executive Editor, DC Comics

DIANE NELSON
President

DAN DiDIO
Publisher

JIM LEE
Publisher

GEOFF JOHNS
President & Chief Creative Officer

AMIT DESAI
Executive VP – Business & Marketing Strategy, Direct to Consumer & Global Franchise Management

SAM ADES
Senior VP & General Manager, Digital Services

BOBBIE CHASE
VP & Executive Editor, Young Reader & Talent Development

MARK CHIARELLO
Senior VP – Art, Design & Collected Editions

JOHN CUNNINGHAM
Senior VP – Sales & Trade Marketing

ANNE DePIES
Senior VP – Business Strategy, Finance & Administration

DON FALLETTI
VP – Manufacturing Operations

LAWRENCE GANEM
VP – Editorial Administration & Talent Relations

ALISON GILL
Senior VP – Manufacturing & Operations

HANK KANALZ
Senior VP – Editorial Strategy & Administration

JAY KOGAN
VP – Legal Affairs

JACK MAHAN
VP – Business Affairs

NICK J. NAPOLITANO
VP – Manufacturing Administration

EDDIE SCANNELL
VP – Consumer Marketing

COURTNEY SIMMONS
Senior VP – Publicity & Communications

JIM (SKI) SOKOLOWSKI
VP – Comic Book Specialty Sales & Trade Marketing

NANCY SPEARS
VP – Mass, Book, Digital Sales & Trade Marketing

MICHELE R. WELLS
VP – Content Strategy

FLASHPOINT

Published by DC Comics. Cover and compilation Copyright © 2011 DC Comics. All Rights Reserved.
Originally published in single magazine form in FLASHPOINT 1-5 © 2011 DC Comics.
All Rights Reserved. All characters, their distinctive likenesses and related elements featured
in this publication are trademarks of DC Comics. The stories, characters and incidents featured
in this publication are entirely fictional. DC Comics does not read or accept
unsolicited submissions of ideas, stories or artwork.

DC Comics, 2900 W. Alameda Avenue, Burbank, CA 91505
Printed by Transcontinental Interglobe, Beauceville, QC, Canada. 3/23/18. Eighth Printing.
ISBN: 978-1-4012-3338-9

Library of Congress Cataloging-in-Publication Data

Johns, Geoff, author.
Flashpoint/ Geoff Johns, Andy Kubert.
pages cm
"Originally published in single magazine form as Flashpoint #1-5"–Tp verso.
ISBN 9781401233389
1. Graphic novels. I. Kubert, Andy illustrator. II. Title.
PN6728.F53 J78 2011
741.5'973–dc23

2012450062

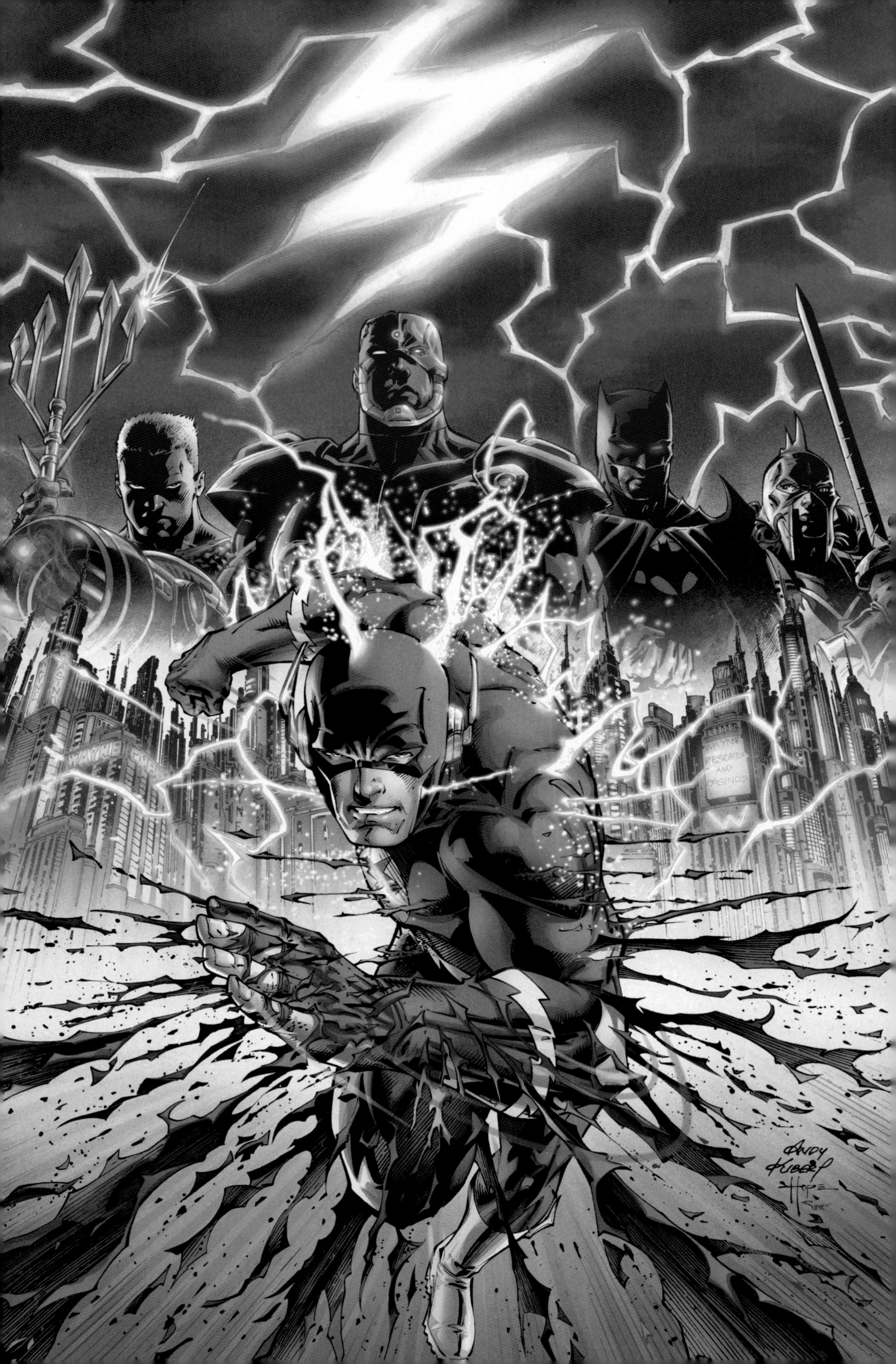
WAYNE
RESORTS AND CASINOS
ANDY KUBERT

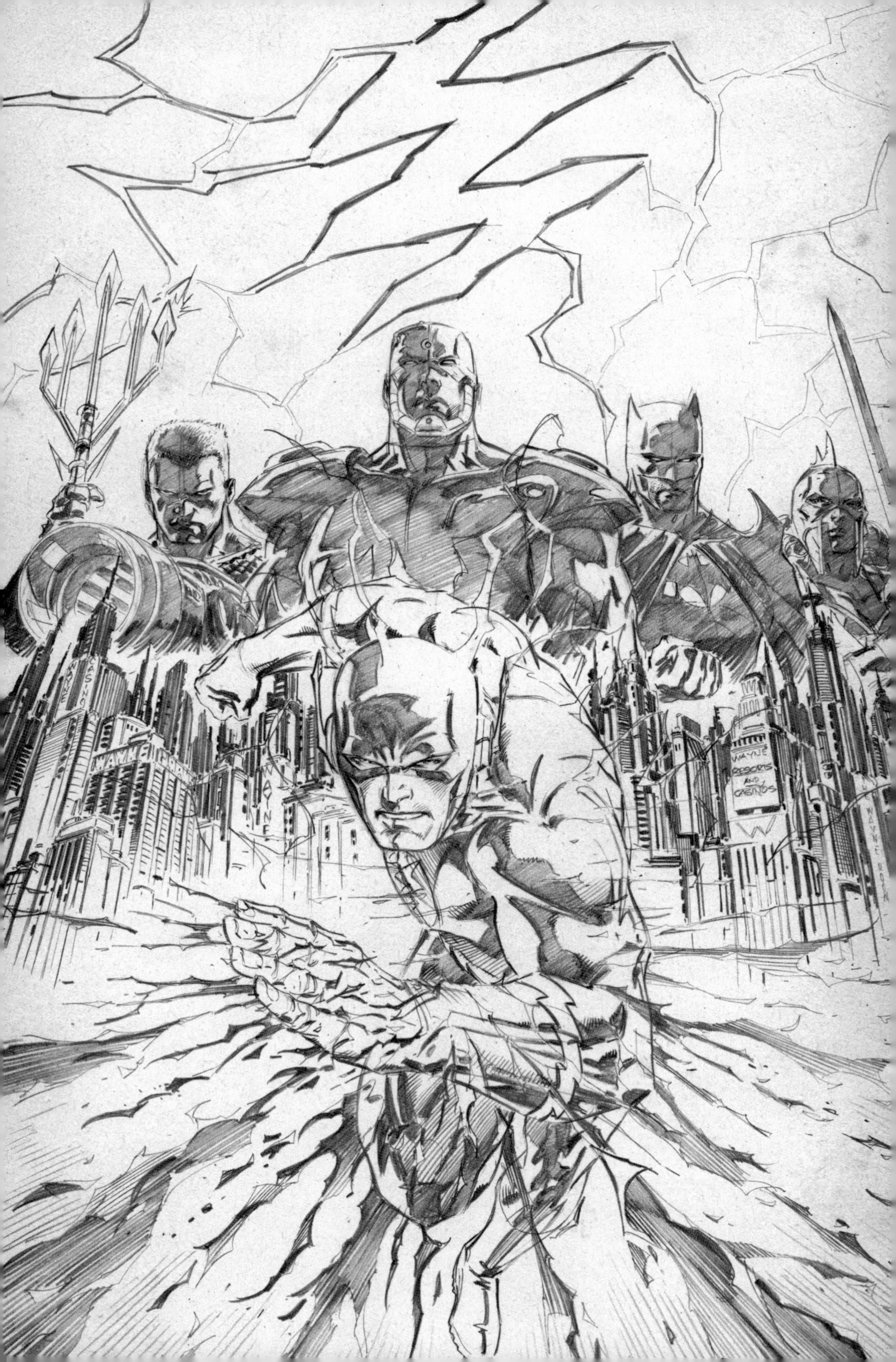
WAYNE
RESORTS AND CASINOS
WAYNE

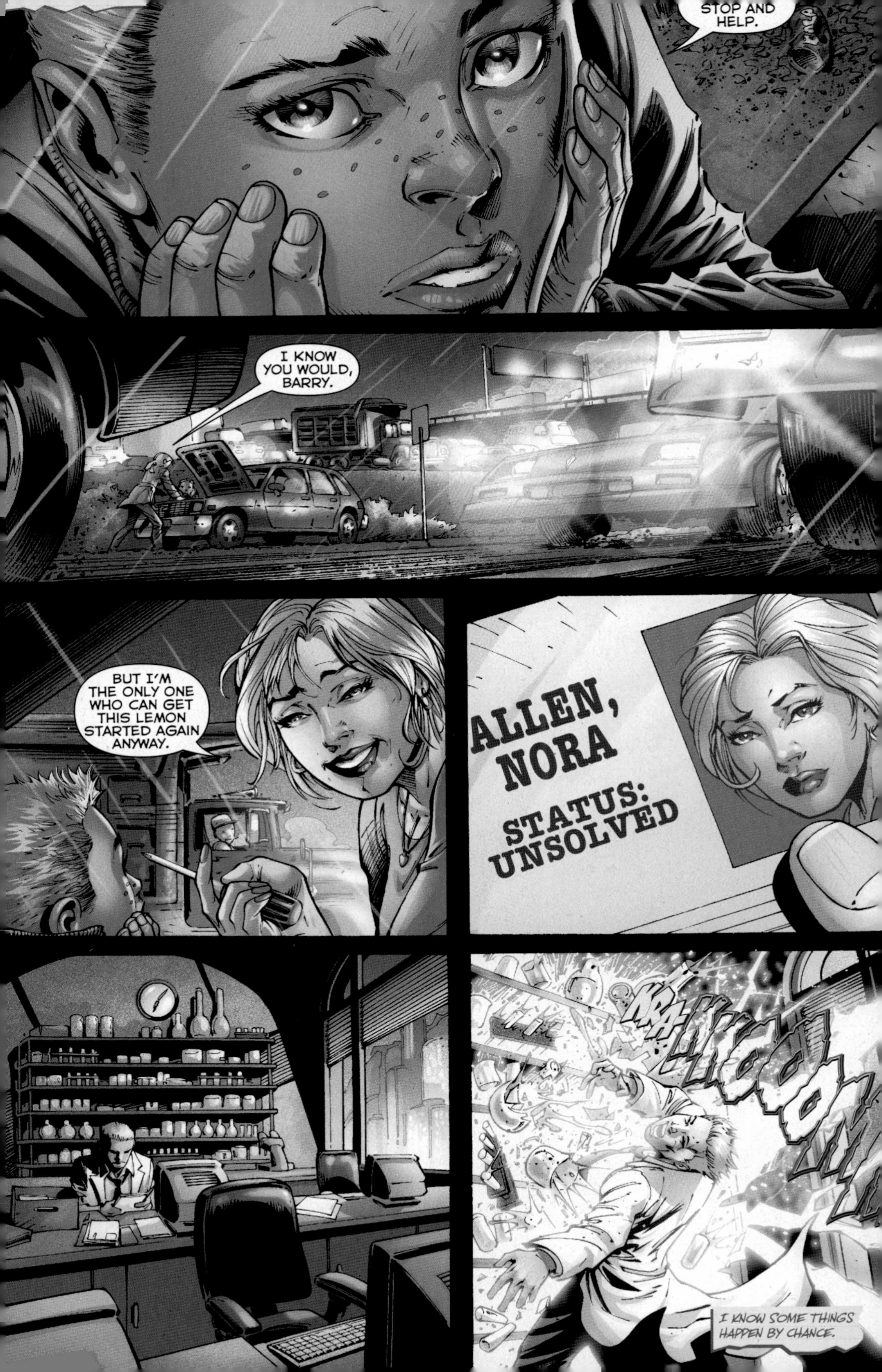
STOP AND HELP.
I KNOW YOU WOULD, BARRY.
BUT I'M THE ONLY ONE WHO CAN GET THIS LEMON STARTED AGAIN ANYWAY.
ALLEN, NORA
STATUS: UNSOLVED
KRA
I KNOW SOME THINGS HAPPEN BY CHANCE.

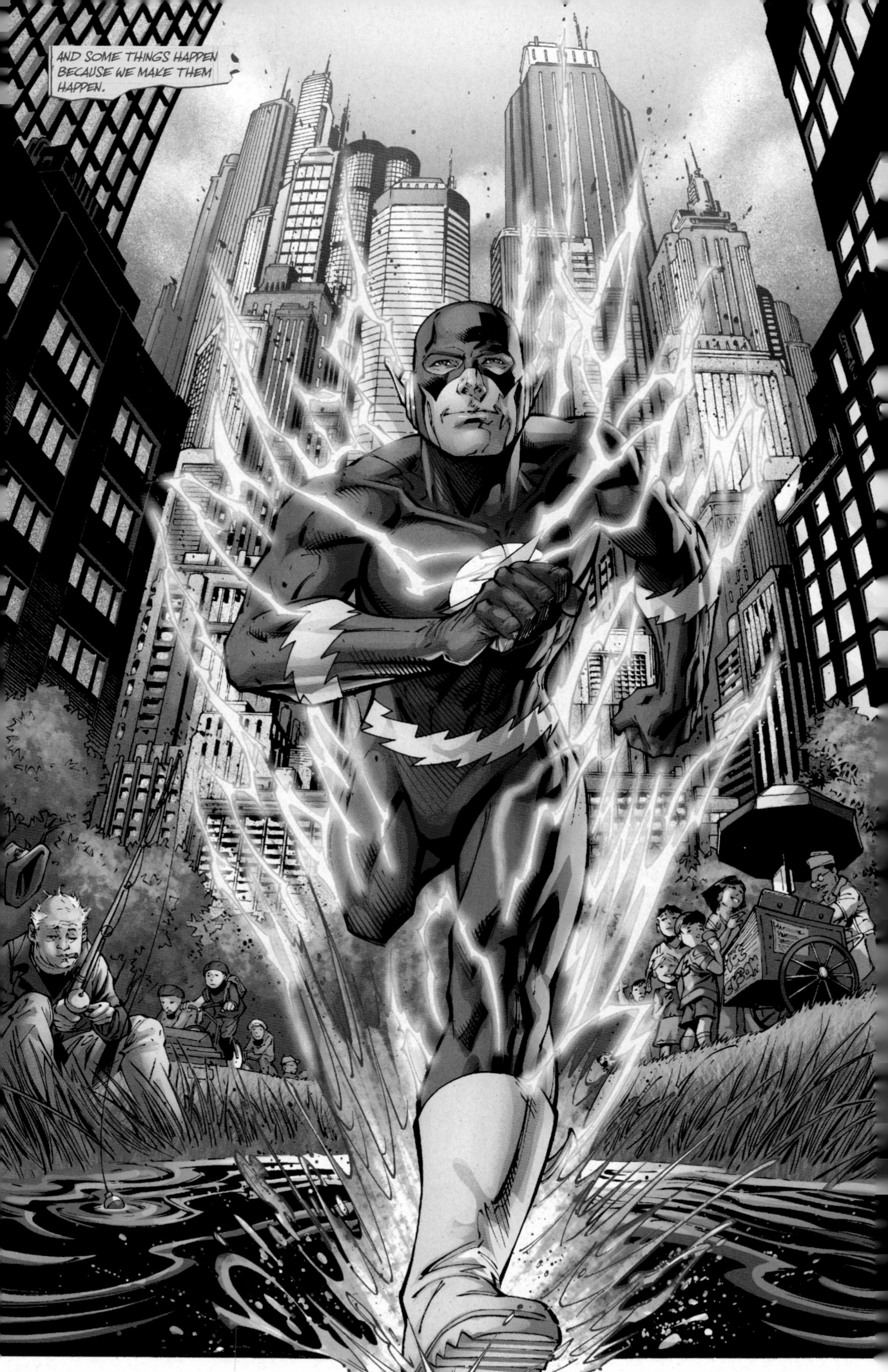
AND SOME THINGS HAPPEN BECAUSE WE MAKE THEM HAPPEN.

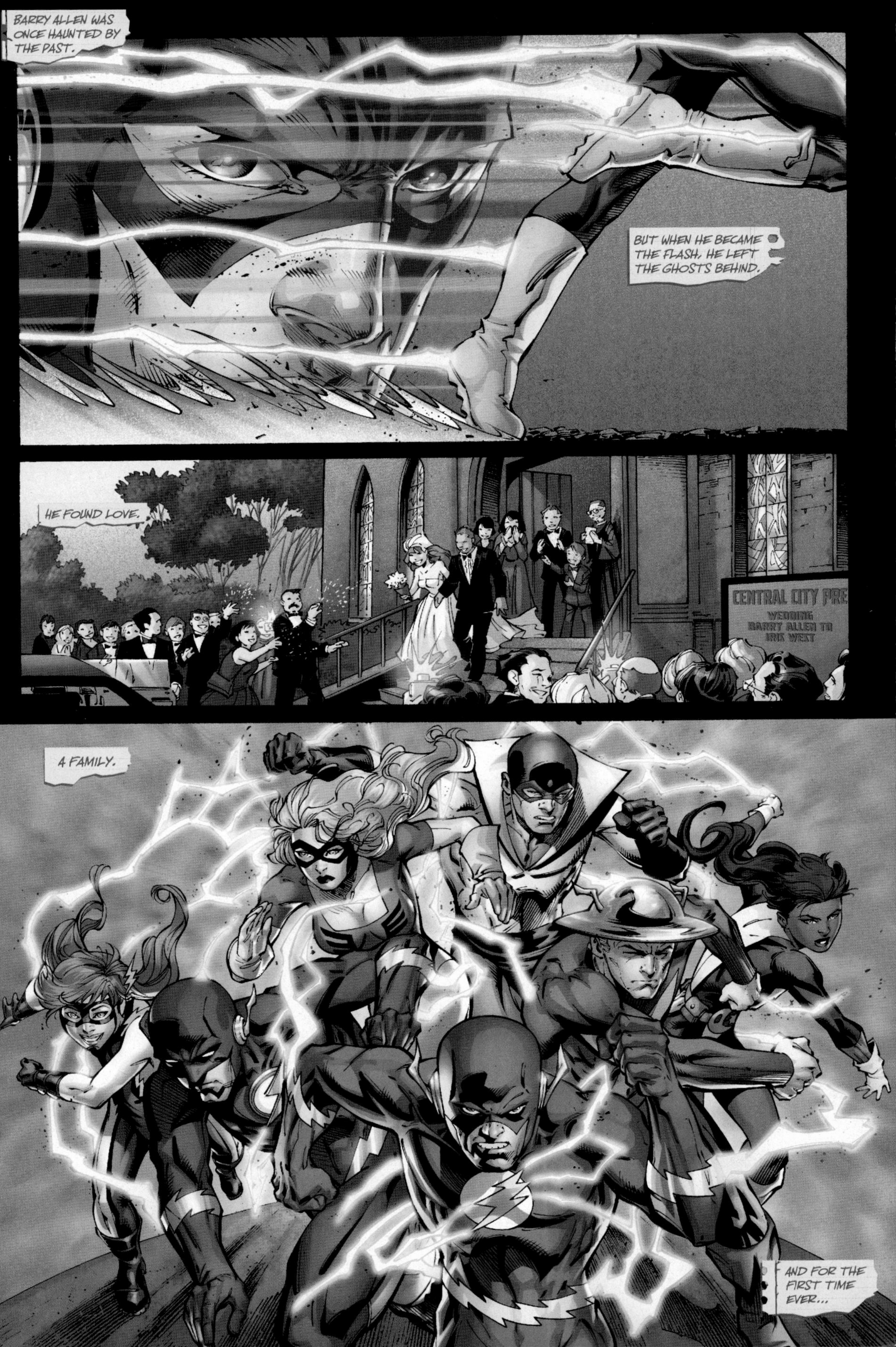
BARRY ALLEN WAS ONCE HAUNTED BY THE PAST.
BUT WHEN HE BECAME THE FLASH, HE LEFT THE GHOSTS BEHIND.
HE FOUND LOVE.
CENTRAL CITY PRE
WEDDING BARRY ALLEN TO IRIS WEST
A FAMILY.
AND FOR THE FIRST TIME EVER...

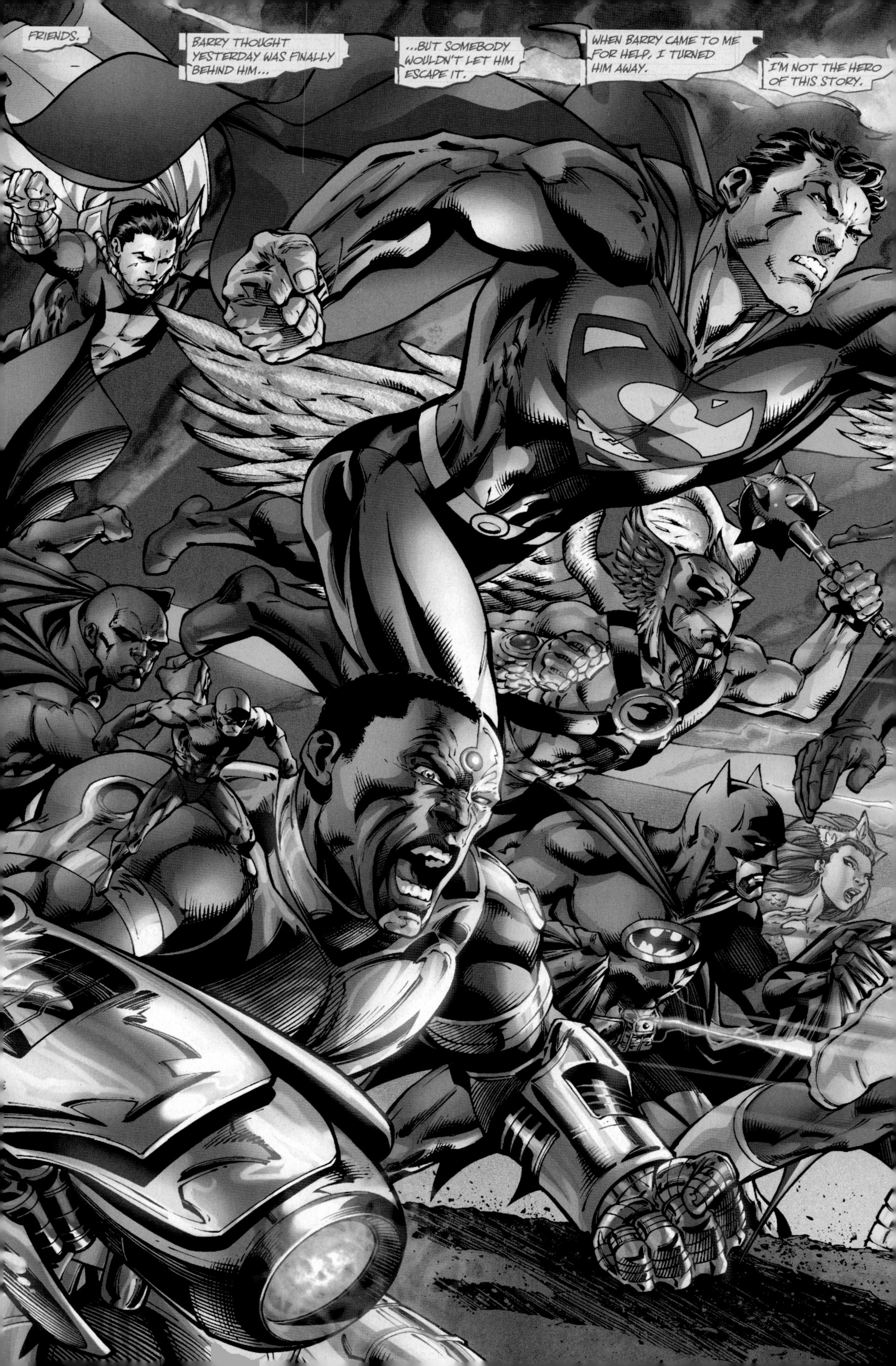
FRIENDS.
BARRY THOUGHT YESTERDAY WAS FINALLY BEHIND HIM...
...BUT SOMEBODY WOULDN'T LET HIM ESCAPE IT.
WHEN BARRY CAME TO ME FOR HELP, I TURNED HIM AWAY.
I'M NOT THE HERO OF THIS STORY.

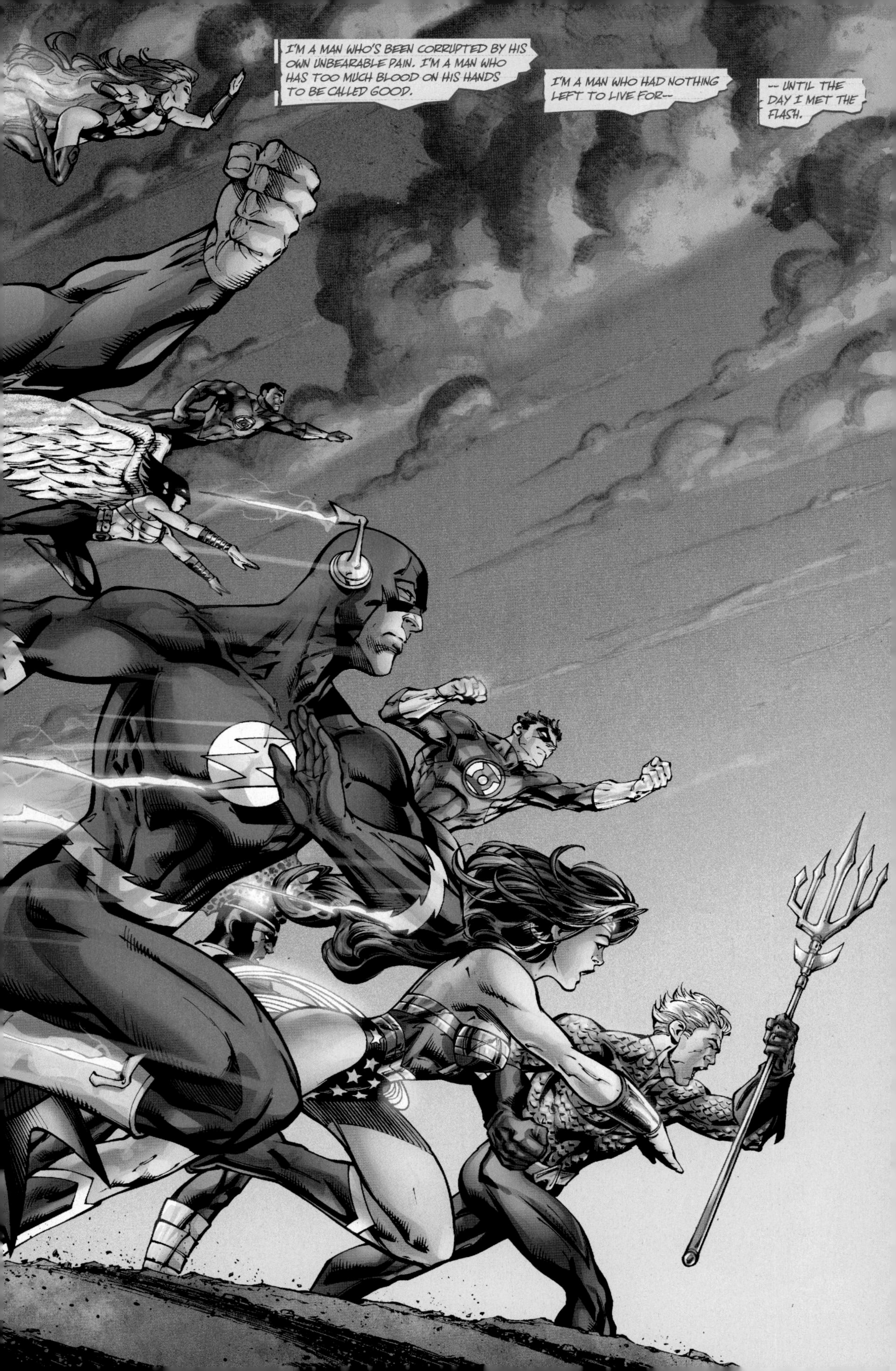
I'M A MAN WHO'S BEEN CORRUPTED BY HIS OWN UNBEARABLE PAIN. I'M A MAN WHO HAS TOO MUCH BLOOD ON HIS HANDS TO BE CALLED GOOD.
I'M A MAN WHO HAD NOTHING LEFT TO LIVE FOR--
-- UNTIL THE DAY I MET THE FLASH.

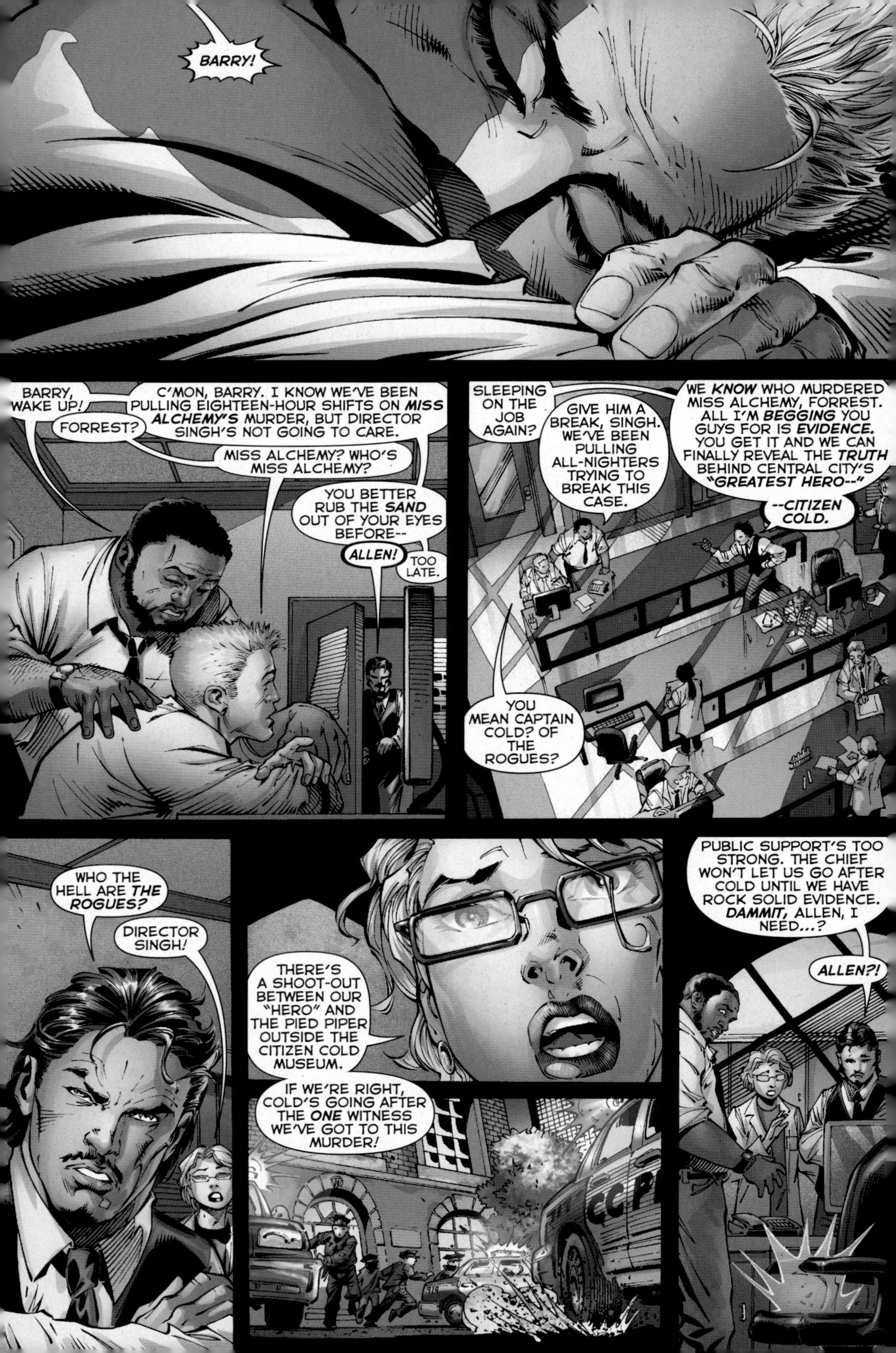
BARRY!
BARRY, WAKE UP!
C'MON, BARRY. I KNOW WE'VE BEEN PULLING EIGHTEEN-HOUR SHIFTS ON MISS ALCHEMY'S MURDER, BUT DIRECTOR SINGH'S NOT GOING TO CARE.
FORREST?
MISS ALCHEMY? WHO'S MISS ALCHEMY?
YOU BETTER RUB THE SAND OUT OF YOUR EYES BEFORE--
ALLEN!
TOO LATE.
SLEEPING ON THE JOB AGAIN?
GIVE HIM A BREAK, SINGH. WE'VE BEEN PULLING ALL-NIGHTERS TRYING TO BREAK THIS CASE.
WE KNOW WHO MURDERED MISS ALCHEMY, FORREST. ALL I'M BEGGING YOU GUYS FOR IS EVIDENCE. YOU GET IT AND WE CAN FINALLY REVEAL THE TRUTH BEHIND CENTRAL CITY'S "GREATEST HERO--"
--CITIZEN COLD.
YOU MEAN CAPTAIN COLD? OF THE ROGUES?
WHO THE HELL ARE THE ROGUES?
DIRECTOR SINGH!
THERE'S A SHOOT-OUT BETWEEN OUR "HERO" AND THE PIED PIPER OUTSIDE THE CITIZEN COLD MUSEUM.
IF WE'RE RIGHT, COLD'S GOING AFTER THE ONE WITNESS WE'VE GOT TO THIS MURDER!
PUBLIC SUPPORT'S TOO STRONG. THE CHIEF WON'T LET US GO AFTER COLD UNTIL WE HAVE ROCK SOLID EVIDENCE. DAMMIT, ALLEN, I NEED...?
ALLEN?!

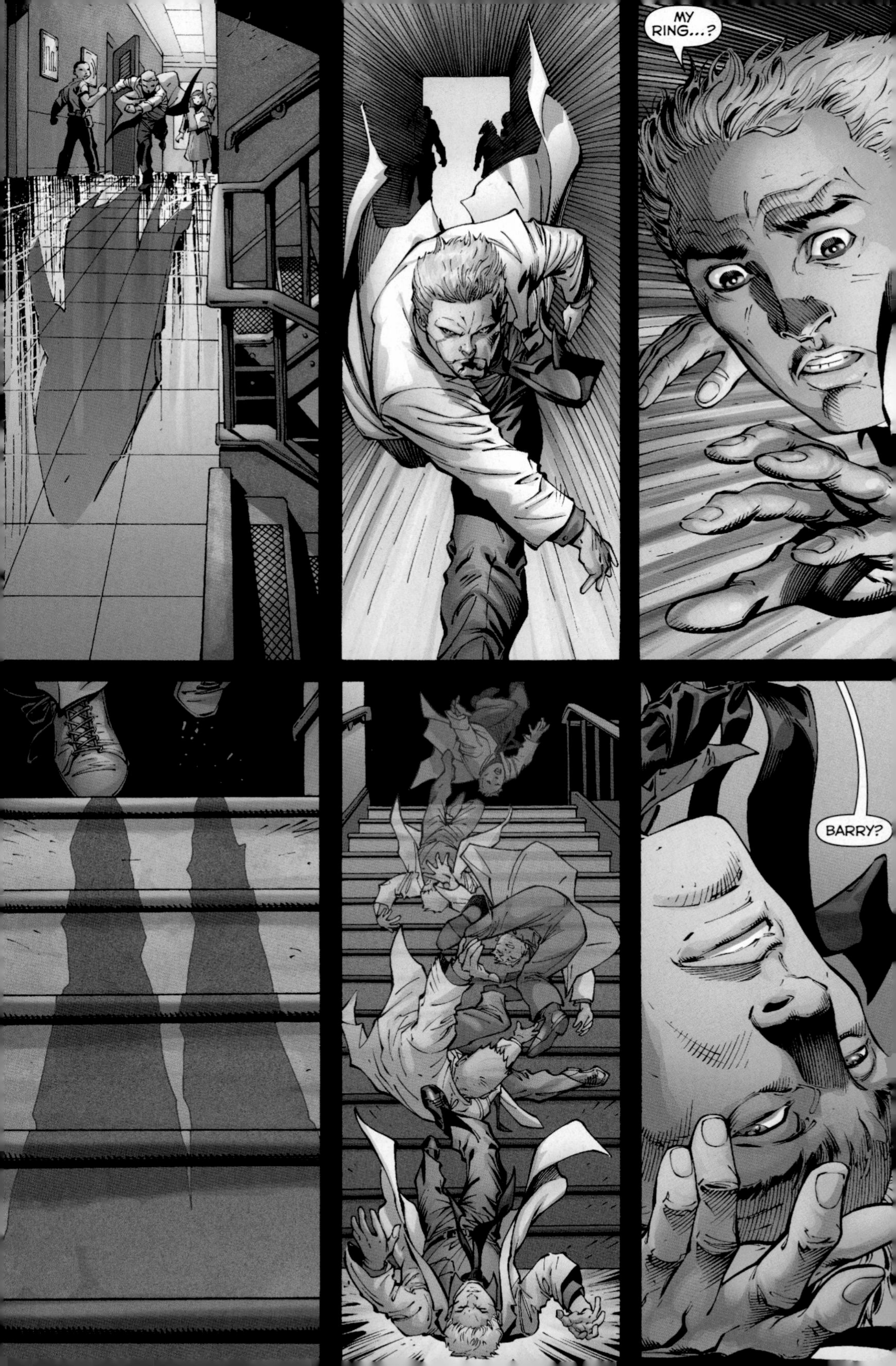
MY RING...?
BARRY?

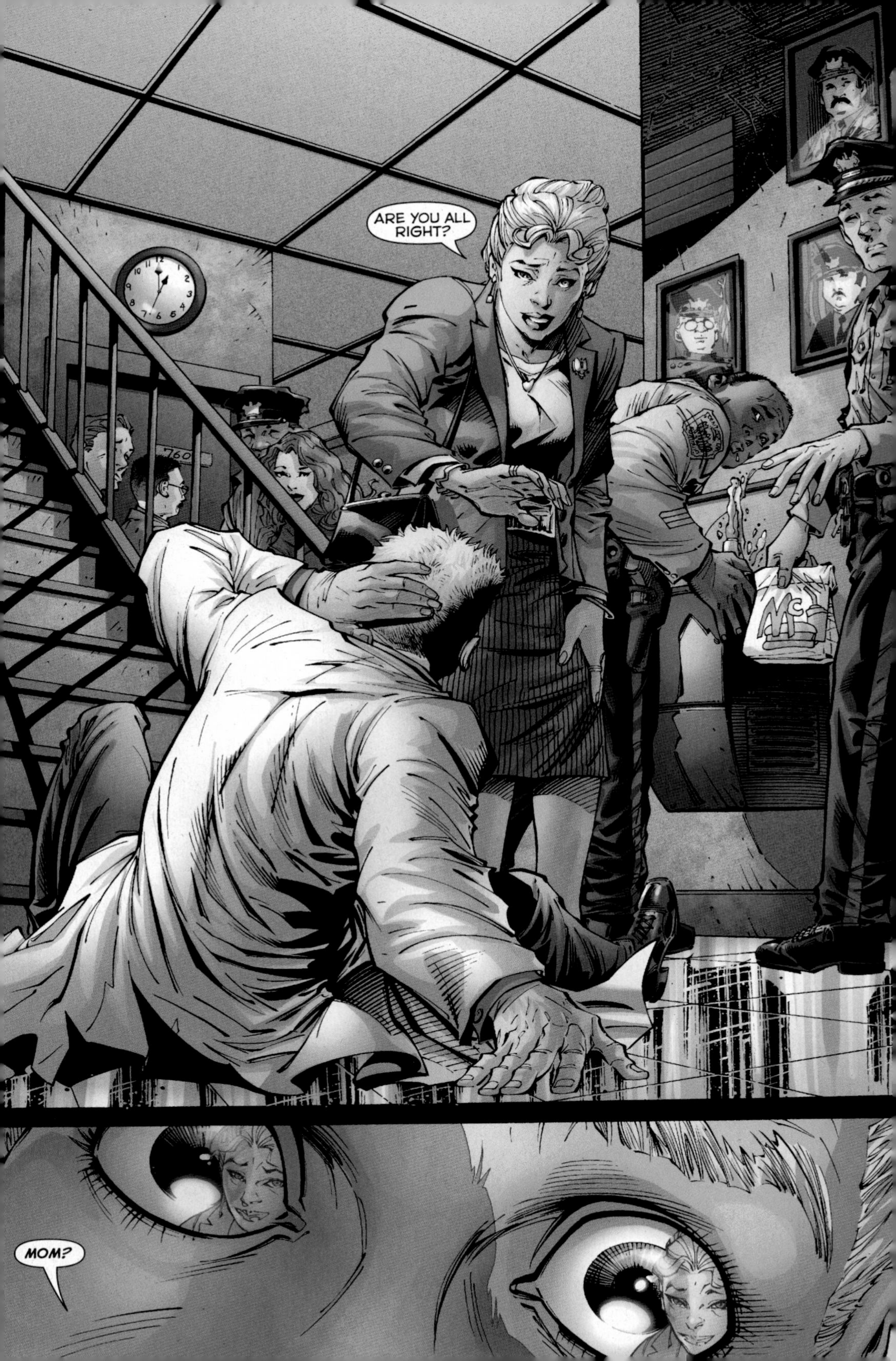
ARE YOU ALL RIGHT?
MOM?

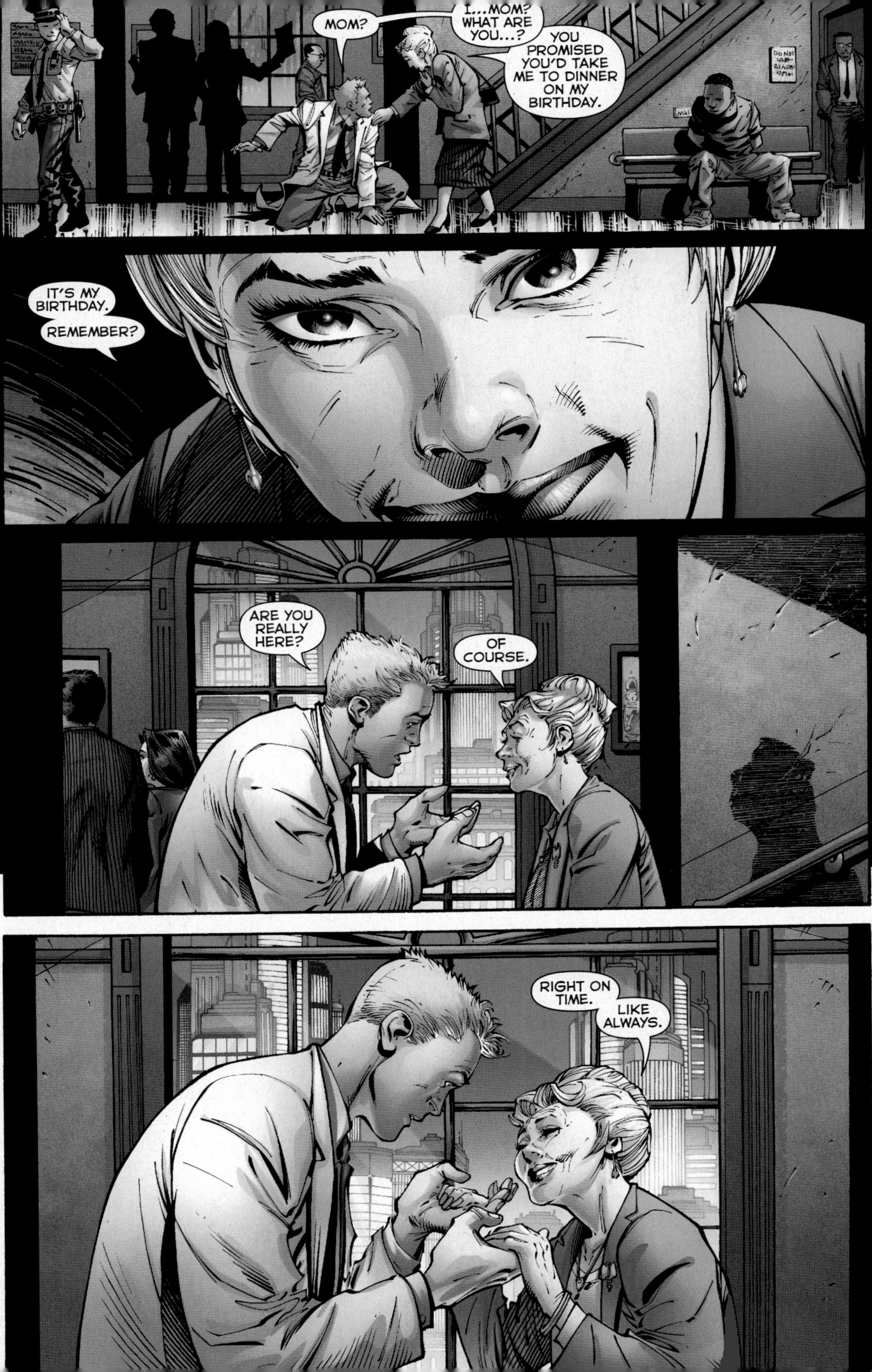
MOM?
I...MOM? WHAT ARE YOU...?
YOU PROMISED YOU'D TAKE ME TO DINNER ON MY BIRTHDAY.
IT'S MY BIRTHDAY.
REMEMBER?
ARE YOU REALLY HERE?
OF COURSE.
RIGHT ON TIME.
LIKE ALWAYS.

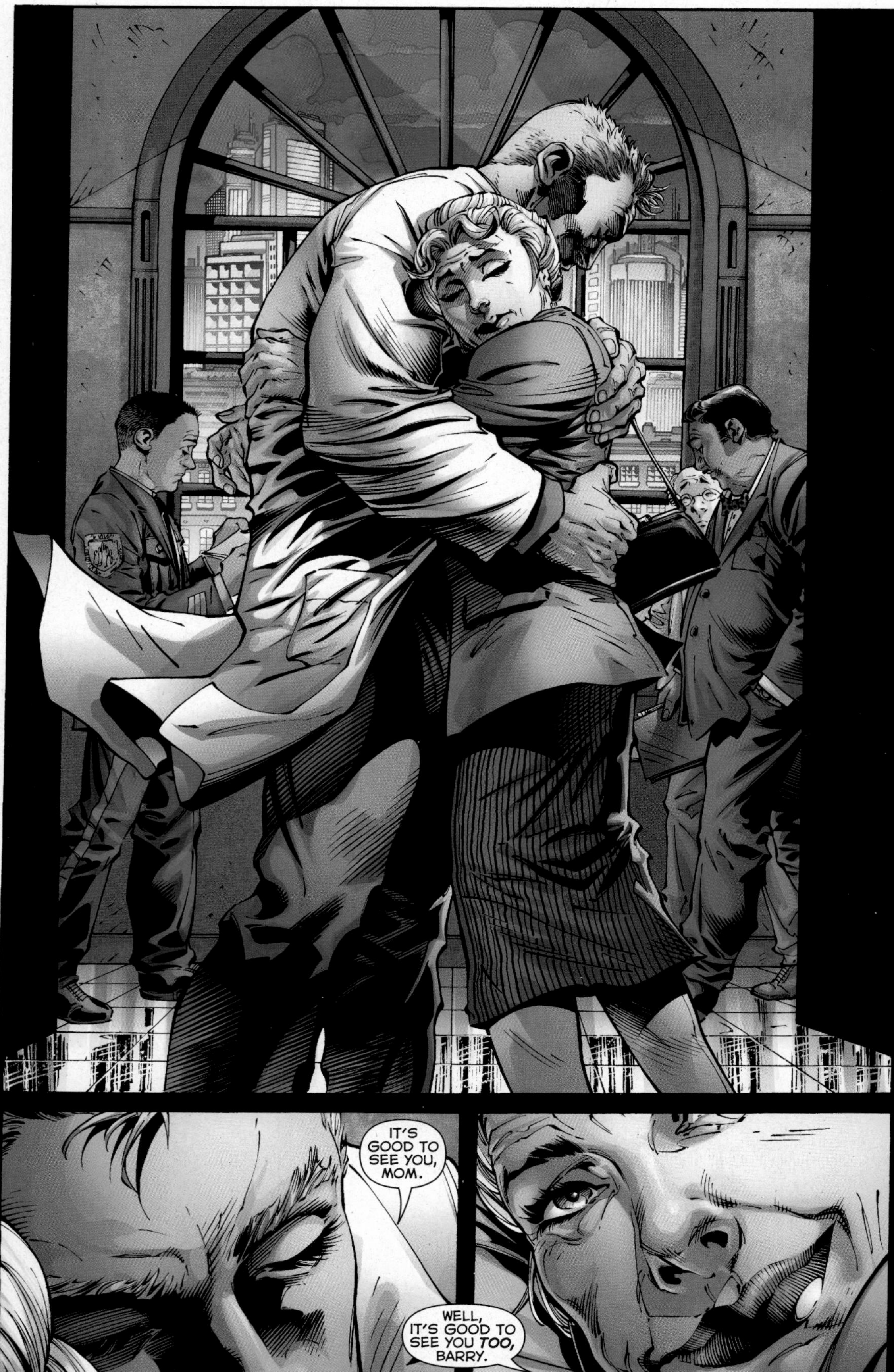
IT'S GOOD TO SEE YOU, MOM.
WELL, IT'S GOOD TO SEE YOU *TOO,* BARRY.

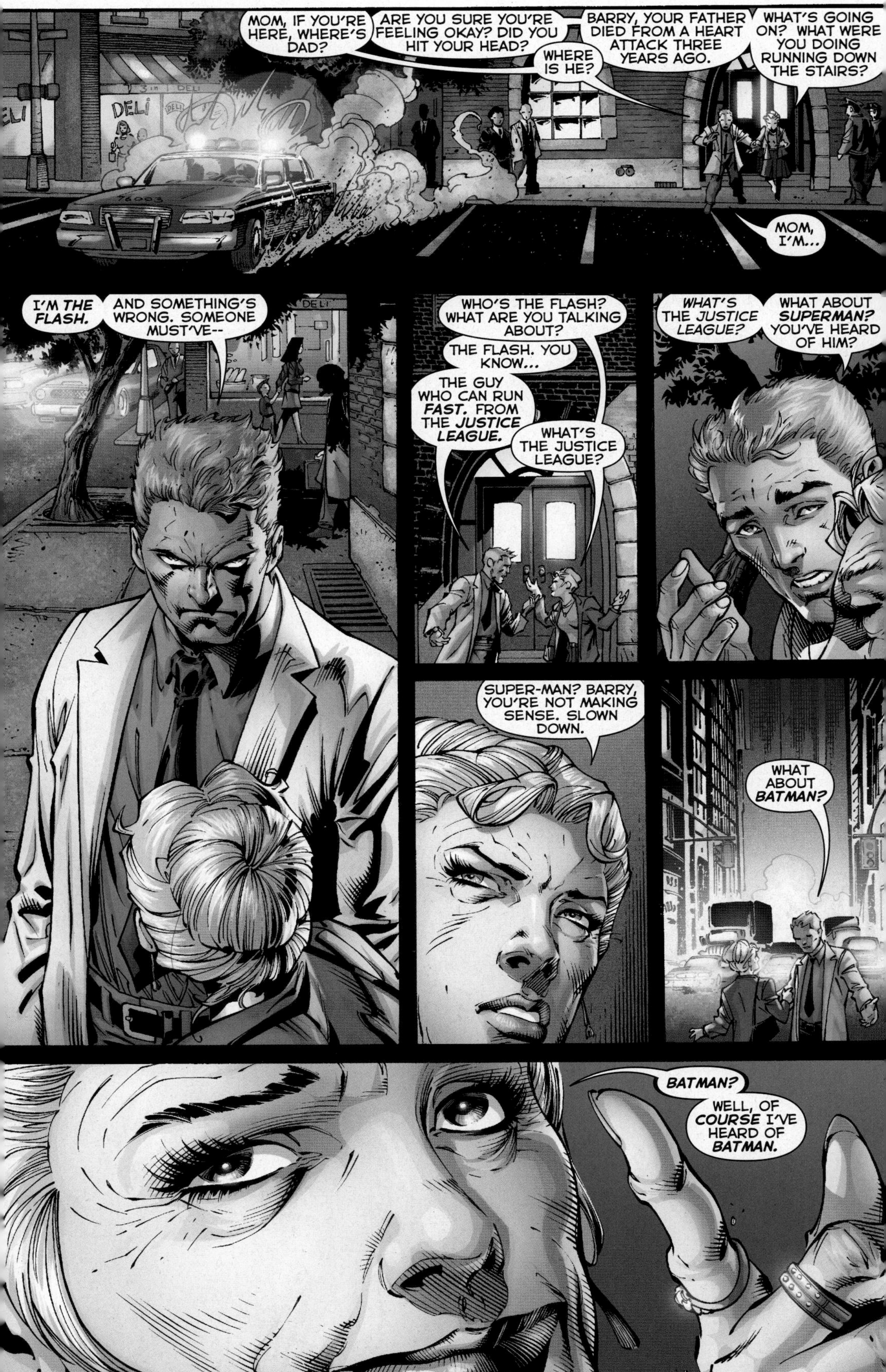

MOM, IF YOU'RE HERE, WHERE'S DAD?
ARE YOU SURE YOU'RE FEELING OKAY? DID YOU HIT YOUR HEAD?
WHERE IS HE?
BARRY, YOUR FATHER DIED FROM A HEART ATTACK THREE YEARS AGO.
WHAT'S GOING ON? WHAT WERE YOU DOING RUNNING DOWN THE STAIRS?
MOM, I'M...
I'M *THE FLASH.*
AND SOMETHING'S WRONG. SOMEONE MUST'VE--
WHO'S THE FLASH? WHAT ARE YOU TALKING ABOUT?
THE FLASH. YOU KNOW...
THE GUY WHO CAN RUN *FAST.* FROM THE *JUSTICE LEAGUE.*
WHAT'S THE JUSTICE LEAGUE?
WHAT'S THE *JUSTICE LEAGUE?*
WHAT ABOUT *SUPERMAN?* YOU'VE HEARD OF HIM?
SUPER-MAN? BARRY, YOU'RE NOT MAKING SENSE. SLOW DOWN.
WHAT ABOUT *BATMAN?*
BATMAN?
WELL, OF *COURSE* I'VE HEARD OF *BATMAN.*

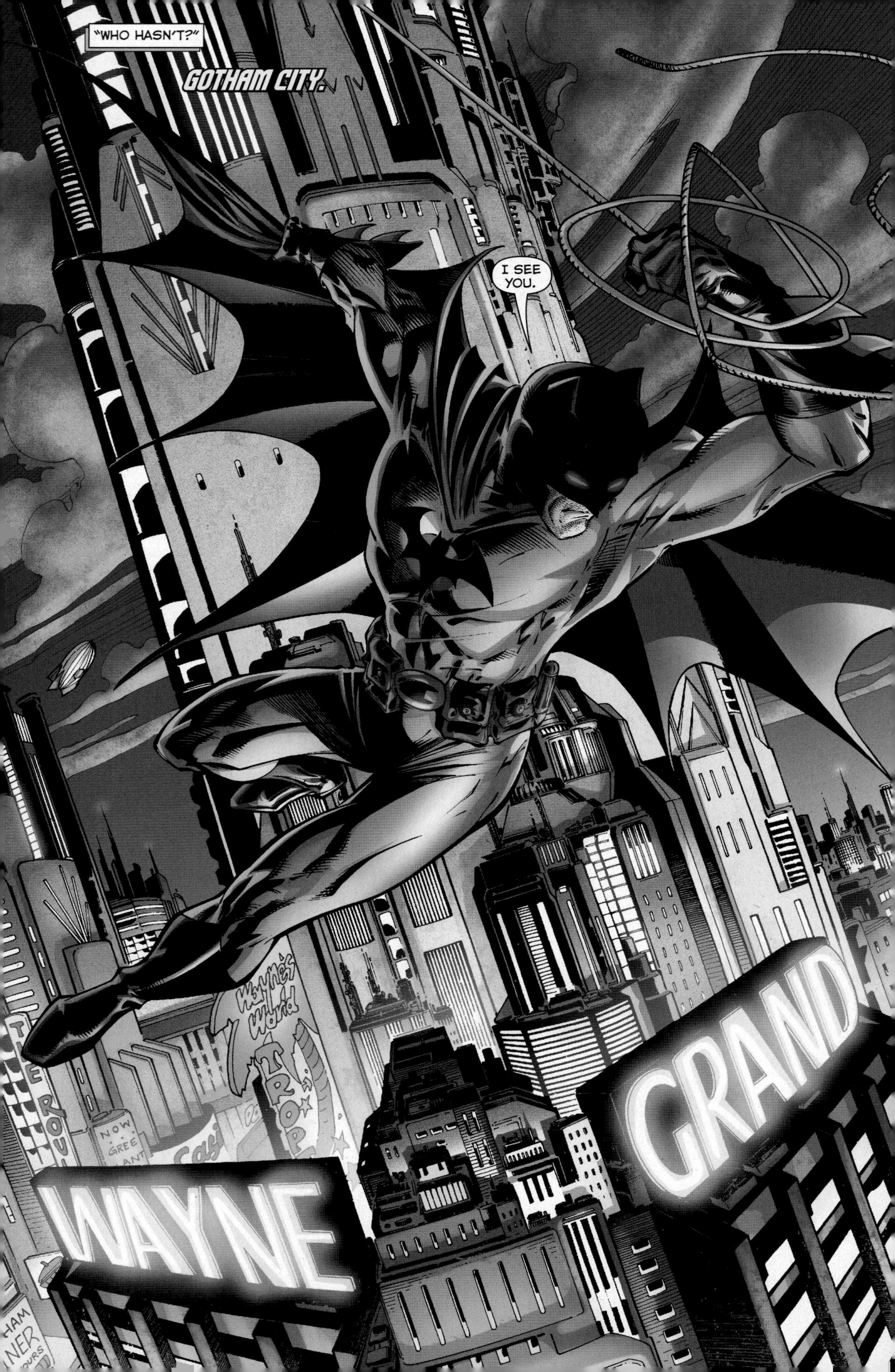
"WHO HASN'T?"
GOTHAM CITY.
I SEE YOU.
Wayne's World
WAYNE
GRAND

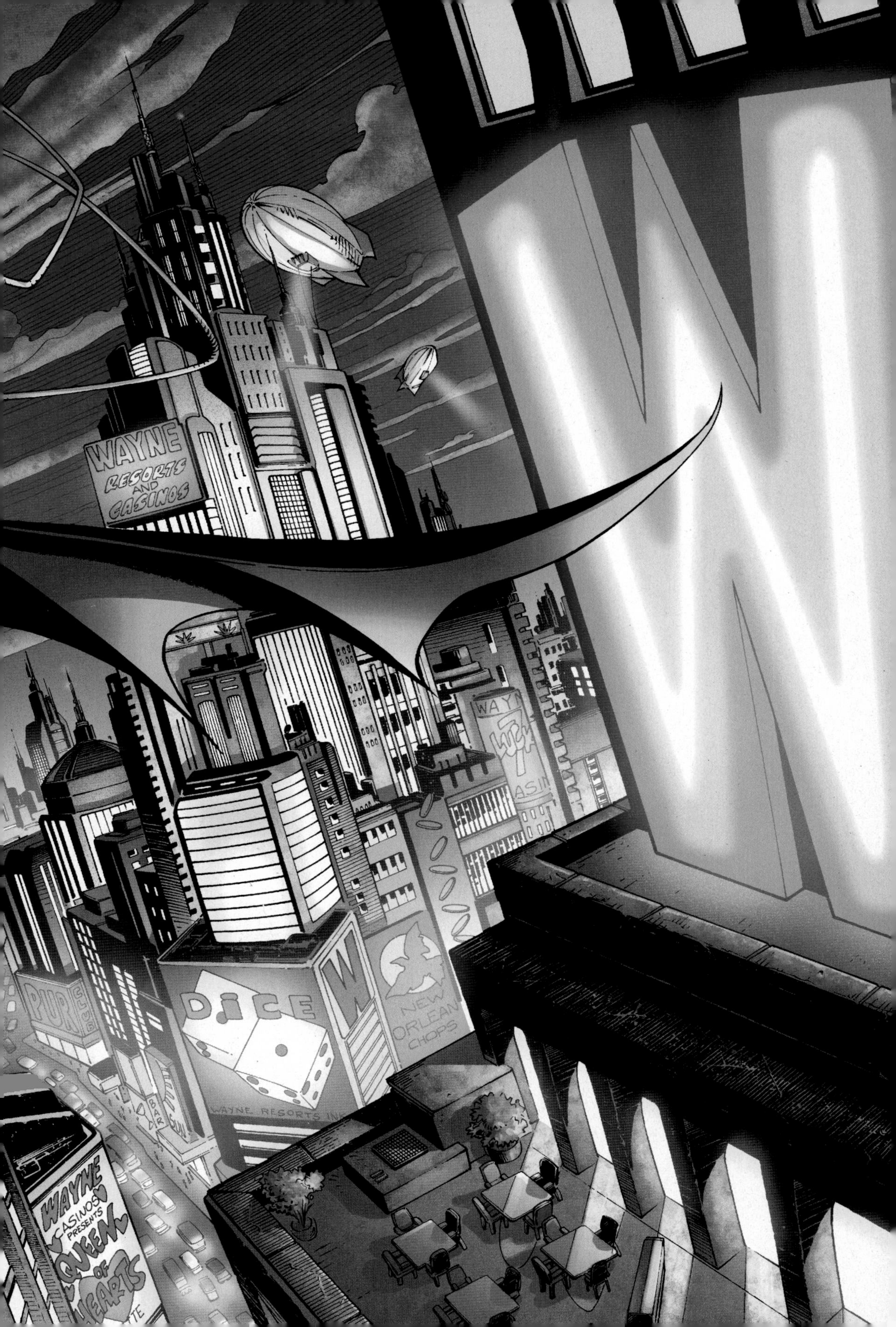
WAYNE RESORTS AND CASINOS
WAYNE
CASINO
PURE CLUB
DICE
W
NEW ORLEAN CHOPS
WAYNE RESORTS INC
BAR
WAYNE CASINOS PRESENTS QUEEN OF HEARTS

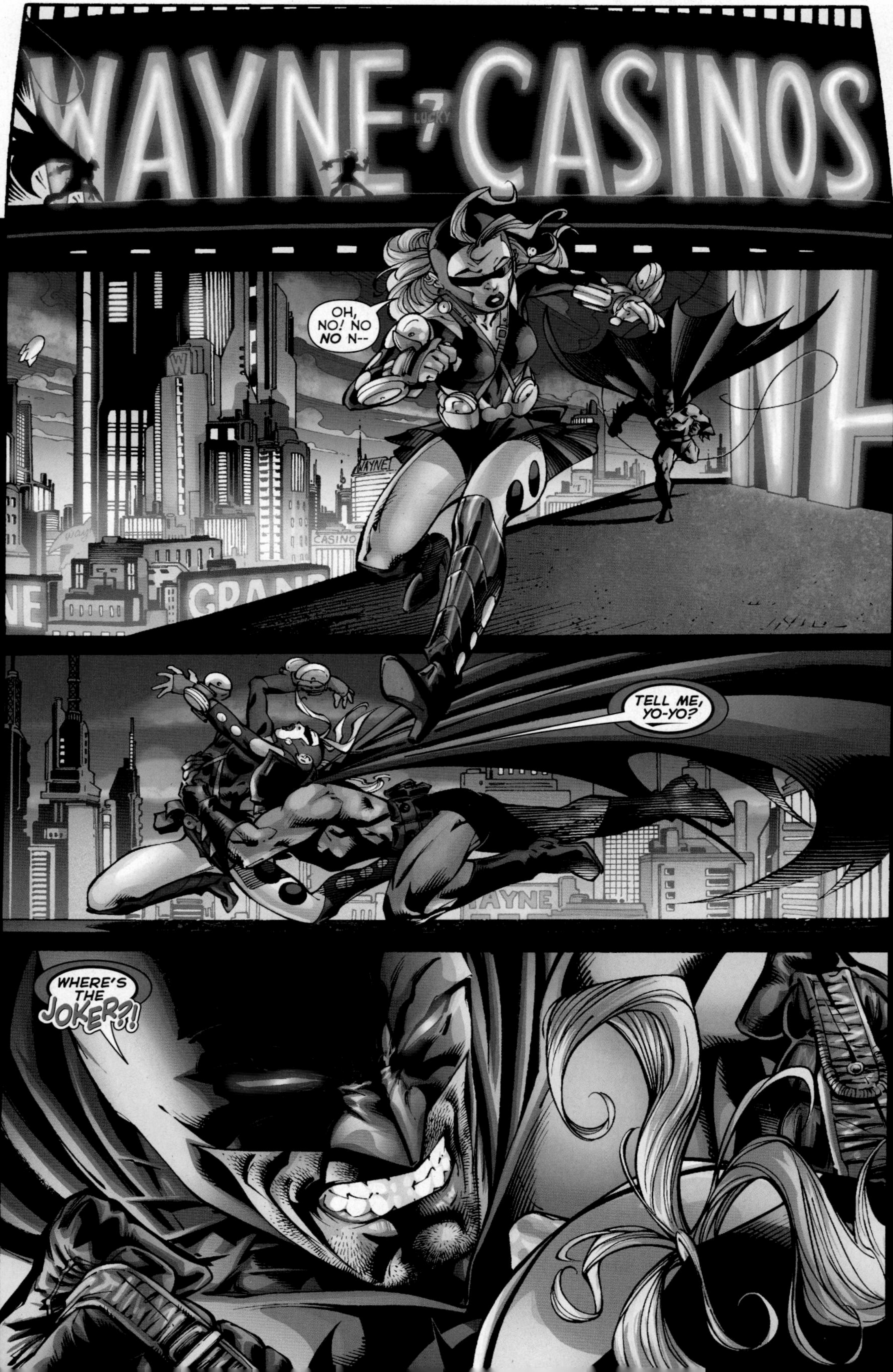
WAYNE
LUCKY 7
CASINOS
OH, NO! NO NO N--
TELL ME, YO-YO?
WHERE'S THE JOKER?!

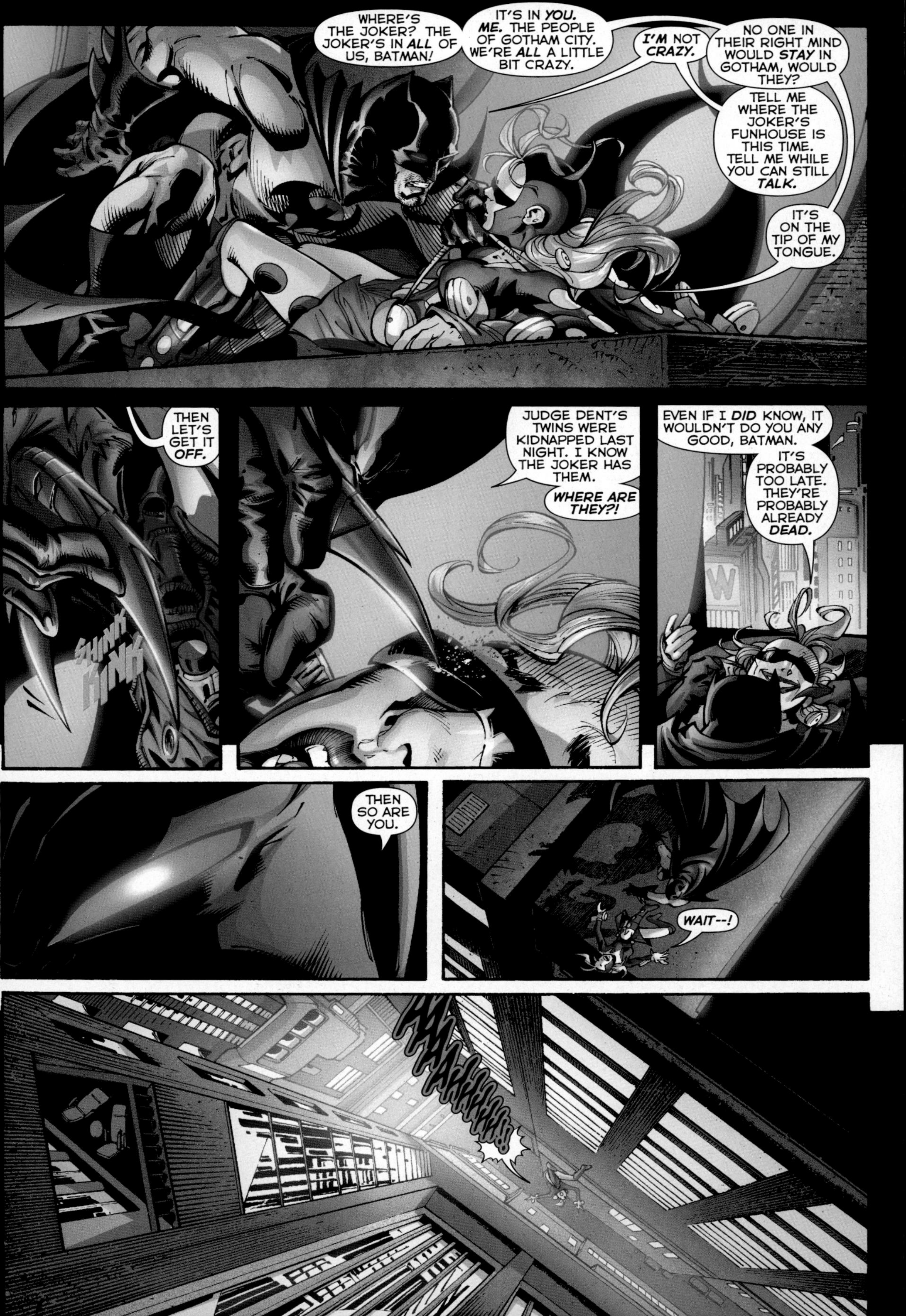
WHERE'S THE JOKER? THE JOKER'S IN ALL OF US, BATMAN!
IT'S IN YOU. ME. THE PEOPLE OF GOTHAM CITY. WE'RE ALL A LITTLE BIT CRAZY.
I'M NOT CRAZY.
NO ONE IN THEIR RIGHT MIND WOULD STAY IN GOTHAM, WOULD THEY?
TELL ME WHERE THE JOKER'S FUNHOUSE IS THIS TIME. TELL ME WHILE YOU CAN STILL TALK.
IT'S ON THE TIP OF MY TONGUE.
THEN LET'S GET IT OFF.
SHINK KINK
JUDGE DENT'S TWINS WERE KIDNAPPED LAST NIGHT. I KNOW THE JOKER HAS THEM.
WHERE ARE THEY?!
EVEN IF I DID KNOW, IT WOULDN'T DO YOU ANY GOOD, BATMAN.
IT'S PROBABLY TOO LATE. THEY'RE PROBABLY ALREADY DEAD.
THEN SO ARE YOU.
WAIT--!

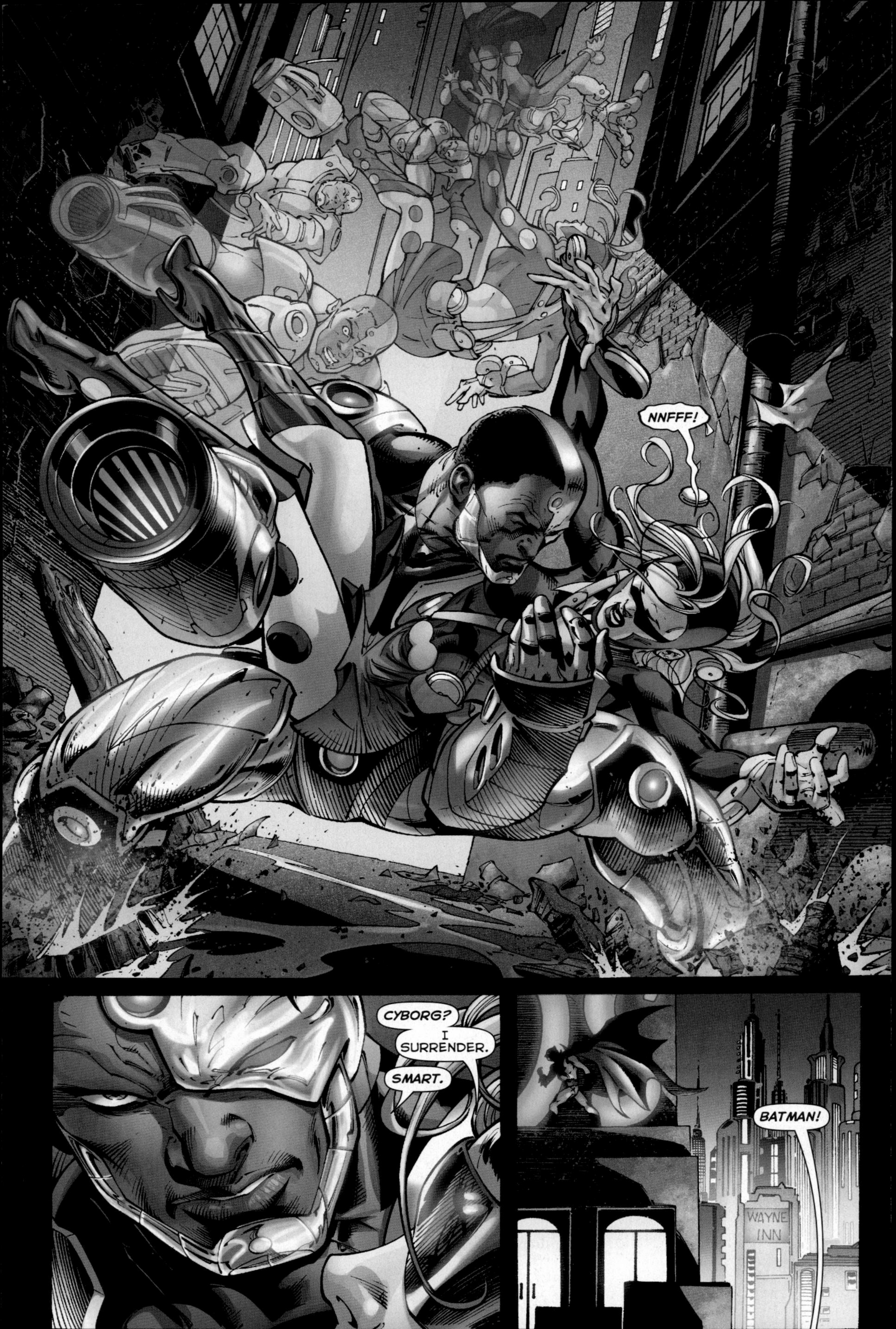
NNFFF!
CYBORG?
I SURRENDER.
SMART.
BATMAN!
WAYNE INN

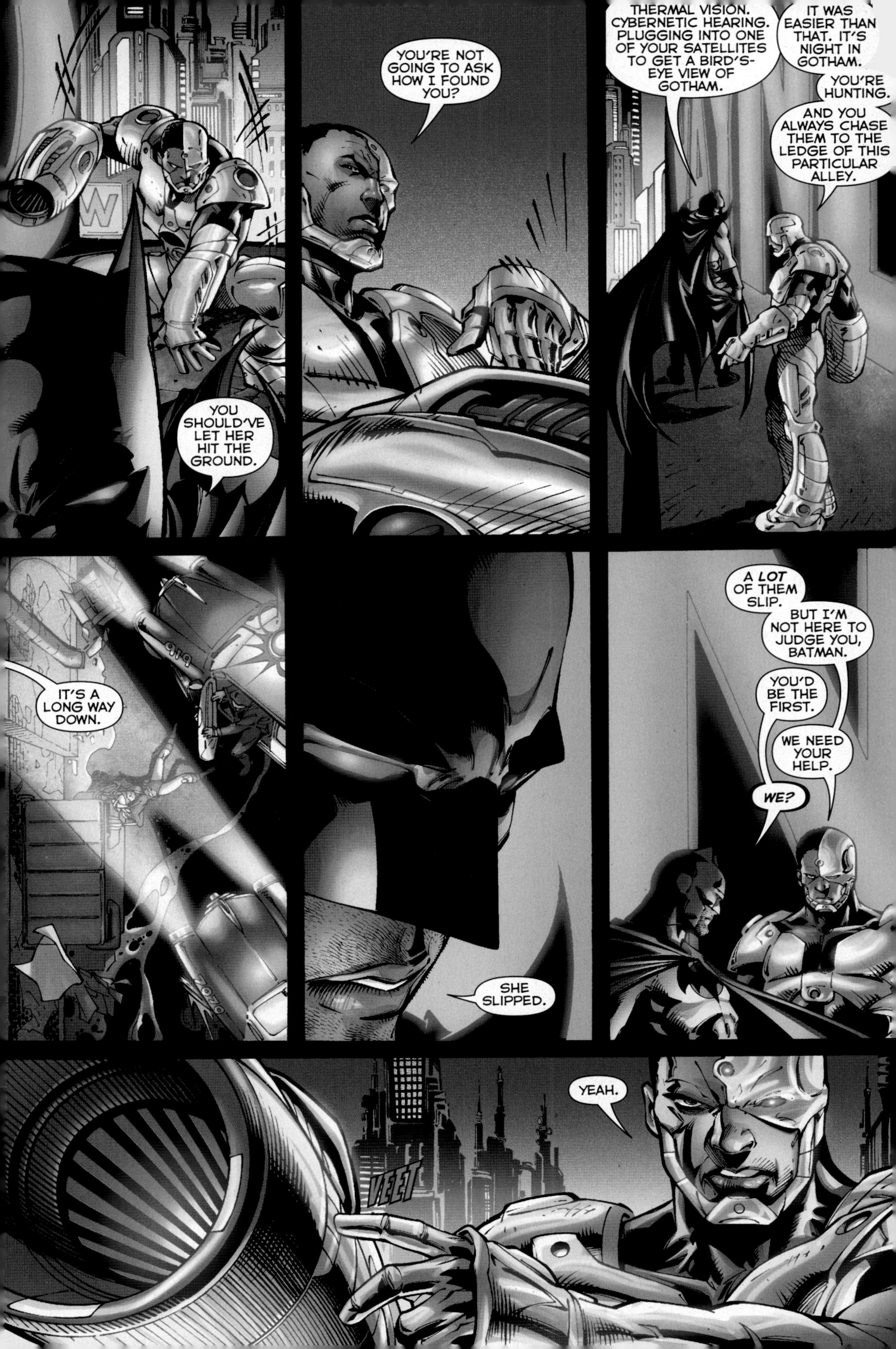
YOU SHOULD'VE LET HER HIT THE GROUND.
YOU'RE NOT GOING TO ASK HOW I FOUND YOU?
THERMAL VISION. CYBERNETIC HEARING. PLUGGING INTO ONE OF YOUR SATELLITES TO GET A BIRD'S-EYE VIEW OF GOTHAM.
IT WAS EASIER THAN THAT. IT'S NIGHT IN GOTHAM.
YOU'RE HUNTING.
AND YOU ALWAYS CHASE THEM TO THE LEDGE OF THIS PARTICULAR ALLEY.
IT'S A LONG WAY DOWN.
SHE SLIPPED.
A *LOT* OF THEM SLIP.
BUT I'M NOT HERE TO JUDGE YOU, BATMAN.
YOU'D BE THE FIRST.
WE NEED YOUR HELP.
WE?
YEAH.
VEET

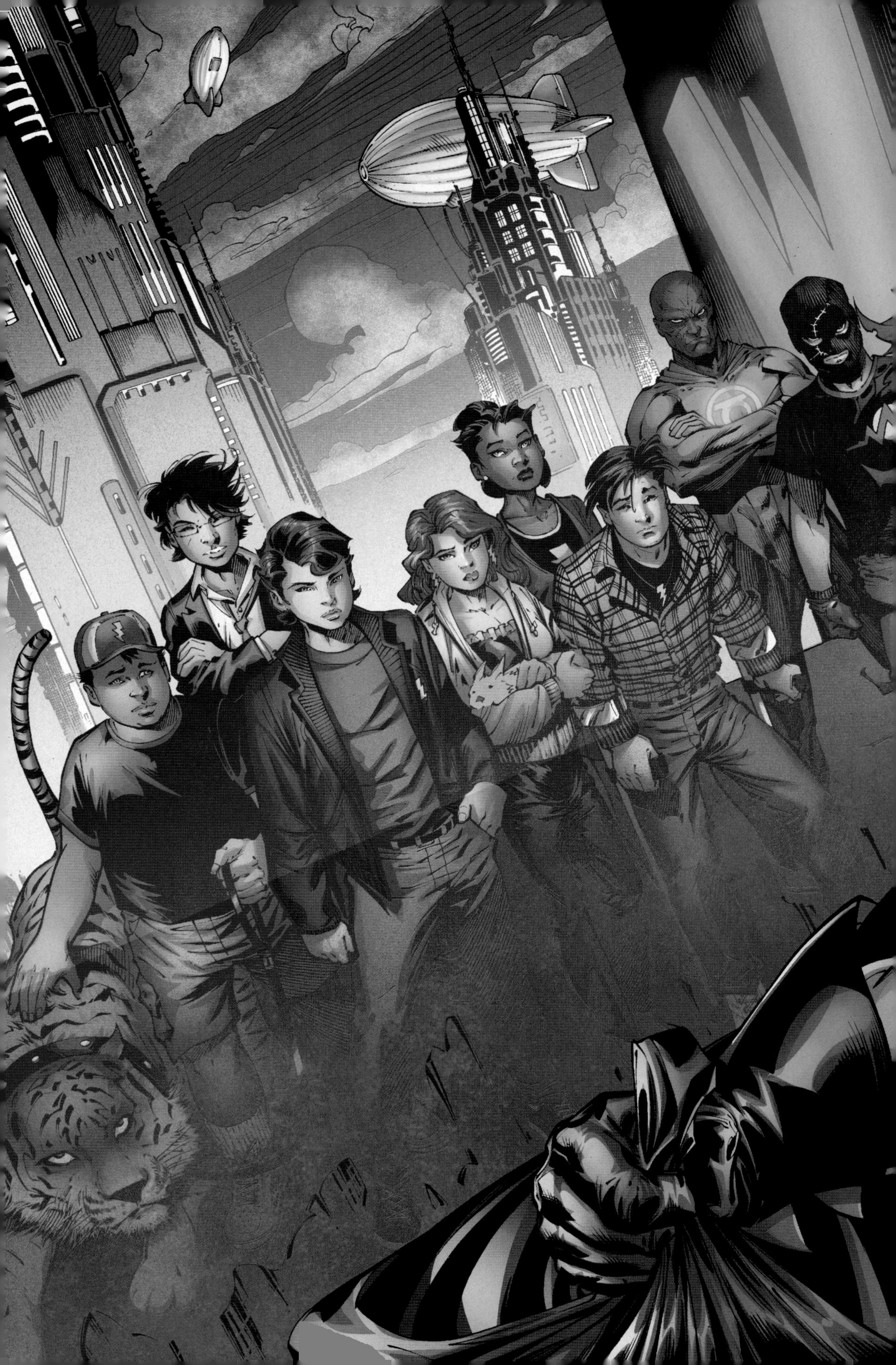

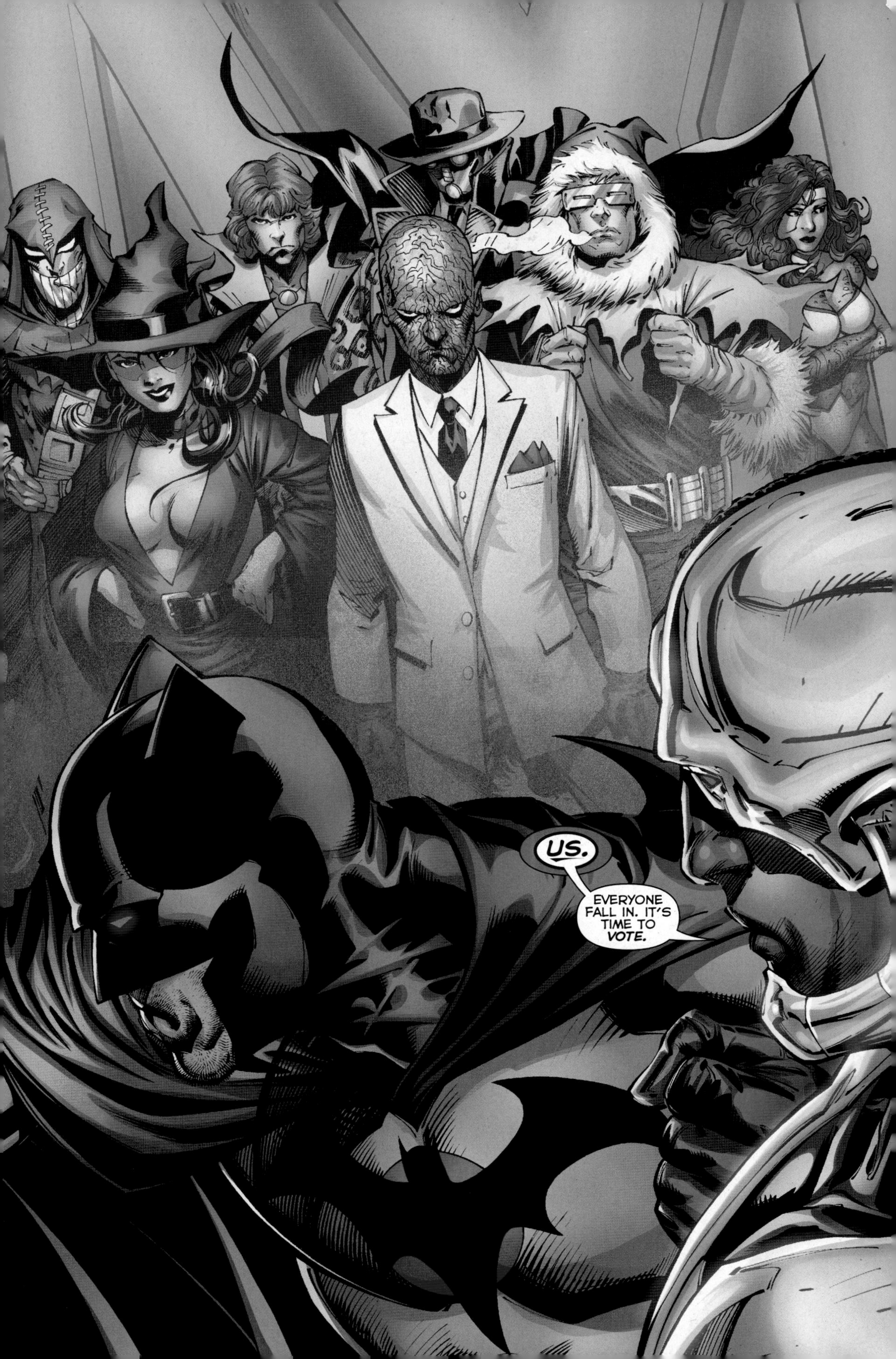
US.
EVERYONE FALL IN. IT'S TIME TO *VOTE.*

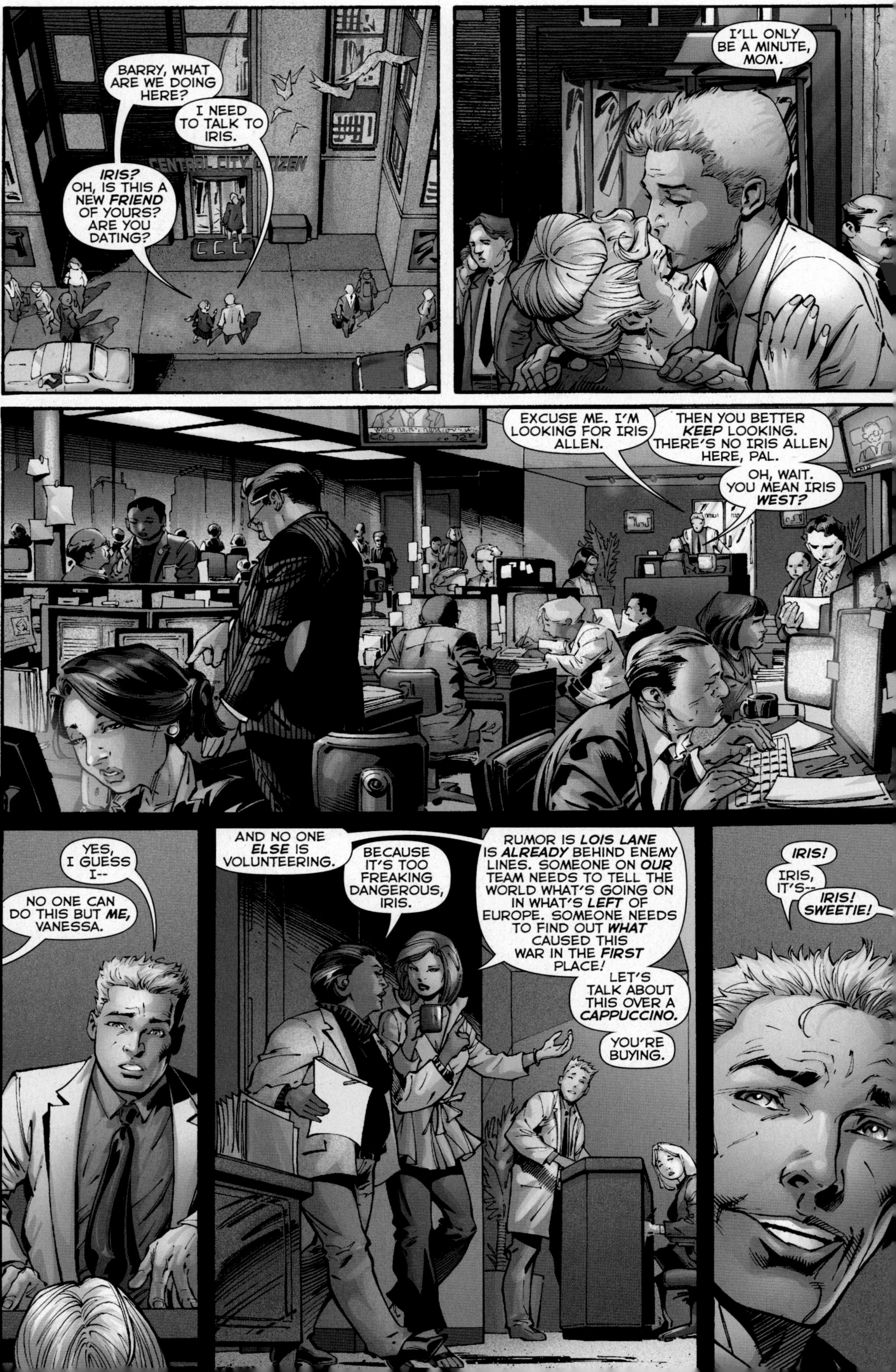
BARRY, WHAT ARE WE DOING HERE?
I NEED TO TALK TO IRIS.
IRIS? OH, IS THIS A NEW FRIEND OF YOURS? ARE YOU DATING?
CENTRAL CITY CITIZEN
I'LL ONLY BE A MINUTE, MOM.
EXCUSE ME. I'M LOOKING FOR IRIS ALLEN.
THEN YOU BETTER KEEP LOOKING. THERE'S NO IRIS ALLEN HERE, PAL.
OH, WAIT. YOU MEAN IRIS WEST?
YES, I GUESS I--
NO ONE CAN DO THIS BUT ME, VANESSA.
AND NO ONE ELSE IS VOLUNTEERING.
BECAUSE IT'S TOO FREAKING DANGEROUS, IRIS.
RUMOR IS LOIS LANE IS ALREADY BEHIND ENEMY LINES. SOMEONE ON OUR TEAM NEEDS TO TELL THE WORLD WHAT'S GOING ON IN WHAT'S LEFT OF EUROPE. SOMEONE NEEDS TO FIND OUT WHAT CAUSED THIS WAR IN THE FIRST PLACE!
LET'S TALK ABOUT THIS OVER A CAPPUCCINO.
YOU'RE BUYING.
IRIS!
IRIS, IT'S--
IRIS! SWEETIE!

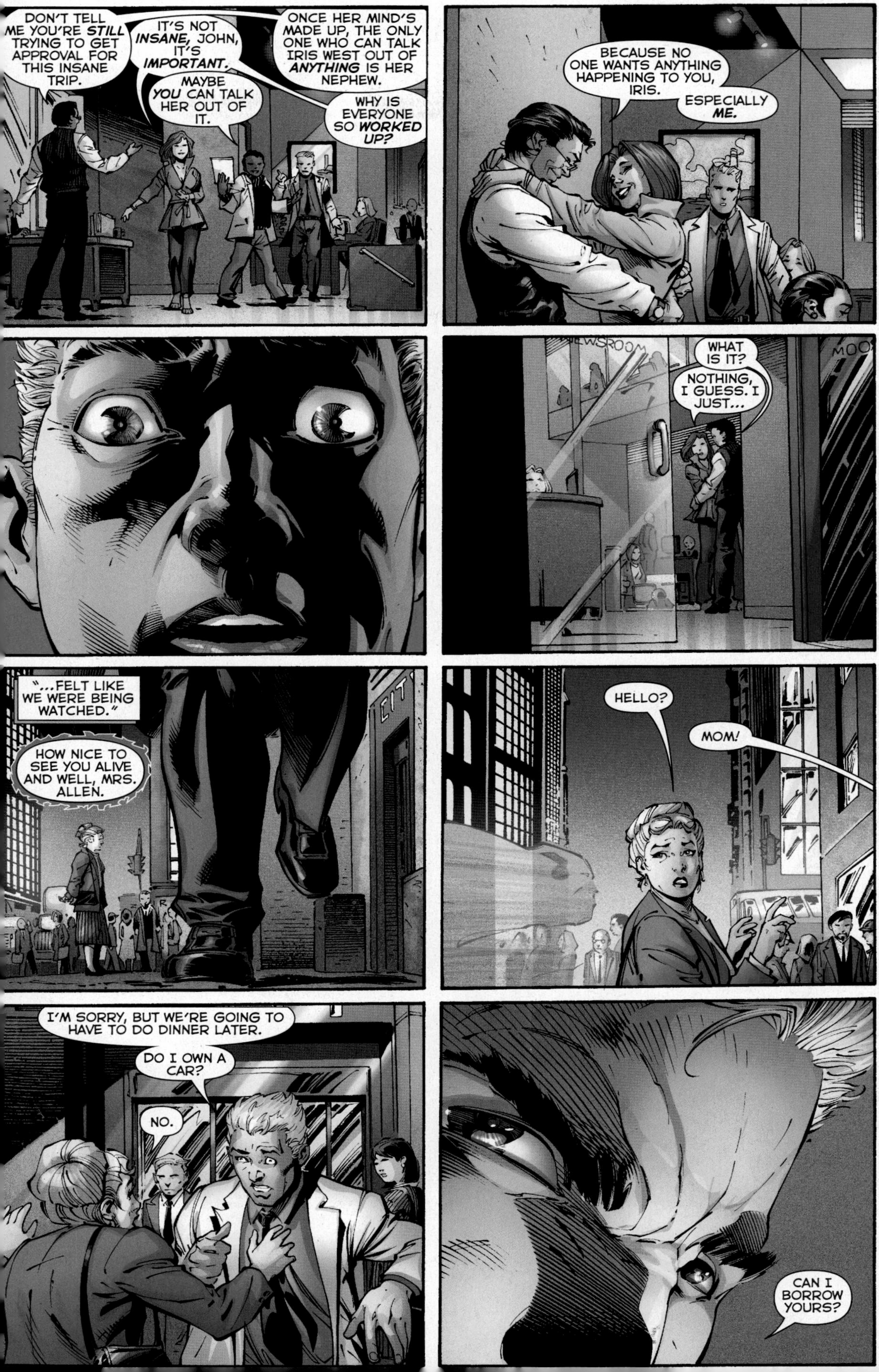
DON'T TELL ME YOU'RE STILL TRYING TO GET APPROVAL FOR THIS INSANE TRIP.
IT'S NOT INSANE, JOHN, IT'S IMPORTANT.
ONCE HER MIND'S MADE UP, THE ONLY ONE WHO CAN TALK IRIS WEST OUT OF ANYTHING IS HER NEPHEW.
MAYBE YOU CAN TALK HER OUT OF IT.
WHY IS EVERYONE SO WORKED UP?
BECAUSE NO ONE WANTS ANYTHING HAPPENING TO YOU, IRIS.
ESPECIALLY ME.
NEWSROOM
WHAT IS IT?
NOTHING, I GUESS. I JUST...
"...FELT LIKE WE WERE BEING WATCHED."
HOW NICE TO SEE YOU ALIVE AND WELL, MRS. ALLEN.
HELLO?
MOM!
I'M SORRY, BUT WE'RE GOING TO HAVE TO DO DINNER LATER.
DO I OWN A CAR?
NO.
CAN I BORROW YOURS?

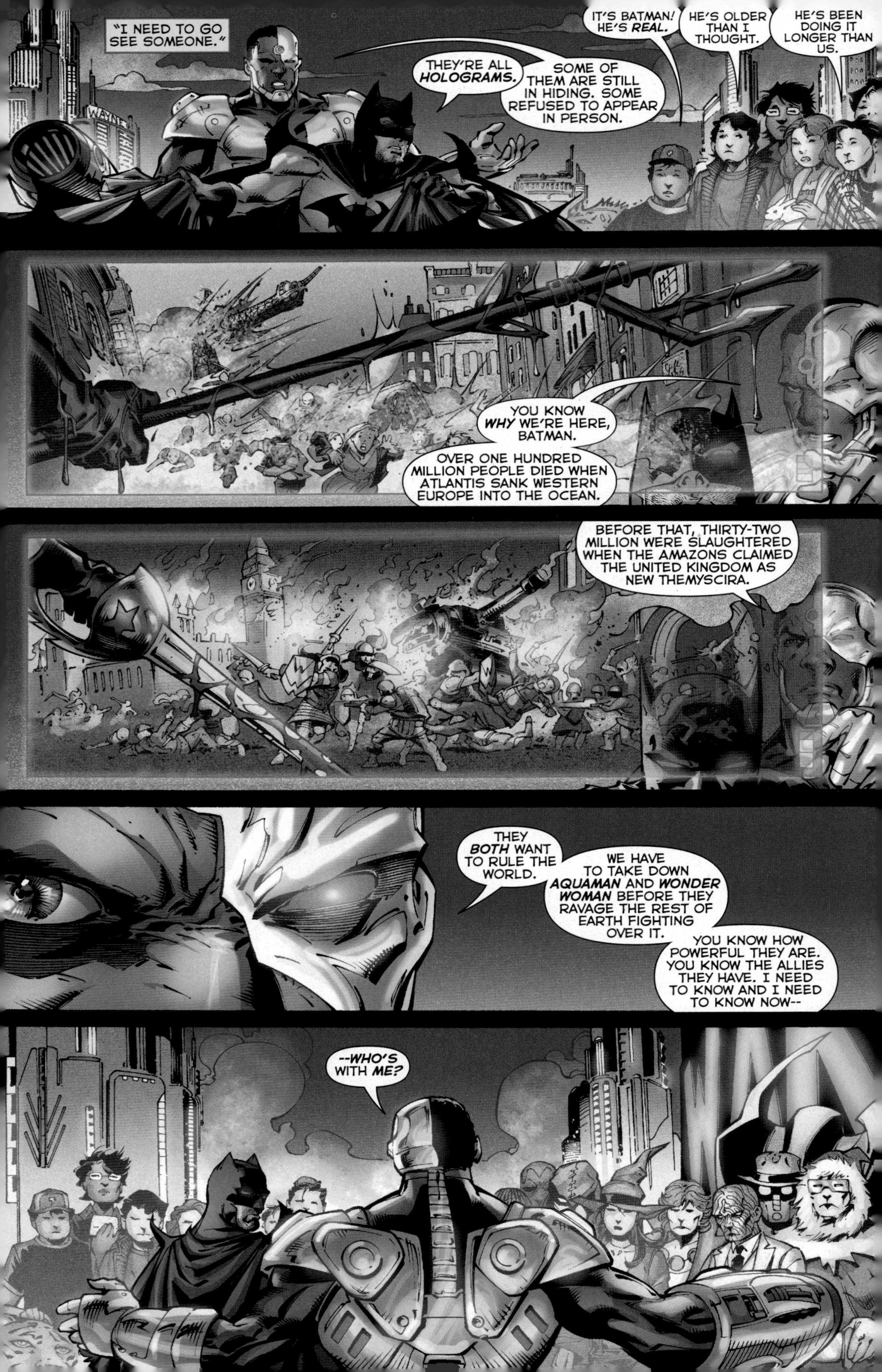
"I NEED TO GO SEE SOMEONE."
THEY'RE ALL HOLOGRAMS.
SOME OF THEM ARE STILL IN HIDING. SOME REFUSED TO APPEAR IN PERSON.
IT'S BATMAN! HE'S REAL.
HE'S OLDER THAN I THOUGHT.
HE'S BEEN DOING IT LONGER THAN US.
YOU KNOW WHY WE'RE HERE, BATMAN.
OVER ONE HUNDRED MILLION PEOPLE DIED WHEN ATLANTIS SANK WESTERN EUROPE INTO THE OCEAN.
BEFORE THAT, THIRTY-TWO MILLION WERE SLAUGHTERED WHEN THE AMAZONS CLAIMED THE UNITED KINGDOM AS NEW THEMYSCIRA.
THEY BOTH WANT TO RULE THE WORLD.
WE HAVE TO TAKE DOWN AQUAMAN AND WONDER WOMAN BEFORE THEY RAVAGE THE REST OF EARTH FIGHTING OVER IT.
YOU KNOW HOW POWERFUL THEY ARE. YOU KNOW THE ALLIES THEY HAVE. I NEED TO KNOW AND I NEED TO KNOW NOW--
--WHO'S WITH ME?

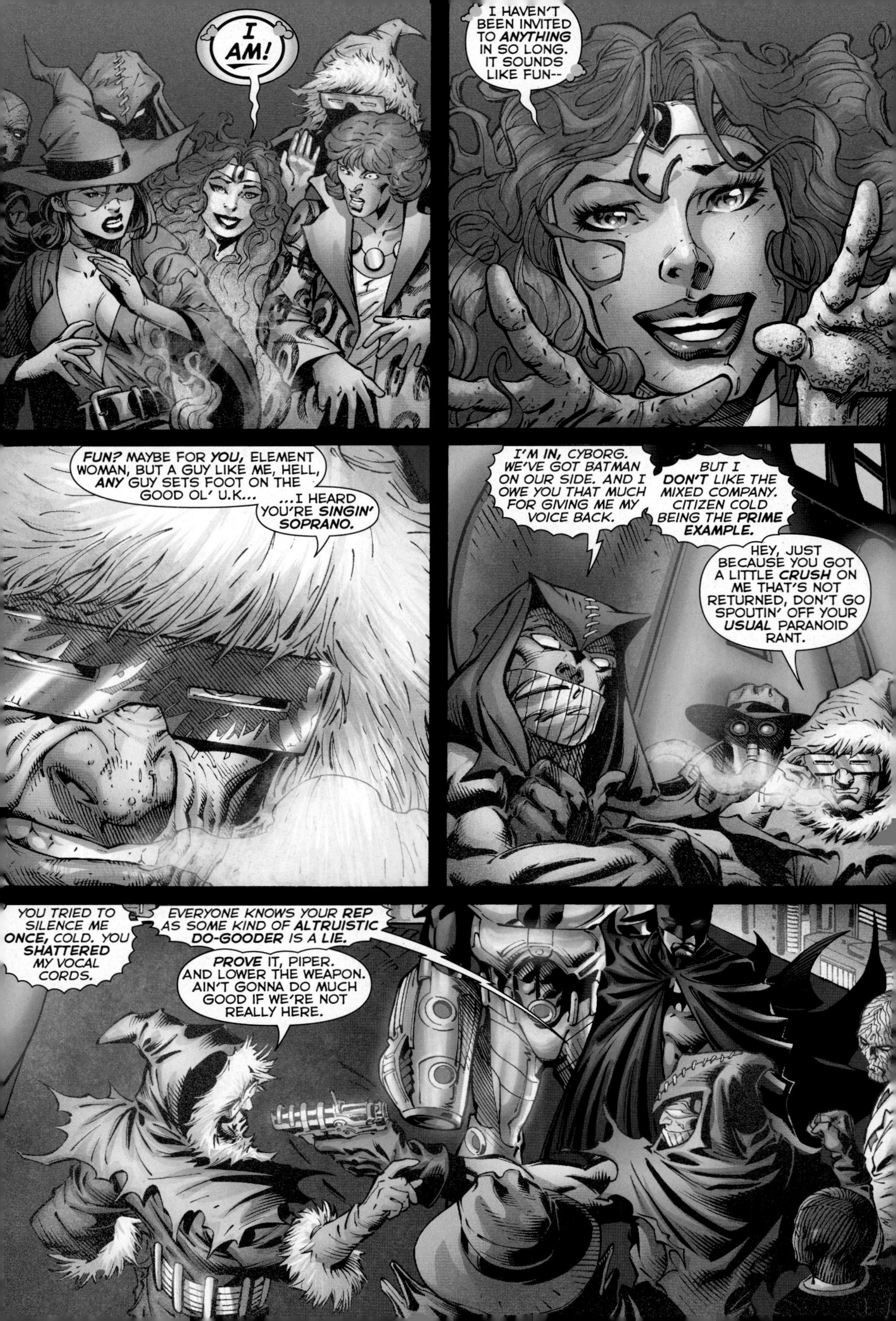
I AM!
I HAVEN'T BEEN INVITED TO ANYTHING IN SO LONG. IT SOUNDS LIKE FUN--
FUN? MAYBE FOR YOU, ELEMENT WOMAN, BUT A GUY LIKE ME, HELL, ANY GUY SETS FOOT ON THE GOOD OL' U.K...
...I HEARD YOU'RE SINGIN' SOPRANO.
I'M IN, CYBORG. WE'VE GOT BATMAN ON OUR SIDE. AND I OWE YOU THAT MUCH FOR GIVING ME MY VOICE BACK.
BUT I DON'T LIKE THE MIXED COMPANY. CITIZEN COLD BEING THE PRIME EXAMPLE.
HEY, JUST BECAUSE YOU GOT A LITTLE CRUSH ON ME THAT'S NOT RETURNED, DON'T GO SPOUTIN' OFF YOUR USUAL PARANOID RANT.
YOU TRIED TO SILENCE ME ONCE, COLD. YOU SHATTERED MY VOCAL CORDS.
EVERYONE KNOWS YOUR REP AS SOME KIND OF ALTRUISTIC DO-GOODER IS A LIE.
PROVE IT, PIPER. AND LOWER THE WEAPON. AIN'T GONNA DO MUCH GOOD IF WE'RE NOT REALLY HERE.

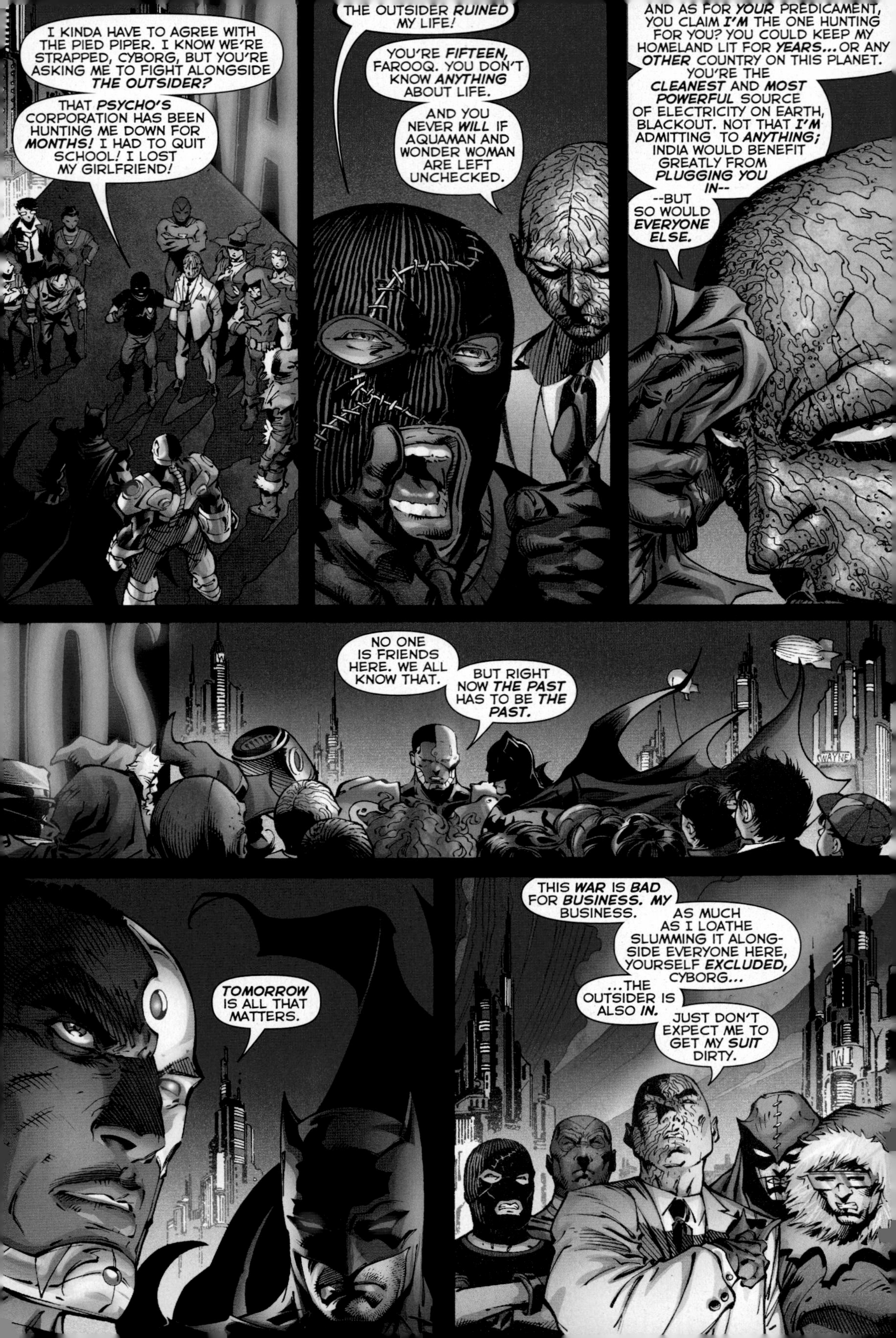
I KINDA HAVE TO AGREE WITH THE PIED PIPER. I KNOW WE'RE STRAPPED, CYBORG, BUT YOU'RE ASKING ME TO FIGHT ALONGSIDE THE OUTSIDER?
THAT PSYCHO'S CORPORATION HAS BEEN HUNTING ME DOWN FOR MONTHS! I HAD TO QUIT SCHOOL! I LOST MY GIRLFRIEND!
THE OUTSIDER RUINED MY LIFE!
YOU'RE FIFTEEN, FAROOQ. YOU DON'T KNOW ANYTHING ABOUT LIFE.
AND YOU NEVER WILL IF AQUAMAN AND WONDER WOMAN ARE LEFT UNCHECKED.
AND AS FOR YOUR PREDICAMENT, YOU CLAIM I'M THE ONE HUNTING FOR YOU? YOU COULD KEEP MY HOMELAND LIT FOR YEARS... OR ANY OTHER COUNTRY ON THIS PLANET.
YOU'RE THE CLEANEST AND MOST POWERFUL SOURCE OF ELECTRICITY ON EARTH, BLACKOUT. NOT THAT I'M ADMITTING TO ANYTHING; INDIA WOULD BENEFIT GREATLY FROM PLUGGING YOU IN--
--BUT SO WOULD EVERYONE ELSE.
NO ONE IS FRIENDS HERE. WE ALL KNOW THAT.
BUT RIGHT NOW THE PAST HAS TO BE THE PAST.
WAYNE
TOMORROW IS ALL THAT MATTERS.
THIS WAR IS BAD FOR BUSINESS. MY BUSINESS.
AS MUCH AS I LOATHE SLUMMING IT ALONG-SIDE EVERYONE HERE, YOURSELF EXCLUDED, CYBORG...
...THE OUTSIDER IS ALSO IN.
JUST DON'T EXPECT ME TO GET MY SUIT DIRTY.

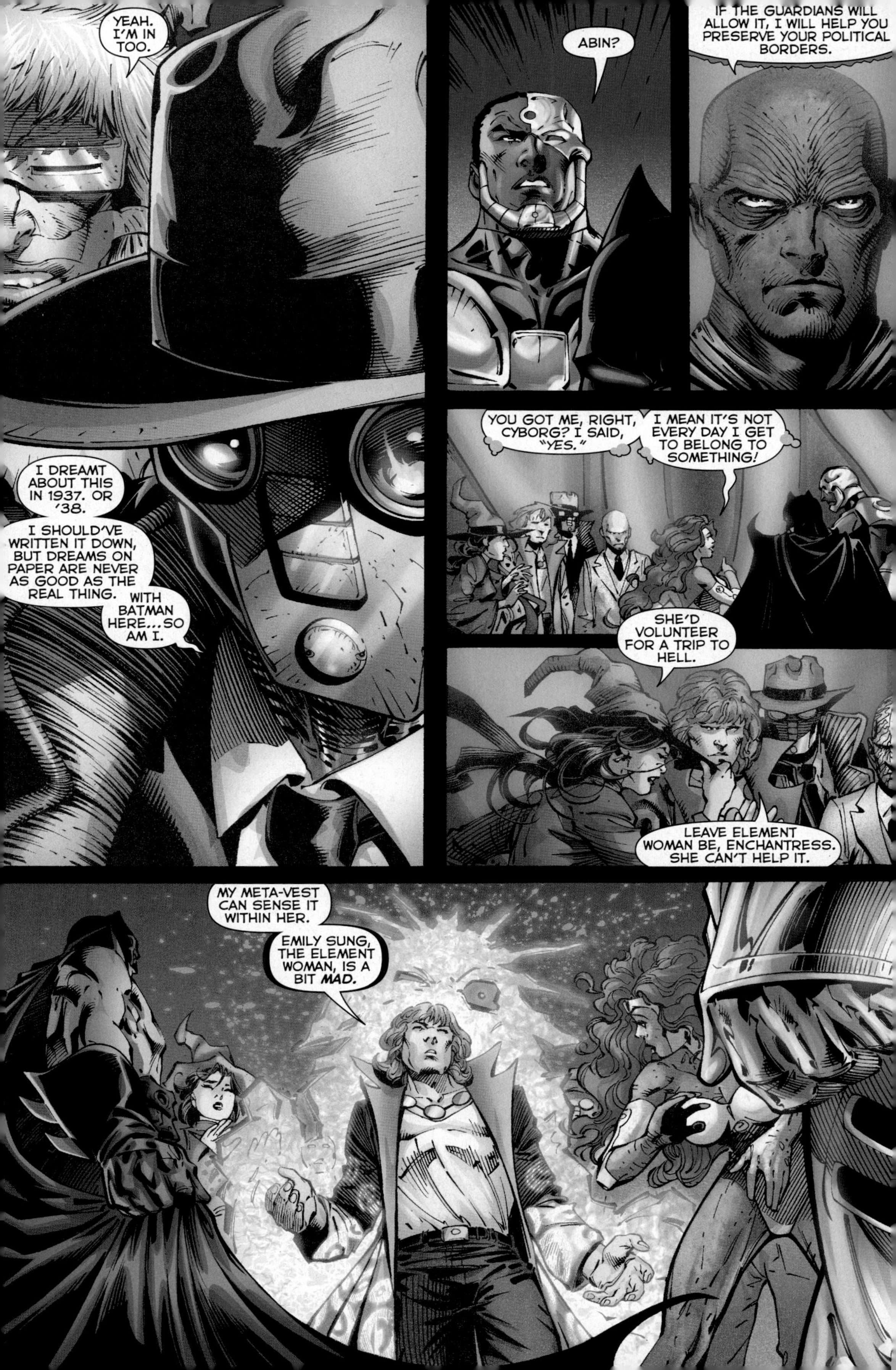
YEAH. I'M IN TOO.
ABIN?
IF THE GUARDIANS WILL ALLOW IT, I WILL HELP YOU PRESERVE YOUR POLITICAL BORDERS.
I DREAMT ABOUT THIS IN 1937. OR '38.
I SHOULD'VE WRITTEN IT DOWN, BUT DREAMS ON PAPER ARE NEVER AS GOOD AS THE REAL THING.
WITH BATMAN HERE...SO AM I.
YOU GOT ME, RIGHT, CYBORG? I SAID, "YES."
I MEAN IT'S NOT EVERY DAY I GET TO BELONG TO SOMETHING!
SHE'D VOLUNTEER FOR A TRIP TO HELL.
LEAVE ELEMENT WOMAN BE, ENCHANTRESS. SHE CAN'T HELP IT.
MY META-VEST CAN SENSE IT WITHIN HER.
EMILY SUNG, THE ELEMENT WOMAN, IS A BIT MAD.

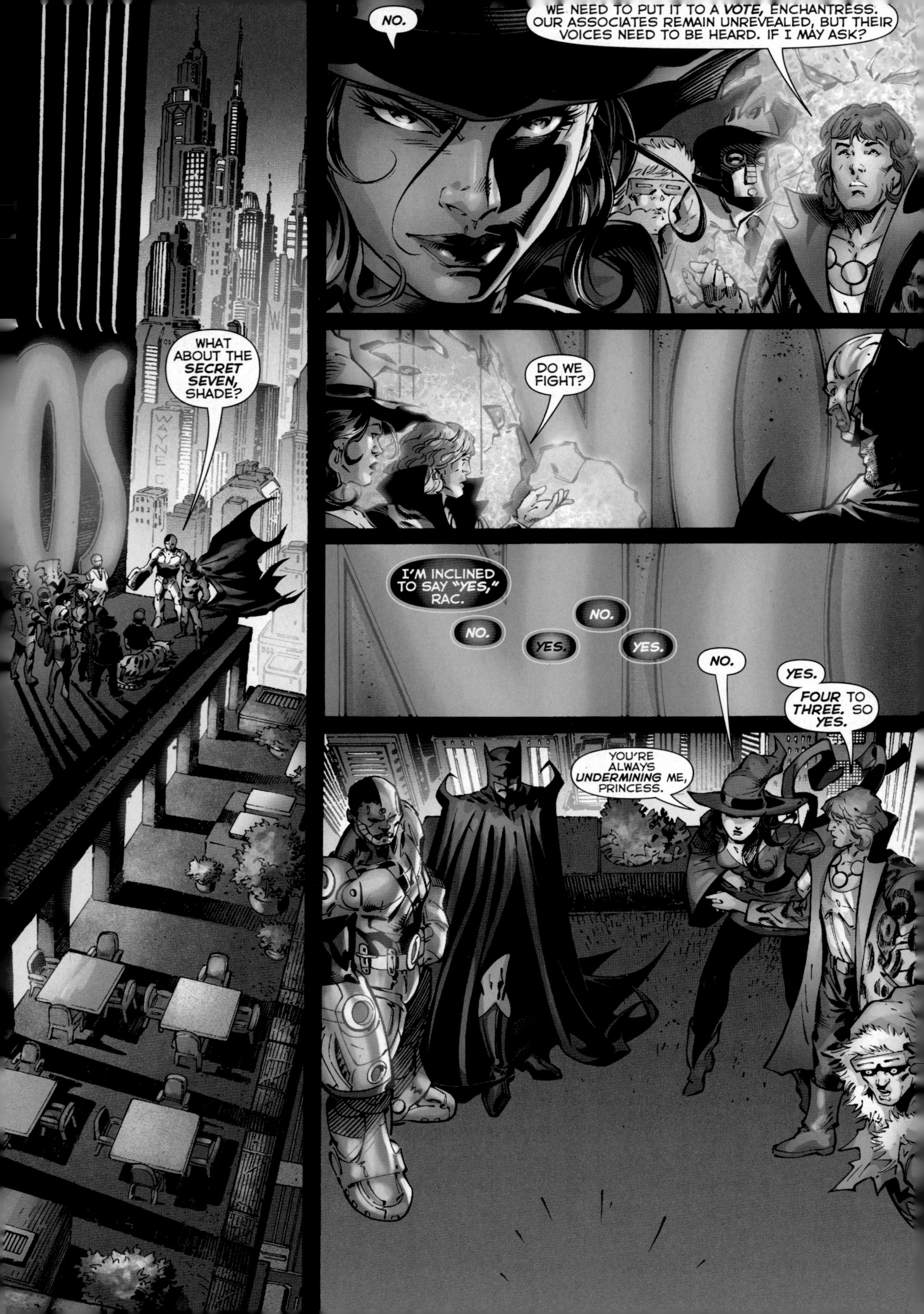
WHAT ABOUT THE SECRET SEVEN, SHADE?
NO.
WE NEED TO PUT IT TO A VOTE, ENCHANTRESS. OUR ASSOCIATES REMAIN UNREVEALED, BUT THEIR VOICES NEED TO BE HEARD. IF I MAY ASK?
DO WE FIGHT?
I'M INCLINED TO SAY "YES," RAC.
NO.
YES.
NO.
YES.
NO.
YES.
FOUR TO THREE. SO YES.
YOU'RE ALWAYS UNDERMINING ME, PRINCESS.

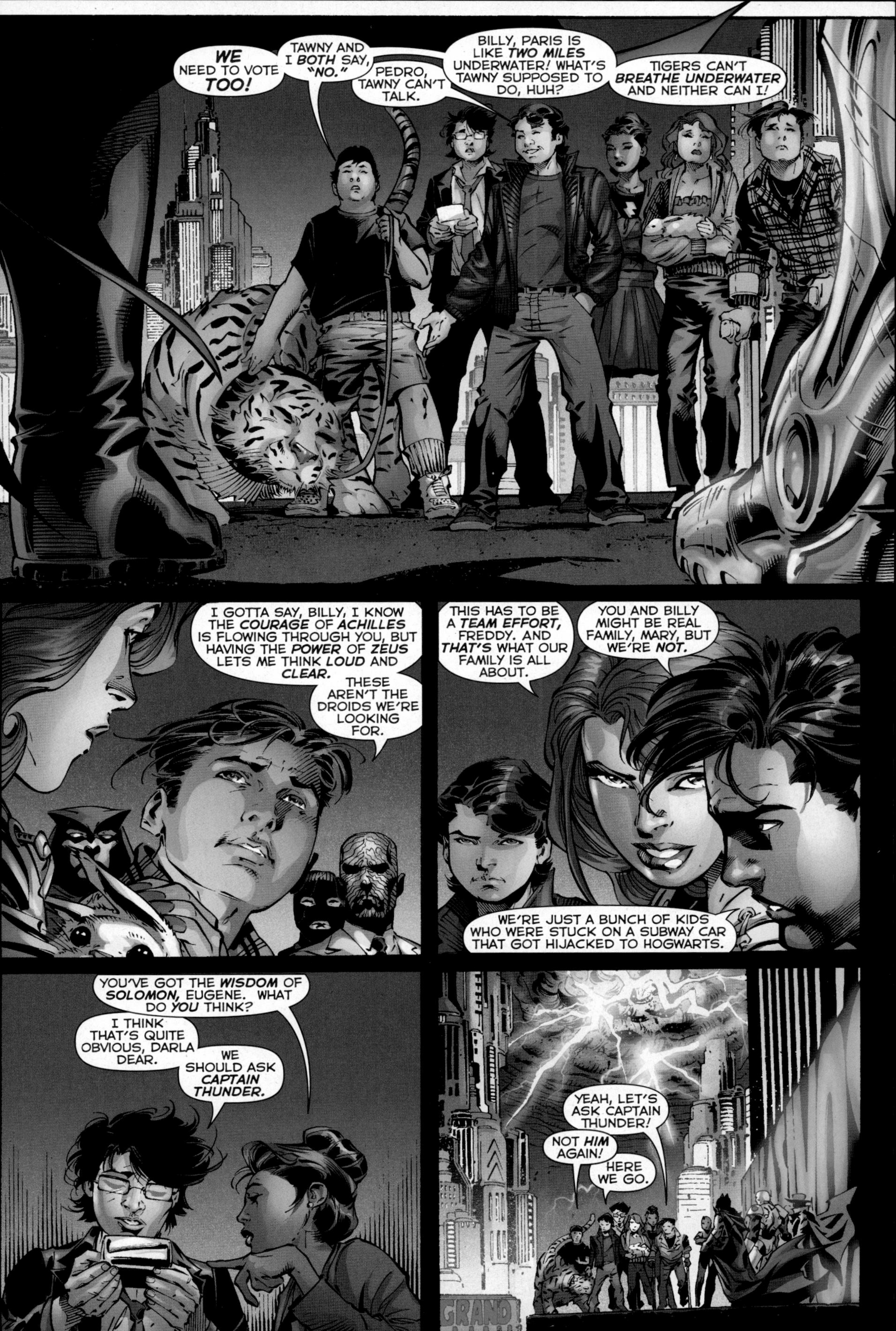

WE NEED TO VOTE TOO!
TAWNY AND I BOTH SAY, "NO."
PEDRO, TAWNY CAN'T TALK.
BILLY, PARIS IS LIKE TWO MILES UNDERWATER! WHAT'S TAWNY SUPPOSED TO DO, HUH?
TIGERS CAN'T BREATHE UNDERWATER AND NEITHER CAN I!
I GOTTA SAY, BILLY, I KNOW THE COURAGE OF ACHILLES IS FLOWING THROUGH YOU, BUT HAVING THE POWER OF ZEUS LETS ME THINK LOUD AND CLEAR.
THESE AREN'T THE DROIDS WE'RE LOOKING FOR.
THIS HAS TO BE A TEAM EFFORT, FREDDY. AND THAT'S WHAT OUR FAMILY IS ALL ABOUT.
YOU AND BILLY MIGHT BE REAL FAMILY, MARY, BUT WE'RE NOT.
WE'RE JUST A BUNCH OF KIDS WHO WERE STUCK ON A SUBWAY CAR THAT GOT HIJACKED TO HOGWARTS.
YOU'VE GOT THE WISDOM OF SOLOMON, EUGENE. WHAT DO YOU THINK?
I THINK THAT'S QUITE OBVIOUS, DARLA DEAR.
WE SHOULD ASK CAPTAIN THUNDER.
YEAH, LET'S ASK CAPTAIN THUNDER!
NOT HIM AGAIN!
HERE WE GO.
GRAND

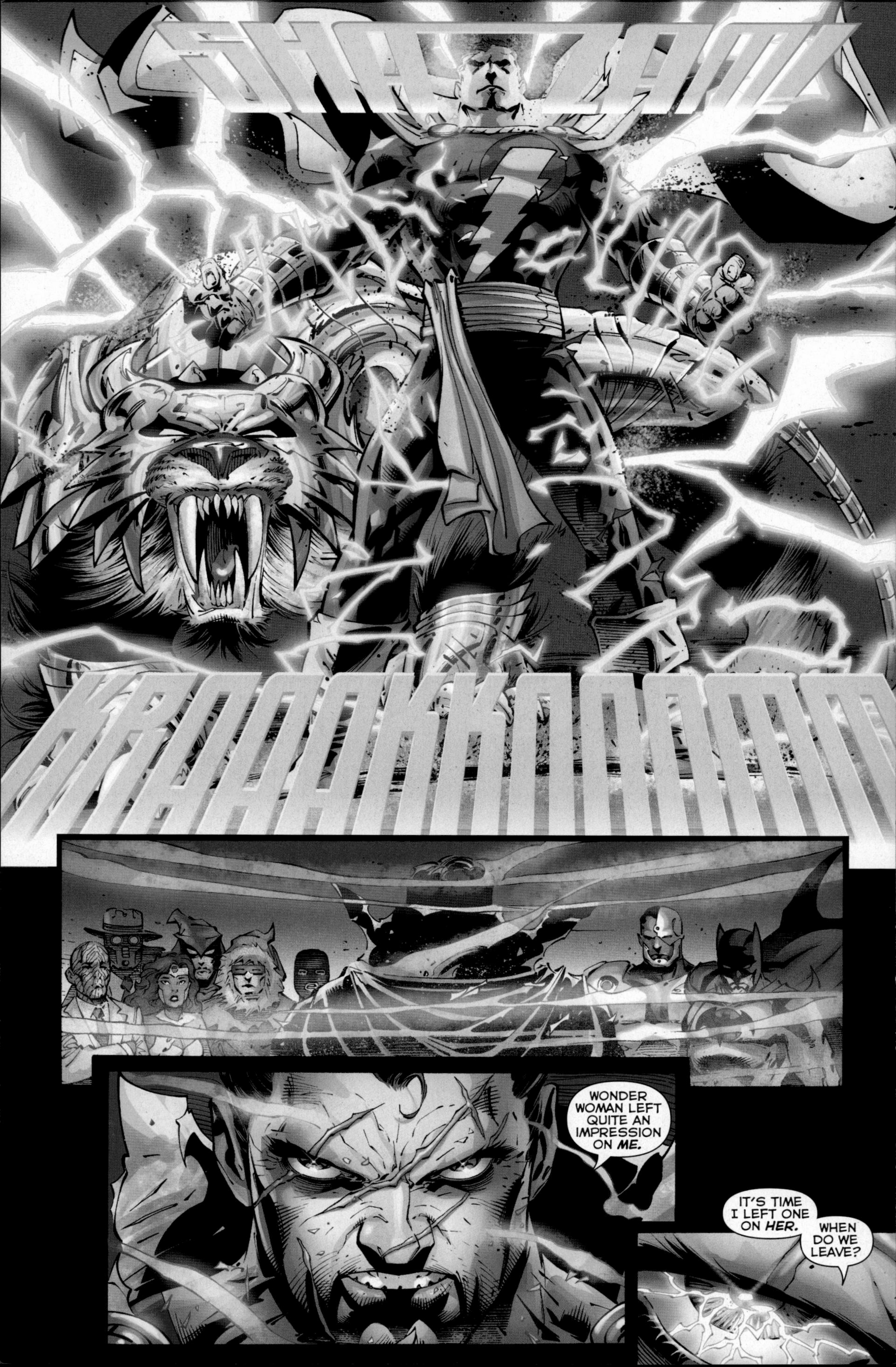
SHAZAM!
KRAAAKKOOOOM
WONDER WOMAN LEFT QUITE AN IMPRESSION ON *ME.*
IT'S TIME I LEFT ONE ON *HER.*
WHEN DO WE LEAVE?

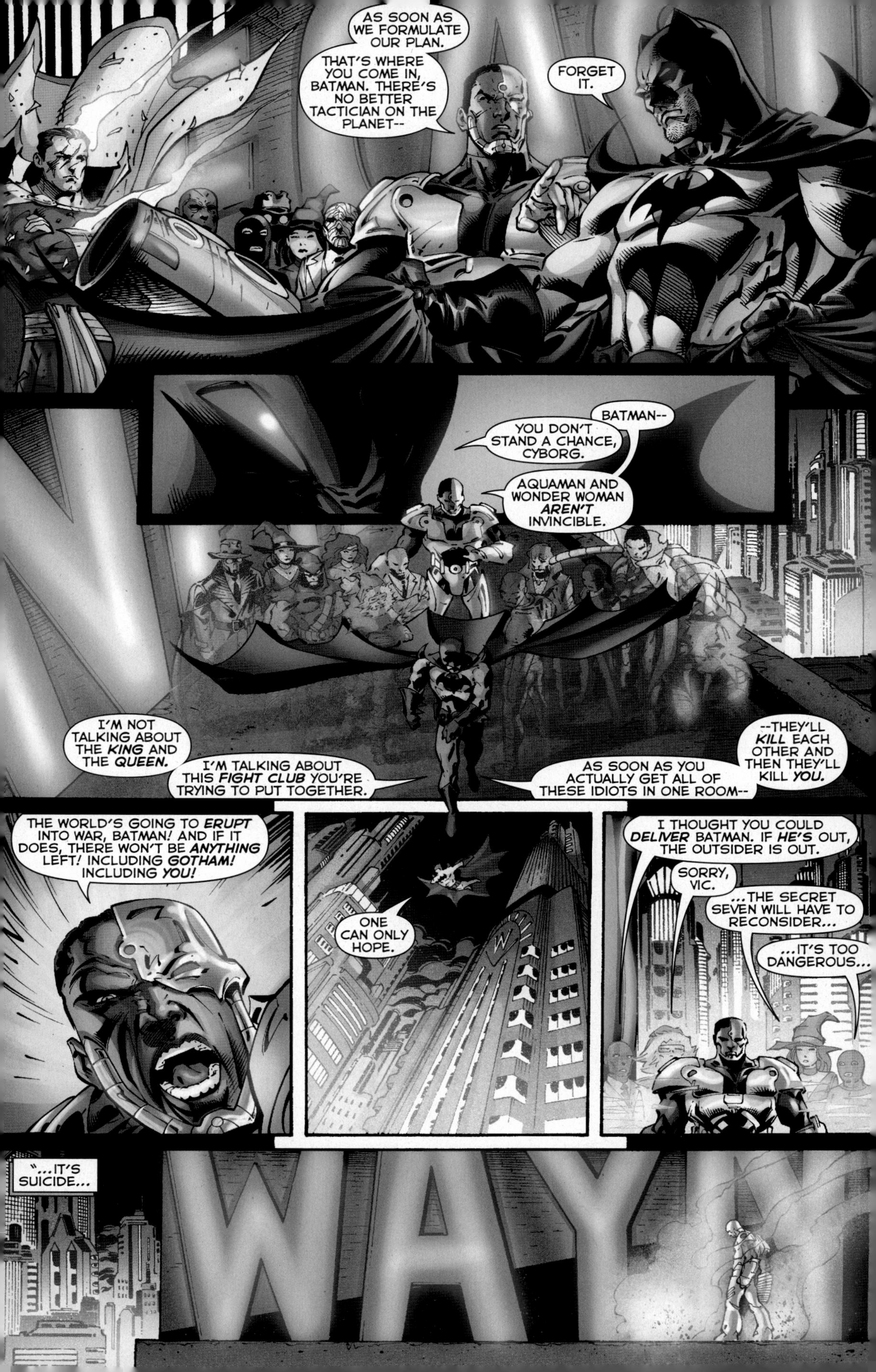
AS SOON AS WE FORMULATE OUR PLAN.
THAT'S WHERE YOU COME IN, BATMAN. THERE'S NO BETTER TACTICIAN ON THE PLANET--
FORGET IT.
BATMAN--
YOU DON'T STAND A CHANCE, CYBORG.
AQUAMAN AND WONDER WOMAN AREN'T INVINCIBLE.
I'M NOT TALKING ABOUT THE KING AND THE QUEEN.
I'M TALKING ABOUT THIS FIGHT CLUB YOU'RE TRYING TO PUT TOGETHER.
AS SOON AS YOU ACTUALLY GET ALL OF THESE IDIOTS IN ONE ROOM--
--THEY'LL KILL EACH OTHER AND THEN THEY'LL KILL YOU.
THE WORLD'S GOING TO ERUPT INTO WAR, BATMAN! AND IF IT DOES, THERE WON'T BE ANYTHING LEFT! INCLUDING GOTHAM! INCLUDING YOU!
ONE CAN ONLY HOPE.
I THOUGHT YOU COULD DELIVER BATMAN. IF HE'S OUT, THE OUTSIDER IS OUT.
SORRY, VIC.
...THE SECRET SEVEN WILL HAVE TO RECONSIDER...
...IT'S TOO DANGEROUS...
"...IT'S SUICIDE...
WAY

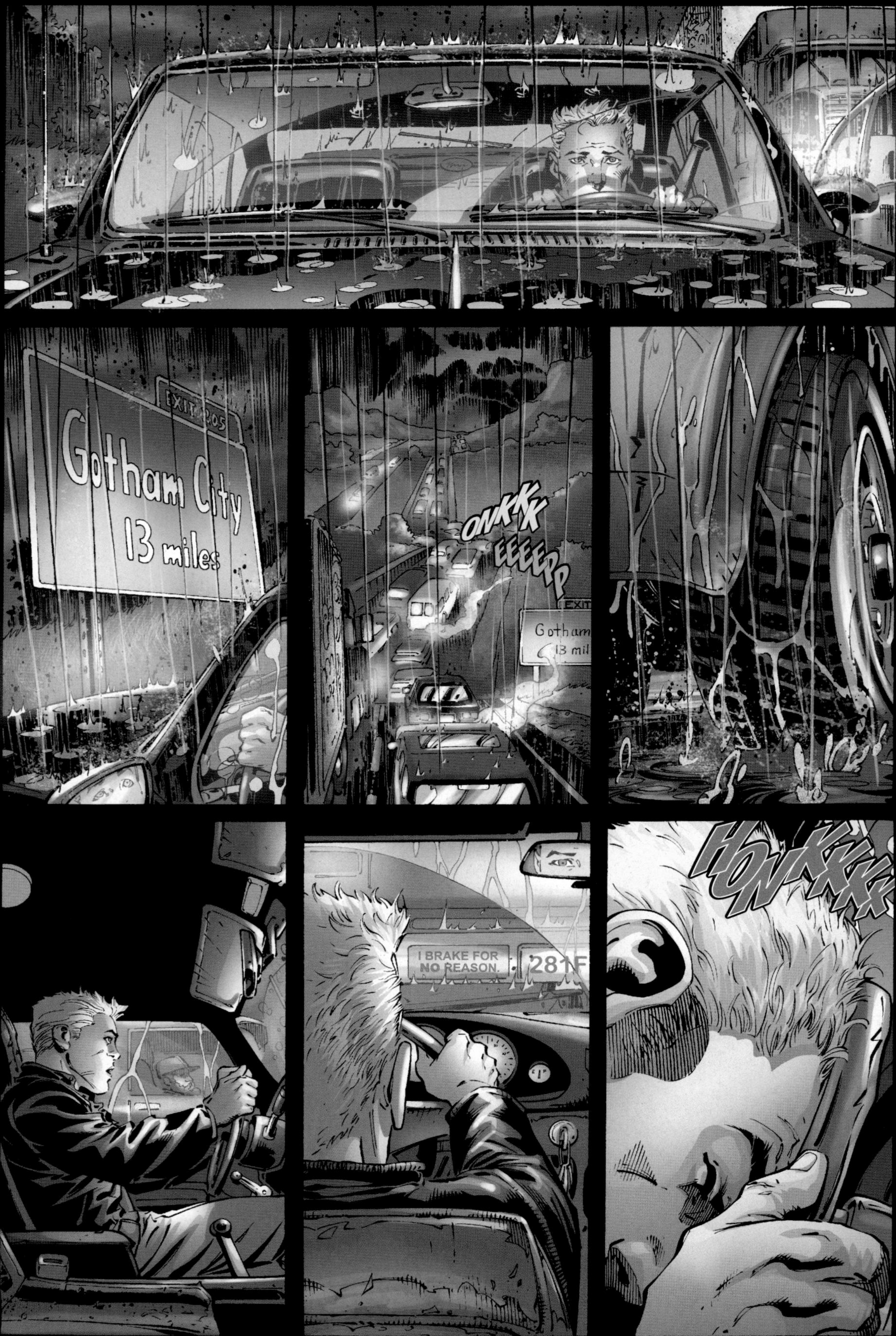
Gotham City
13 miles
ONKKK
EEEEPP
I BRAKE FOR NO REASON.
HONKKKK

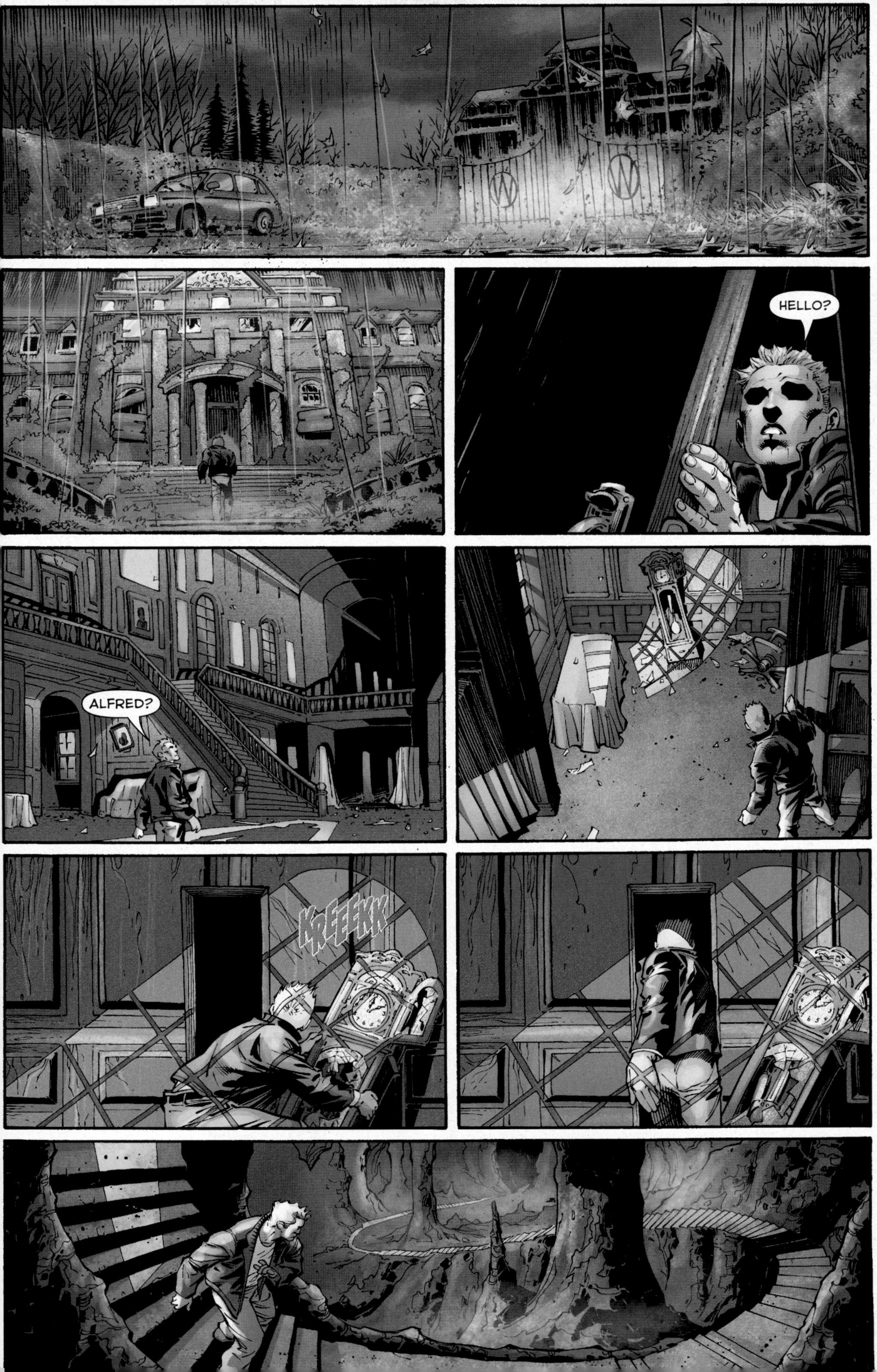
HELLO?
ALFRED?
KREEEKK

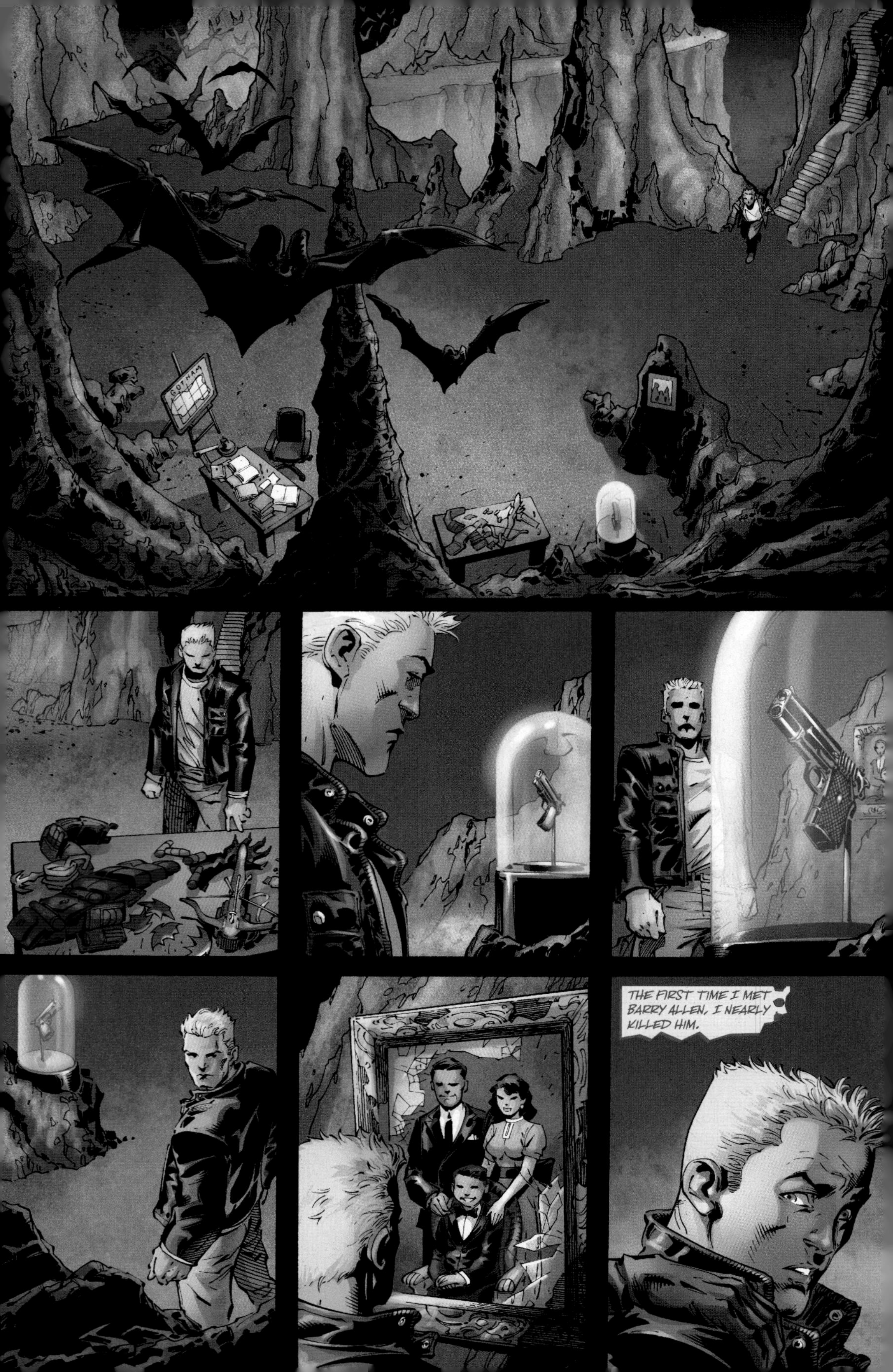
THE FIRST TIME I MET BARRY ALLEN, I NEARLY KILLED HIM.

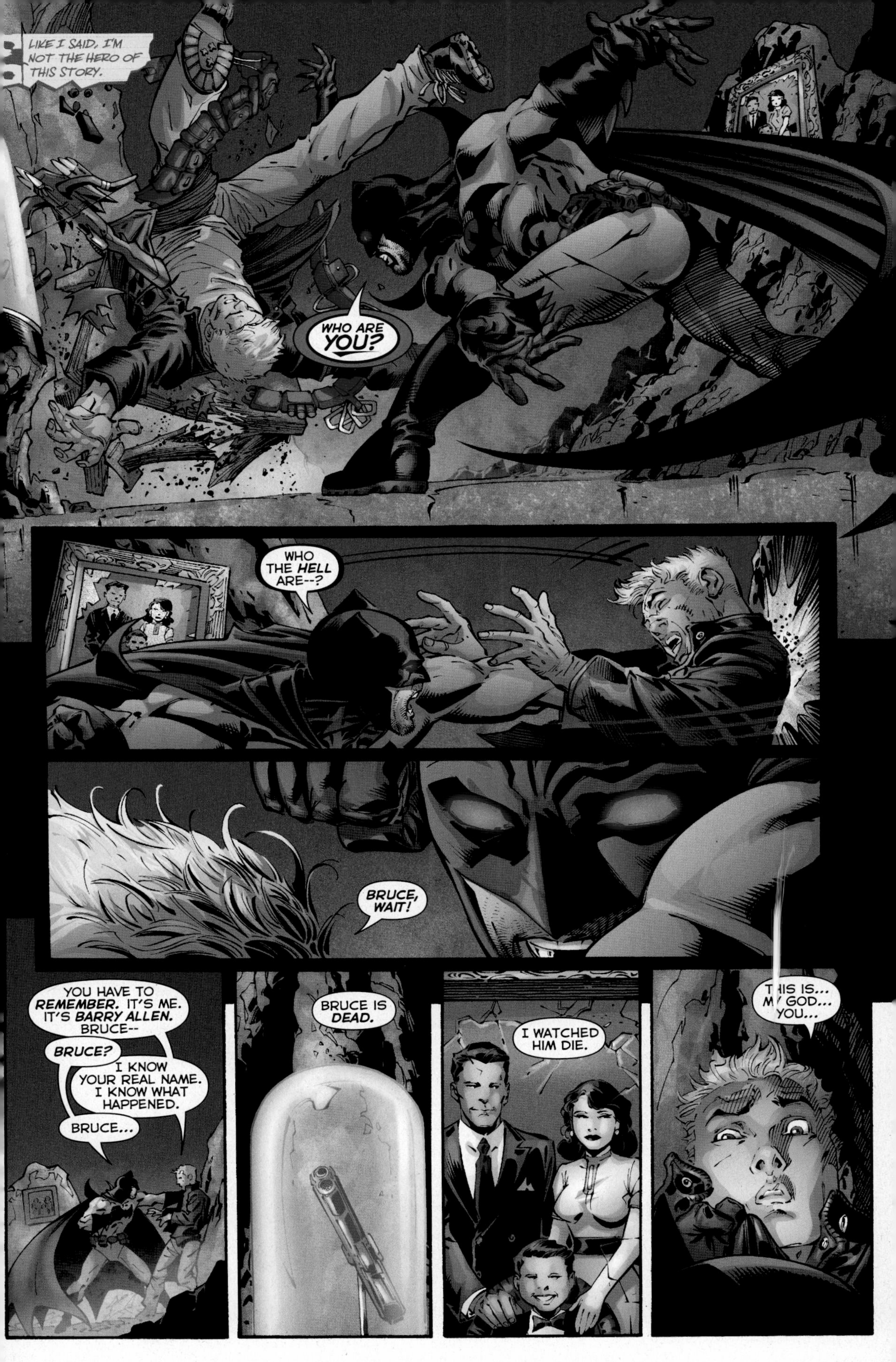
LIKE I SAID, I'M NOT THE HERO OF THIS STORY.
WHO ARE YOU?
WHO THE HELL ARE--?
BRUCE, WAIT!
YOU HAVE TO REMEMBER. IT'S ME. IT'S BARRY ALLEN. BRUCE--
BRUCE?
I KNOW YOUR REAL NAME. I KNOW WHAT HAPPENED.
BRUCE...
BRUCE IS DEAD.
I WATCHED HIM DIE.
THIS IS... MY GOD... YOU...

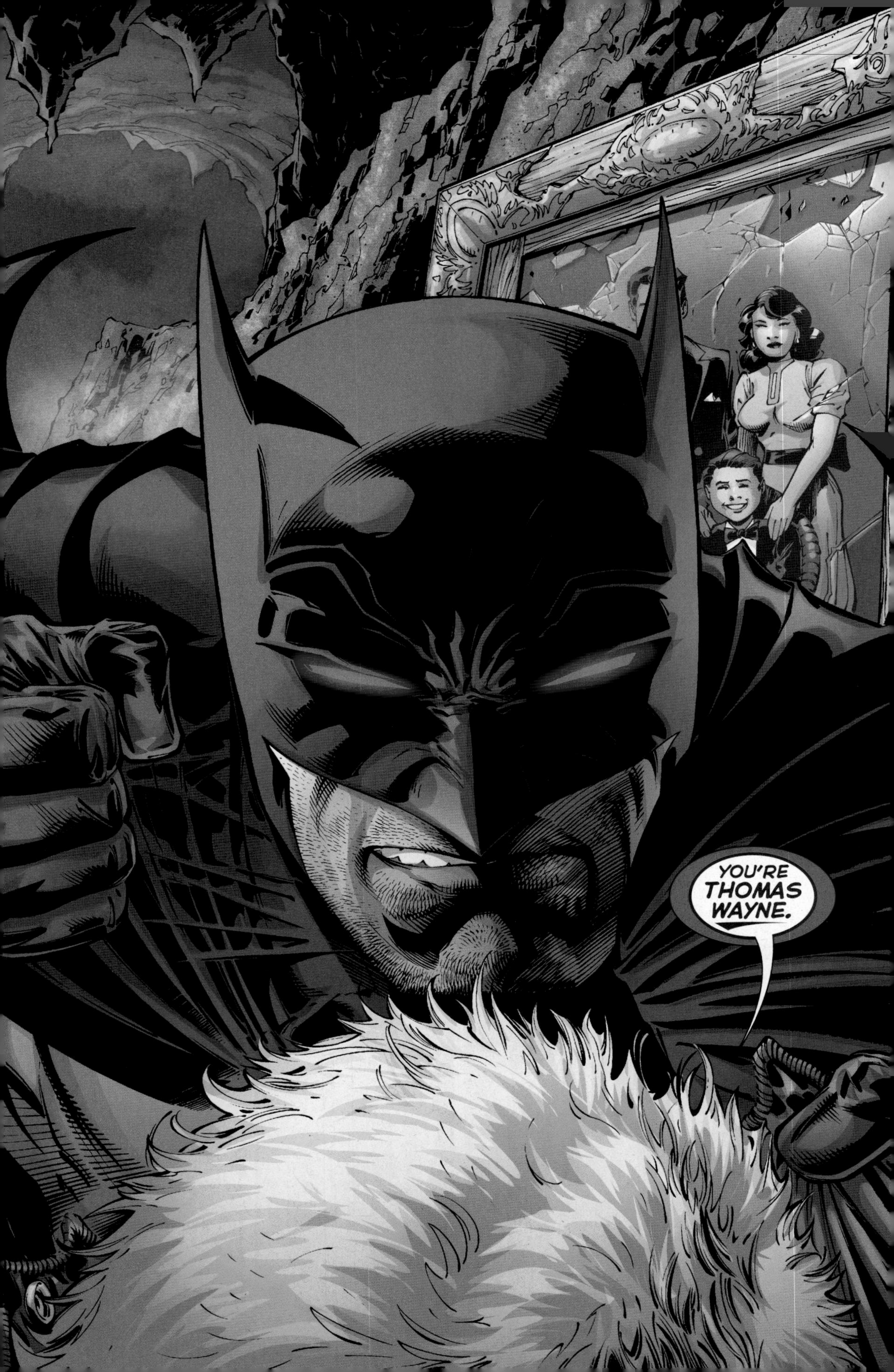
YOU'RE THOMAS WAYNE.

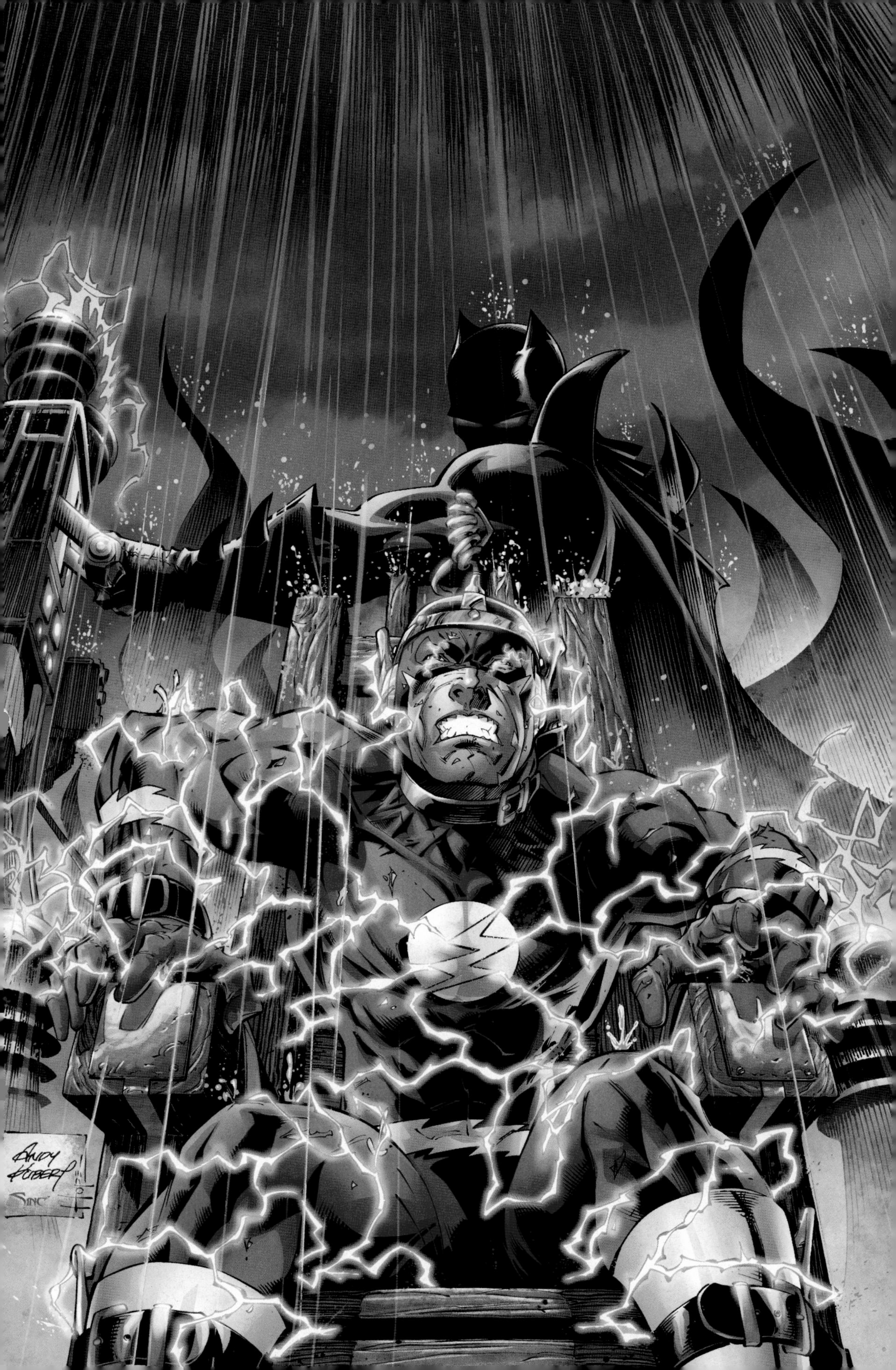
ANDY KUBERT
SINC

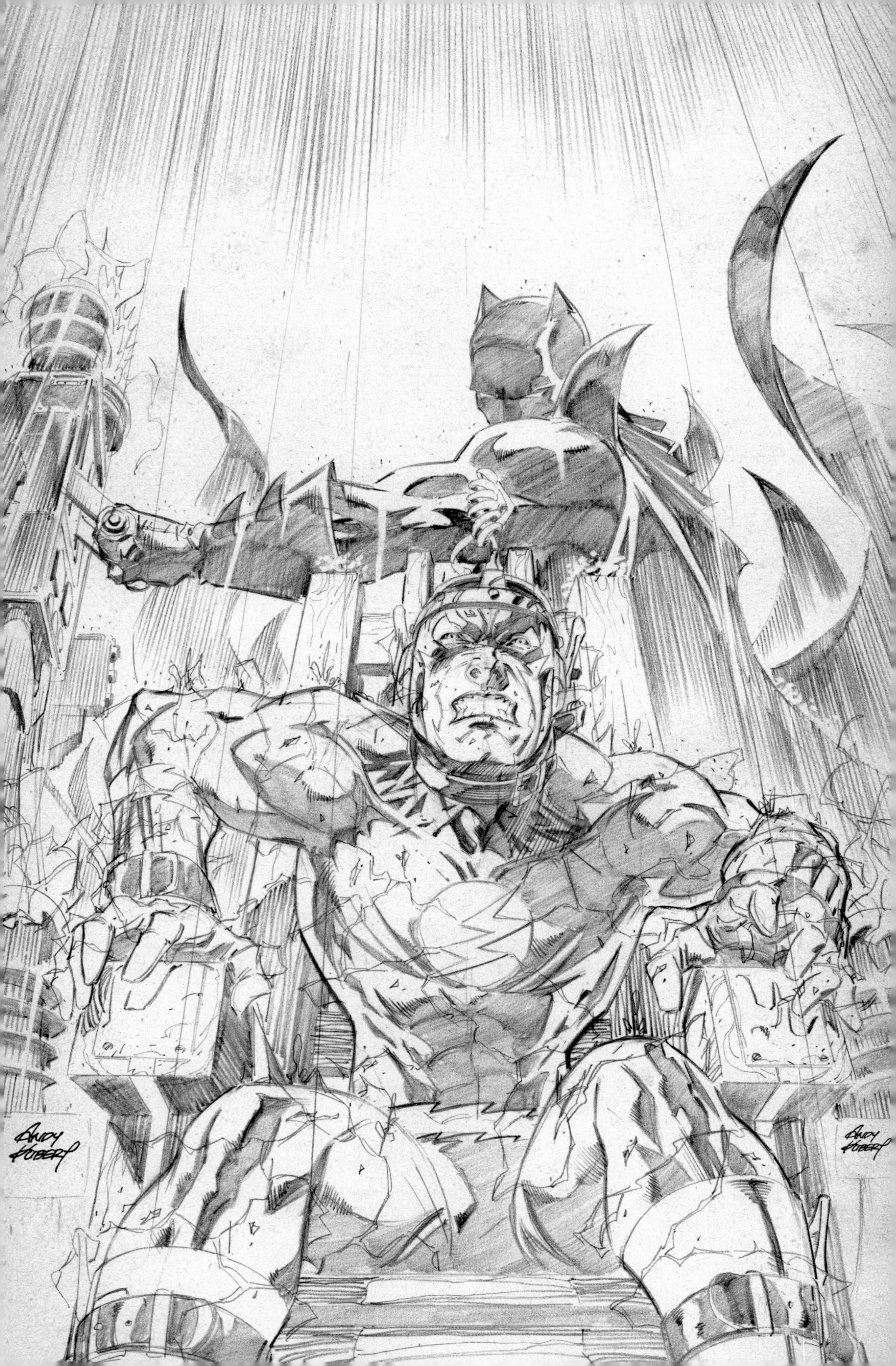
ANDY KUBERT
ANDY KUBERT

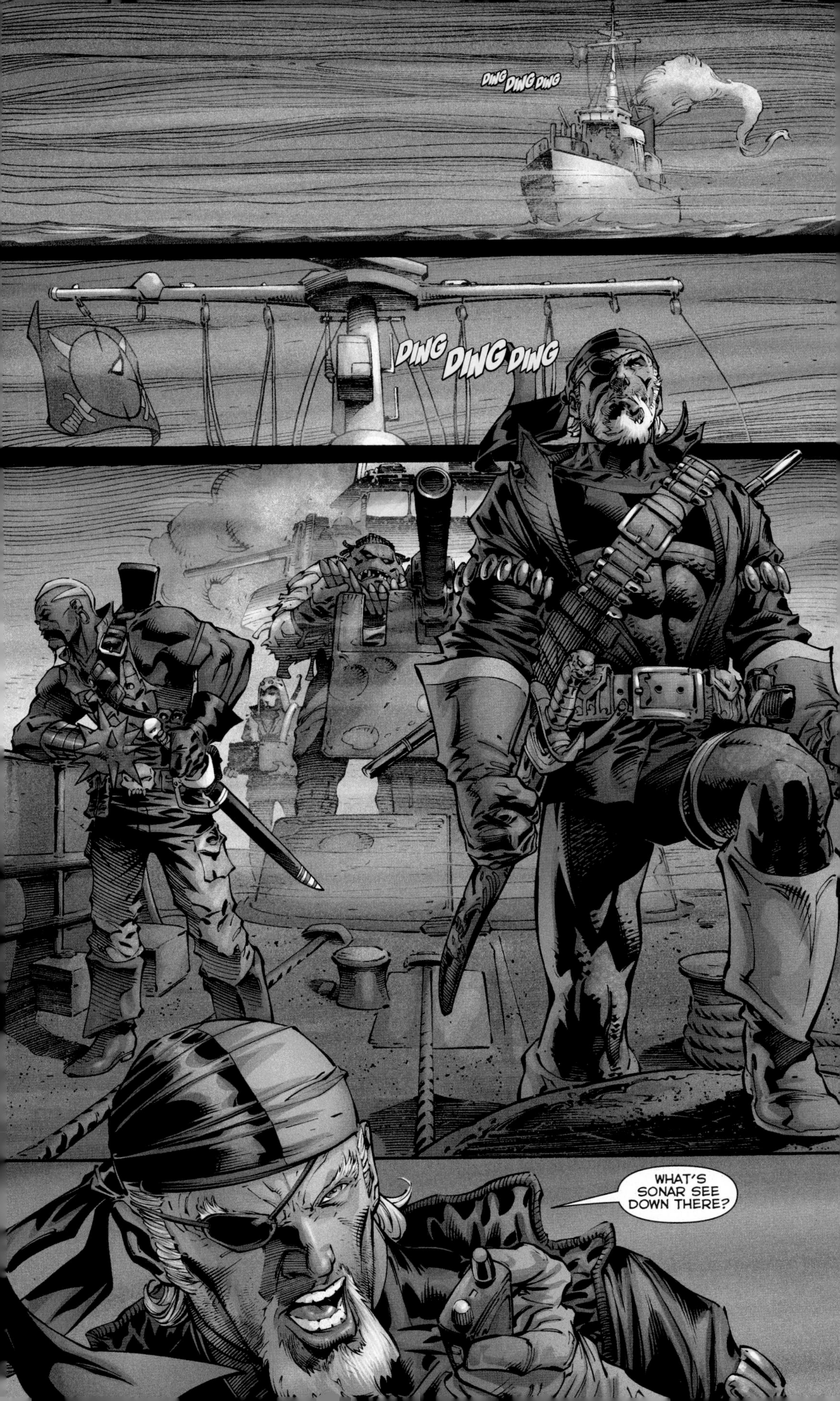
DING DING DING
DING DING DING
WHAT'S SONAR SEE DOWN THERE?

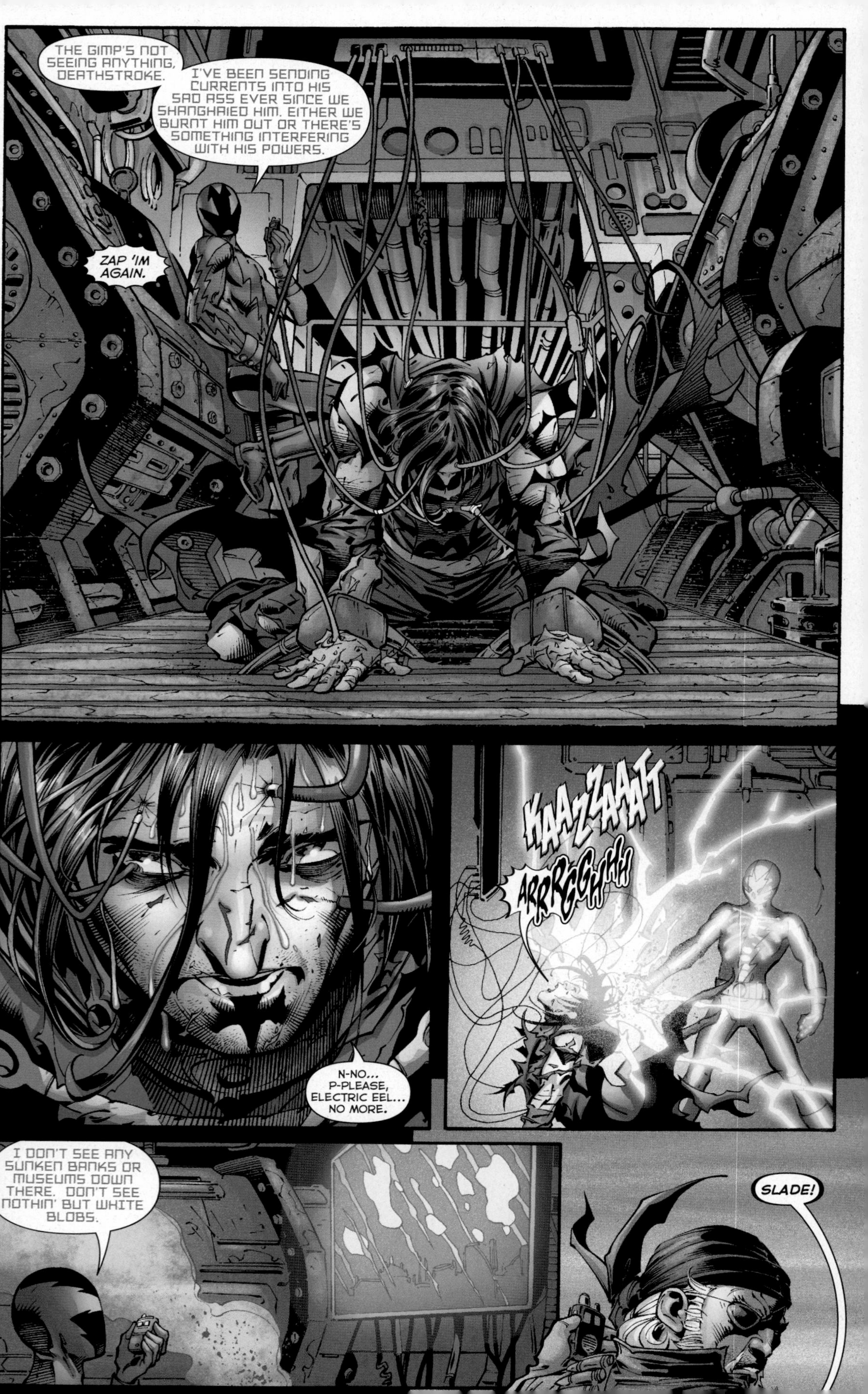
THE GIMP'S NOT SEEING ANYTHING, DEATHSTROKE.
I'VE BEEN SENDING CURRENTS INTO HIS SAD ASS EVER SINCE WE SHANGHAIED HIM. EITHER WE BURNT HIM OUT OR THERE'S SOMETHING INTERFERING WITH HIS POWERS.
ZAP 'IM AGAIN.
N-NO... P-PLEASE, ELECTRIC EEL... NO MORE.
KAAZZAAATT
ARRRGGHHH
I DON'T SEE ANY SUNKEN BANKS OR MUSEUMS DOWN THERE. DON'T SEE NOTHIN' BUT WHITE BLOBS.
SLADE!

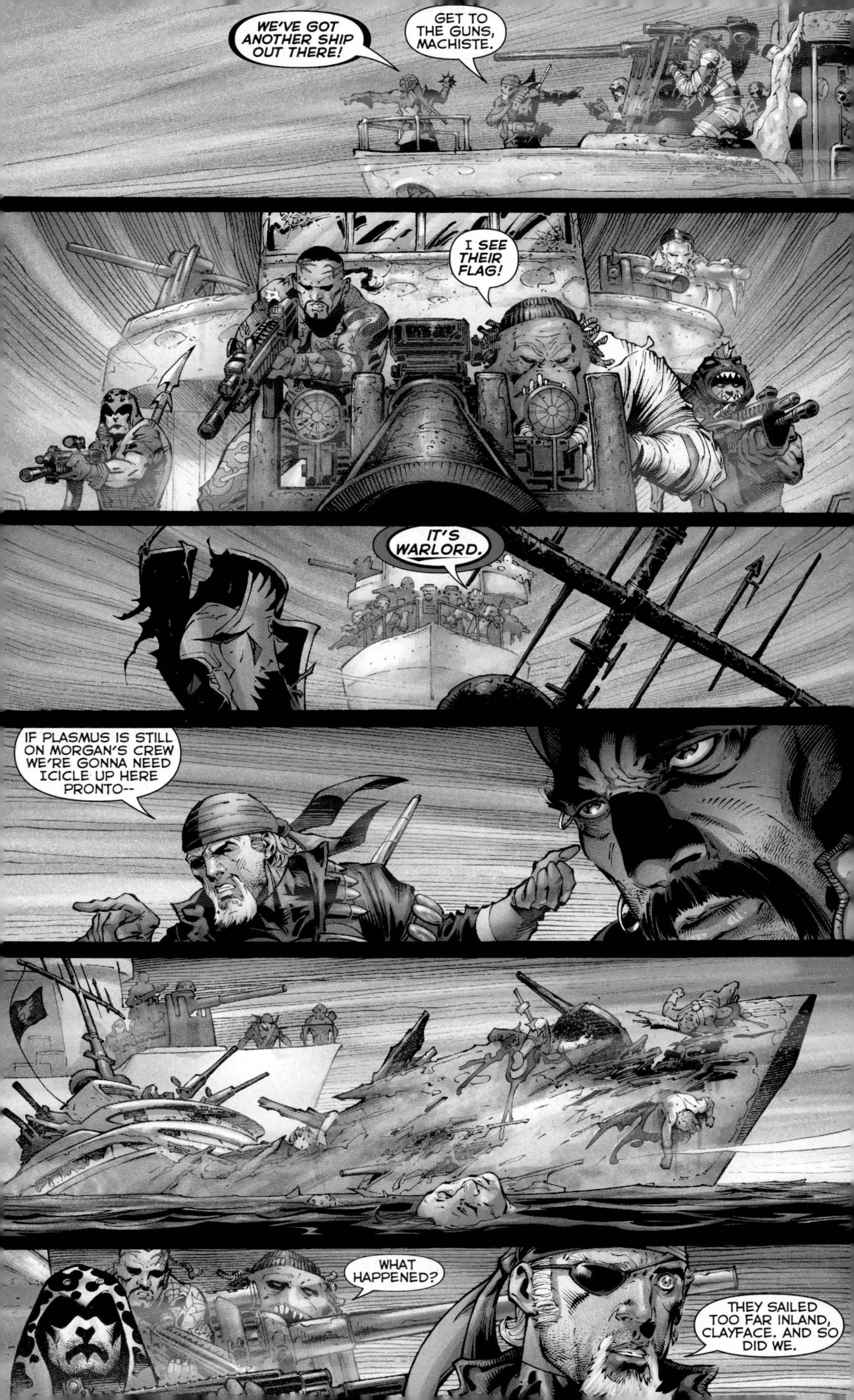
WE'VE GOT ANOTHER SHIP OUT THERE!
GET TO THE GUNS, MACHISTE.
I SEE THEIR FLAG!
IT'S WARLORD.
IF PLASMUS IS STILL ON MORGAN'S CREW WE'RE GONNA NEED ICICLE UP HERE PRONTO--
WHAT HAPPENED?
THEY SAILED TOO FAR INLAND, CLAYFACE. AND SO DID WE.

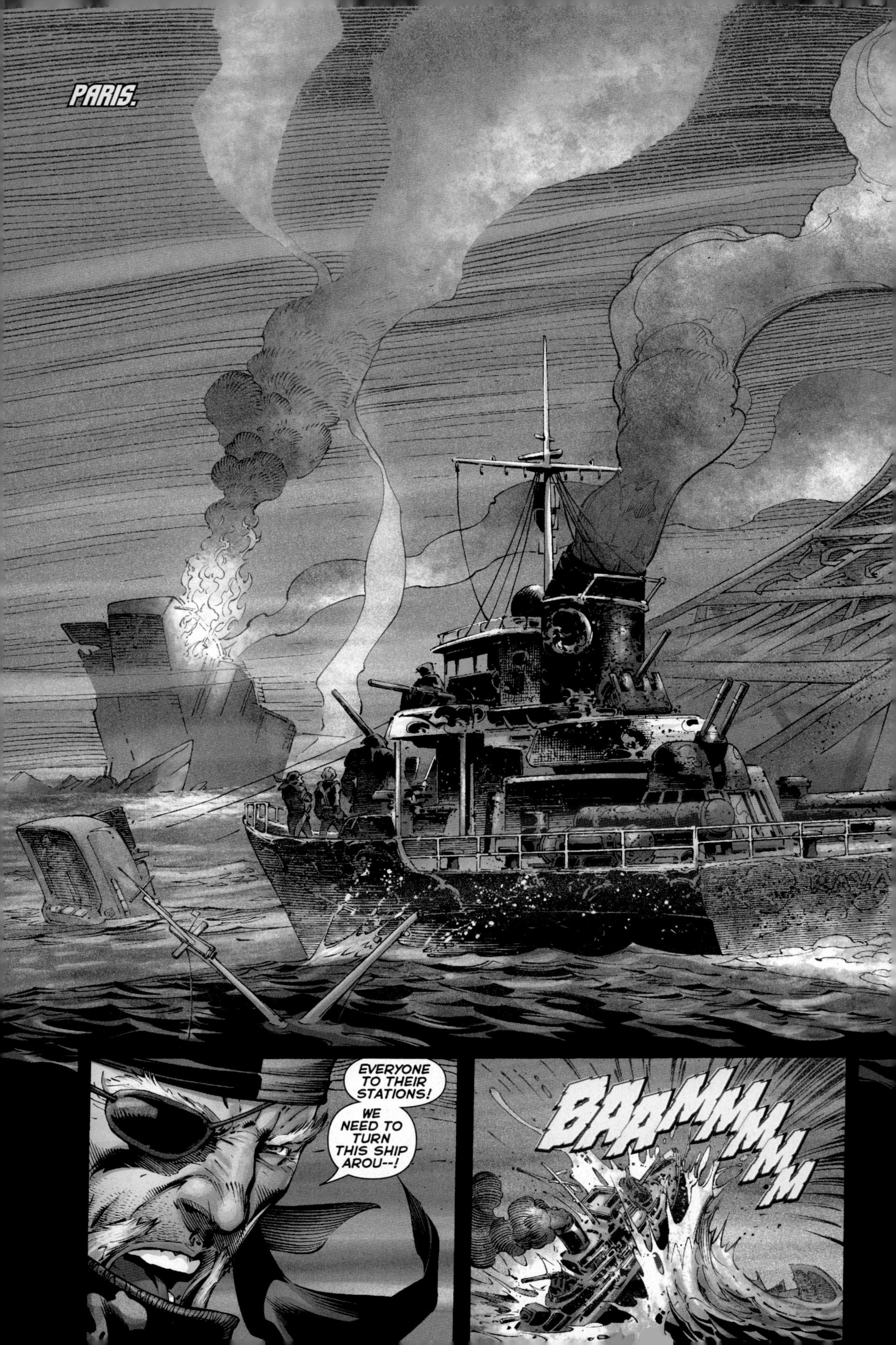
PARIS.
EVERYONE TO THEIR STATIONS!
WE NEED TO TURN THIS SHIP AROU--!
BAAMMMMM

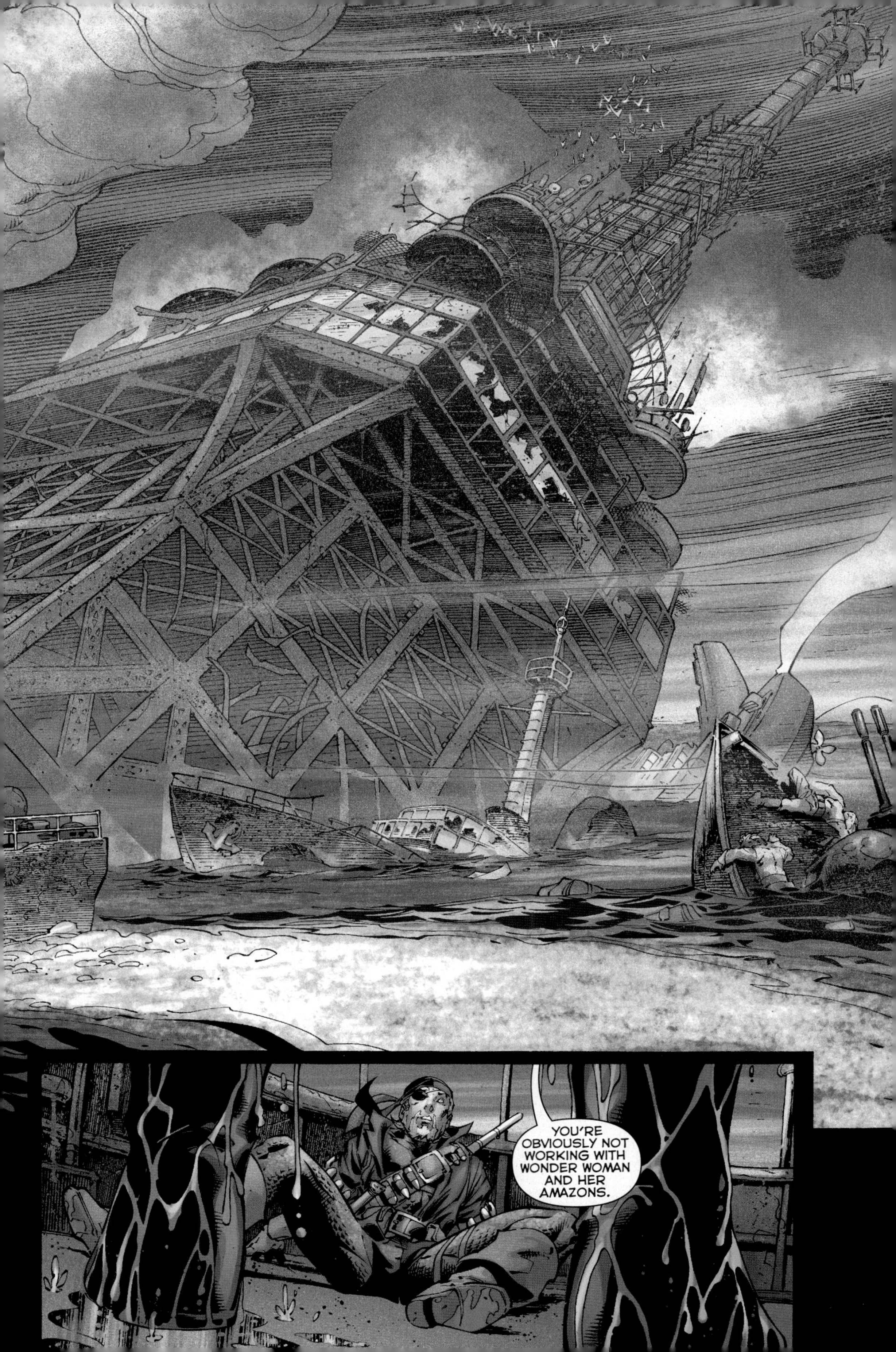
YOU'RE OBVIOUSLY NOT WORKING WITH WONDER WOMAN AND HER AMAZONS.

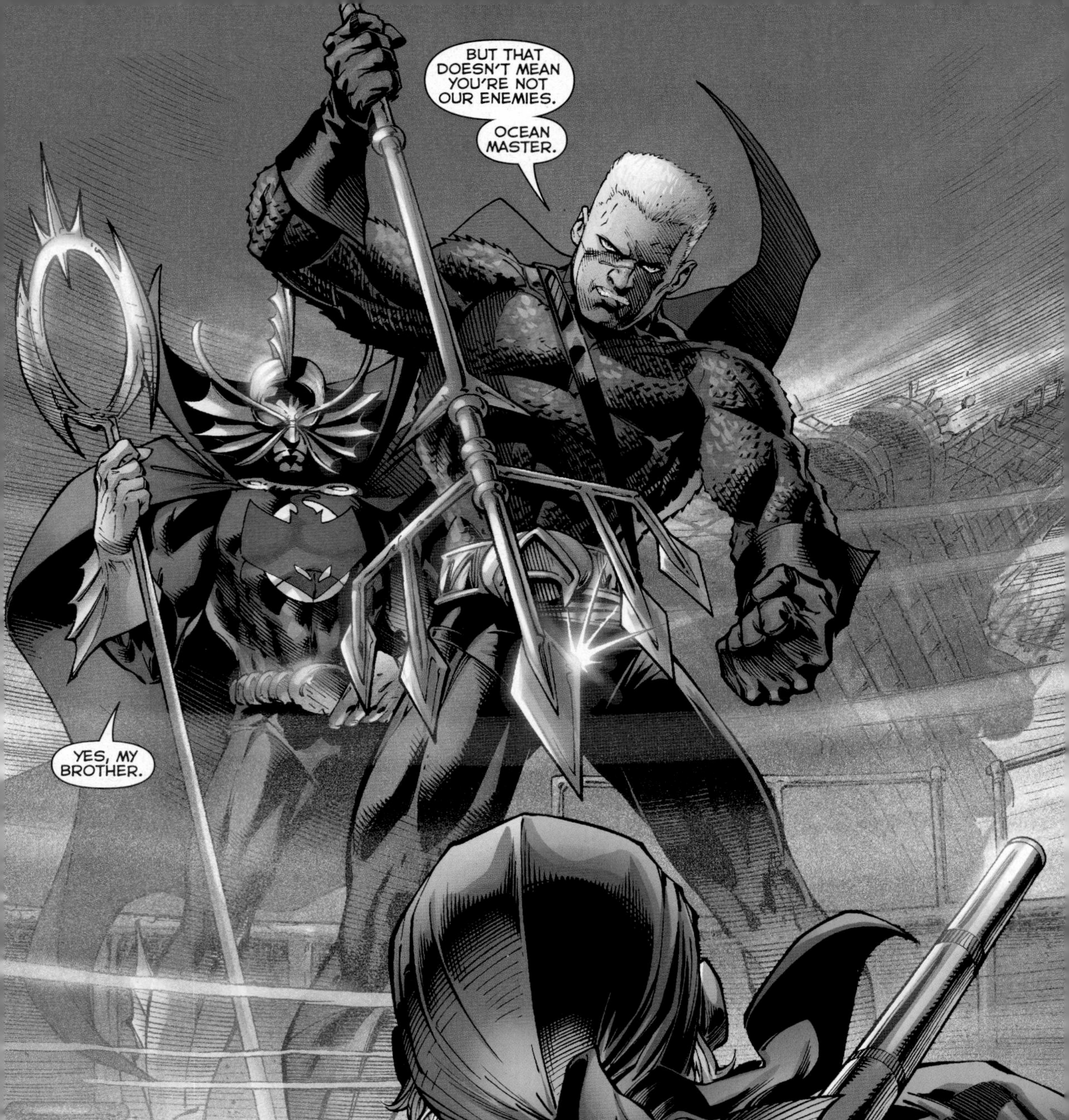
BUT THAT DOESN'T MEAN YOU'RE NOT OUR ENEMIES.
OCEAN MASTER.
YES, MY BROTHER.

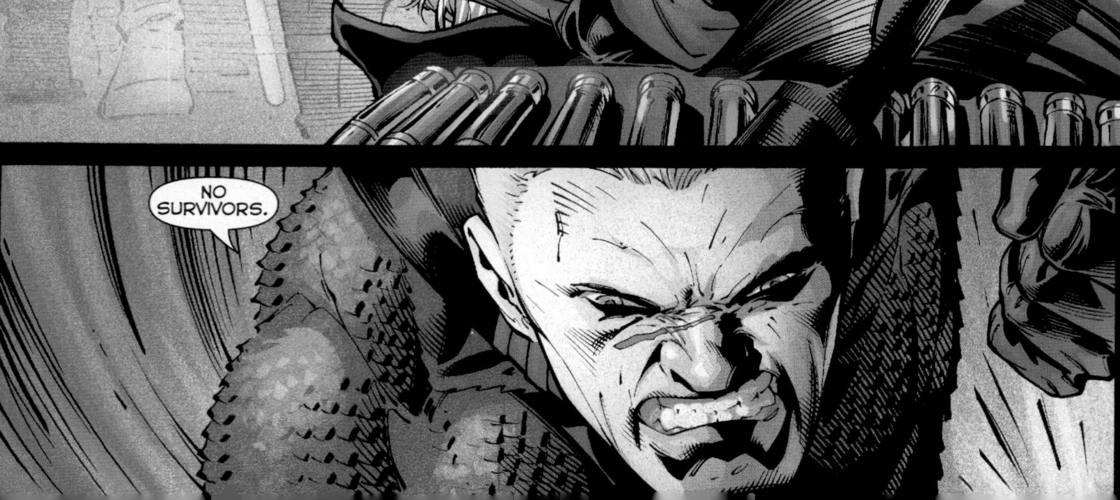
NO SURVIVORS.

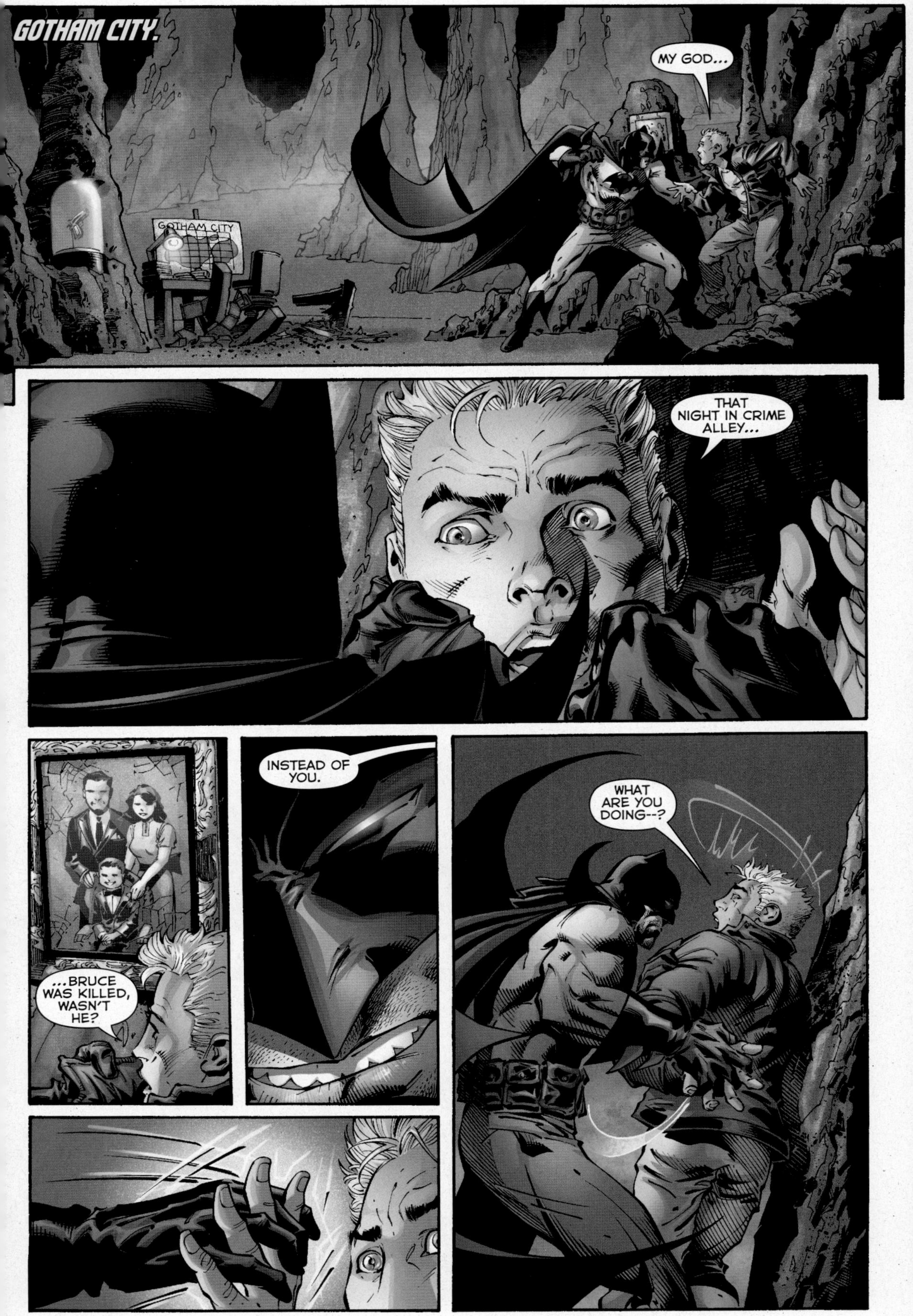
GOTHAM CITY.
MY GOD...
GOTHAM CITY
THAT NIGHT IN CRIME ALLEY...
...BRUCE WAS KILLED, WASN'T HE?
INSTEAD OF YOU.
WHAT ARE YOU DOING--?

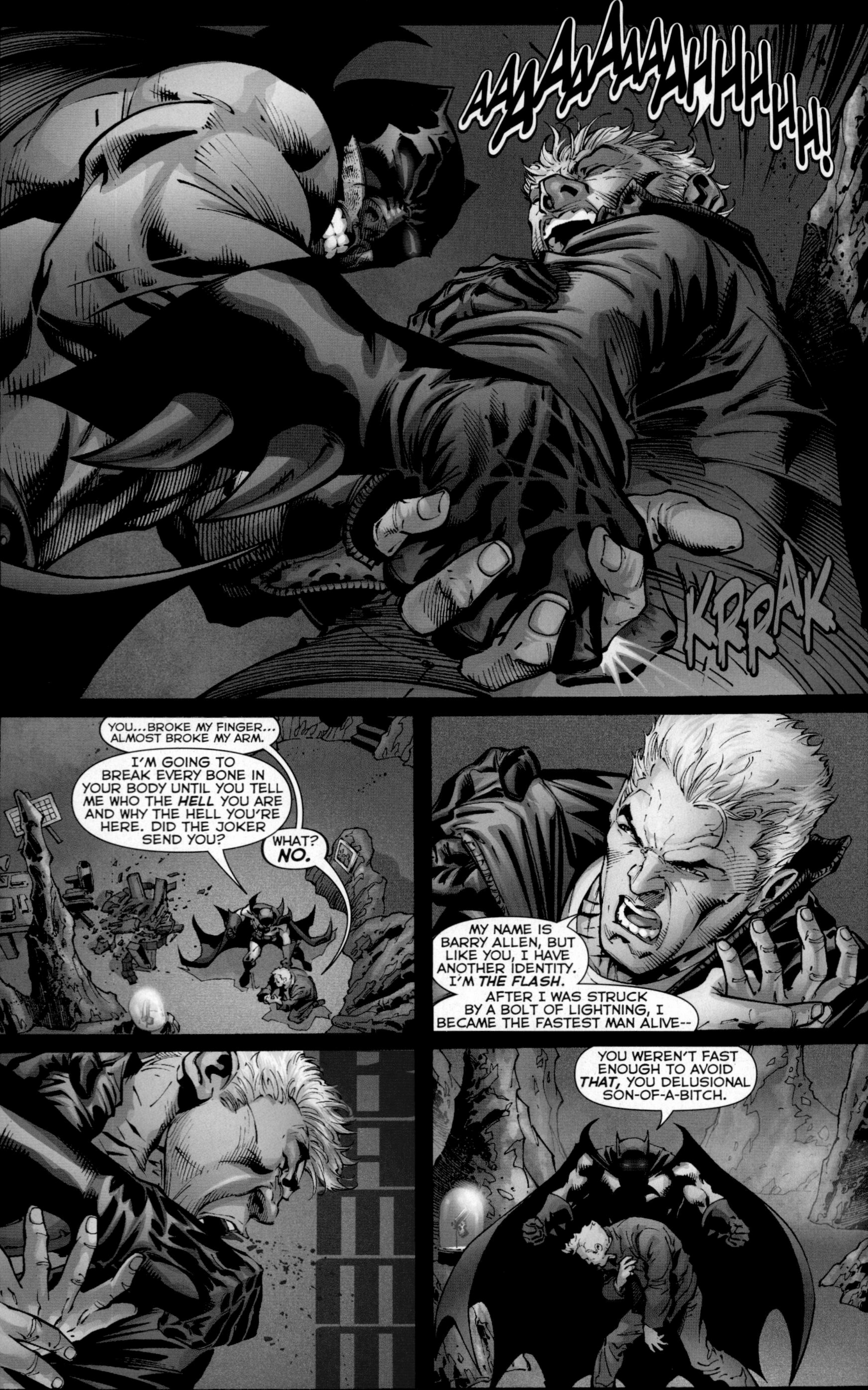

AAAAAAAAHHHHH!
KRRAK
YOU...BROKE MY FINGER... ALMOST BROKE MY ARM.
I'M GOING TO BREAK EVERY BONE IN YOUR BODY UNTIL YOU TELL ME WHO THE *HELL* YOU ARE AND WHY THE HELL YOU'RE HERE. DID THE JOKER SEND YOU?
WHAT? *NO.*
MY NAME IS BARRY ALLEN, BUT LIKE YOU, I HAVE ANOTHER IDENTITY. I'M *THE FLASH*.
AFTER I WAS STRUCK BY A BOLT OF LIGHTNING, I BECAME THE FASTEST MAN ALIVE--
YOU WEREN'T FAST ENOUGH TO AVOID *THAT,* YOU DELUSIONAL SON-OF-A-BITCH.

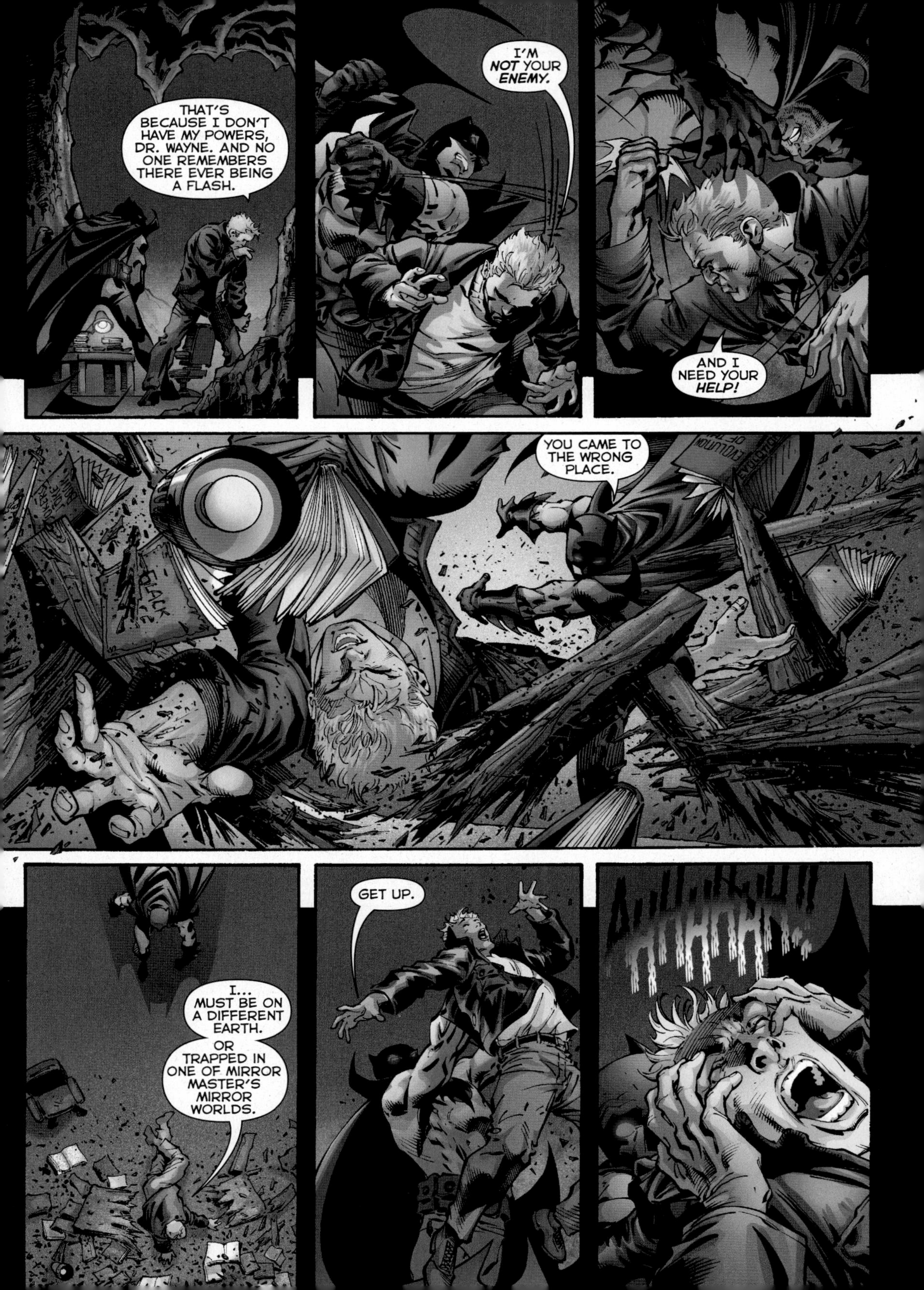
THAT'S BECAUSE I DON'T HAVE MY POWERS, DR. WAYNE. AND NO ONE REMEMBERS THERE EVER BEING A FLASH.
I'M NOT YOUR ENEMY.
AND I NEED YOUR HELP!
YOU CAME TO THE WRONG PLACE.
I... MUST BE ON A DIFFERENT EARTH.
OR TRAPPED IN ONE OF MIRROR MASTER'S MIRROR WORLDS.
GET UP.

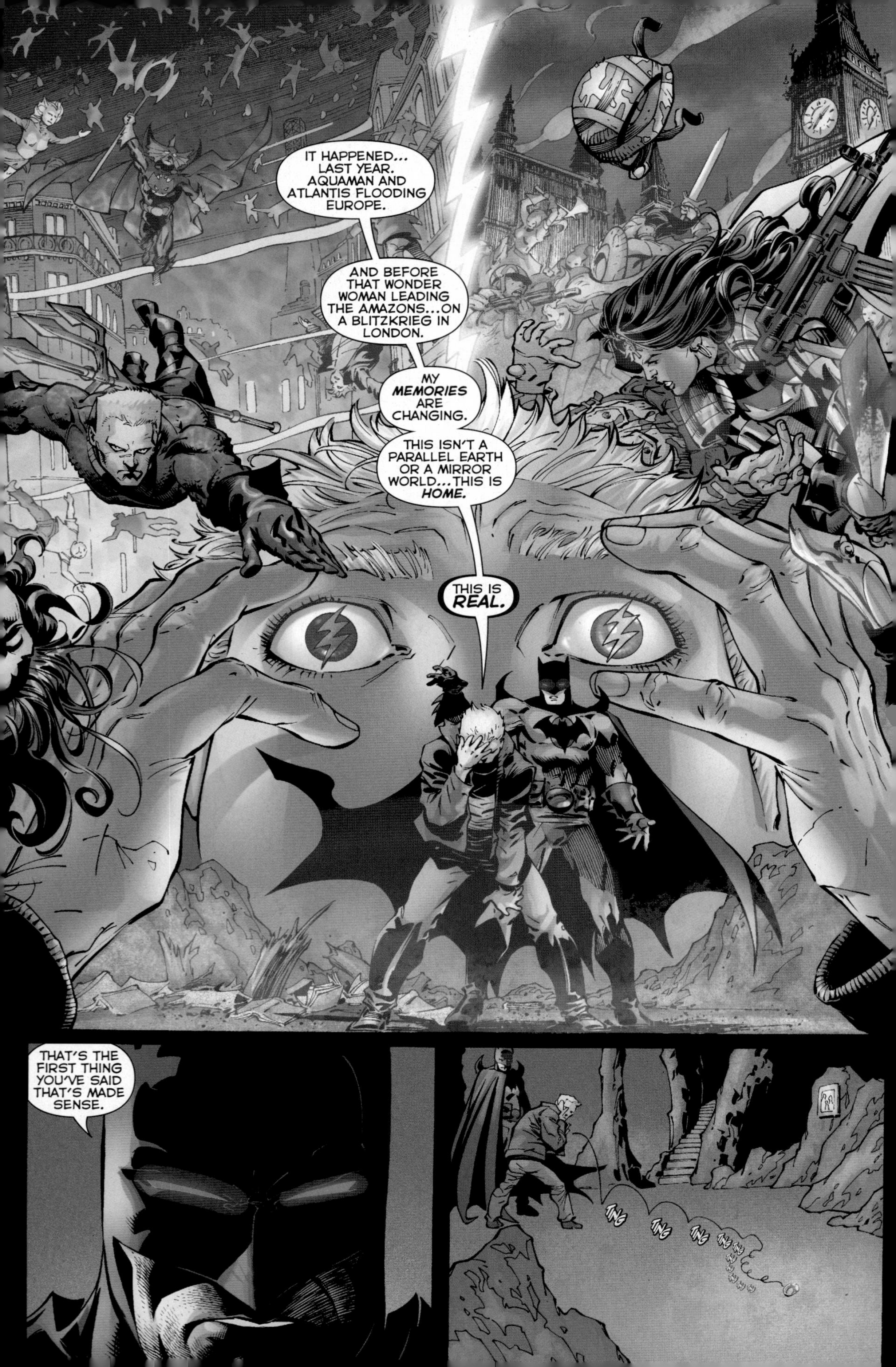
IT HAPPENED... LAST YEAR. AQUAMAN AND ATLANTIS FLOODING EUROPE.
AND BEFORE THAT WONDER WOMAN LEADING THE AMAZONS...ON A BLITZKRIEG IN LONDON.
MY MEMORIES ARE CHANGING.
THIS ISN'T A PARALLEL EARTH OR A MIRROR WORLD...THIS IS HOME.
THIS IS REAL.
THAT'S THE FIRST THING YOU'VE SAID THAT'S MADE SENSE.
TING TING TING TING TING

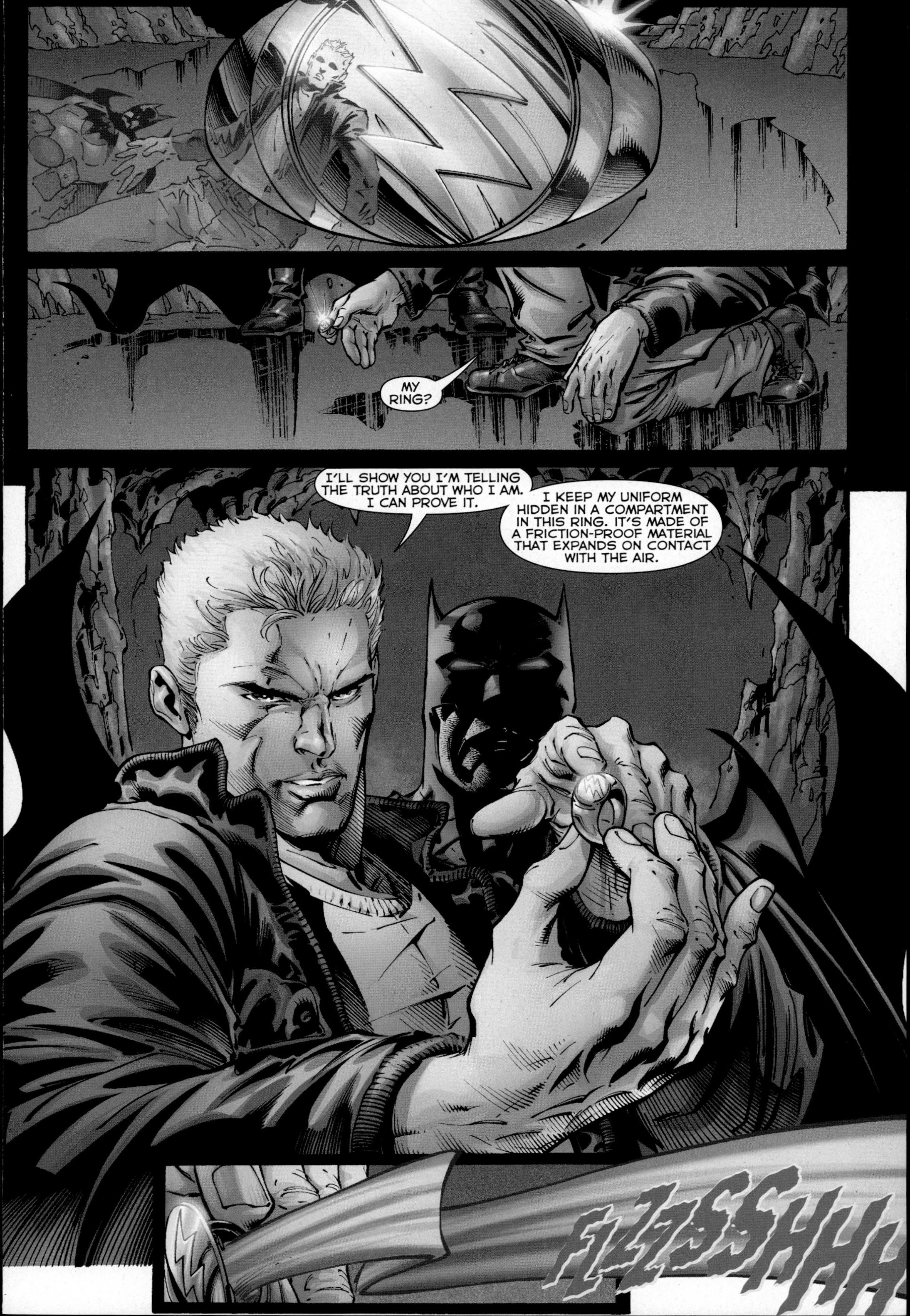
MY RING?
I'LL SHOW YOU I'M TELLING THE TRUTH ABOUT WHO I AM. I CAN PROVE IT.
I KEEP MY UNIFORM HIDDEN IN A COMPARTMENT IN THIS RING. IT'S MADE OF A FRICTION-PROOF MATERIAL THAT EXPANDS ON CONTACT WITH THE AIR.
FIZZSSHHH

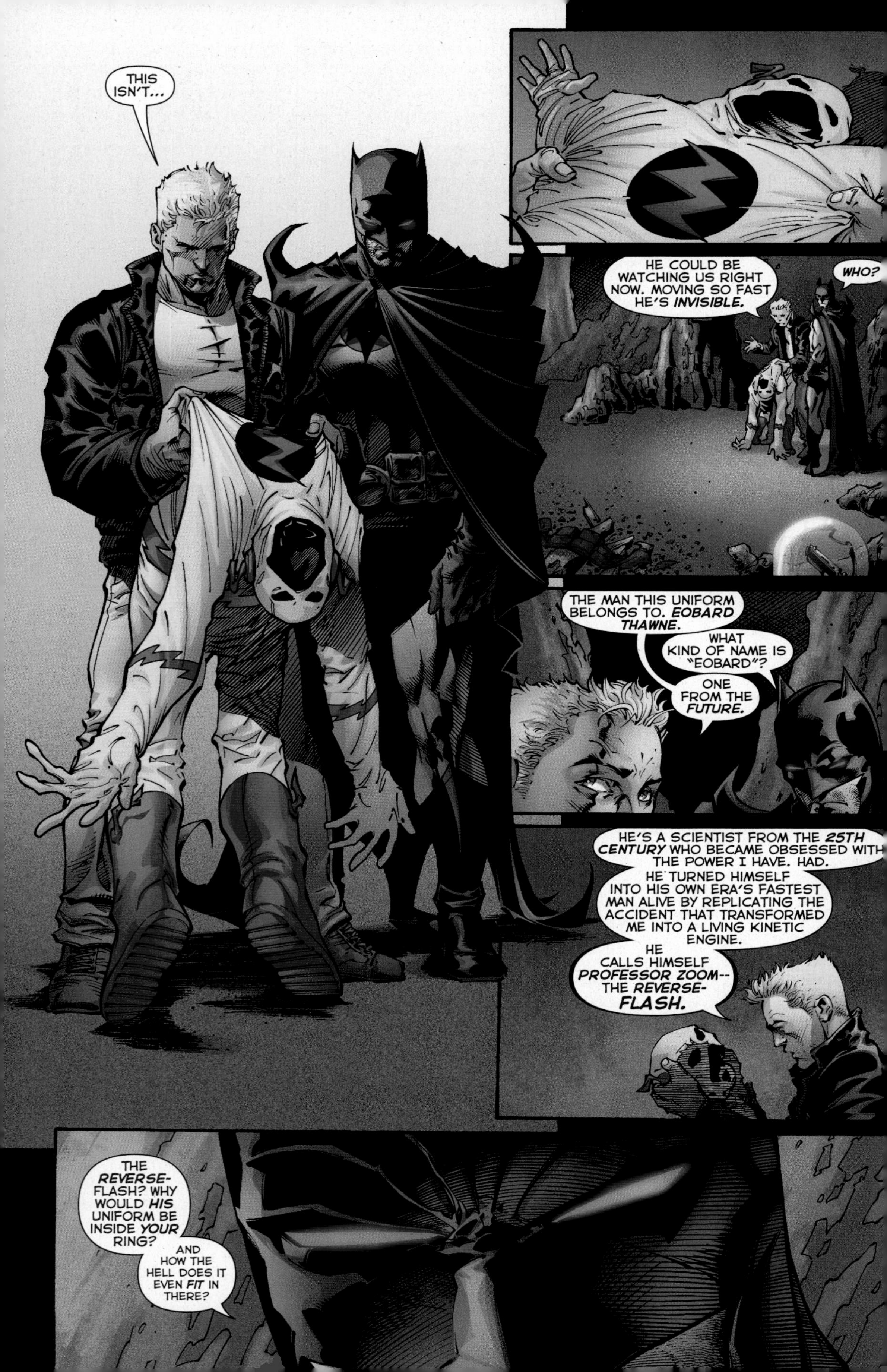
THIS ISN'T...
HE COULD BE WATCHING US RIGHT NOW. MOVING SO FAST HE'S INVISIBLE.
WHO?
THE MAN THIS UNIFORM BELONGS TO. EOBARD THAWNE.
WHAT KIND OF NAME IS "EOBARD"?
ONE FROM THE FUTURE.
HE'S A SCIENTIST FROM THE 25TH CENTURY WHO BECAME OBSESSED WITH THE POWER I HAVE. HAD.
HE TURNED HIMSELF INTO HIS OWN ERA'S FASTEST MAN ALIVE BY REPLICATING THE ACCIDENT THAT TRANSFORMED ME INTO A LIVING KINETIC ENGINE.
HE CALLS HIMSELF PROFESSOR ZOOM-- THE REVERSE-FLASH.
THE REVERSE-FLASH? WHY WOULD HIS UNIFORM BE INSIDE YOUR RING?
AND HOW THE HELL DOES IT EVEN FIT IN THERE?

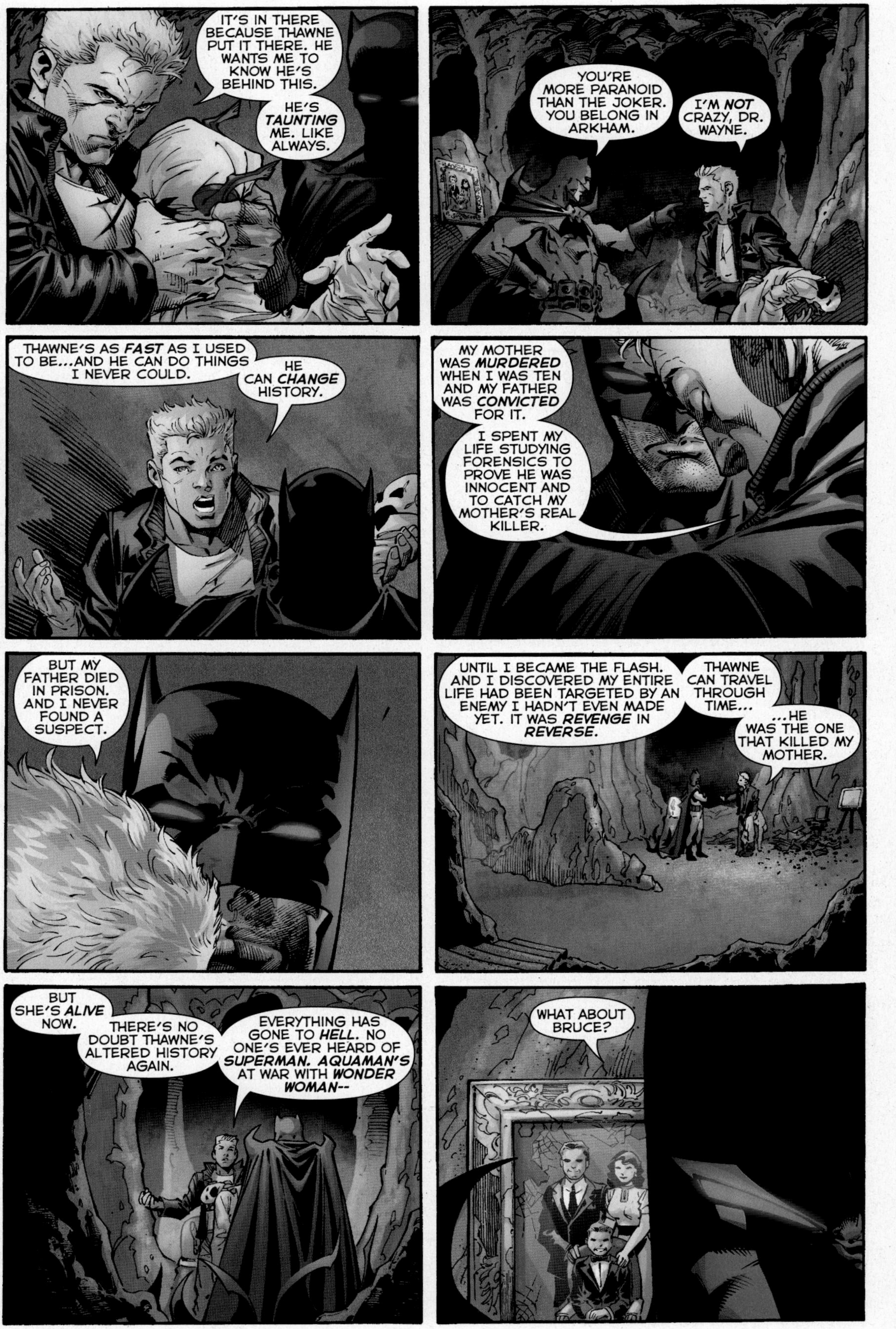
IT'S IN THERE BECAUSE THAWNE PUT IT THERE. HE WANTS ME TO KNOW HE'S BEHIND THIS.
HE'S *TAUNTING* ME. LIKE ALWAYS.
YOU'RE MORE PARANOID THAN THE JOKER. YOU BELONG IN ARKHAM.
I'M *NOT* CRAZY, DR. WAYNE.
THAWNE'S AS *FAST* AS I USED TO BE...AND HE CAN DO THINGS I NEVER COULD.
HE CAN *CHANGE* HISTORY.
MY MOTHER WAS *MURDERED* WHEN I WAS TEN AND MY FATHER WAS *CONVICTED* FOR IT.
I SPENT MY LIFE STUDYING FORENSICS TO PROVE HE WAS INNOCENT AND TO CATCH MY MOTHER'S REAL KILLER.
BUT MY FATHER DIED IN PRISON. AND I NEVER FOUND A SUSPECT.
UNTIL I BECAME THE FLASH. AND I DISCOVERED MY ENTIRE LIFE HAD BEEN TARGETED BY AN ENEMY I HADN'T EVEN MADE YET. IT WAS *REVENGE* IN *REVERSE*.
THAWNE CAN TRAVEL THROUGH TIME...
...HE WAS THE ONE THAT KILLED MY MOTHER.
BUT SHE'S *ALIVE* NOW.
THERE'S NO DOUBT THAWNE'S ALTERED HISTORY AGAIN.
EVERYTHING HAS GONE TO *HELL*. NO ONE'S EVER HEARD OF *SUPERMAN*. *AQUAMAN'S* AT WAR WITH *WONDER WOMAN*--
WHAT ABOUT BRUCE?

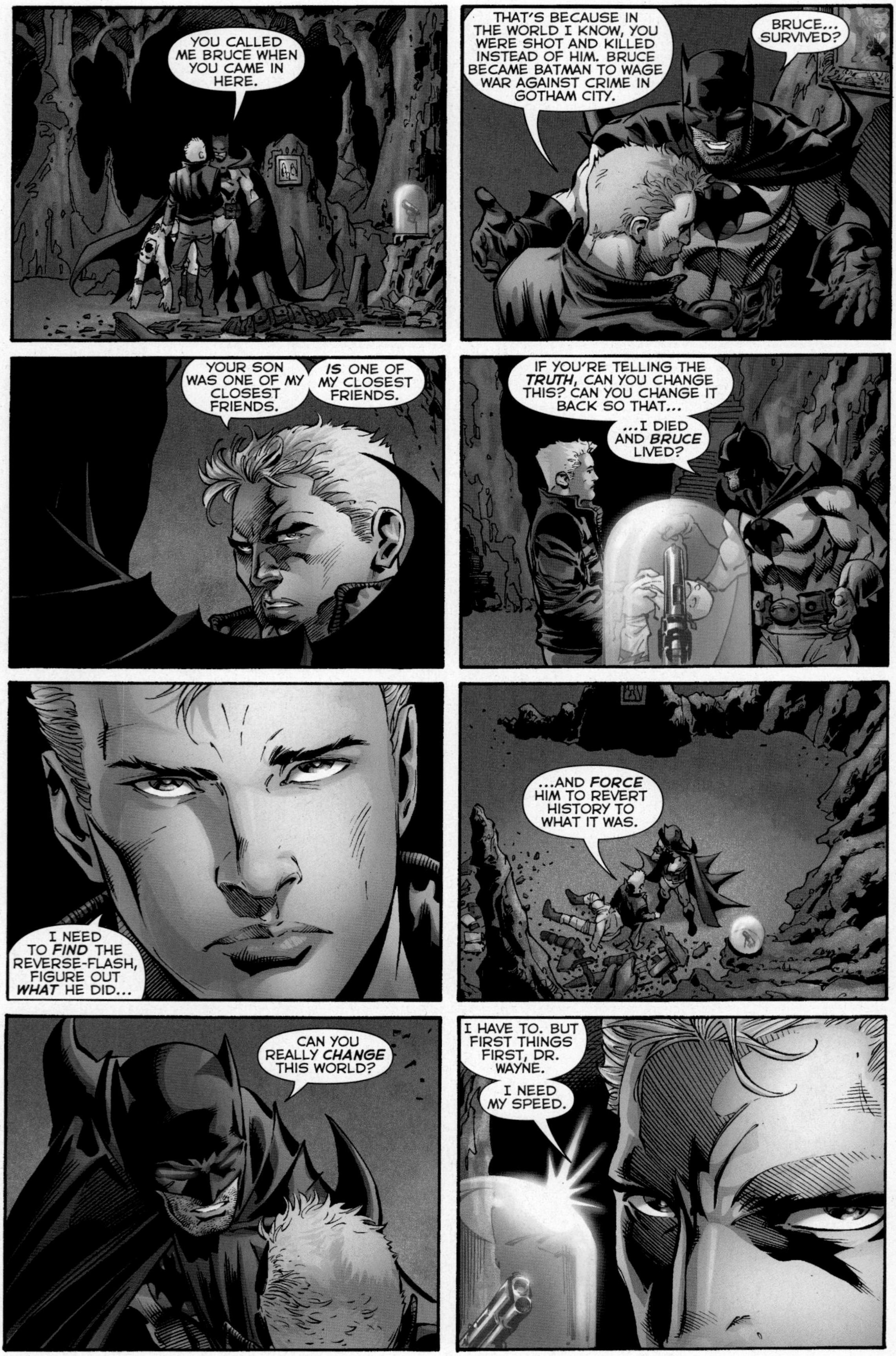
YOU CALLED ME BRUCE WHEN YOU CAME IN HERE.
THAT'S BECAUSE IN THE WORLD I KNOW, YOU WERE SHOT AND KILLED INSTEAD OF HIM. BRUCE BECAME BATMAN TO WAGE WAR AGAINST CRIME IN GOTHAM CITY.
BRUCE... SURVIVED?
YOUR SON WAS ONE OF MY CLOSEST FRIENDS.
IS ONE OF MY CLOSEST FRIENDS.
IF YOU'RE TELLING THE TRUTH, CAN YOU CHANGE THIS? CAN YOU CHANGE IT BACK SO THAT...
...I DIED AND BRUCE LIVED?
I NEED TO FIND THE REVERSE-FLASH, FIGURE OUT WHAT HE DID...
...AND FORCE HIM TO REVERT HISTORY TO WHAT IT WAS.
CAN YOU REALLY CHANGE THIS WORLD?
I HAVE TO. BUT FIRST THINGS FIRST, DR. WAYNE.
I NEED MY SPEED.

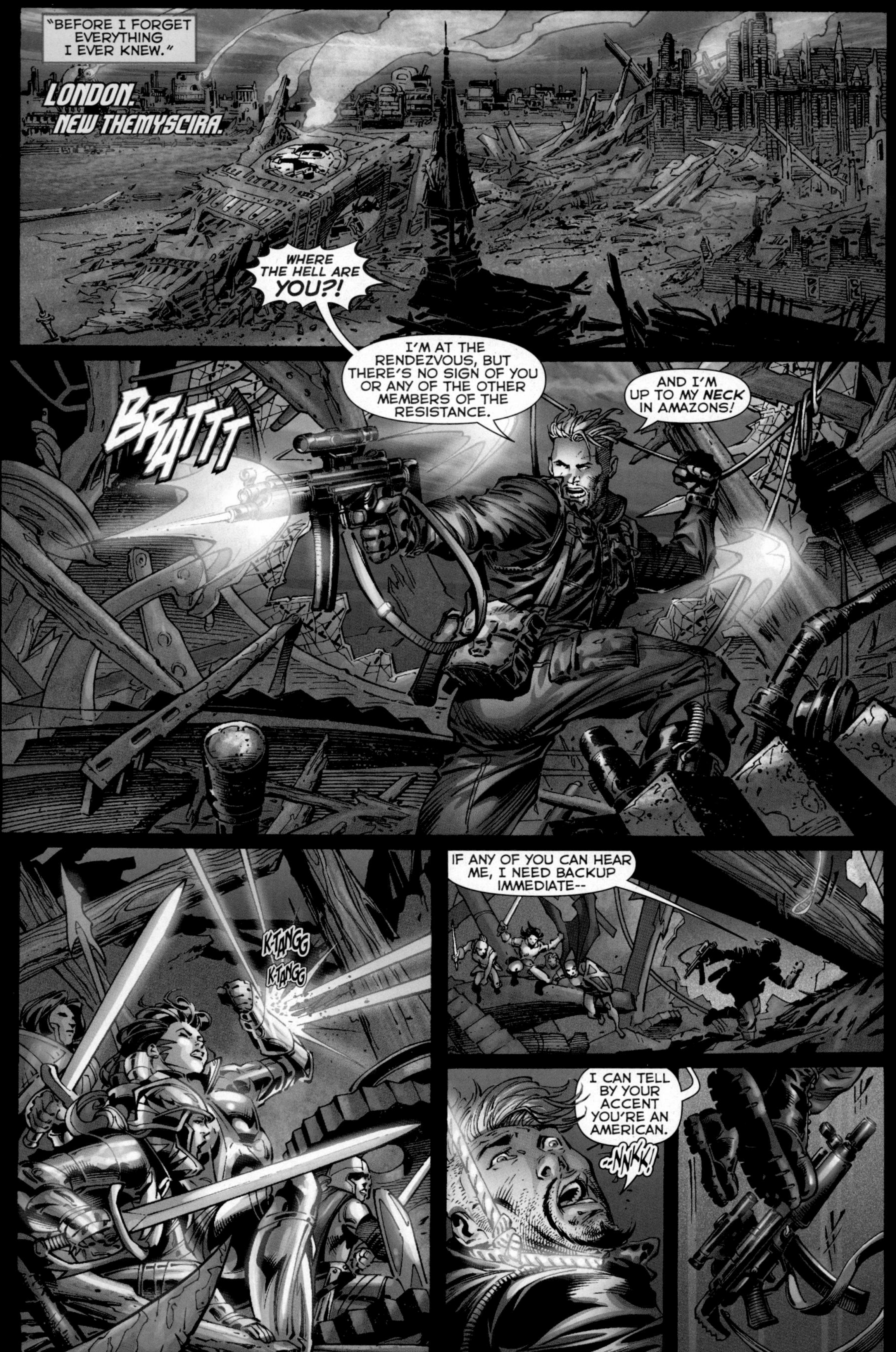
"BEFORE I FORGET EVERYTHING I EVER KNEW."
LONDON. NEW THEMYSCIRA.
WHERE THE HELL ARE YOU?!
I'M AT THE RENDEZVOUS, BUT THERE'S NO SIGN OF YOU OR ANY OF THE OTHER MEMBERS OF THE RESISTANCE.
AND I'M UP TO MY NECK IN AMAZONS!
BRATTT
K-TANGG
K-TANGG
IF ANY OF YOU CAN HEAR ME, I NEED BACKUP IMMEDIATE--
I CAN TELL BY YOUR ACCENT YOU'RE AN AMERICAN.
--NNKK!

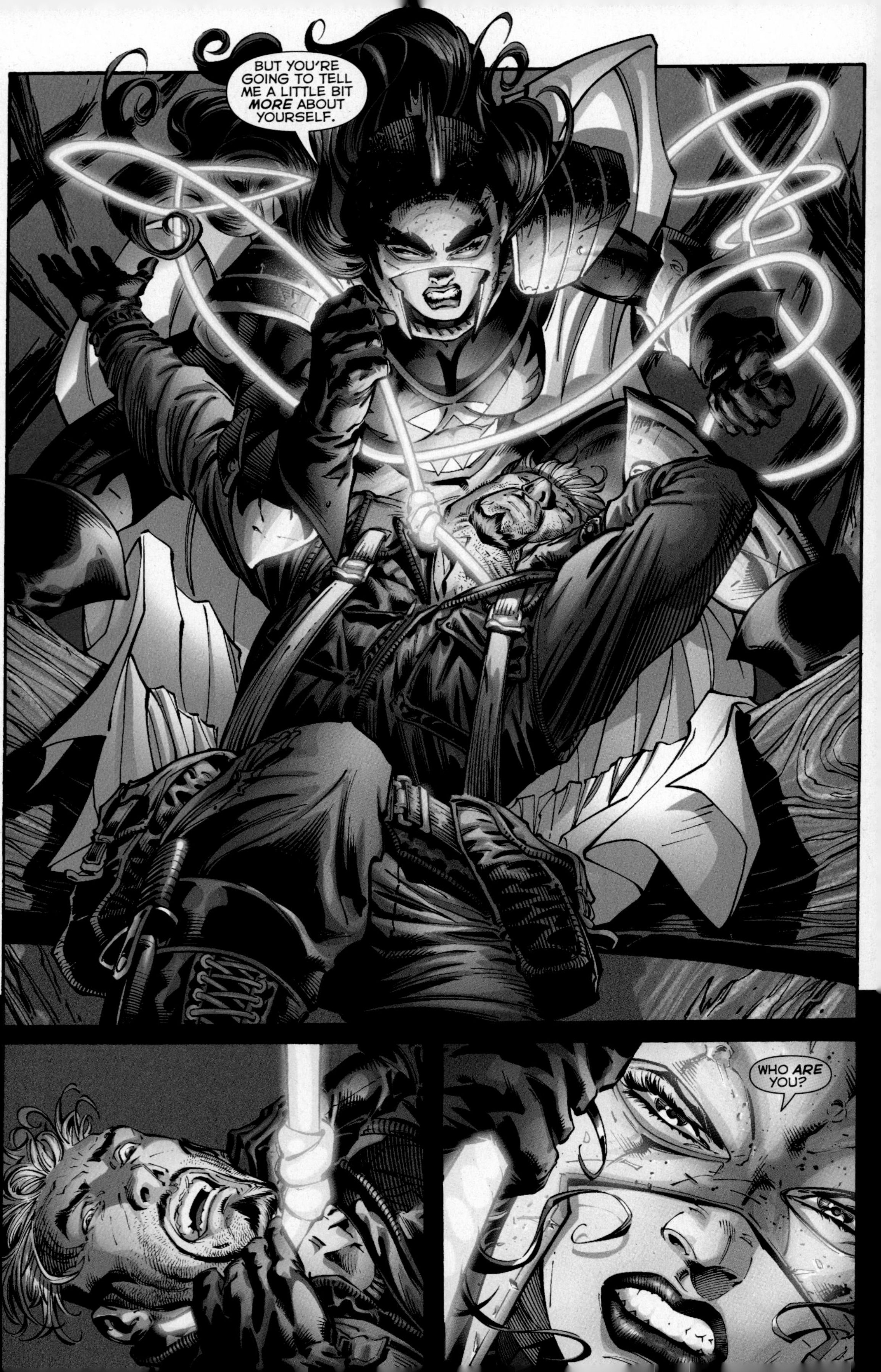
BUT YOU'RE GOING TO TELL ME A LITTLE BIT MORE ABOUT YOURSELF.
WHO ARE YOU?

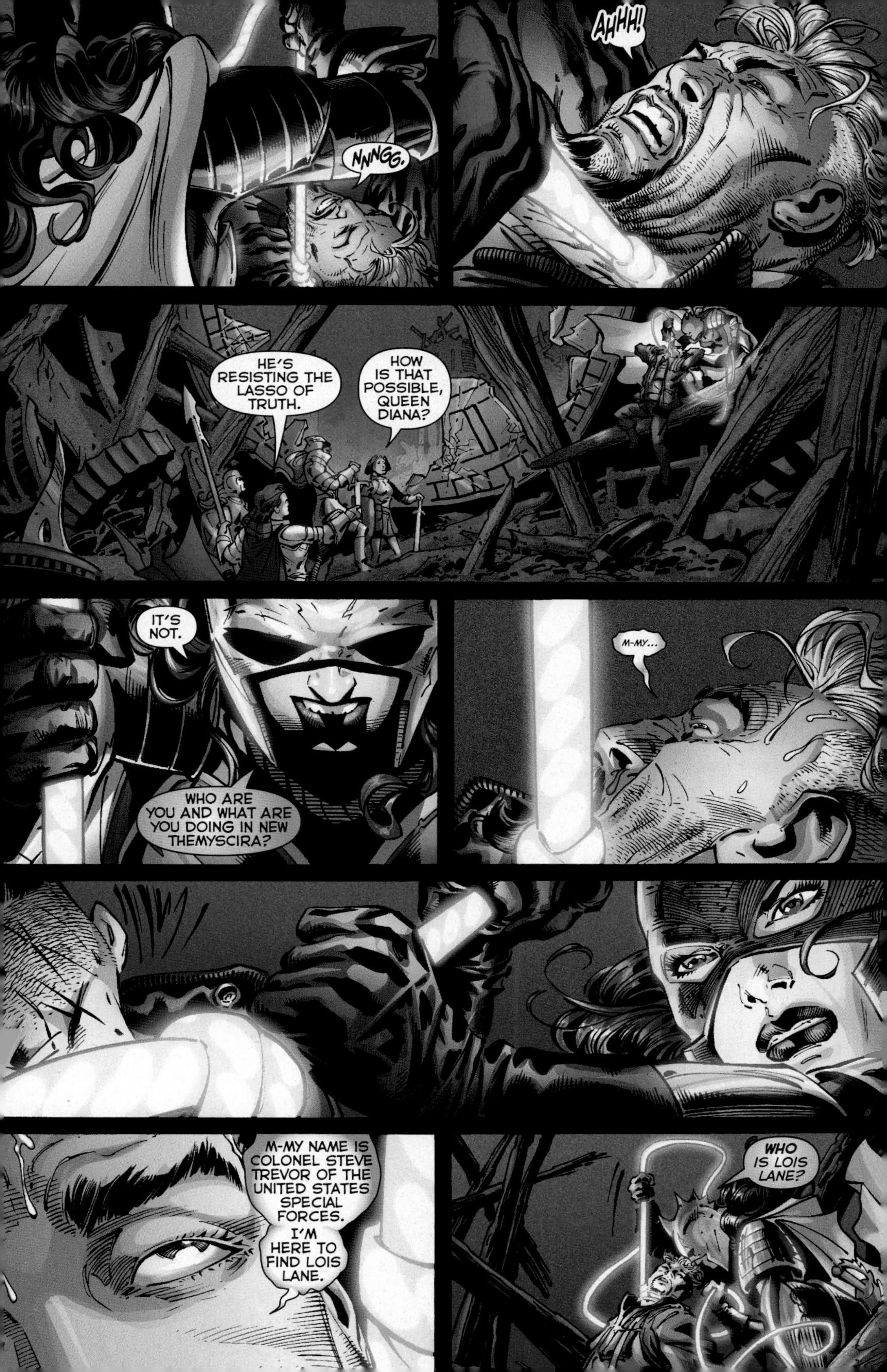
NNNGG.
AHHH!
HE'S RESISTING THE LASSO OF TRUTH.
HOW IS THAT POSSIBLE, QUEEN DIANA?
IT'S NOT.
WHO ARE YOU AND WHAT ARE YOU DOING IN NEW THEMYSCIRA?
M-MY...
M-MY NAME IS COLONEL STEVE TREVOR OF THE UNITED STATES SPECIAL FORCES.
I'M HERE TO FIND LOIS LANE.
WHO IS LOIS LANE?

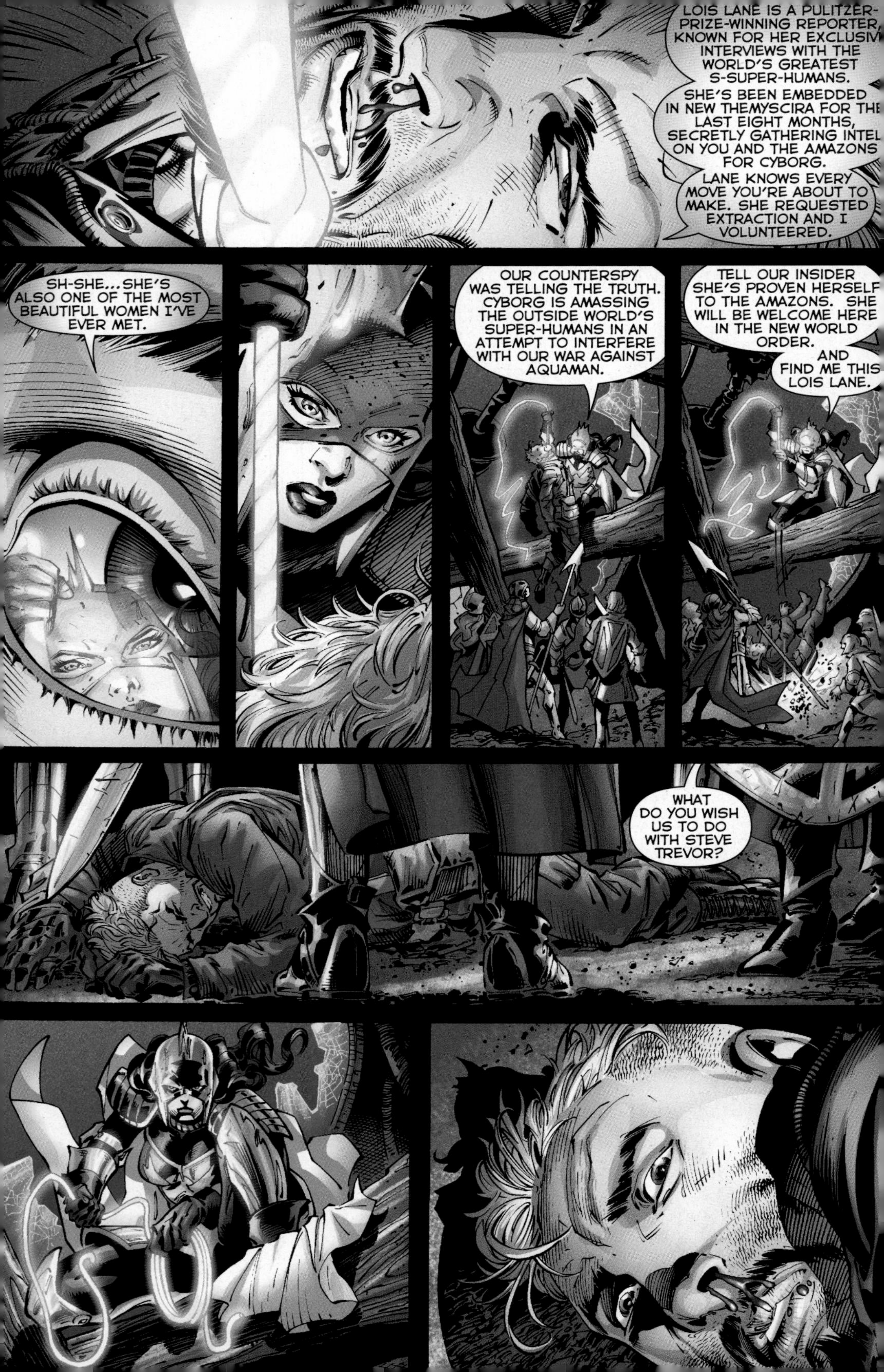
LOIS LANE IS A PULITZER-PRIZE-WINNING REPORTER, KNOWN FOR HER EXCLUSIVE INTERVIEWS WITH THE WORLD'S GREATEST S-SUPER-HUMANS.
SHE'S BEEN EMBEDDED IN NEW THEMYSCIRA FOR THE LAST EIGHT MONTHS, SECRETLY GATHERING INTEL ON YOU AND THE AMAZONS FOR CYBORG.
LANE KNOWS EVERY MOVE YOU'RE ABOUT TO MAKE. SHE REQUESTED EXTRACTION AND I VOLUNTEERED.
SH-SHE...SHE'S ALSO ONE OF THE MOST BEAUTIFUL WOMEN I'VE EVER MET.
OUR COUNTERSPY WAS TELLING THE TRUTH. CYBORG IS AMASSING THE OUTSIDE WORLD'S SUPER-HUMANS IN AN ATTEMPT TO INTERFERE WITH OUR WAR AGAINST AQUAMAN.
TELL OUR INSIDER SHE'S PROVEN HERSELF TO THE AMAZONS. SHE WILL BE WELCOME HERE IN THE NEW WORLD ORDER.
AND FIND ME THIS LOIS LANE.
WHAT DO YOU WISH US TO DO WITH STEVE TREVOR?

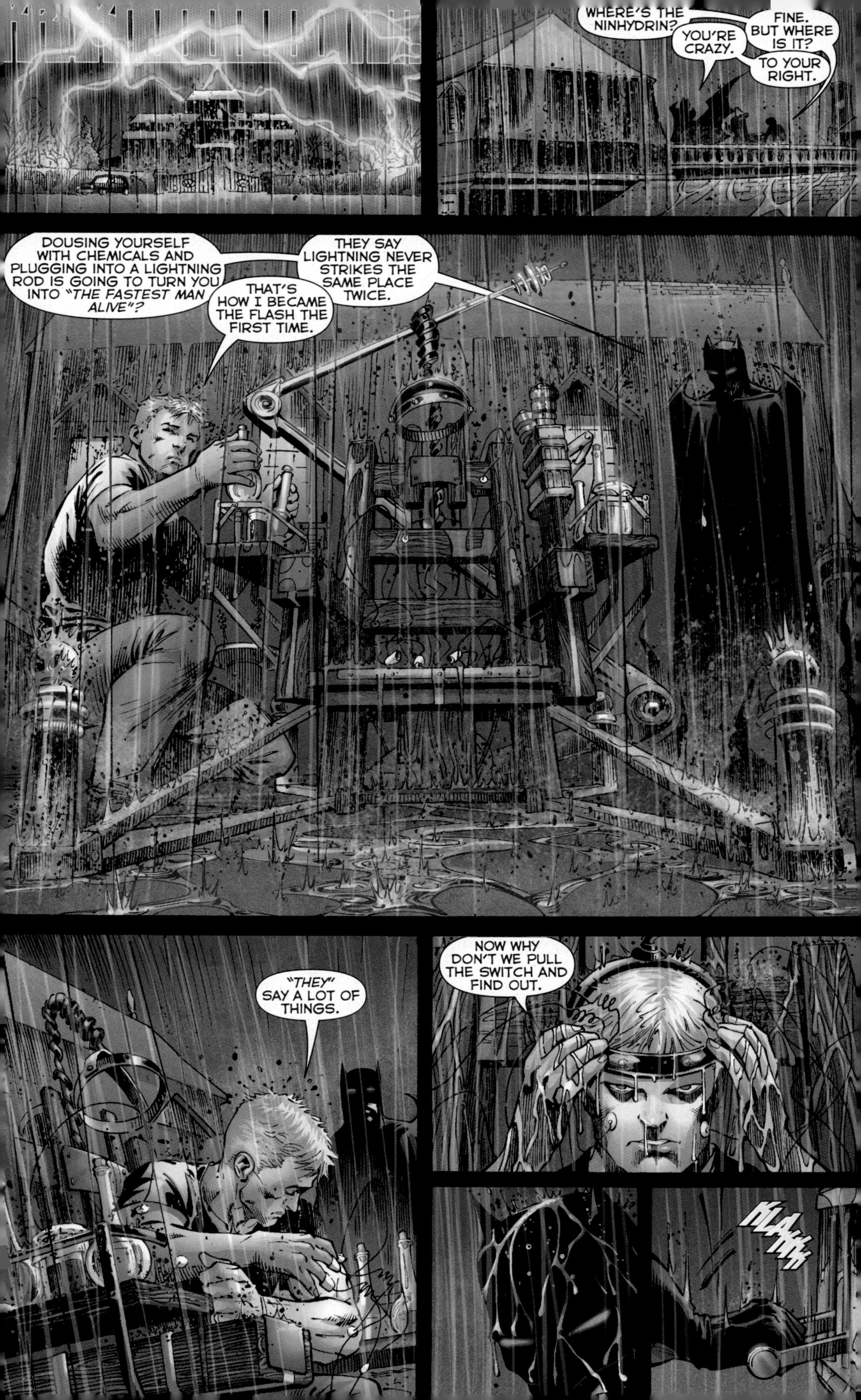
WHERE'S THE NINHYDRIN?
YOU'RE CRAZY.
FINE. BUT WHERE IS IT?
TO YOUR RIGHT.
DOUSING YOURSELF WITH CHEMICALS AND PLUGGING INTO A LIGHTNING ROD IS GOING TO TURN YOU INTO *"THE FASTEST MAN ALIVE"*?
THAT'S HOW I BECAME THE FLASH THE FIRST TIME.
THEY SAY LIGHTNING NEVER STRIKES THE SAME PLACE TWICE.
"THEY" SAY A LOT OF THINGS.
NOW WHY DON'T WE PULL THE SWITCH AND FIND OUT.
KLAKK

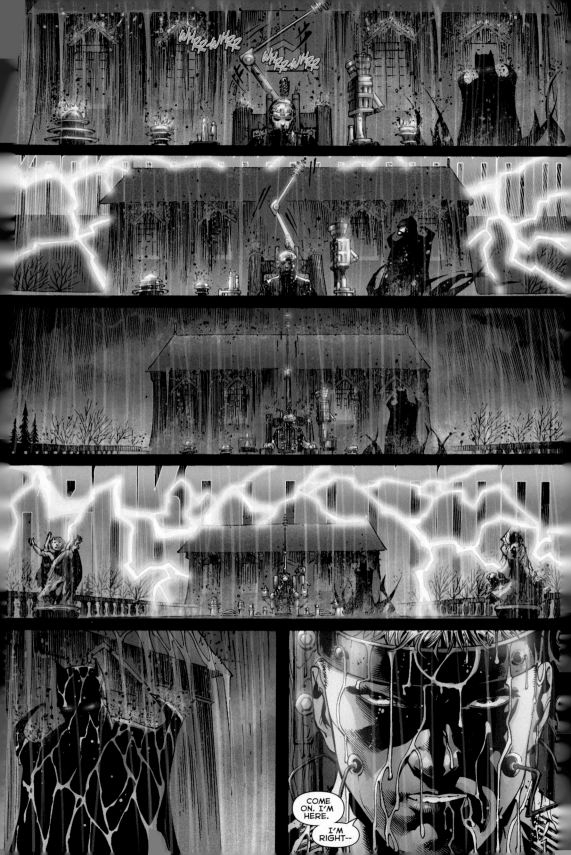

WHRR-WHRR
WHRR-WHRR

COME
ON. I'M
HERE.

I'M
RIGHT--

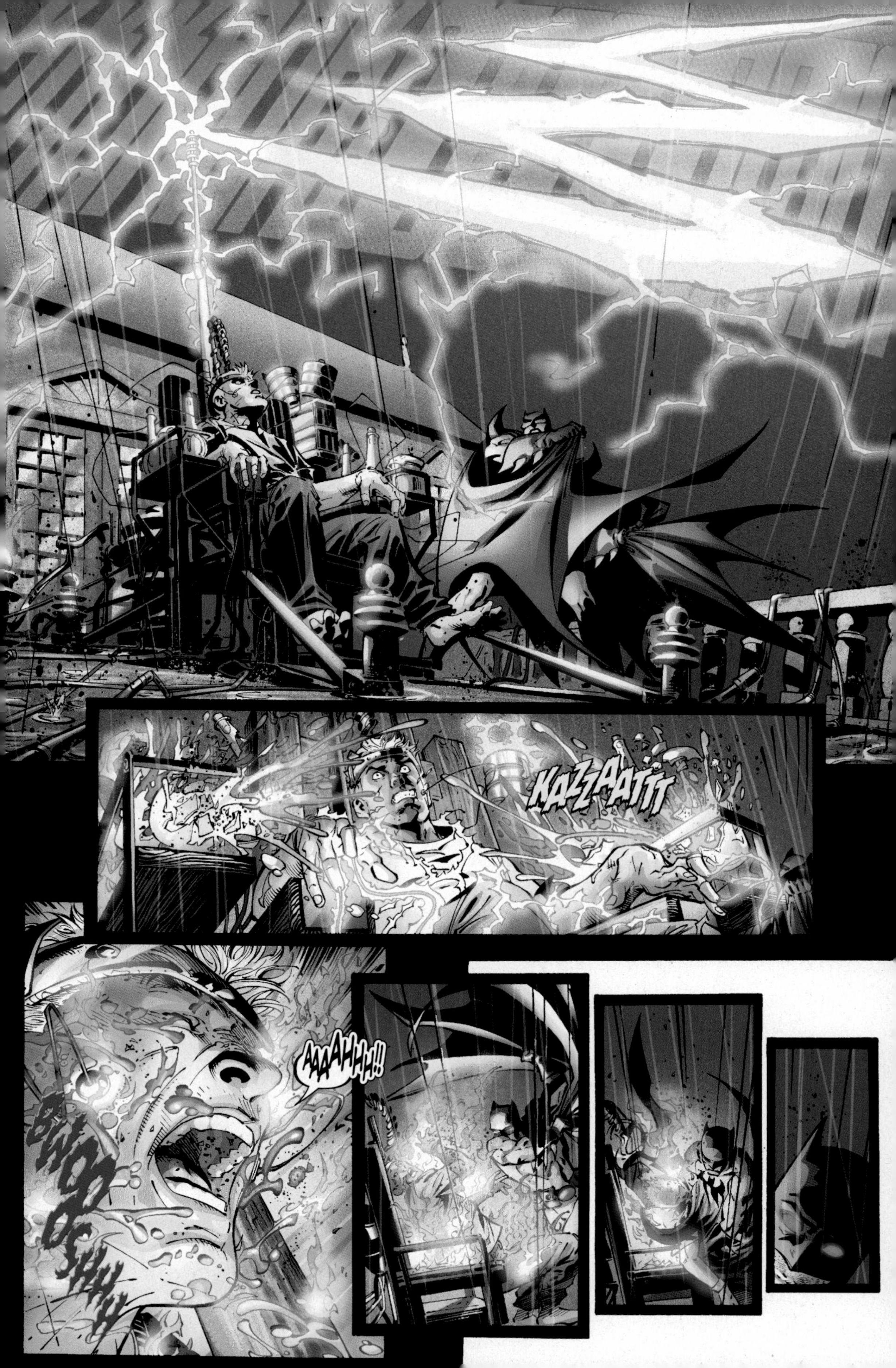
KAZZAATTT
AAAAHHH!!
BWOOOSHHH

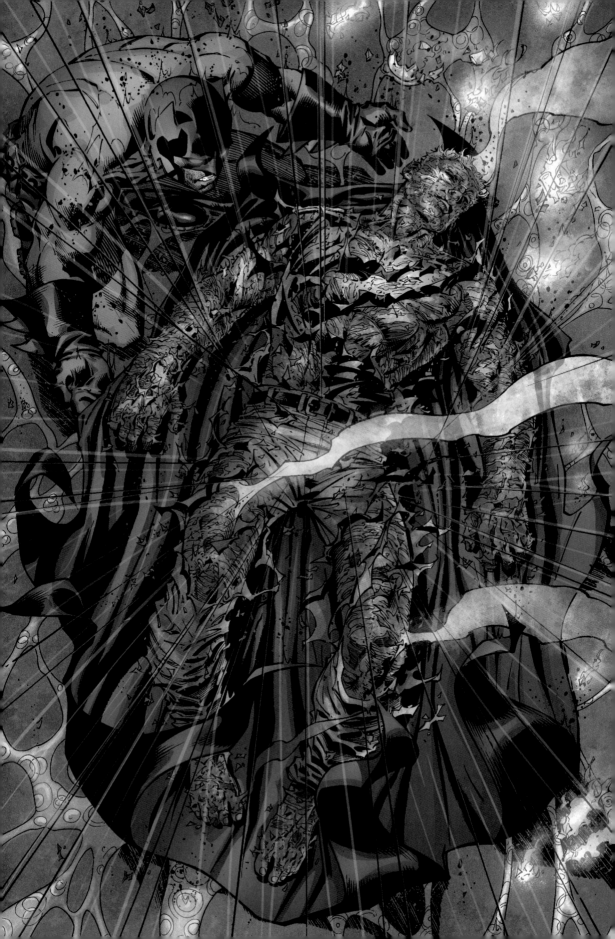

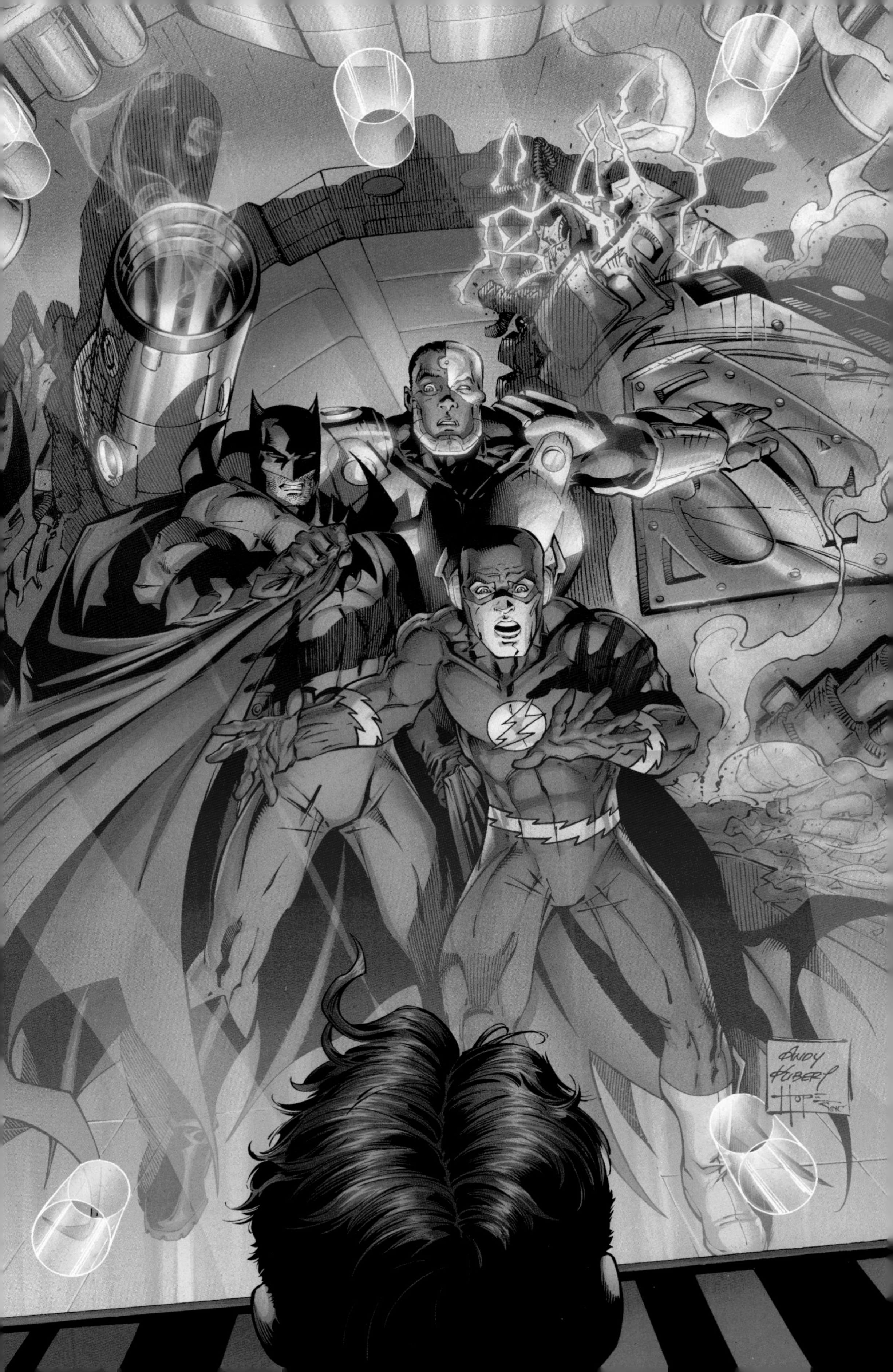
ANDY KUBERT
HOPE

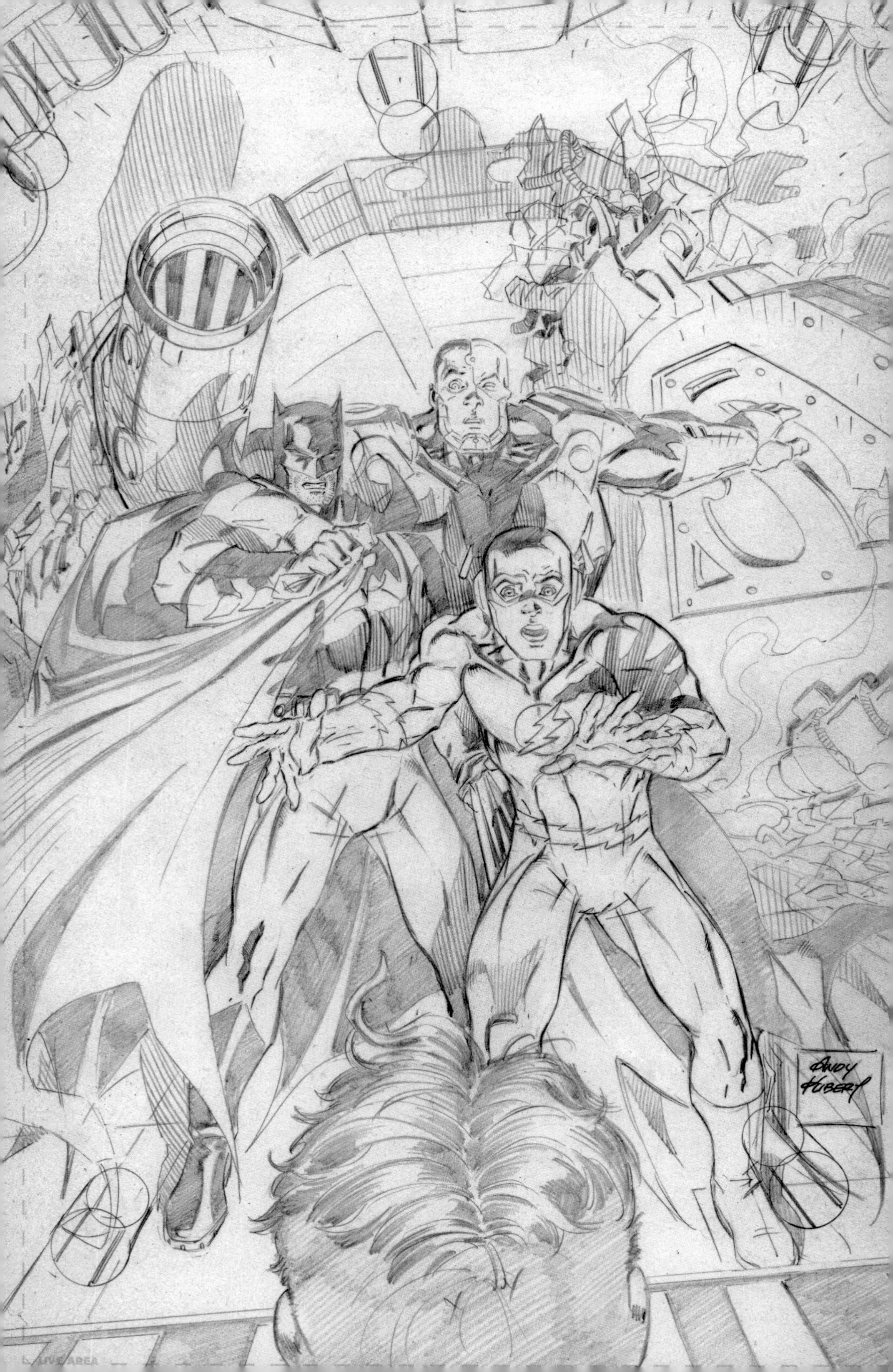
ANDY KUBERT

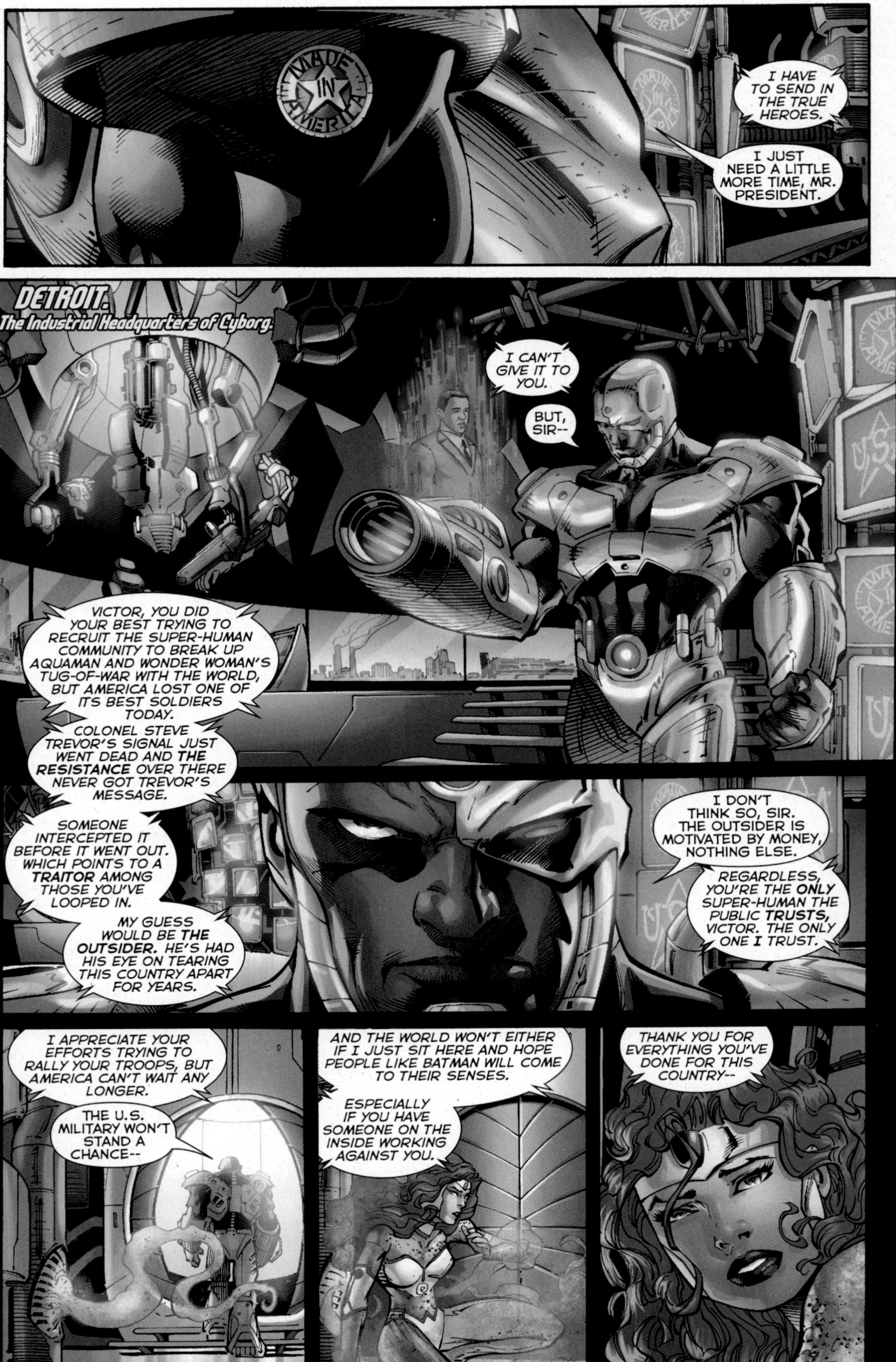
MADE IN AMERICA
I HAVE TO SEND IN THE TRUE HEROES.
I JUST NEED A LITTLE MORE TIME, MR. PRESIDENT.
DETROIT.
The Industrial Headquarters of Cyborg.
I CAN'T GIVE IT TO YOU.
BUT, SIR--
VICTOR, YOU DID YOUR BEST TRYING TO RECRUIT THE SUPER-HUMAN COMMUNITY TO BREAK UP AQUAMAN AND WONDER WOMAN'S TUG-OF-WAR WITH THE WORLD, BUT AMERICA LOST ONE OF ITS BEST SOLDIERS TODAY.
COLONEL STEVE TREVOR'S SIGNAL JUST WENT DEAD AND THE RESISTANCE OVER THERE NEVER GOT TREVOR'S MESSAGE.
SOMEONE INTERCEPTED IT BEFORE IT WENT OUT. WHICH POINTS TO A TRAITOR AMONG THOSE YOU'VE LOOPED IN.
MY GUESS WOULD BE THE OUTSIDER. HE'S HAD HIS EYE ON TEARING THIS COUNTRY APART FOR YEARS.
I DON'T THINK SO, SIR. THE OUTSIDER IS MOTIVATED BY MONEY, NOTHING ELSE.
REGARDLESS, YOU'RE THE ONLY SUPER-HUMAN THE PUBLIC TRUSTS, VICTOR. THE ONLY ONE I TRUST.
I APPRECIATE YOUR EFFORTS TRYING TO RALLY YOUR TROOPS, BUT AMERICA CAN'T WAIT ANY LONGER.
THE U.S. MILITARY WON'T STAND A CHANCE--
AND THE WORLD WON'T EITHER IF I JUST SIT HERE AND HOPE PEOPLE LIKE BATMAN WILL COME TO THEIR SENSES.
ESPECIALLY IF YOU HAVE SOMEONE ON THE INSIDE WORKING AGAINST YOU.
THANK YOU FOR EVERYTHING YOU'VE DONE FOR THIS COUNTRY--

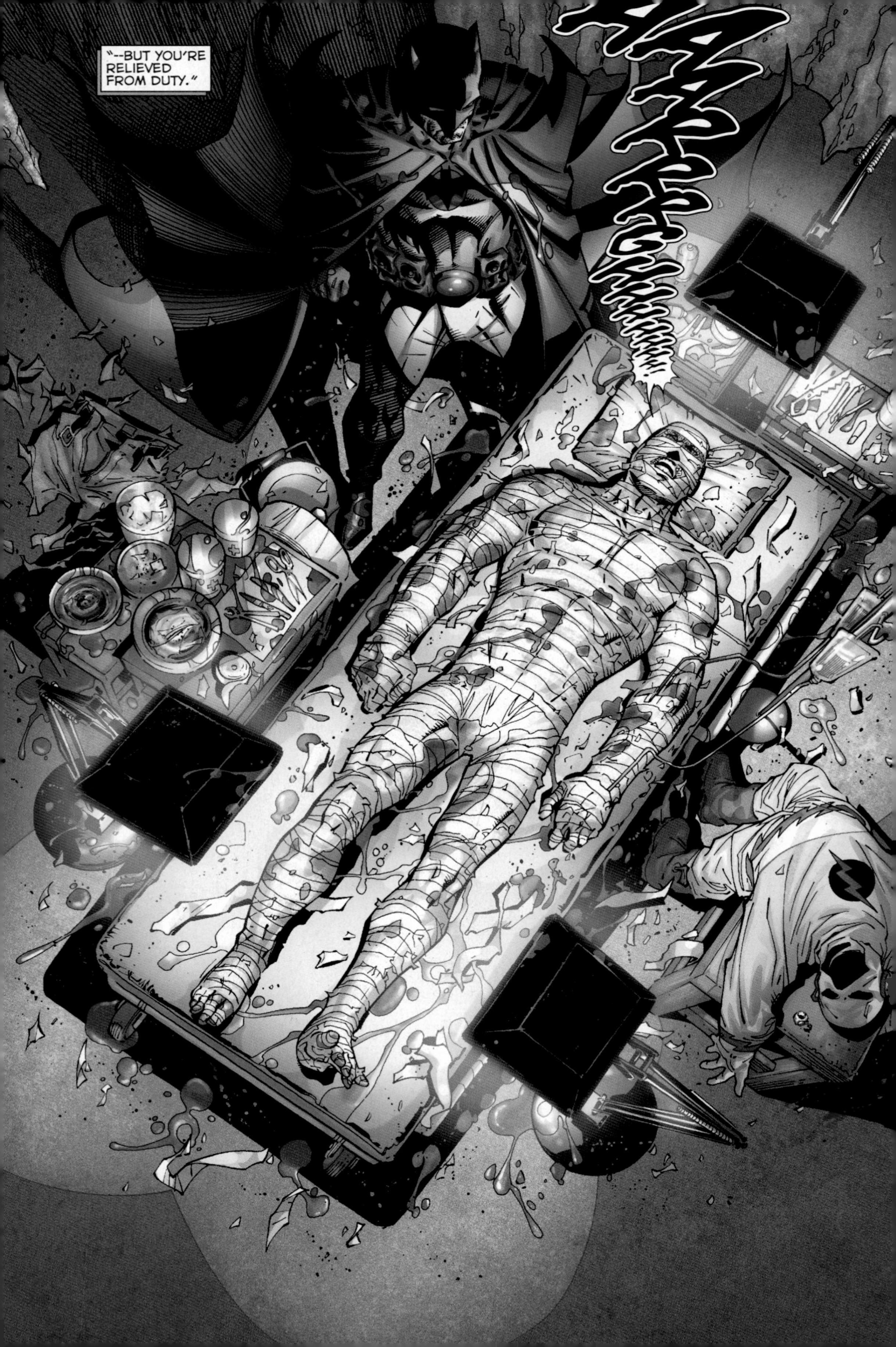
"--BUT YOU'RE RELIEVED FROM DUTY."
AAARRRGHHHHHH

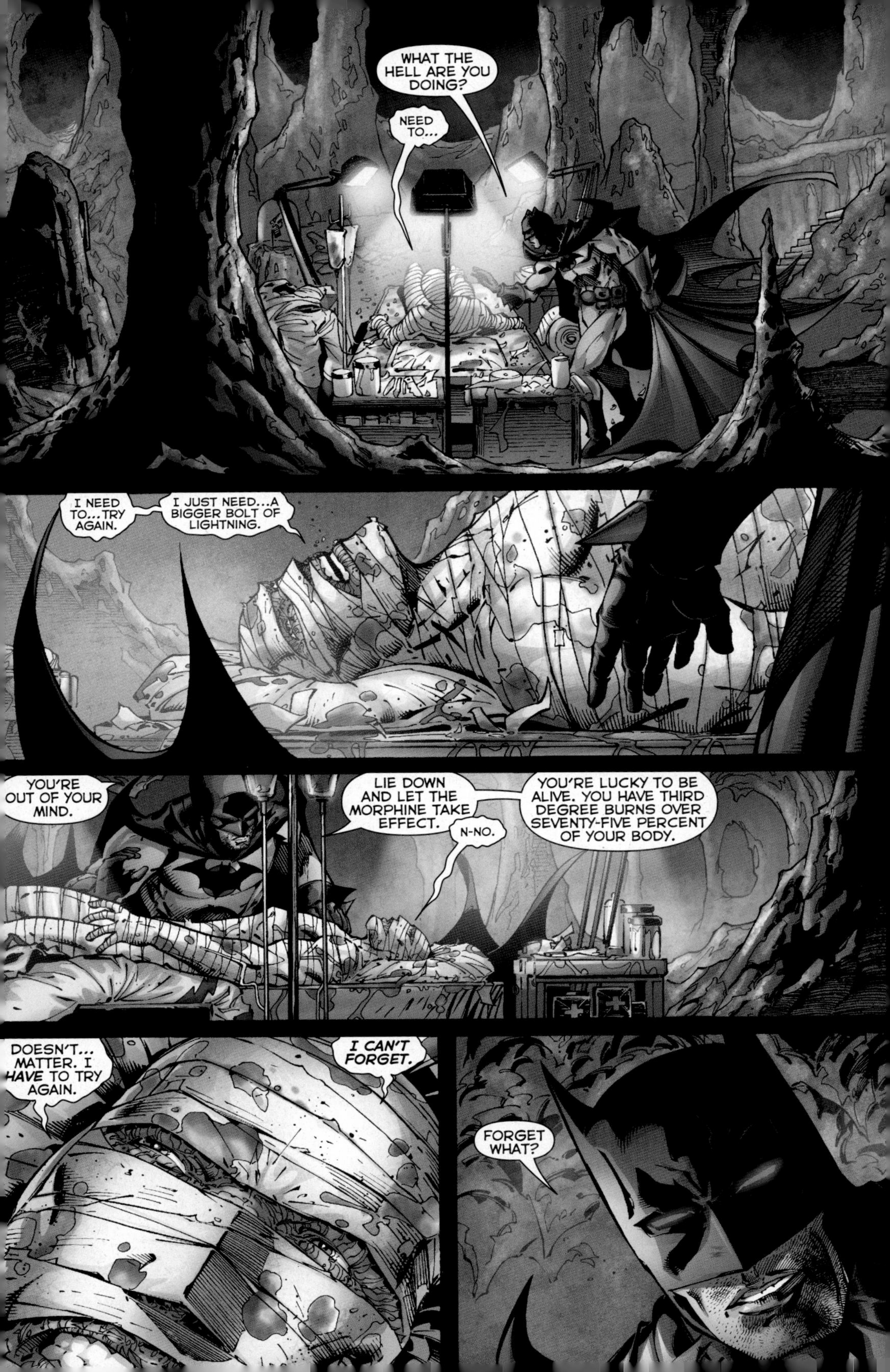
WHAT THE HELL ARE YOU DOING?
NEED TO...
I NEED TO...TRY AGAIN.
I JUST NEED...A BIGGER BOLT OF LIGHTNING.
YOU'RE OUT OF YOUR MIND.
LIE DOWN AND LET THE MORPHINE TAKE EFFECT.
N-NO.
YOU'RE LUCKY TO BE ALIVE. YOU HAVE THIRD DEGREE BURNS OVER SEVENTY-FIVE PERCENT OF YOUR BODY.
DOESN'T... MATTER. I *HAVE* TO TRY AGAIN.
I CAN'T FORGET.
FORGET WHAT?

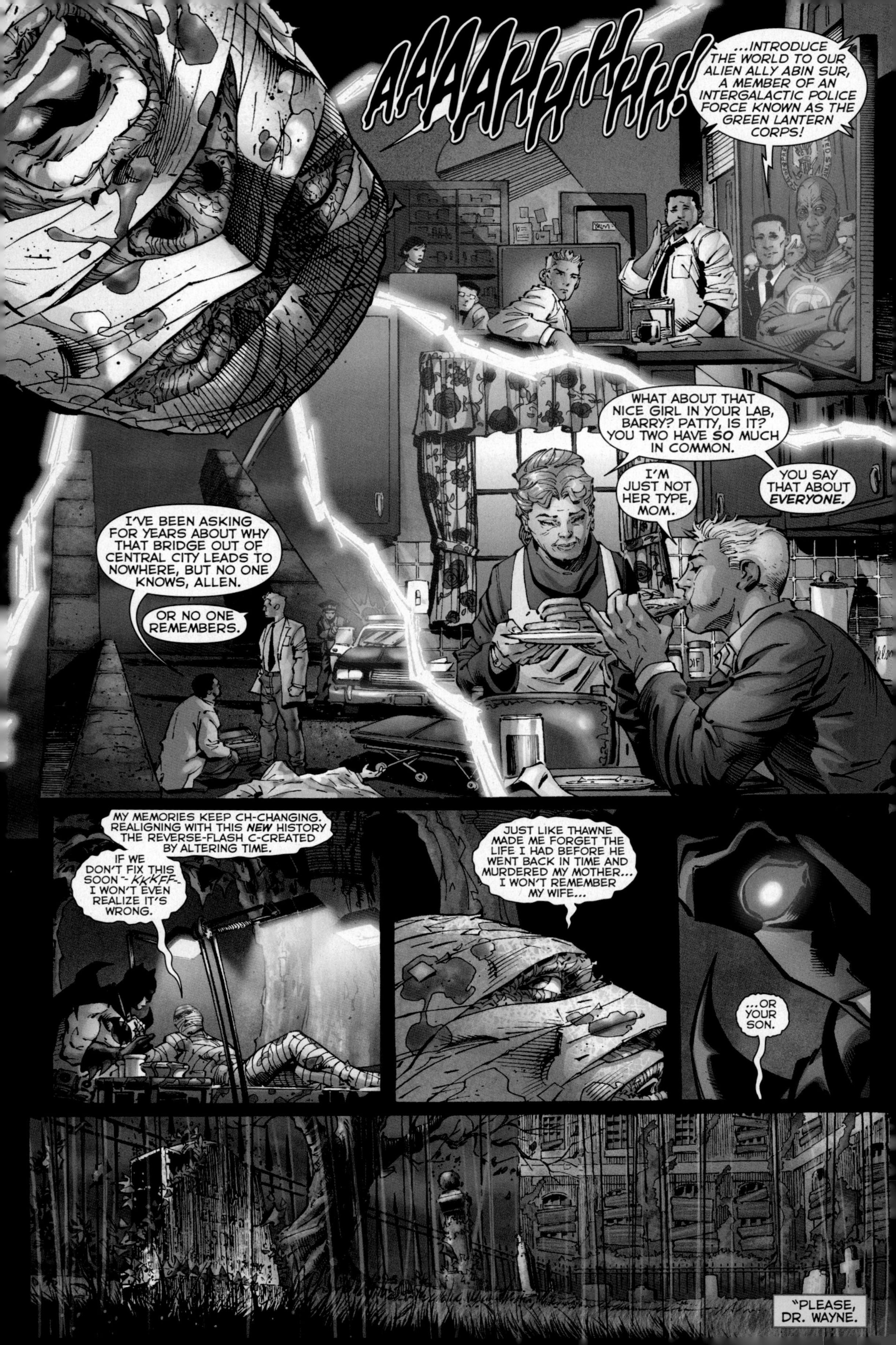
AAAAHHHHHH!
...INTRODUCE THE WORLD TO OUR ALIEN ALLY ABIN SUR, A MEMBER OF AN INTERGALACTIC POLICE FORCE KNOWN AS THE GREEN LANTERN CORPS!
WHAT ABOUT THAT NICE GIRL IN YOUR LAB, BARRY? PATTY, IS IT? YOU TWO HAVE SO MUCH IN COMMON.
I'M JUST NOT HER TYPE, MOM.
YOU SAY THAT ABOUT EVERYONE.
I'VE BEEN ASKING FOR YEARS ABOUT WHY THAT BRIDGE OUT OF CENTRAL CITY LEADS TO NOWHERE, BUT NO ONE KNOWS, ALLEN.
OR NO ONE REMEMBERS.
MY MEMORIES KEEP CH-CHANGING. REALIGNING WITH THIS NEW HISTORY THE REVERSE-FLASH C-CREATED BY ALTERING TIME.
IF WE DON'T FIX THIS SOON--KKKFF--I WON'T EVEN REALIZE IT'S WRONG.
JUST LIKE THAWNE MADE ME FORGET THE LIFE I HAD BEFORE HE WENT BACK IN TIME AND MURDERED MY MOTHER... I WON'T REMEMBER MY WIFE...
...OR YOUR SON.
"PLEASE, DR. WAYNE.

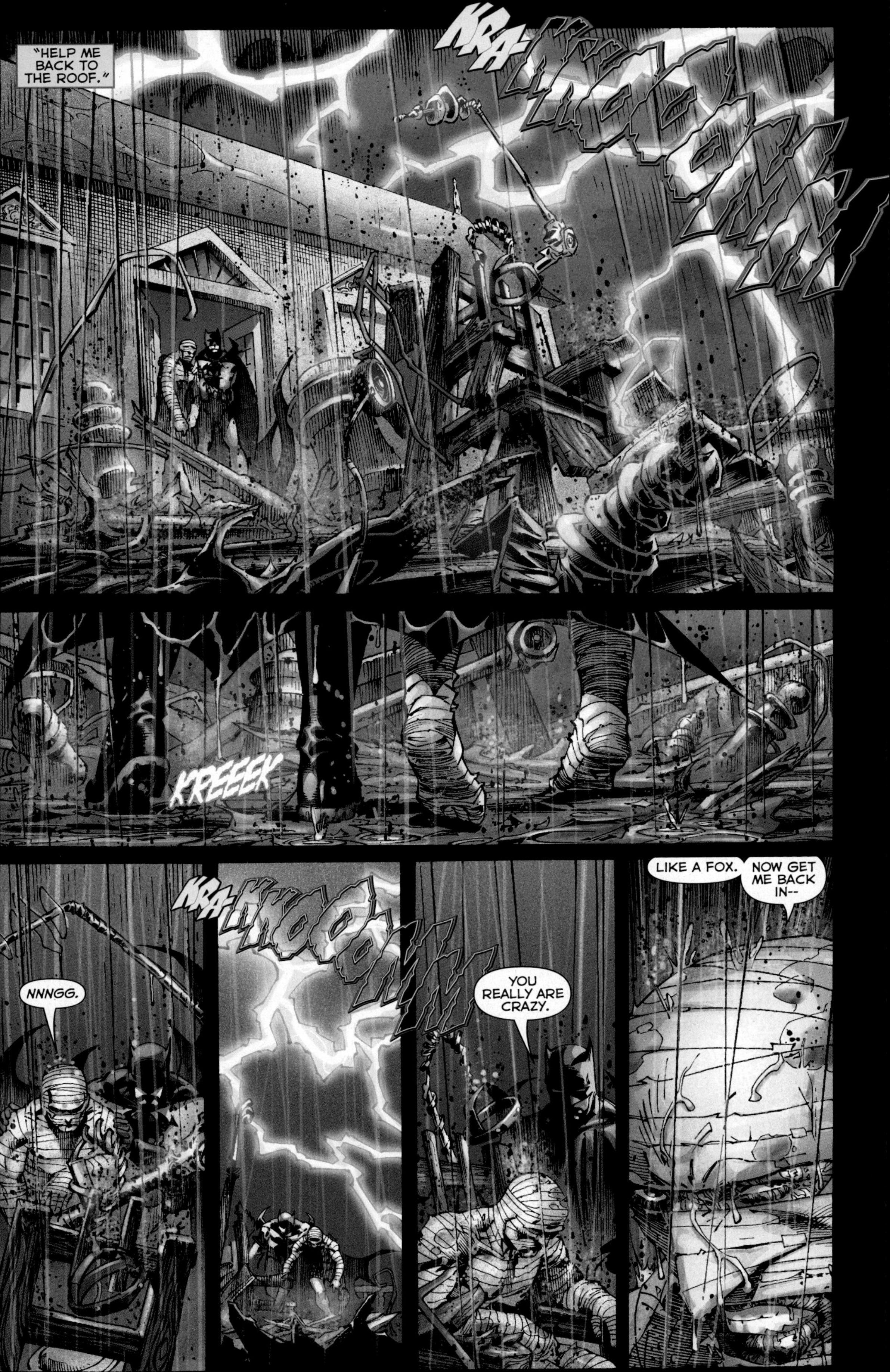
"HELP ME BACK TO THE ROOF."
KREEEK
NNNGG.
YOU REALLY ARE CRAZY.
LIKE A FOX.
NOW GET ME BACK IN--

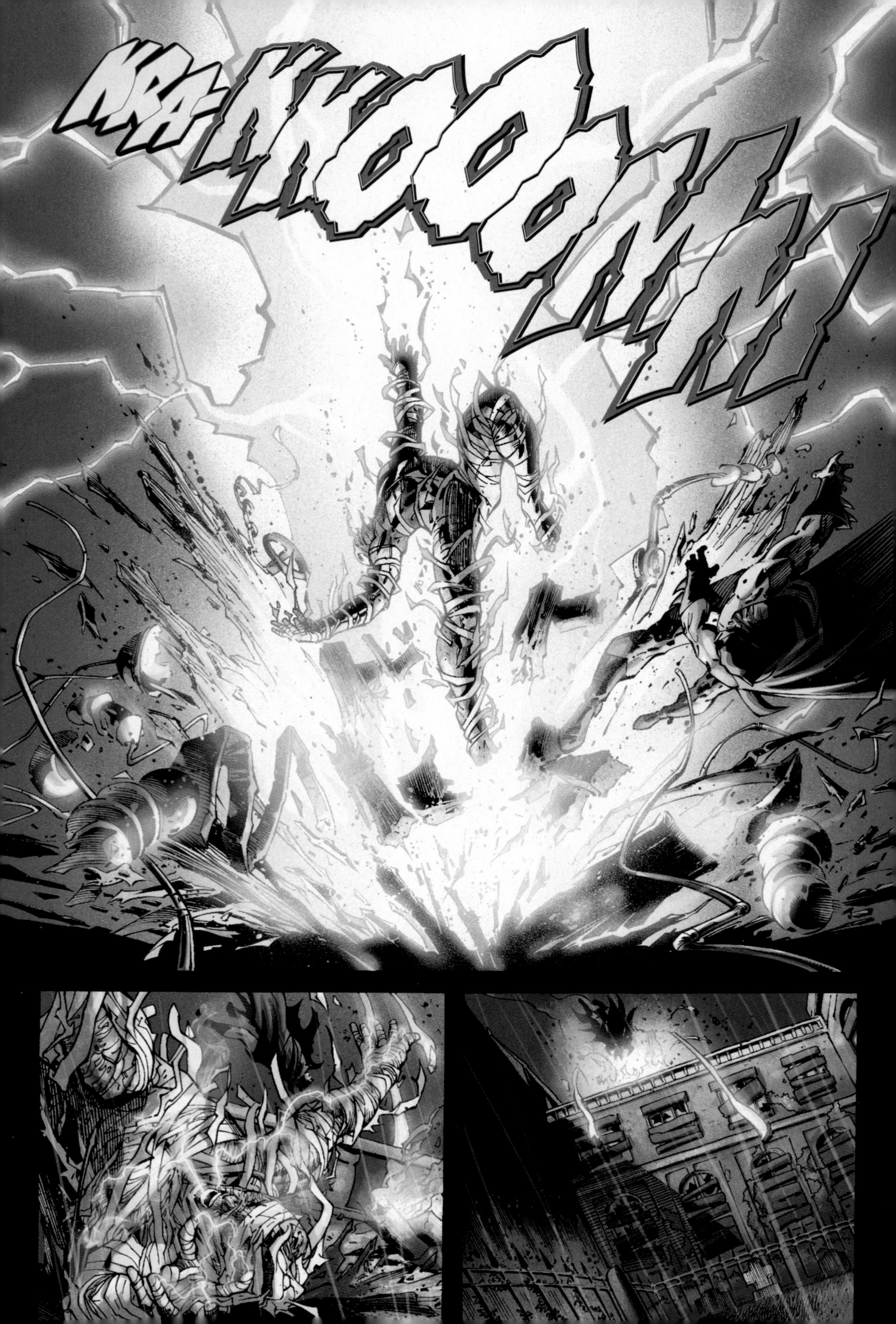
KRA-KOOOM

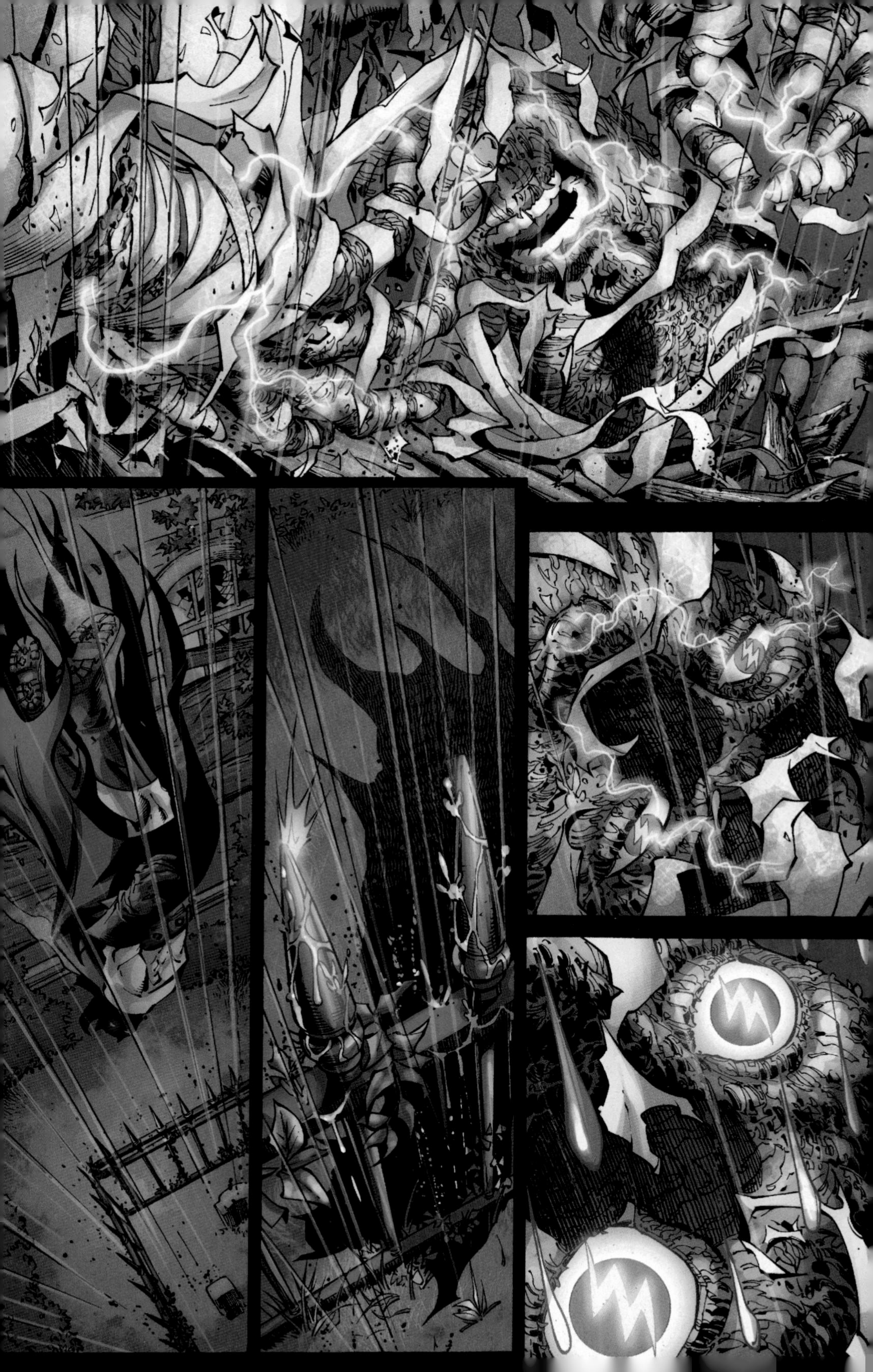

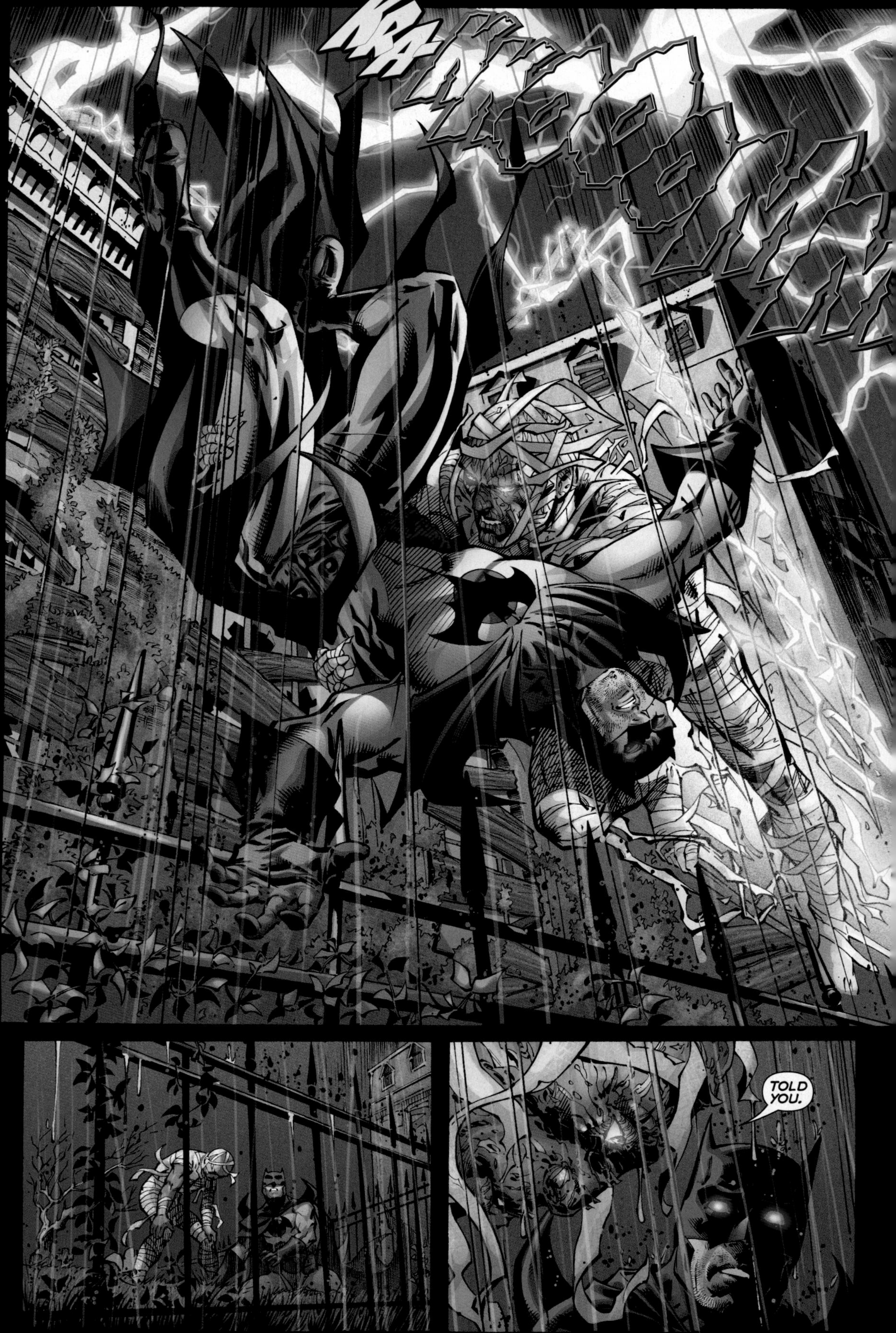
KRA
TOLD YOU.

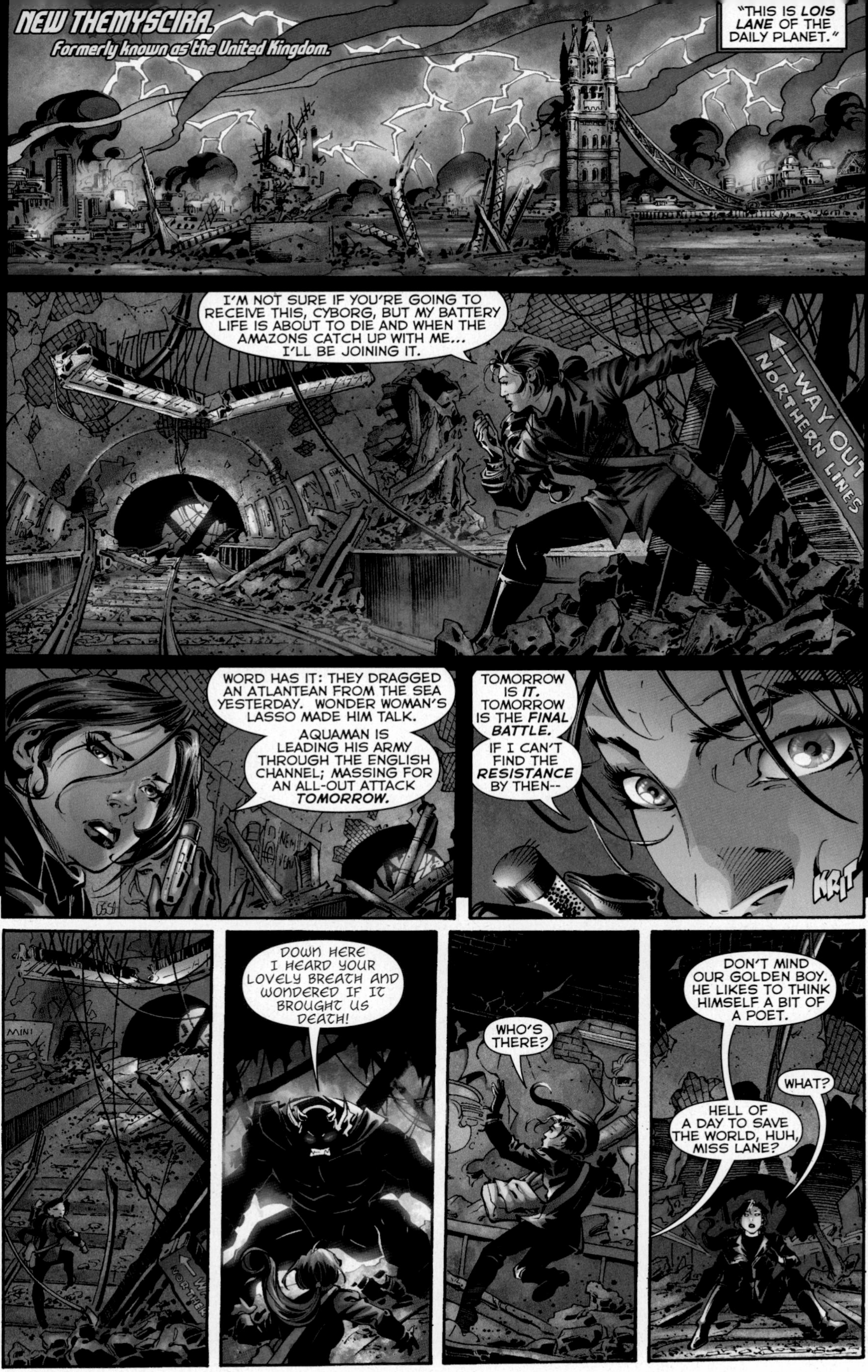
NEW THEMYSCIRA.
Formerly known as the United Kingdom.
"THIS IS LOIS LANE OF THE DAILY PLANET."
I'M NOT SURE IF YOU'RE GOING TO RECEIVE THIS, CYBORG, BUT MY BATTERY LIFE IS ABOUT TO DIE AND WHEN THE AMAZONS CATCH UP WITH ME... I'LL BE JOINING IT.
WAY OUT
NORTHERN LINES
WORD HAS IT: THEY DRAGGED AN ATLANTEAN FROM THE SEA YESTERDAY. WONDER WOMAN'S LASSO MADE HIM TALK.
AQUAMAN IS LEADING HIS ARMY THROUGH THE ENGLISH CHANNEL; MASSING FOR AN ALL-OUT ATTACK TOMORROW.
TOMORROW IS IT. TOMORROW IS THE FINAL BATTLE.
IF I CAN'T FIND THE RESISTANCE BY THEN--
MINI
DOWN HERE I HEARD YOUR LOVELY BREATH AND WONDERED IF IT BROUGHT US DEATH!
WHO'S THERE?
DON'T MIND OUR GOLDEN BOY. HE LIKES TO THINK HIMSELF A BIT OF A POET.
WHAT?
HELL OF A DAY TO SAVE THE WORLD, HUH, MISS LANE?

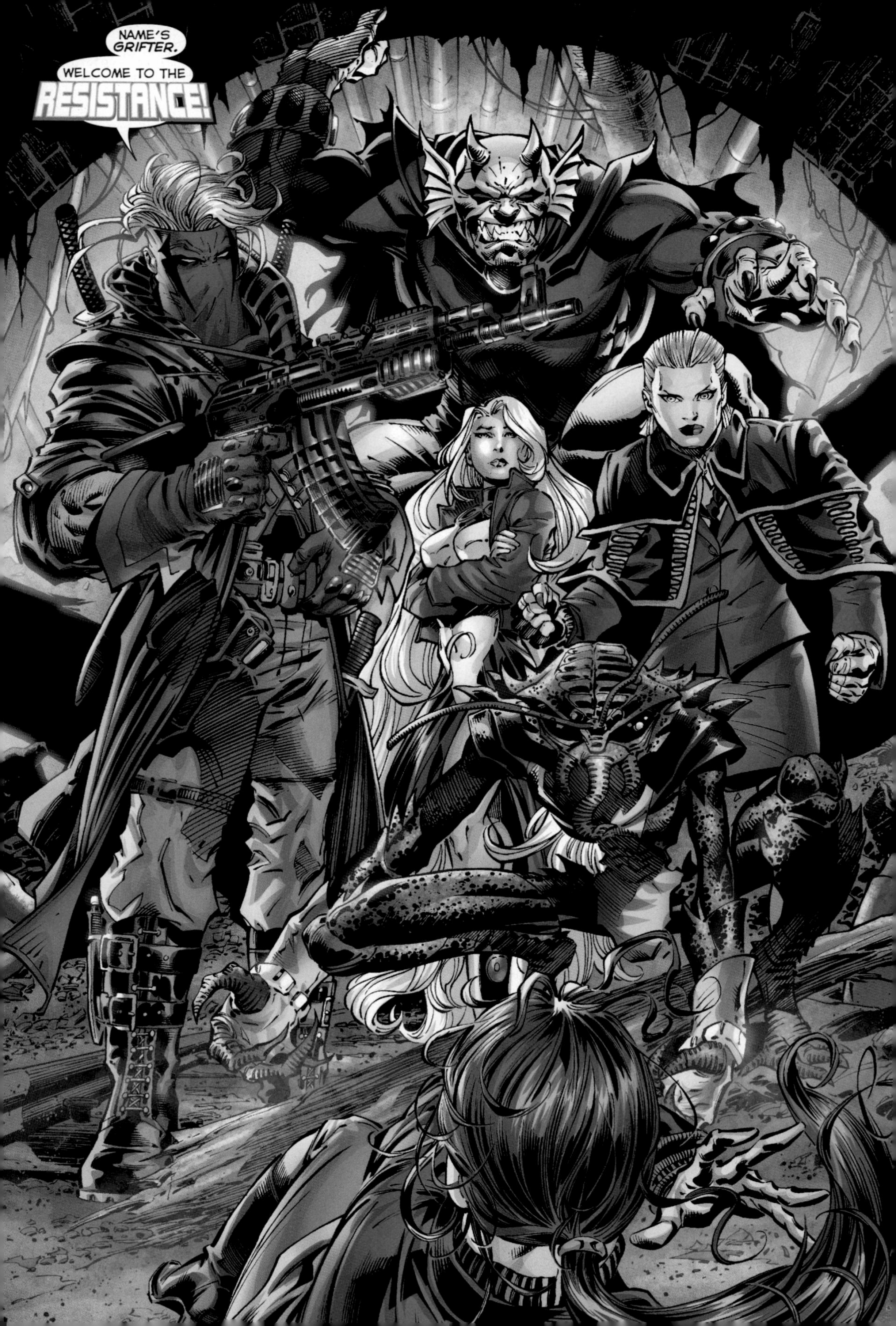
NAME'S GRIFTER.
WELCOME TO THE RESISTANCE!

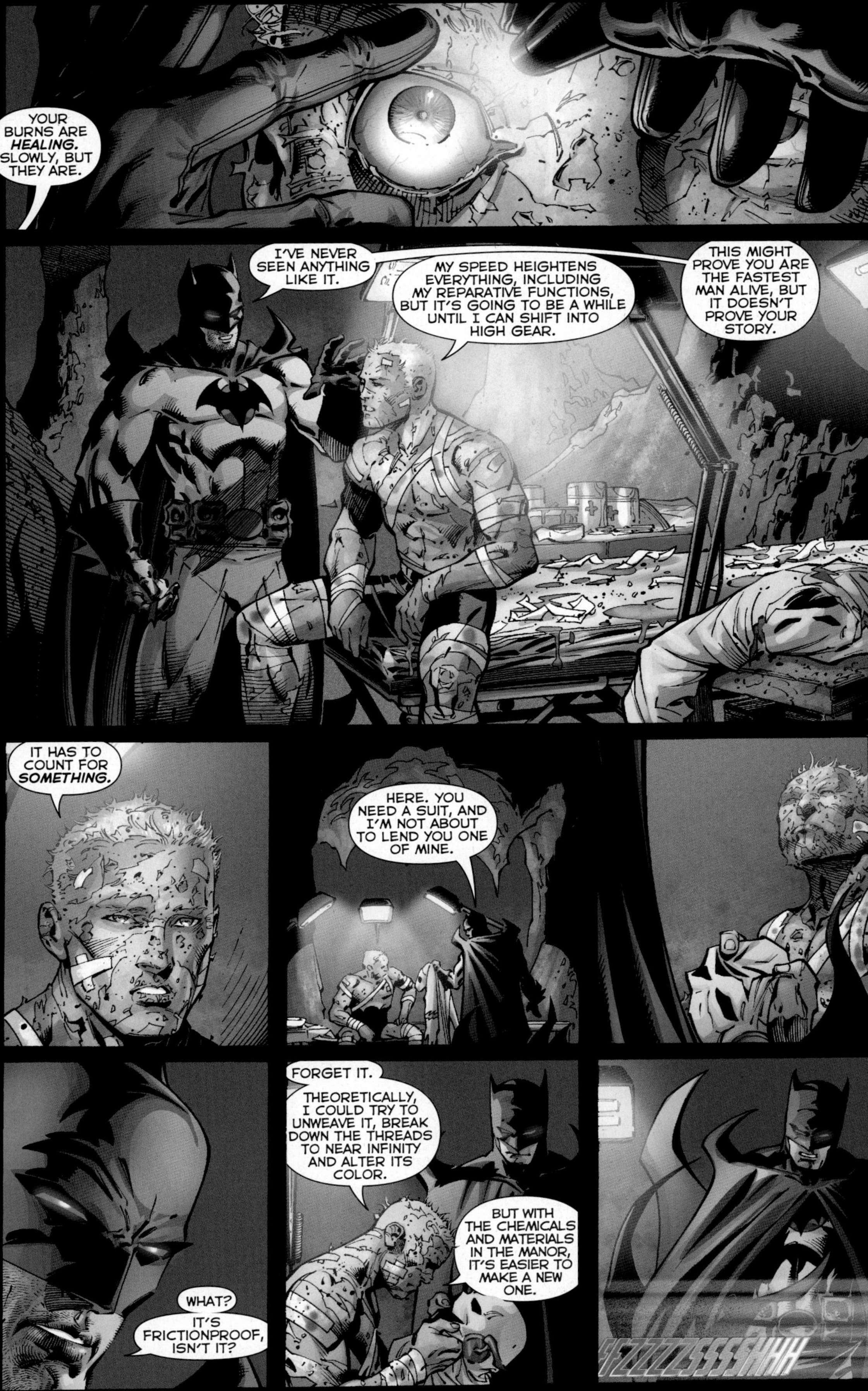
YOUR BURNS ARE HEALING. SLOWLY, BUT THEY ARE.
I'VE NEVER SEEN ANYTHING LIKE IT.
MY SPEED HEIGHTENS EVERYTHING, INCLUDING MY REPARATIVE FUNCTIONS, BUT IT'S GOING TO BE A WHILE UNTIL I CAN SHIFT INTO HIGH GEAR.
THIS MIGHT PROVE YOU ARE THE FASTEST MAN ALIVE, BUT IT DOESN'T PROVE YOUR STORY.
IT HAS TO COUNT FOR SOMETHING.
HERE. YOU NEED A SUIT, AND I'M NOT ABOUT TO LEND YOU ONE OF MINE.
WHAT?
IT'S FRICTIONPROOF, ISN'T IT?
FORGET IT.
THEORETICALLY, I COULD TRY TO UNWEAVE IT, BREAK DOWN THE THREADS TO NEAR INFINITY AND ALTER ITS COLOR.
BUT WITH THE CHEMICALS AND MATERIALS IN THE MANOR, IT'S EASIER TO MAKE A NEW ONE.
SZZZZZSSSSSHHH

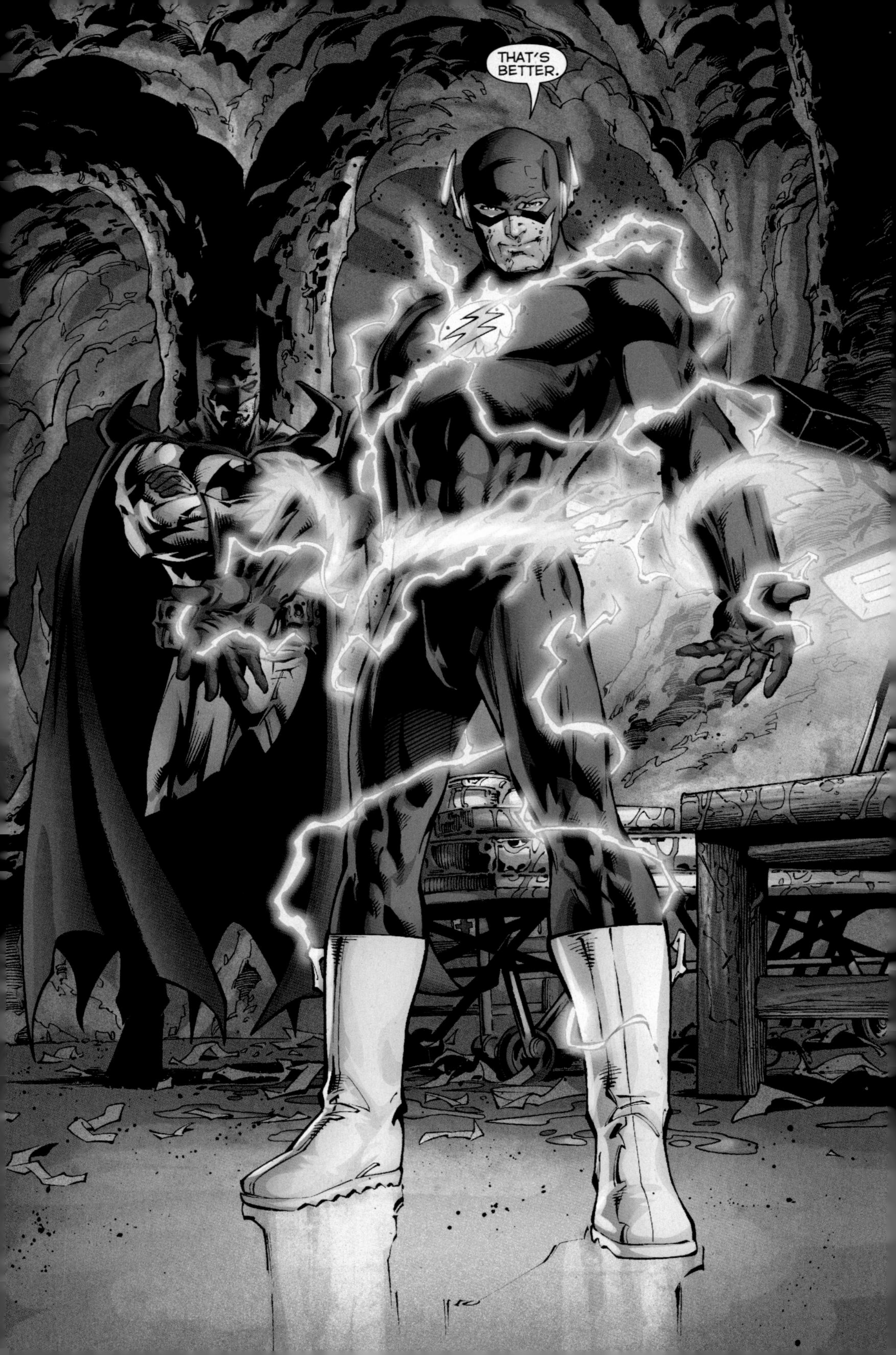
THAT'S BETTER.

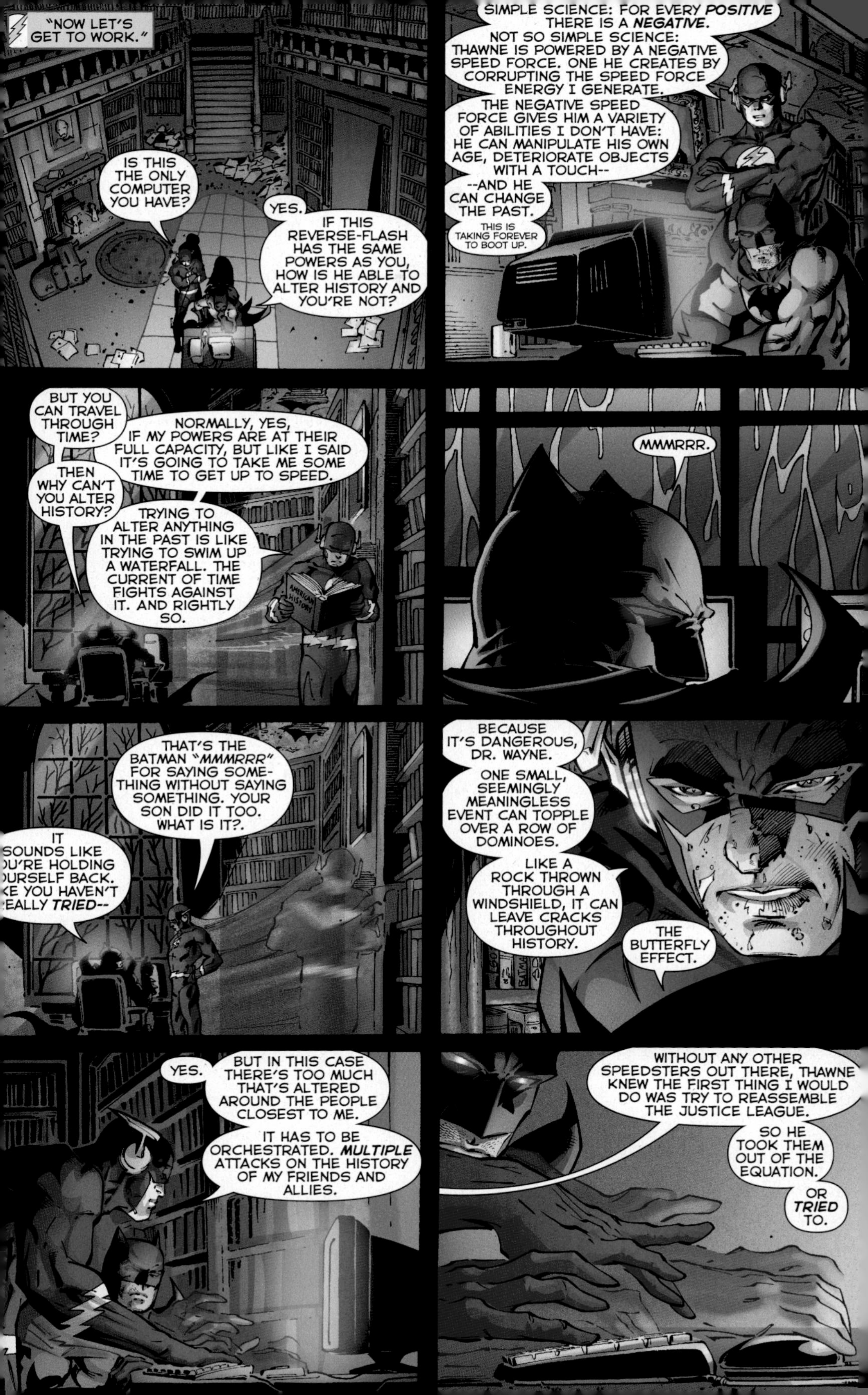

"NOW LET'S GET TO WORK."
IS THIS THE ONLY COMPUTER YOU HAVE?
YES.
IF THIS REVERSE-FLASH HAS THE SAME POWERS AS YOU, HOW IS HE ABLE TO ALTER HISTORY AND YOU'RE NOT?
SIMPLE SCIENCE: FOR EVERY *POSITIVE* THERE IS A *NEGATIVE*.
NOT SO SIMPLE SCIENCE: THAWNE IS POWERED BY A NEGATIVE SPEED FORCE. ONE HE CREATES BY CORRUPTING THE SPEED FORCE ENERGY I GENERATE.
THE NEGATIVE SPEED FORCE GIVES HIM A VARIETY OF ABILITIES I DON'T HAVE: HE CAN MANIPULATE HIS OWN AGE, DETERIORATE OBJECTS WITH A TOUCH--
--AND HE CAN CHANGE THE PAST.
THIS IS TAKING FOREVER TO BOOT UP.
BUT YOU CAN TRAVEL THROUGH TIME?
NORMALLY, YES, IF MY POWERS ARE AT THEIR FULL CAPACITY, BUT LIKE I SAID IT'S GOING TO TAKE ME SOME TIME TO GET UP TO SPEED.
THEN WHY CAN'T YOU ALTER HISTORY?
TRYING TO ALTER ANYTHING IN THE PAST IS LIKE TRYING TO SWIM UP A WATERFALL. THE CURRENT OF TIME FIGHTS AGAINST IT. AND RIGHTLY SO.
AMERICAN HISTORY
MMMRRR.
THAT'S THE BATMAN *"MMMRRR"* FOR SAYING SOMETHING WITHOUT SAYING SOMETHING. YOUR SON DID IT TOO. WHAT IS IT?.
IT SOUNDS LIKE OU'RE HOLDING OURSELF BACK. KE YOU HAVEN'T EALLY *TRIED*--
BECAUSE IT'S DANGEROUS, DR. WAYNE.
ONE SMALL, SEEMINGLY MEANINGLESS EVENT CAN TOPPLE OVER A ROW OF DOMINOES.
LIKE A ROCK THROWN THROUGH A WINDSHIELD, IT CAN LEAVE CRACKS THROUGHOUT HISTORY.
THE BUTTERFLY EFFECT.
YES.
BUT IN THIS CASE THERE'S TOO MUCH THAT'S ALTERED AROUND THE PEOPLE CLOSEST TO ME.
IT HAS TO BE ORCHESTRATED. *MULTIPLE* ATTACKS ON THE HISTORY OF MY FRIENDS AND ALLIES.
WITHOUT ANY OTHER SPEEDSTERS OUT THERE, THAWNE KNEW THE FIRST THING I WOULD DO WAS TRY TO REASSEMBLE THE JUSTICE LEAGUE.
SO HE TOOK THEM OUT OF THE EQUATION.
OR *TRIED* TO.

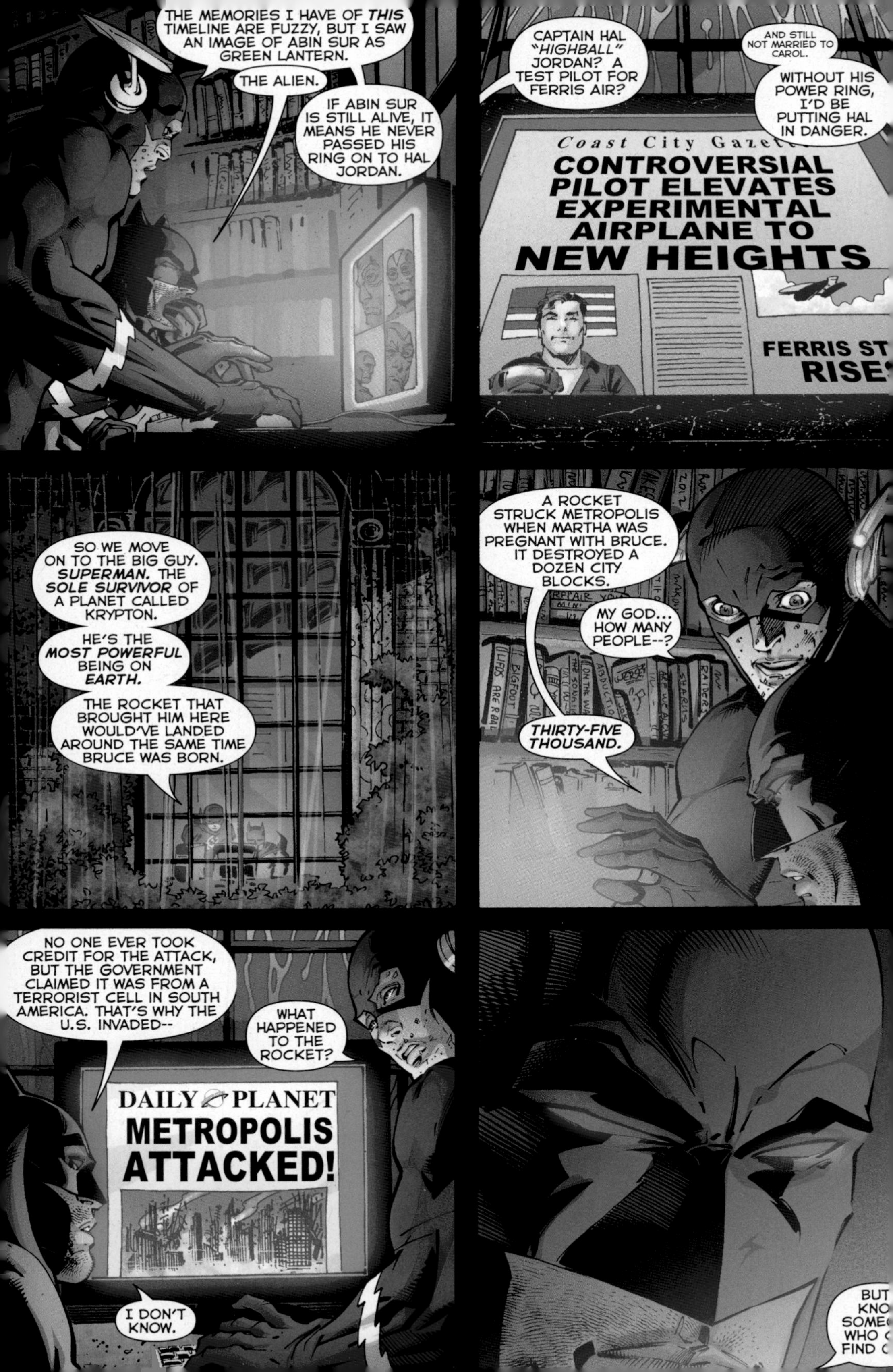
THE MEMORIES I HAVE OF THIS TIMELINE ARE FUZZY, BUT I SAW AN IMAGE OF ABIN SUR AS GREEN LANTERN.
THE ALIEN.
IF ABIN SUR IS STILL ALIVE, IT MEANS HE NEVER PASSED HIS RING ON TO HAL JORDAN.
CAPTAIN HAL "HIGHBALL" JORDAN? A TEST PILOT FOR FERRIS AIR?
AND STILL NOT MARRIED TO CAROL.
WITHOUT HIS POWER RING, I'D BE PUTTING HAL IN DANGER.
Coast City Gazet
CONTROVERSIAL PILOT ELEVATES EXPERIMENTAL AIRPLANE TO NEW HEIGHTS
FERRIS ST
RISE
SO WE MOVE ON TO THE BIG GUY. SUPERMAN. THE SOLE SURVIVOR OF A PLANET CALLED KRYPTON.
HE'S THE MOST POWERFUL BEING ON EARTH.
THE ROCKET THAT BROUGHT HIM HERE WOULD'VE LANDED AROUND THE SAME TIME BRUCE WAS BORN.
A ROCKET STRUCK METROPOLIS WHEN MARTHA WAS PREGNANT WITH BRUCE. IT DESTROYED A DOZEN CITY BLOCKS.
MY GOD... HOW MANY PEOPLE--?
THIRTY-FIVE THOUSAND.
NO ONE EVER TOOK CREDIT FOR THE ATTACK, BUT THE GOVERNMENT CLAIMED IT WAS FROM A TERRORIST CELL IN SOUTH AMERICA. THAT'S WHY THE U.S. INVADED--
WHAT HAPPENED TO THE ROCKET?
DAILY PLANET
METROPOLIS ATTACKED!
I DON'T KNOW.
BUT
KNO
SOME
WHO
FIND

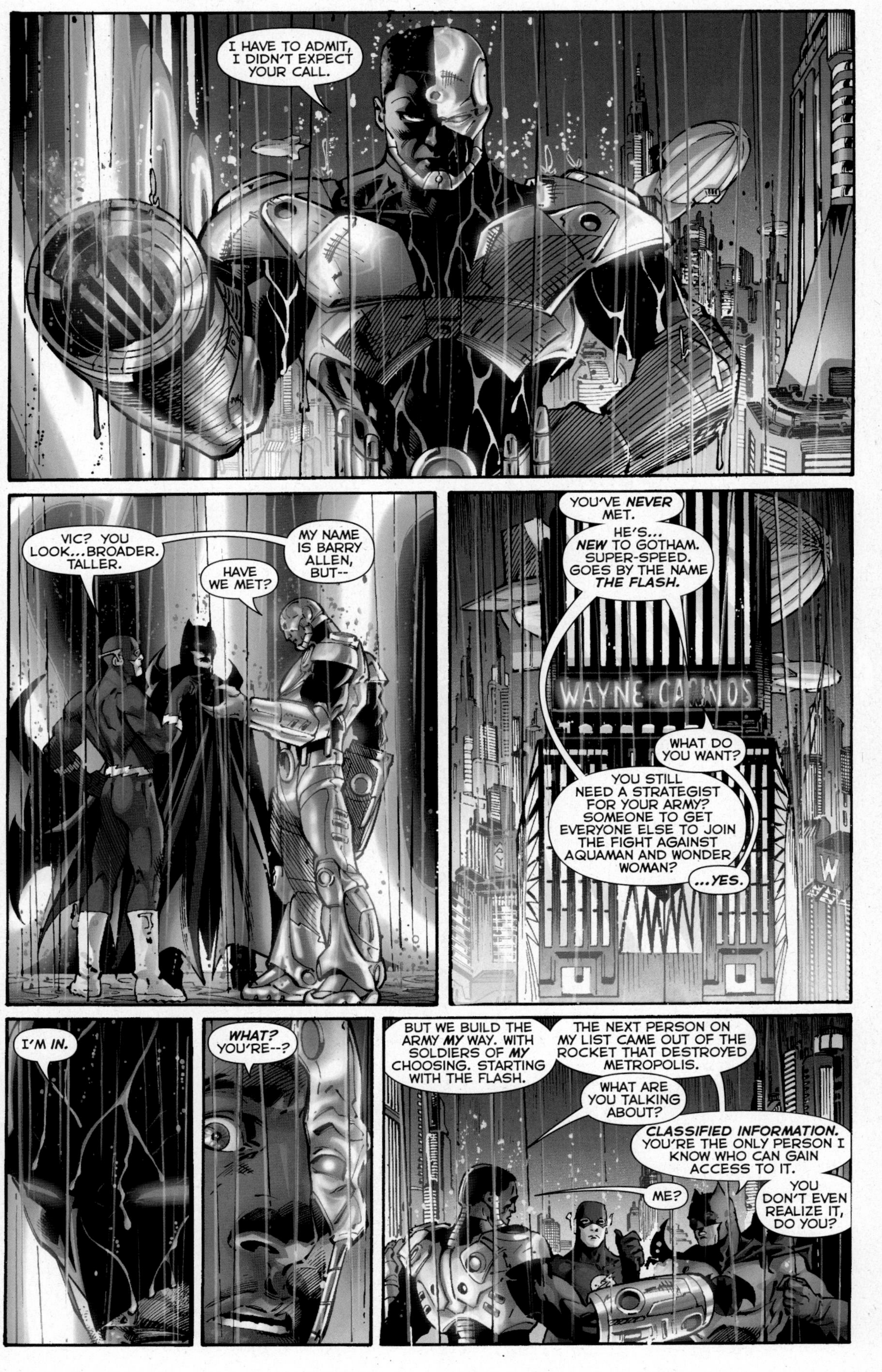
I HAVE TO ADMIT, I DIDN'T EXPECT YOUR CALL.
VIC? YOU LOOK...BROADER. TALLER.
HAVE WE MET?
MY NAME IS BARRY ALLEN, BUT--
YOU'VE NEVER MET.
HE'S... NEW TO GOTHAM. SUPER-SPEED. GOES BY THE NAME THE FLASH.
WAYNE CASINOS
WHAT DO YOU WANT?
YOU STILL NEED A STRATEGIST FOR YOUR ARMY? SOMEONE TO GET EVERYONE ELSE TO JOIN THE FIGHT AGAINST AQUAMAN AND WONDER WOMAN?
...YES.
I'M IN.
WHAT? YOU'RE--?
BUT WE BUILD THE ARMY MY WAY. WITH SOLDIERS OF MY CHOOSING. STARTING WITH THE FLASH.
THE NEXT PERSON ON MY LIST CAME OUT OF THE ROCKET THAT DESTROYED METROPOLIS.
WHAT ARE YOU TALKING ABOUT?
CLASSIFIED INFORMATION. YOU'RE THE ONLY PERSON I KNOW WHO CAN GAIN ACCESS TO IT.
ME?
YOU DON'T EVEN REALIZE IT, DO YOU?

YOU COULD BE THE SINGLE MOST POWERFUL SOURCE OF *INFORMATION* ON THE *PLANET*.

A *PHYSICAL* AND *DIGITAL* TANK.

THERE'S NOT A *BRICK WALL* OR *FIREWALL* ON EARTH THAT CAN KEEP CYBORG *OUT*.

YOU'RE TALKING ABOUT *HACKING* INTO GOVERNMENT SYSTEMS, BATMAN. I *DON'T* HACK INTO GOVERNMENT SYSTEMS.

THIS IS TH *DEAL*. THIS THE *PRICE* F MY *SIGNING UP*.

FIRST, I WANT TO KNOW WHAT THE HELL MADE YOU CHANGE YOUR MIND?

DOES IT *MATTER*?

I'LL SEE WHAT I CAN DO.

WHAT ARE YOU DOING?

GETTING THE INFORMATION WE NEED.

YOU'RE *LYING* TO HIM, DR. WAYNE.

WE SHOULD TELL HIM WHAT WE'RE REALLY UP TO. HE COULD HELP--

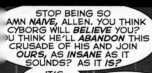

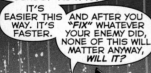

STOP BEING SO AMN *NAIVE*, ALLEN. YOU THINK CYBORG WILL *BELIEVE* YOU? U THINK HE'LL *ABANDON* THIS CRUSADE OF HIS AND JOIN *OURS*, AS *INSANE* AS IT SOUNDS? AS IT *IS*?

IT'S EASIER THIS WAY. IT'S FASTER.

AND AFTER YOU *"FIX"* WHATEVER YOUR ENEMY DID, NONE OF THIS WILL MATTER ANYWAY, *WILL IT*?

DID IT *EVER* MATTER TO YOU?

ACCORDING TO GOVERNMENT FILES, THE ROCKET WAS TAKEN AND TRANSFERRED TO A SECRET UNDERGROUND FACILITY UNDERNEATH METROPOLIS CALLED *PROJECT: SUPERMAN*.

AND THERE *IS* A REPORT, MOSTLY DESTROYED, THAT THEY FOUND SOMETHING *INSIDE* THE ROCKET. THEY CALLED IT *SUBJECT 1*.

HOW THE HELL DID YOU *KNOW* ABOUT THIS?

THAT ALSO DOESN'T MATTER. NOW ARE YOU GOING TO TELL US HOW TO GET INTO PROJECT: SUPERMAN OR NOT?

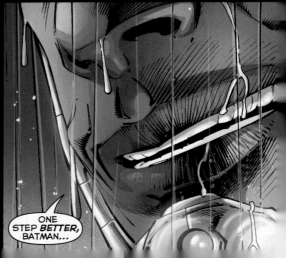

ONE STEP *BETTER*, BATMAN...

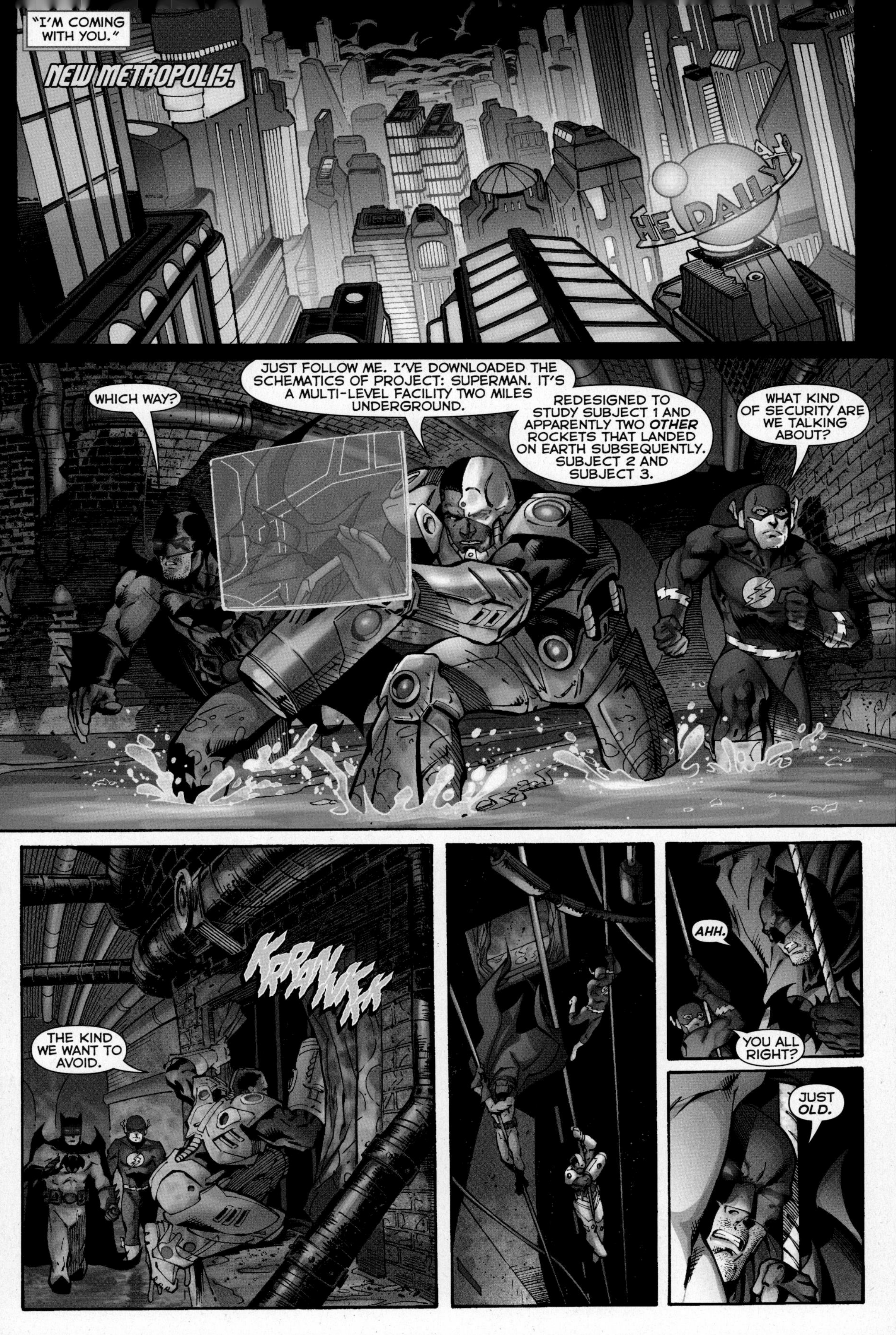
"I'M COMING WITH YOU."
NEW METROPOLIS.
WHICH WAY?
JUST FOLLOW ME. I'VE DOWNLOADED THE SCHEMATICS OF PROJECT: SUPERMAN. IT'S A MULTI-LEVEL FACILITY TWO MILES UNDERGROUND.
REDESIGNED TO STUDY SUBJECT 1 AND APPARENTLY TWO OTHER ROCKETS THAT LANDED ON EARTH SUBSEQUENTLY. SUBJECT 2 AND SUBJECT 3.
WHAT KIND OF SECURITY ARE WE TALKING ABOUT?
KRRAANKK
THE KIND WE WANT TO AVOID.
AHH.
YOU ALL RIGHT?
JUST OLD.

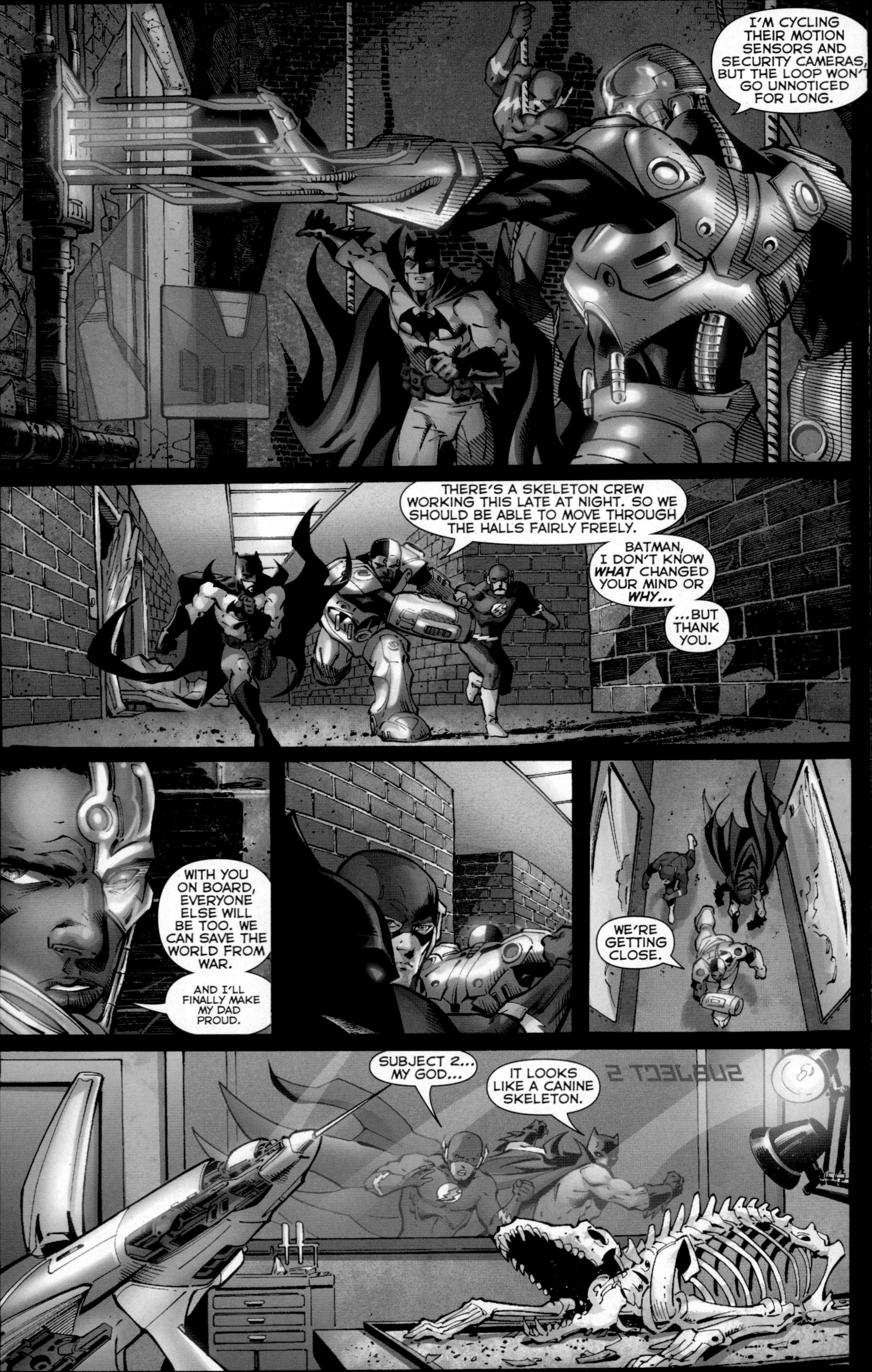
I'M CYCLING THEIR MOTION SENSORS AND SECURITY CAMERAS, BUT THE LOOP WON'T GO UNNOTICED FOR LONG.
THERE'S A SKELETON CREW WORKING THIS LATE AT NIGHT. SO WE SHOULD BE ABLE TO MOVE THROUGH THE HALLS FAIRLY FREELY.
BATMAN, I DON'T KNOW *WHAT* CHANGED YOUR MIND OR *WHY*...
...BUT THANK YOU.
WITH YOU ON BOARD, EVERYONE ELSE WILL BE TOO. WE CAN SAVE THE WORLD FROM WAR.
AND I'LL FINALLY MAKE MY DAD PROUD.
WE'RE GETTING CLOSE.
SUBJECT 2... MY GOD...
IT LOOKS LIKE A CANINE SKELETON.

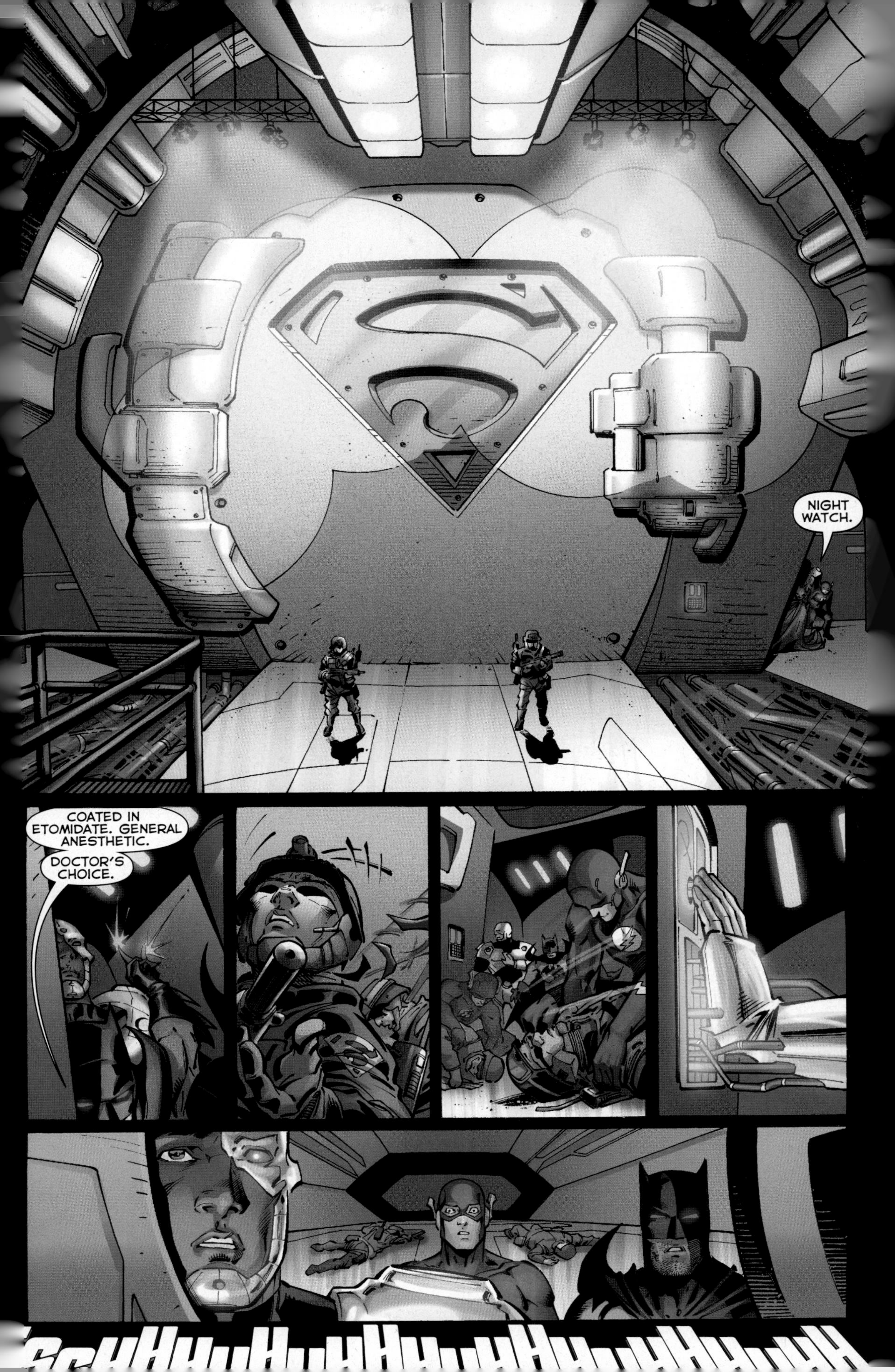
NIGHT WATCH.
COATED IN ETOMIDATE. GENERAL ANESTHETIC.
DOCTOR'S CHOICE.

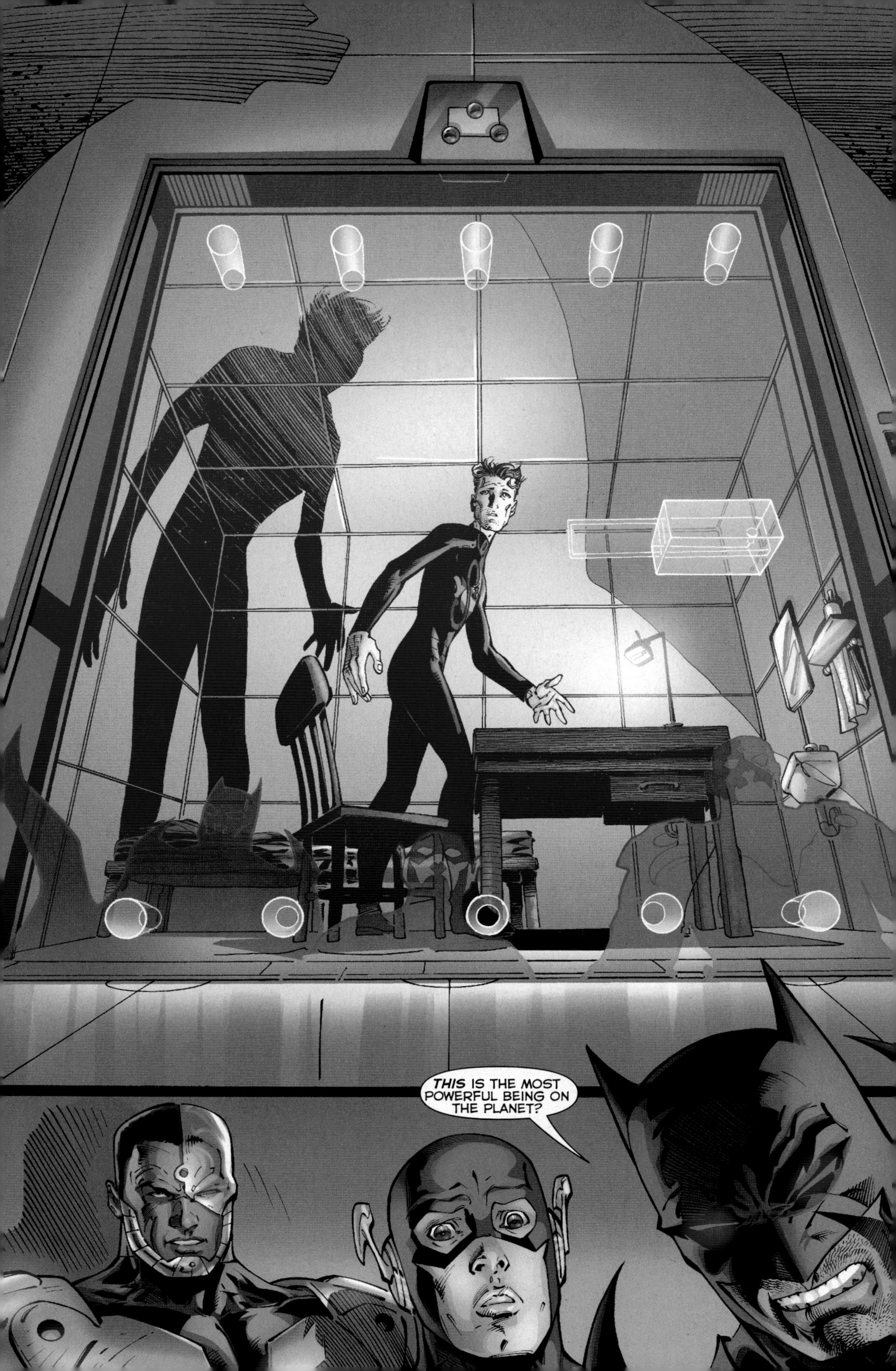
THIS IS THE MOST POWERFUL BEING ON THE PLANET?

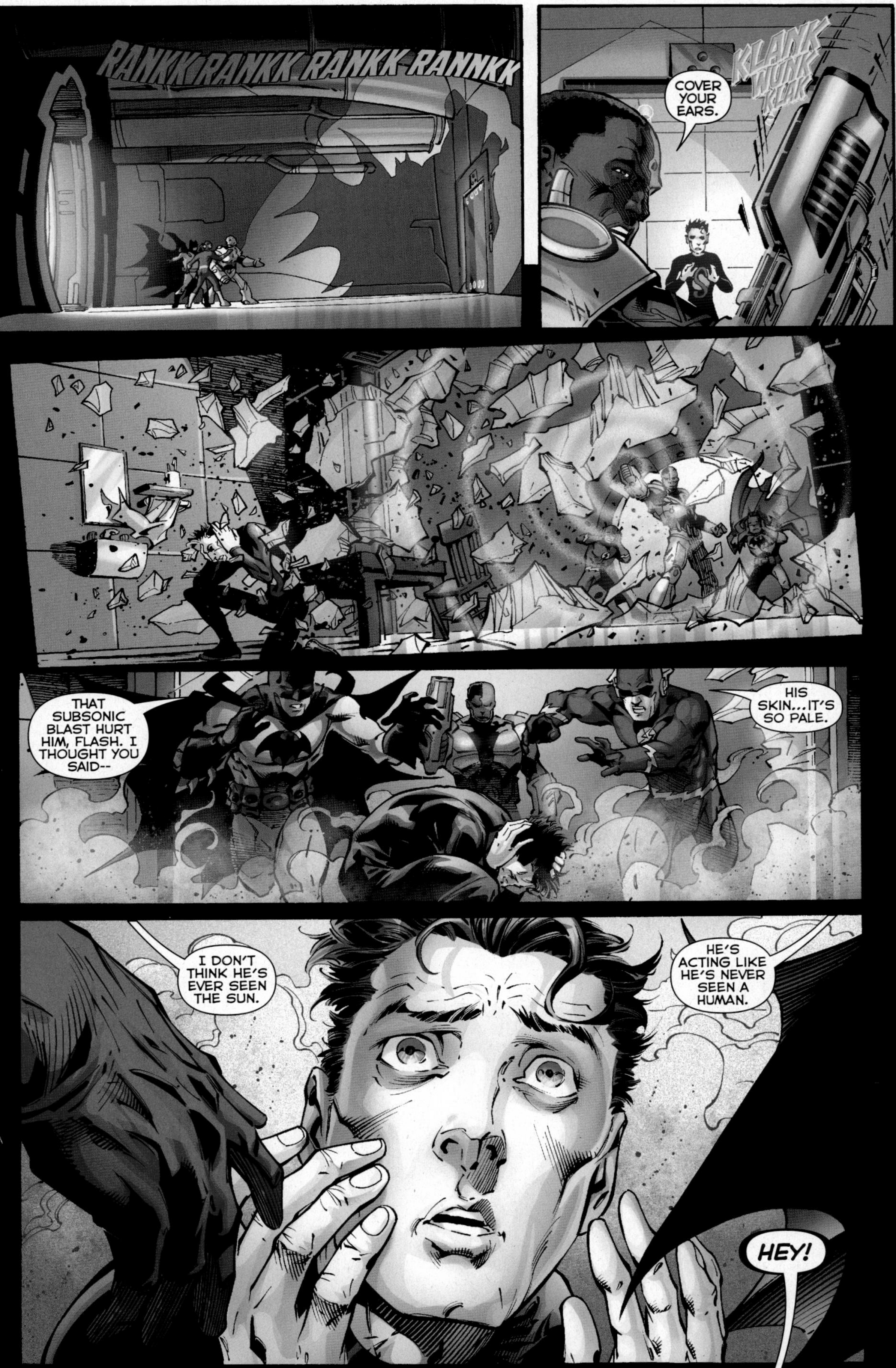
RANKK RANKK RANKK RANNKK
KLANK WUNK KLAK
COVER YOUR EARS.
THAT SUBSONIC BLAST HURT HIM, FLASH. I THOUGHT YOU SAID--
HIS SKIN...IT'S SO PALE.
I DON'T THINK HE'S EVER SEEN THE SUN.
HE'S ACTING LIKE HE'S NEVER SEEN A HUMAN.
HEY!

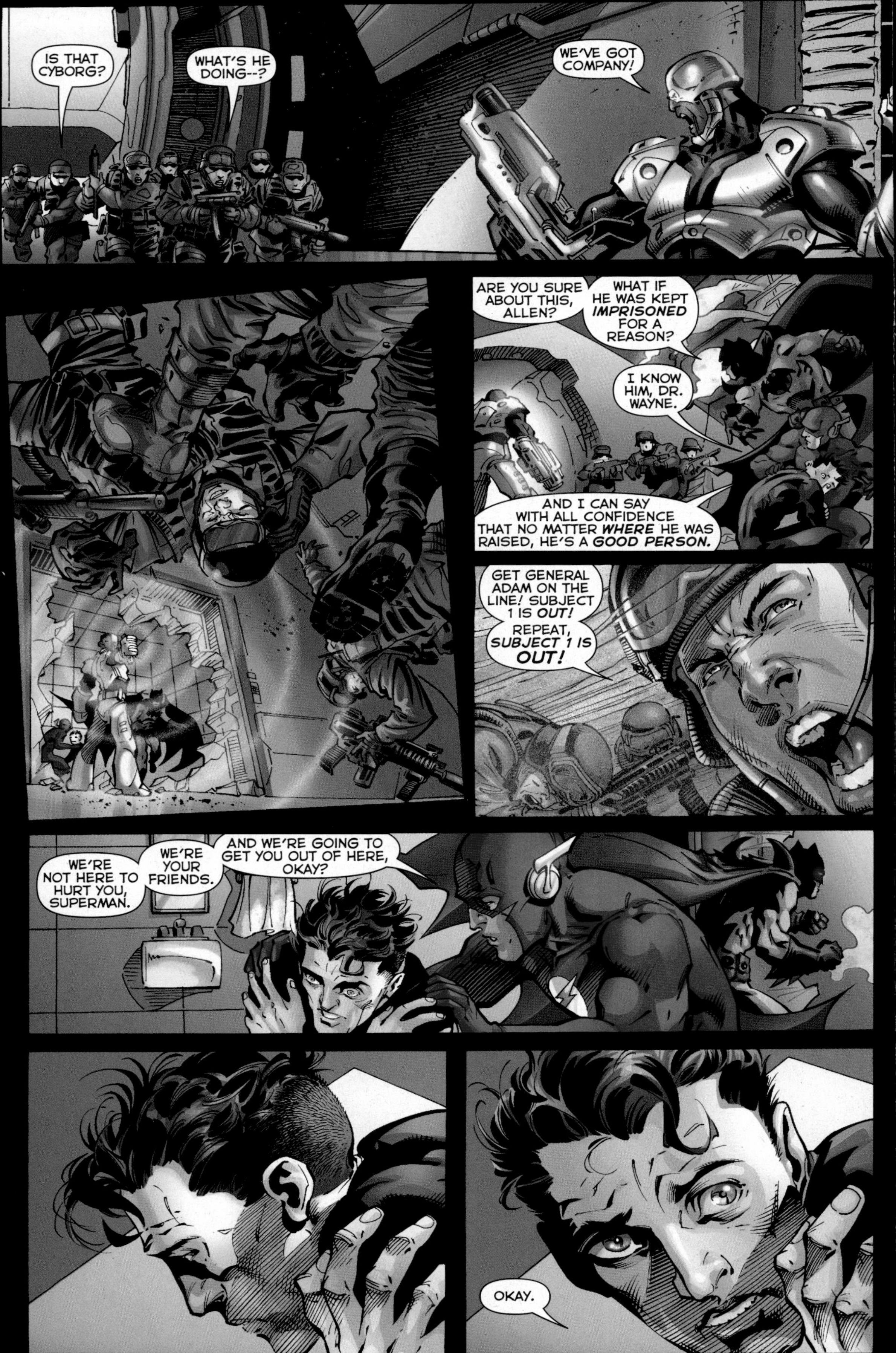
IS THAT CYBORG?
WHAT'S HE DOING--?
WE'VE GOT COMPANY!
ARE YOU SURE ABOUT THIS, ALLEN?
WHAT IF HE WAS KEPT *IMPRISONED* FOR A REASON?
I KNOW HIM, DR. WAYNE.
AND I CAN SAY WITH ALL CONFIDENCE THAT NO MATTER *WHERE* HE WAS RAISED, HE'S A *GOOD PERSON.*
GET GENERAL ADAM ON THE LINE! SUBJECT 1 IS *OUT!*
REPEAT, *SUBJECT 1 IS OUT!*
WE'RE NOT HERE TO HURT YOU, SUPERMAN.
WE'RE YOUR FRIENDS.
AND WE'RE GOING TO GET YOU OUT OF HERE, OKAY?
OKAY.

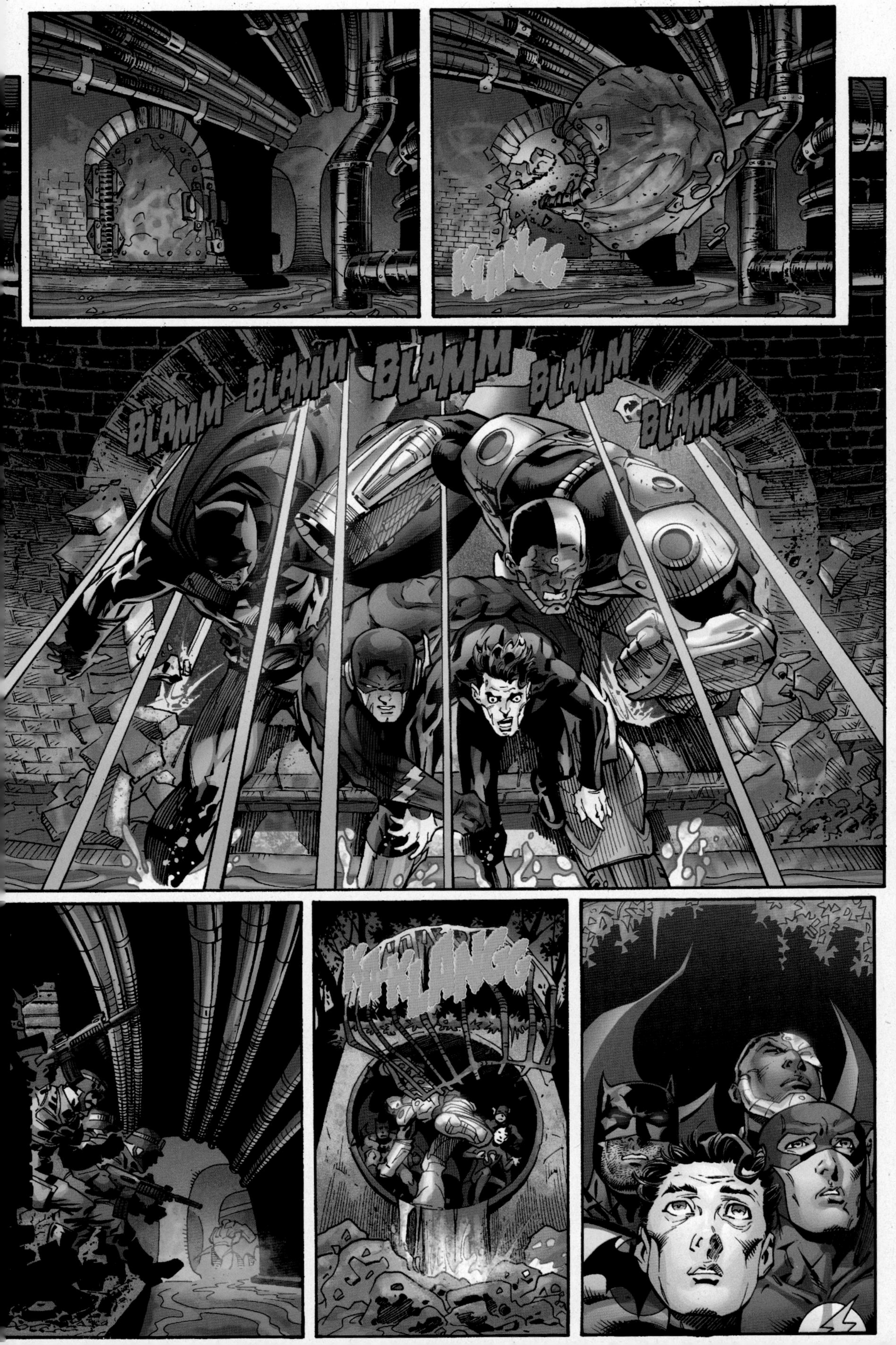
KLANGG
BLAMM
BLAMM
BLAMM
BLAMM
BLAMM
KA-KLANGG

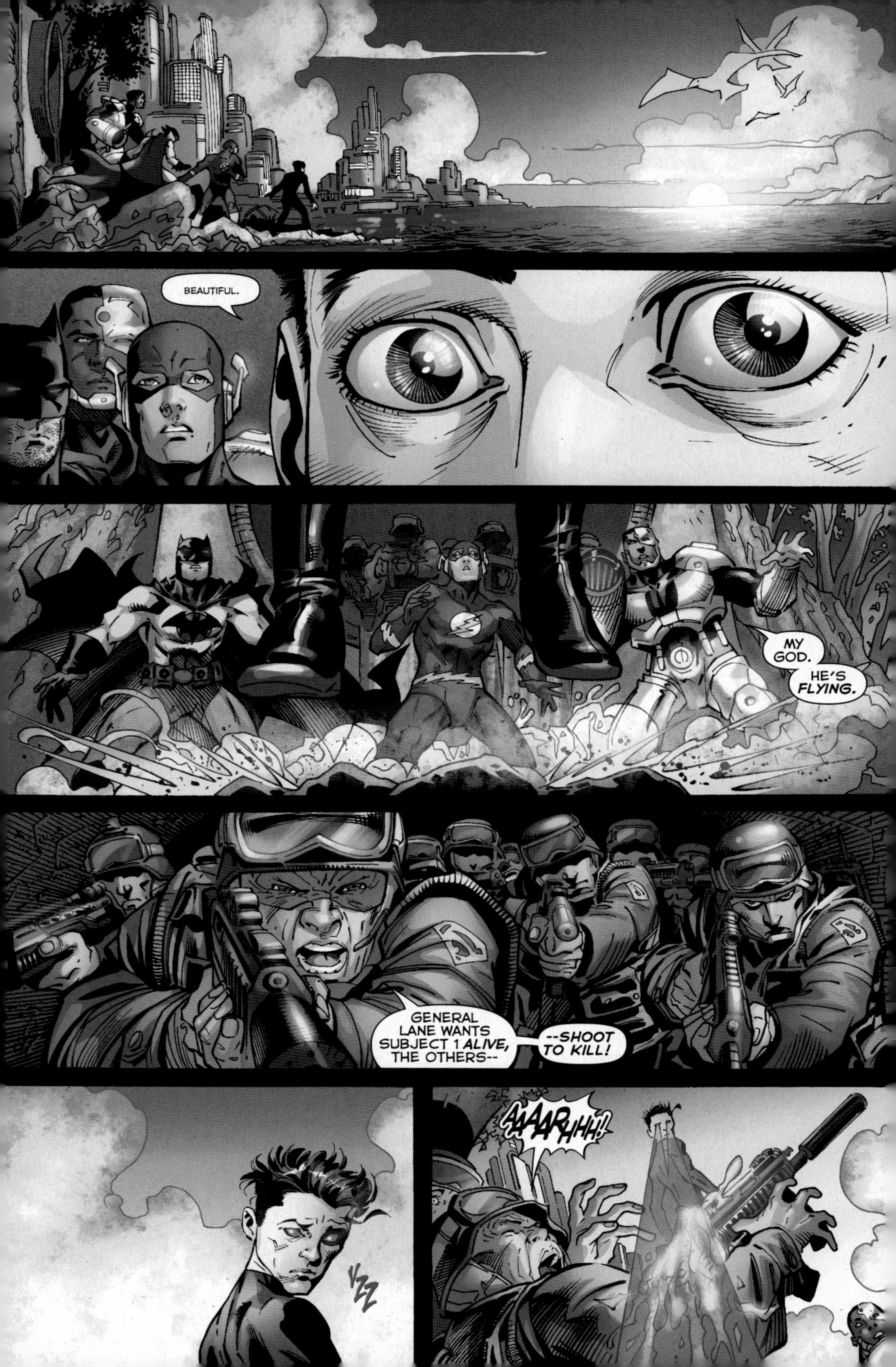
BEAUTIFUL.
MY GOD. HE'S FLYING.
GENERAL LANE WANTS SUBJECT 1 ALIVE, THE OTHERS--
--SHOOT TO KILL!
VZZ
AAAARHHH!

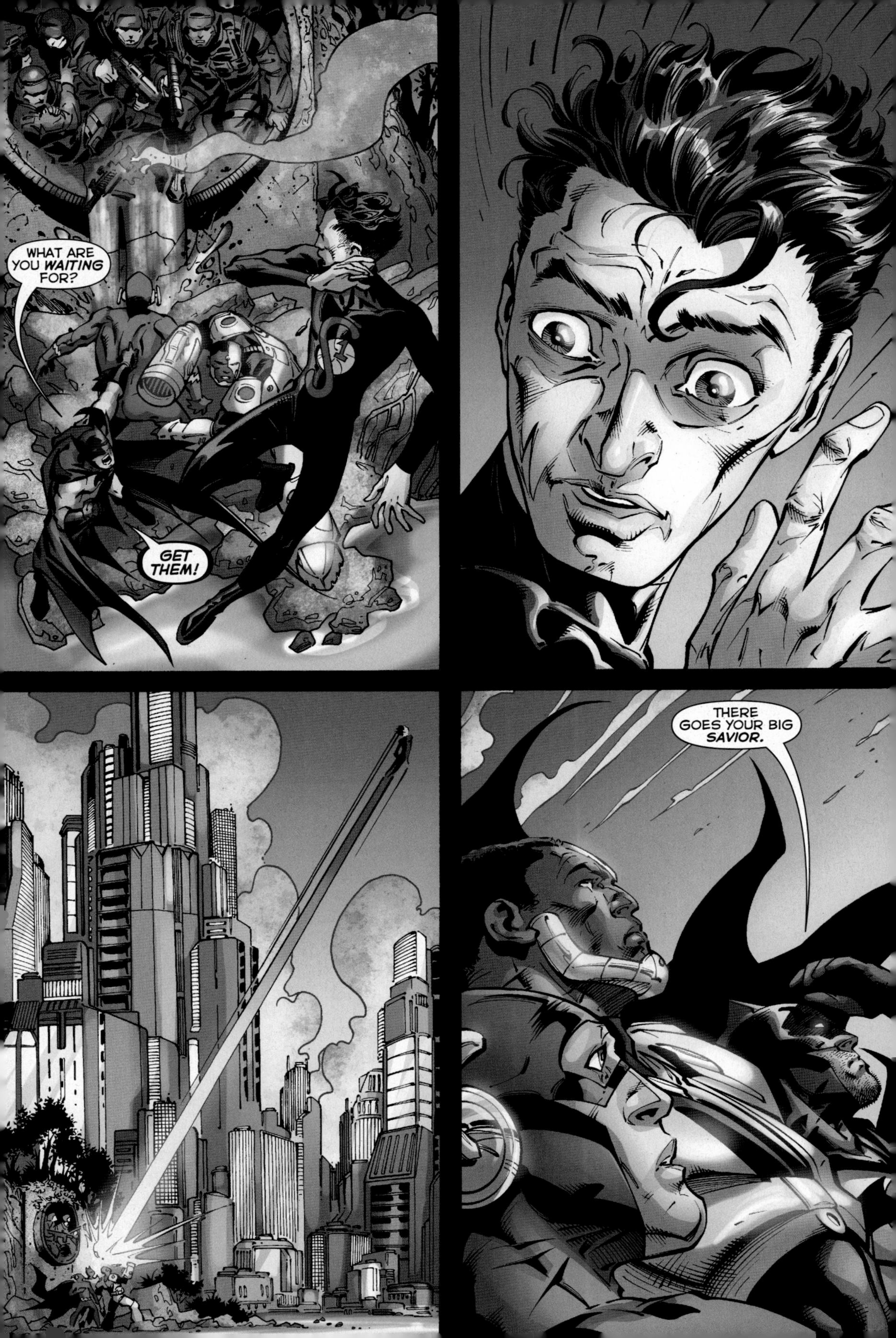
WHAT ARE YOU WAITING FOR?
GET THEM!
THERE GOES YOUR BIG SAVIOR.

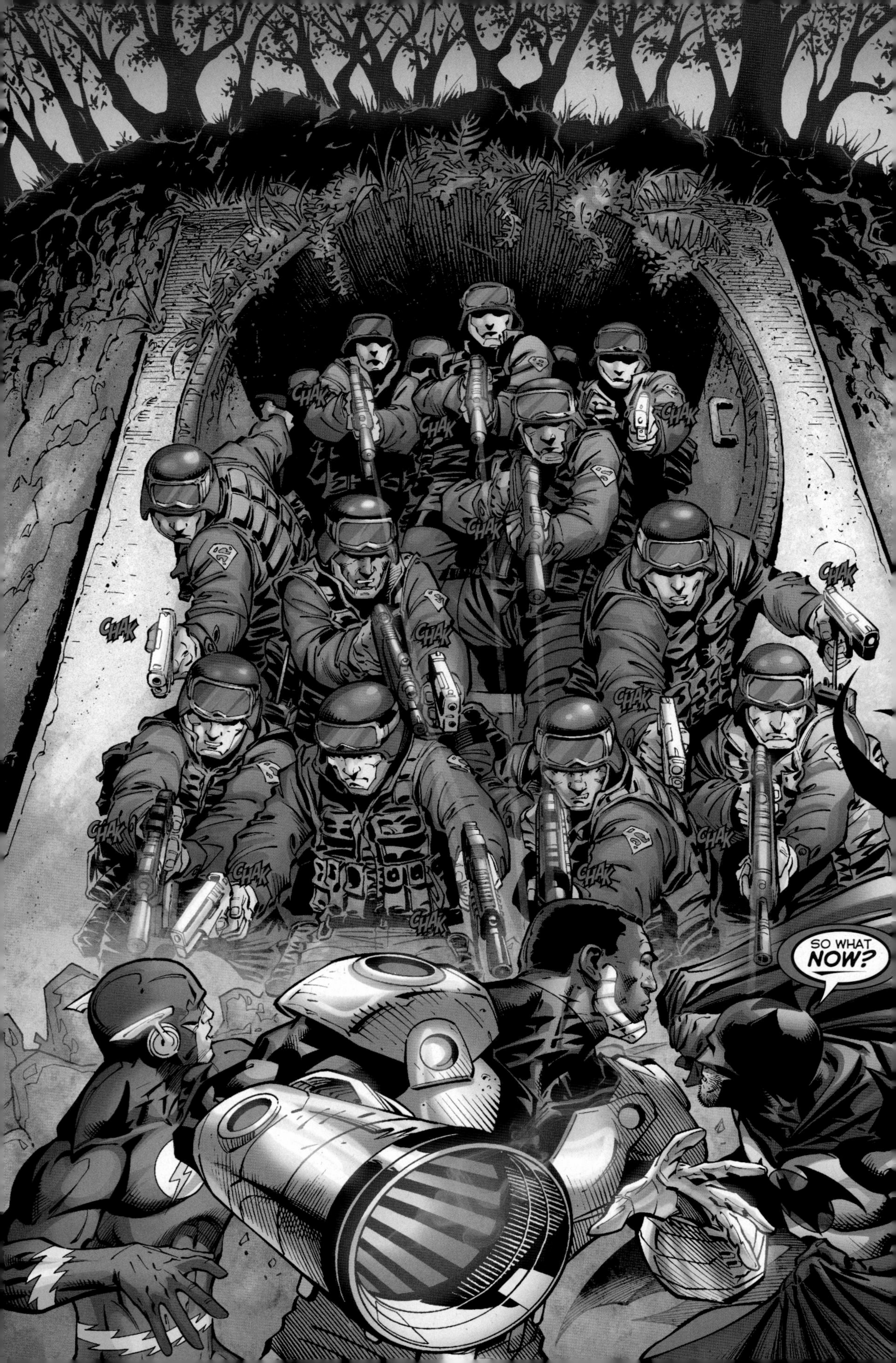
CHAK
CHAK
CHAK
CHAK
CHAK
CHAK
CHAK
CHAK
CHAK
CHAK
CHAK
CHAK
SO WHAT NOW?

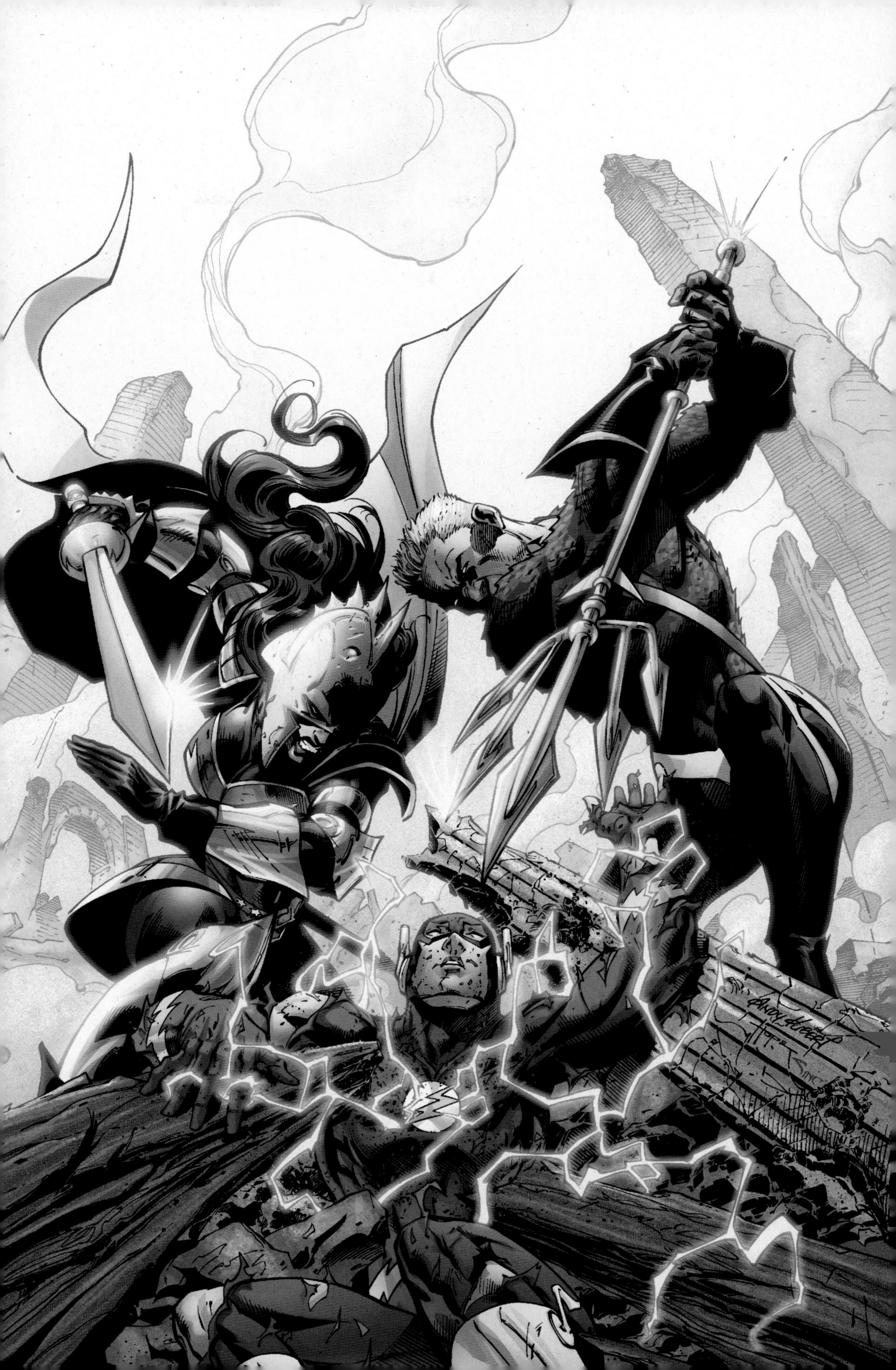

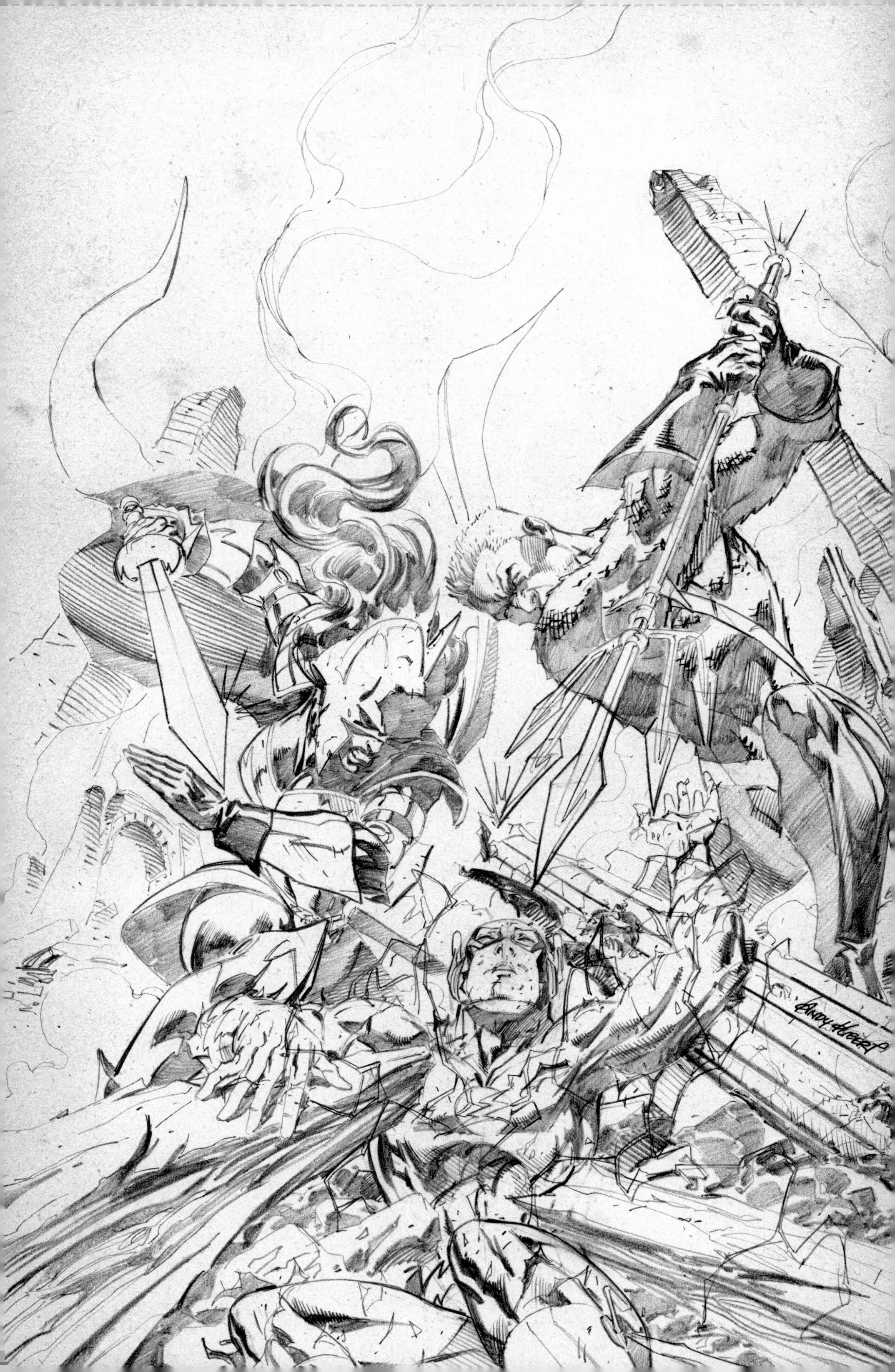

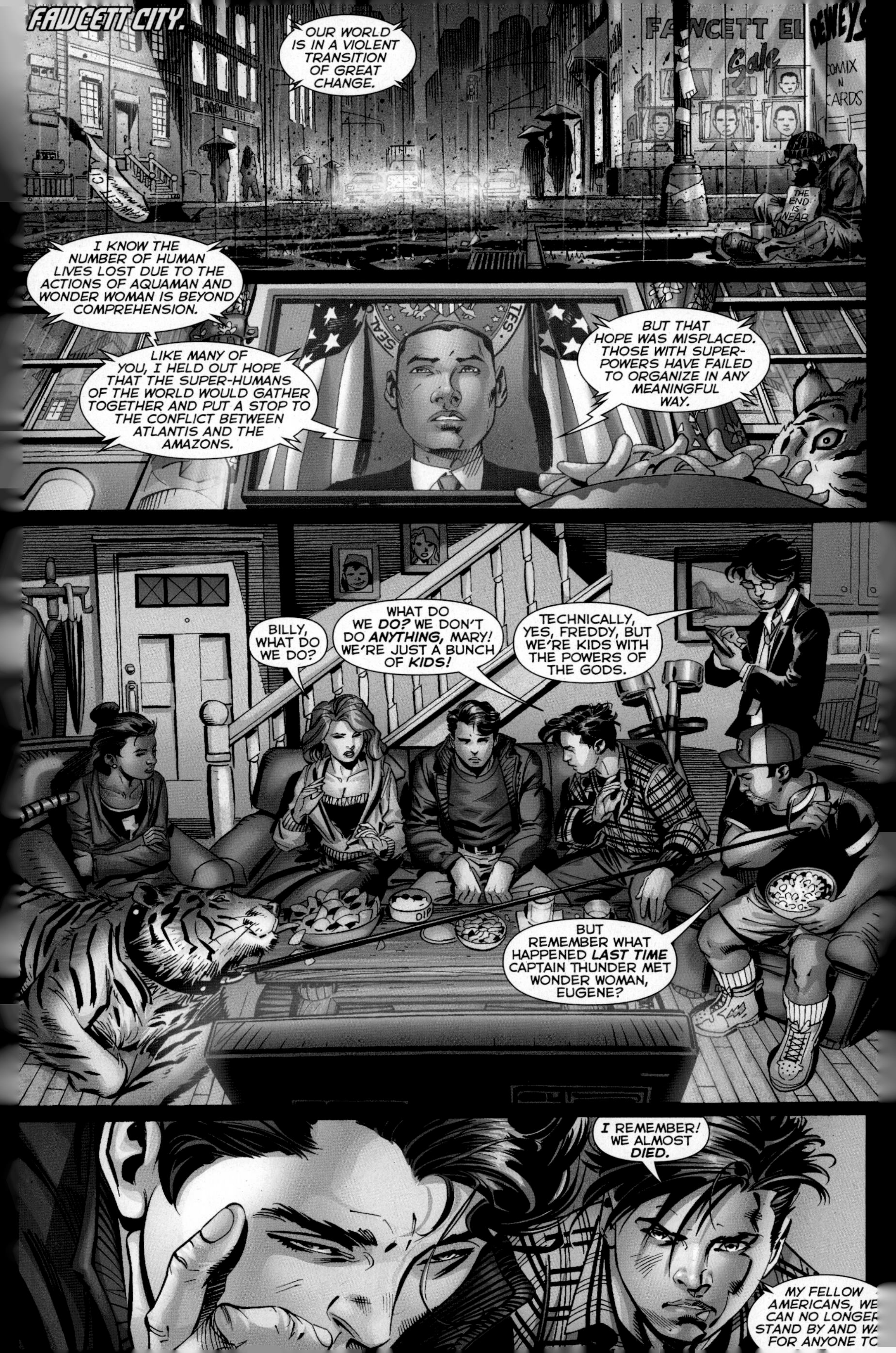
FAWCETT CITY.
OUR WORLD IS IN A VIOLENT TRANSITION OF GREAT CHANGE.
FAWCETT EL
DEWEY'S
Sale
COMIX N CARDS
THE END IS NEAR
I KNOW THE NUMBER OF HUMAN LIVES LOST DUE TO THE ACTIONS OF AQUAMAN AND WONDER WOMAN IS BEYOND COMPREHENSION.
LIKE MANY OF YOU, I HELD OUT HOPE THAT THE SUPER-HUMANS OF THE WORLD WOULD GATHER TOGETHER AND PUT A STOP TO THE CONFLICT BETWEEN ATLANTIS AND THE AMAZONS.
BUT THAT HOPE WAS MISPLACED. THOSE WITH SUPER-POWERS HAVE FAILED TO ORGANIZE IN ANY MEANINGFUL WAY.
BILLY, WHAT DO WE DO?
WHAT DO WE DO? WE DON'T DO ANYTHING, MARY! WE'RE JUST A BUNCH OF KIDS!
TECHNICALLY, YES, FREDDY, BUT WE'RE KIDS WITH THE POWERS OF THE GODS.
DIP
BUT REMEMBER WHAT HAPPENED LAST TIME CAPTAIN THUNDER MET WONDER WOMAN, EUGENE?
I REMEMBER! WE ALMOST DIED.
MY FELLOW AMERICANS, WE CAN NO LONGER STAND BY AND WA FOR ANYONE TO

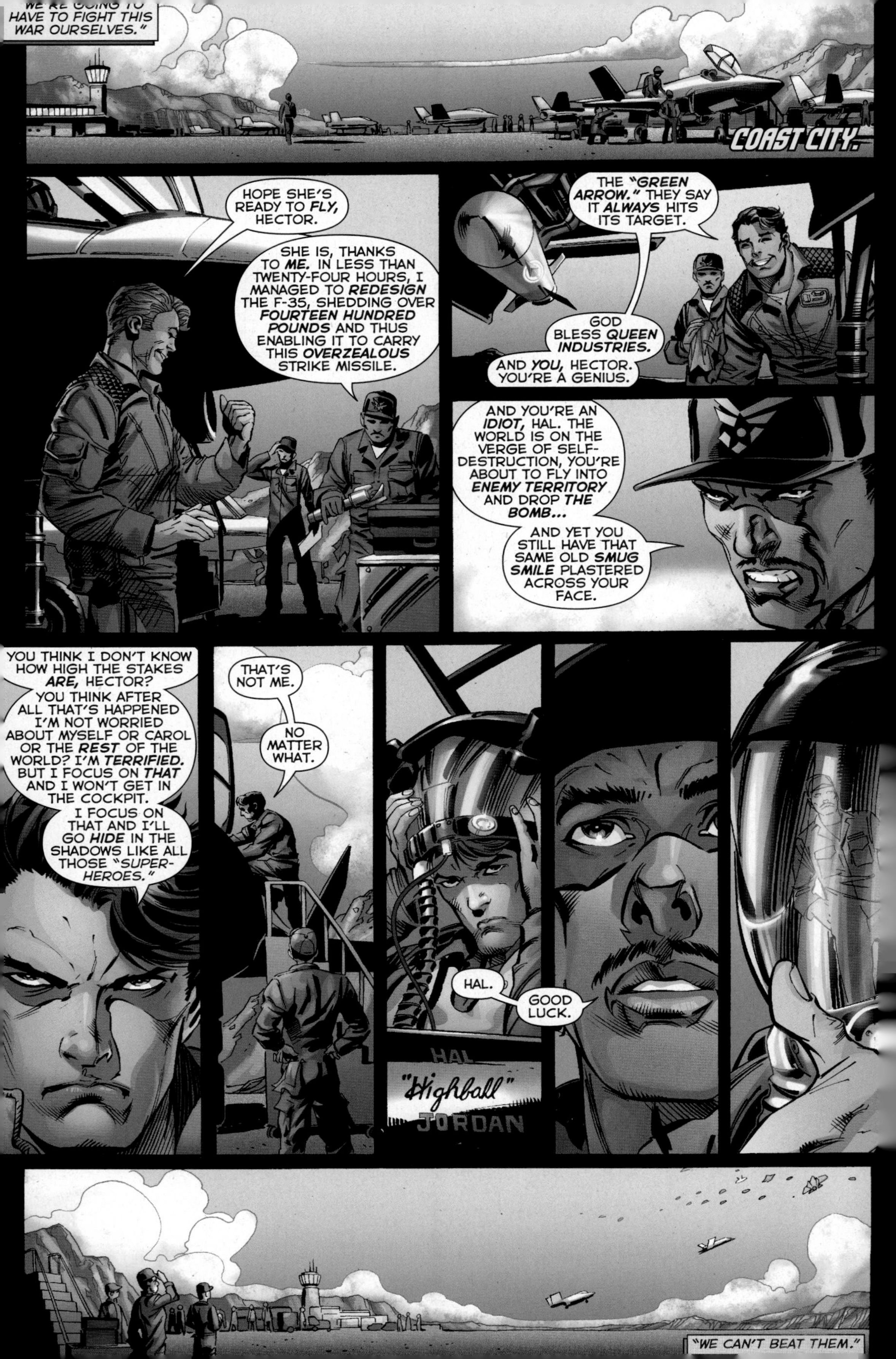

HAVE TO FIGHT THIS WAR OURSELVES."
COAST CITY.
HOPE SHE'S READY TO FLY, HECTOR.
SHE IS, THANKS TO ME. IN LESS THAN TWENTY-FOUR HOURS, I MANAGED TO REDESIGN THE F-35, SHEDDING OVER FOURTEEN HUNDRED POUNDS AND THUS ENABLING IT TO CARRY THIS OVERZEALOUS STRIKE MISSILE.
THE "GREEN ARROW." THEY SAY IT ALWAYS HITS ITS TARGET.
GOD BLESS QUEEN INDUSTRIES.
AND YOU, HECTOR. YOU'RE A GENIUS.
AND YOU'RE AN IDIOT, HAL. THE WORLD IS ON THE VERGE OF SELF-DESTRUCTION, YOU'RE ABOUT TO FLY INTO ENEMY TERRITORY AND DROP THE BOMB...
AND YET YOU STILL HAVE THAT SAME OLD SMUG SMILE PLASTERED ACROSS YOUR FACE.
YOU THINK I DON'T KNOW HOW HIGH THE STAKES ARE, HECTOR?
YOU THINK AFTER ALL THAT'S HAPPENED I'M NOT WORRIED ABOUT MYSELF OR CAROL OR THE REST OF THE WORLD? I'M TERRIFIED.
BUT I FOCUS ON THAT AND I WON'T GET IN THE COCKPIT.
I FOCUS ON THAT AND I'LL GO HIDE IN THE SHADOWS LIKE ALL THOSE "SUPER-HEROES."
THAT'S NOT ME.
NO MATTER WHAT.
HAL.
GOOD LUCK.
HAL "Highball" JORDAN
"WE CAN'T BEAT THEM."

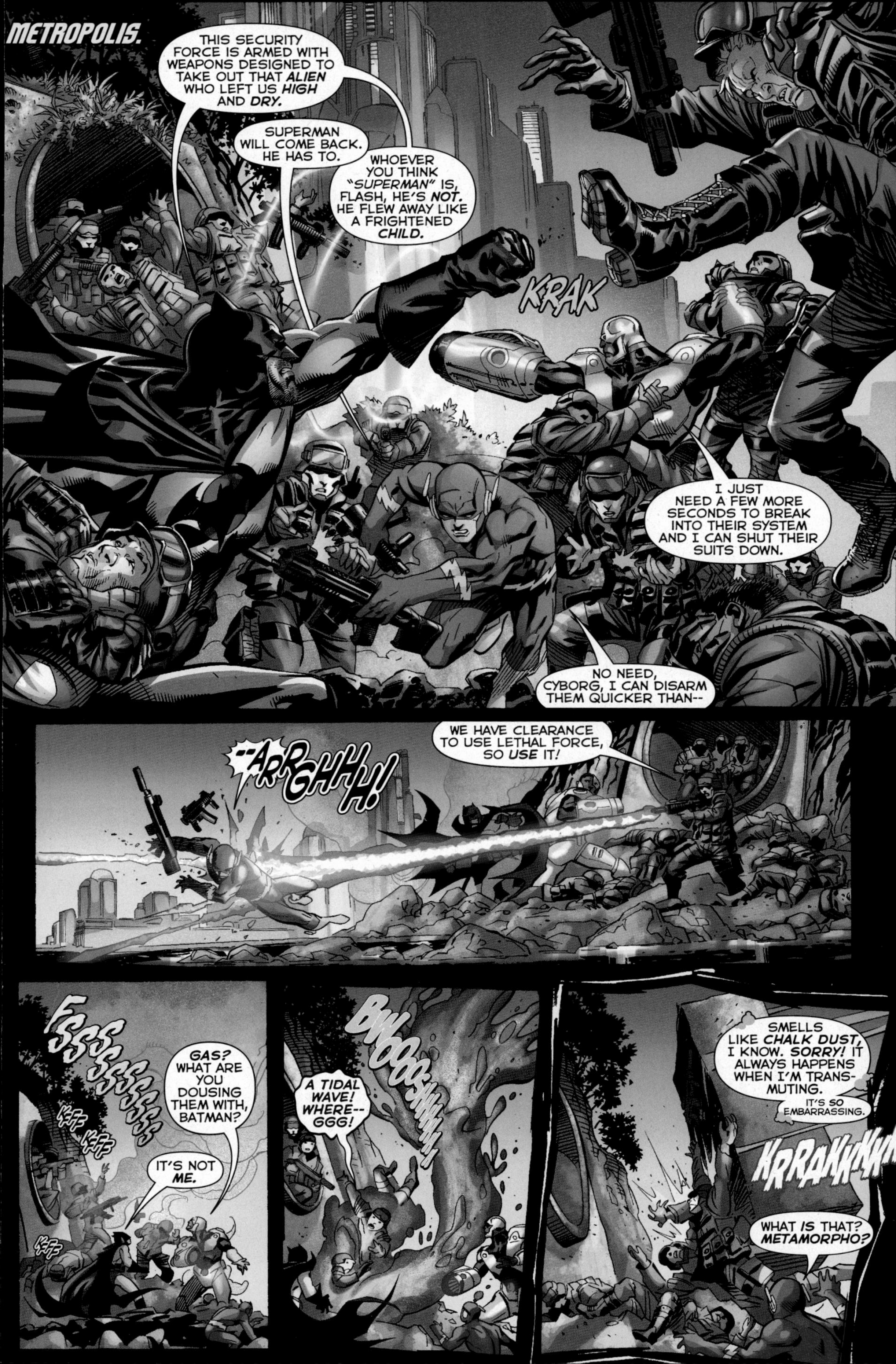
METROPOLIS.
THIS SECURITY FORCE IS ARMED WITH WEAPONS DESIGNED TO TAKE OUT THAT ALIEN WHO LEFT US HIGH AND DRY.
SUPERMAN WILL COME BACK. HE HAS TO.
WHOEVER YOU THINK "SUPERMAN" IS, FLASH, HE'S NOT. HE FLEW AWAY LIKE A FRIGHTENED CHILD.
KRAK
I JUST NEED A FEW MORE SECONDS TO BREAK INTO THEIR SYSTEM AND I CAN SHUT THEIR SUITS DOWN.
NO NEED, CYBORG, I CAN DISARM THEM QUICKER THAN--
--ARRGHHHH!
WE HAVE CLEARANCE TO USE LETHAL FORCE, SO USE IT!
FSSSSSSSSSSS
KFF KFF
KFF
GAS? WHAT ARE YOU DOUSING THEM WITH, BATMAN?
IT'S NOT ME.
BWOOOSHHHH
A TIDAL WAVE! WHERE--GGG!
SMELLS LIKE CHALK DUST, I KNOW. SORRY! IT ALWAYS HAPPENS WHEN I'M TRANSMUTING.
IT'S SO EMBARRASSING.
KRRAKKKK
WHAT IS THAT? METAMORPHO?

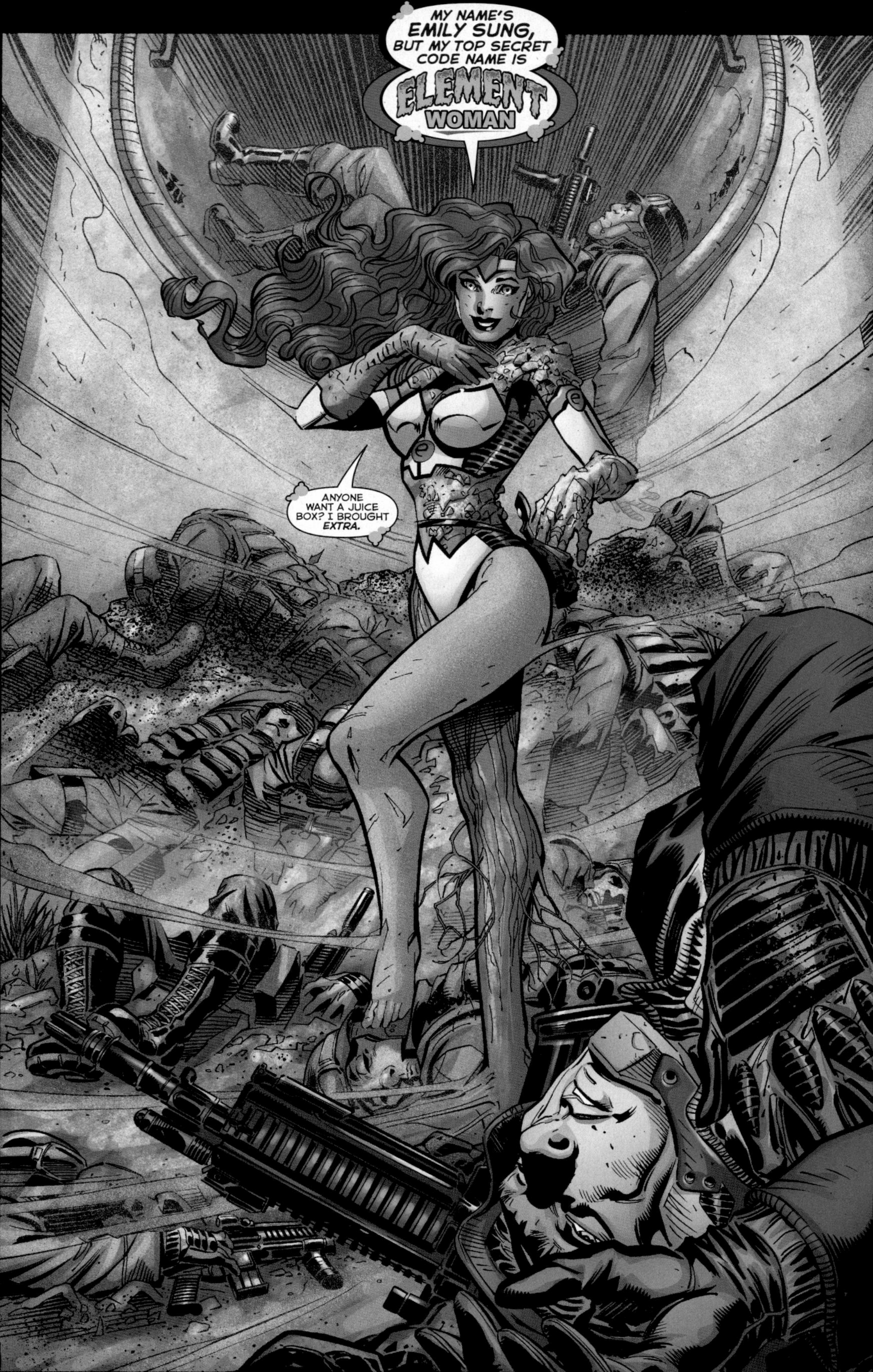
MY NAME'S EMILY SUNG, BUT MY TOP SECRET CODE NAME IS
ELEMENT WOMAN
ANYONE WANT A JUICE BOX? I BROUGHT EXTRA.

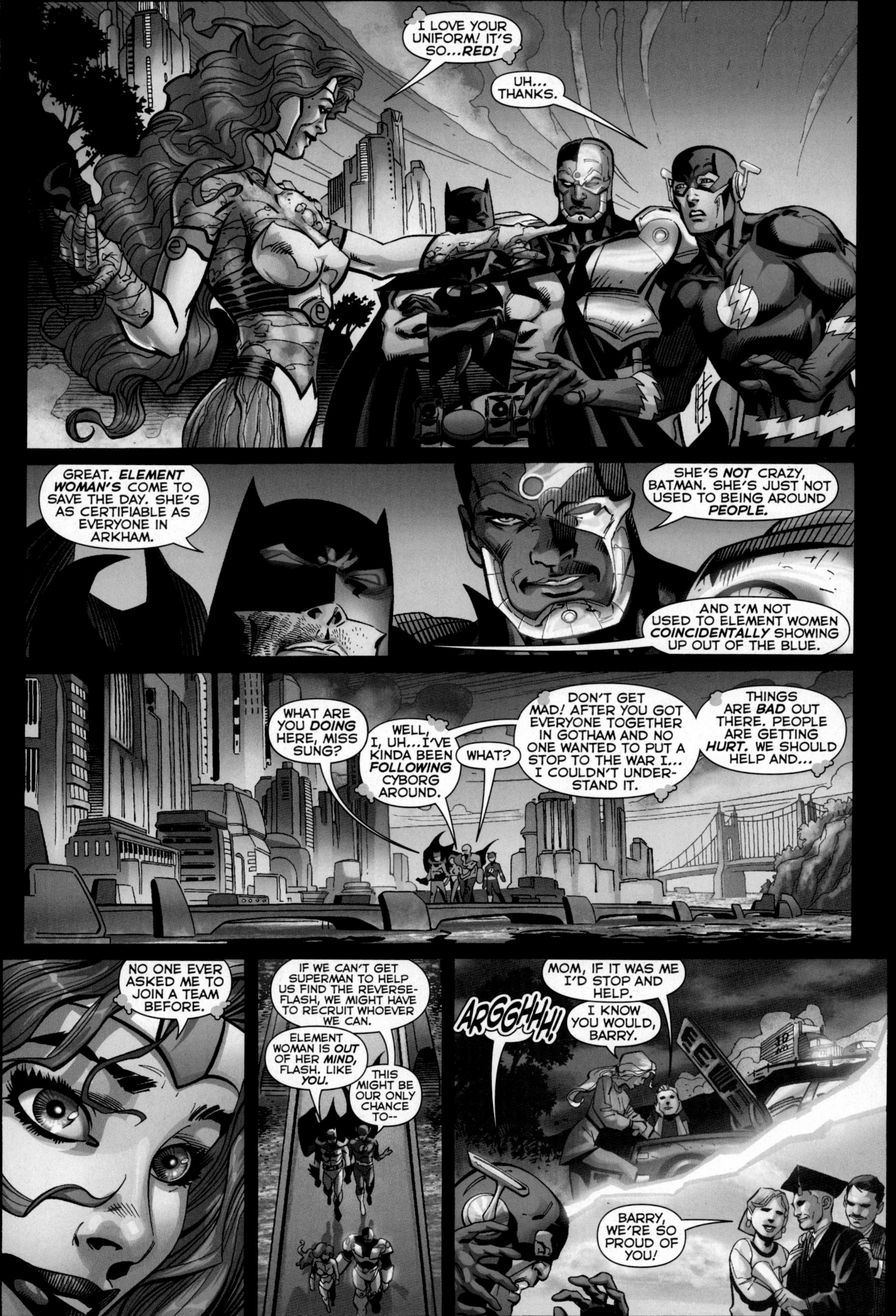
I LOVE YOUR UNIFORM! IT'S SO...RED!
UH... THANKS.
GREAT. ELEMENT WOMAN'S COME TO SAVE THE DAY. SHE'S AS CERTIFIABLE AS EVERYONE IN ARKHAM.
SHE'S NOT CRAZY, BATMAN. SHE'S JUST NOT USED TO BEING AROUND PEOPLE.
AND I'M NOT USED TO ELEMENT WOMEN COINCIDENTALLY SHOWING UP OUT OF THE BLUE.
WHAT ARE YOU DOING HERE, MISS SUNG?
WELL, I, UH...I'VE KINDA BEEN FOLLOWING CYBORG AROUND.
WHAT?
DON'T GET MAD! AFTER YOU GOT EVERYONE TOGETHER IN GOTHAM AND NO ONE WANTED TO PUT A STOP TO THE WAR I... I COULDN'T UNDERSTAND IT.
THINGS ARE BAD OUT THERE. PEOPLE ARE GETTING HURT. WE SHOULD HELP AND...
NO ONE EVER ASKED ME TO JOIN A TEAM BEFORE.
IF WE CAN'T GET SUPERMAN TO HELP US FIND THE REVERSE-FLASH, WE MIGHT HAVE TO RECRUIT WHOEVER WE CAN.
ELEMENT WOMAN IS OUT OF HER MIND, FLASH. LIKE YOU.
THIS MIGHT BE OUR ONLY CHANCE TO--
ARGGHHH!
MOM, IF IT WAS ME I'D STOP AND HELP.
I KNOW YOU WOULD, BARRY.
BARRY, WE'RE SO PROUD OF YOU!

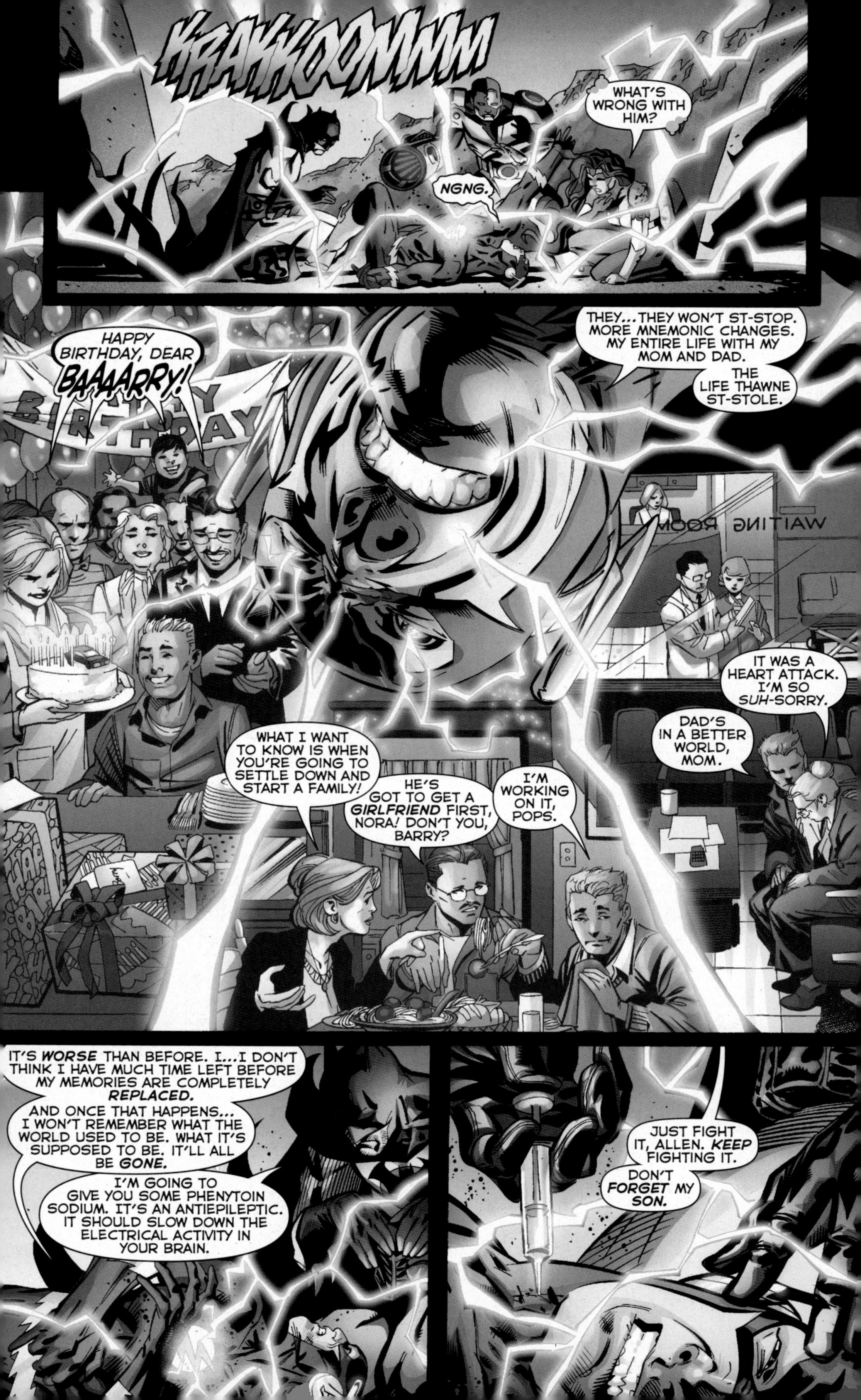
KRAKKOOMMM
WHAT'S WRONG WITH HIM?
NGNG.
THEY... THEY WON'T ST-STOP. MORE MNEMONIC CHANGES. MY ENTIRE LIFE WITH MY MOM AND DAD.
THE LIFE THAWNE ST-STOLE.
HAPPY BIRTHDAY, DEAR BAAAARRY!
HAPPY BIRTHDAY
WAITING ROOM
IT WAS A HEART ATTACK. I'M SO SUH-SORRY.
DAD'S IN A BETTER WORLD, MOM.
WHAT I WANT TO KNOW IS WHEN YOU'RE GOING TO SETTLE DOWN AND START A FAMILY!
HE'S GOT TO GET A GIRLFRIEND FIRST, NORA! DON'T YOU, BARRY?
I'M WORKING ON IT, POPS.
IT'S WORSE THAN BEFORE. I...I DON'T THINK I HAVE MUCH TIME LEFT BEFORE MY MEMORIES ARE COMPLETELY REPLACED.
AND ONCE THAT HAPPENS... I WON'T REMEMBER WHAT THE WORLD USED TO BE. WHAT IT'S SUPPOSED TO BE. IT'LL ALL BE GONE.
I'M GOING TO GIVE YOU SOME PHENYTOIN SODIUM. IT'S AN ANTIEPILEPTIC. IT SHOULD SLOW DOWN THE ELECTRICAL ACTIVITY IN YOUR BRAIN.
JUST FIGHT IT, ALLEN. KEEP FIGHTING IT.
DON'T FORGET MY SON.

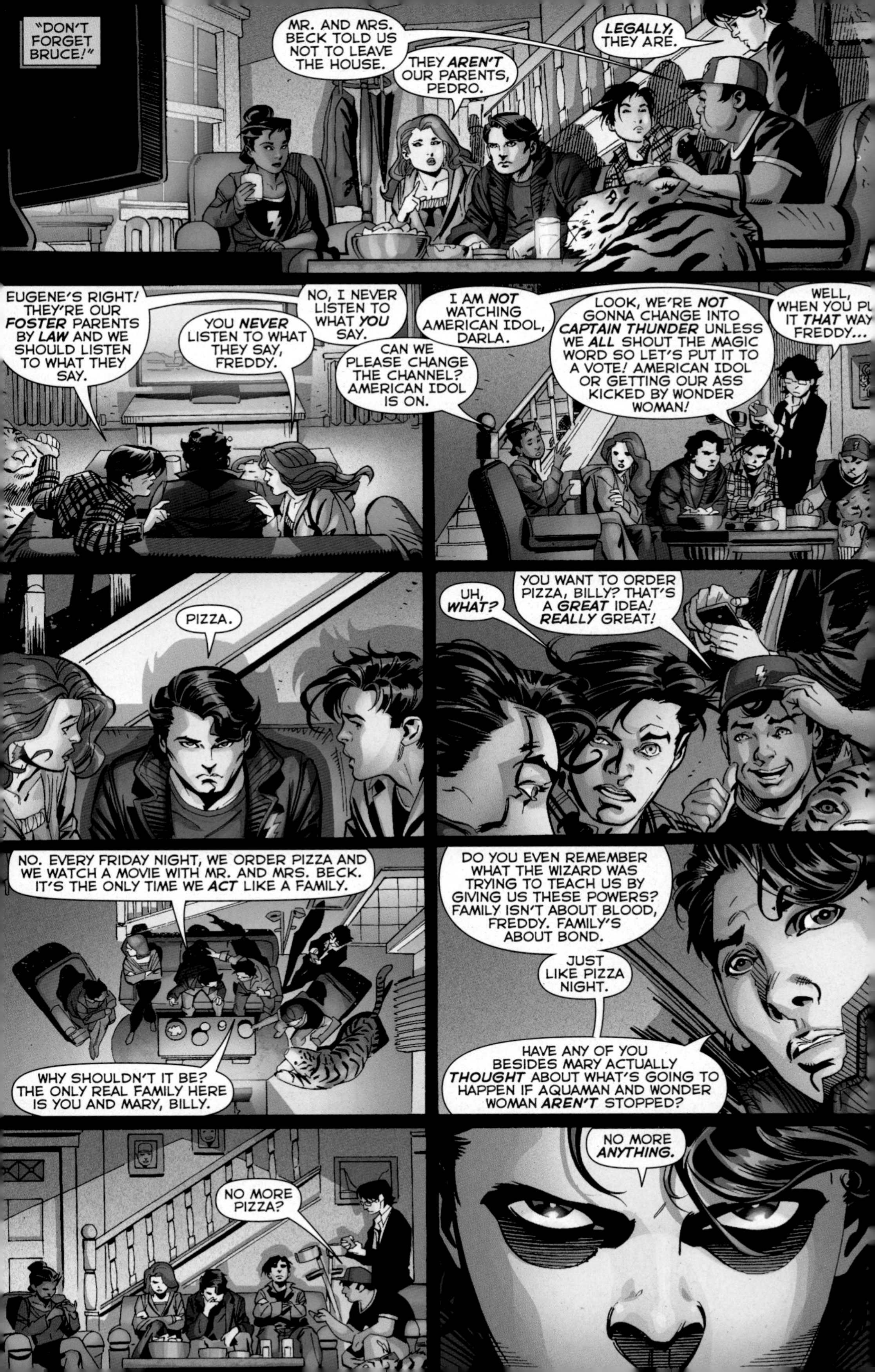
"DON'T FORGET BRUCE!"
MR. AND MRS. BECK TOLD US NOT TO LEAVE THE HOUSE.
THEY *AREN'T* OUR PARENTS, PEDRO.
LEGALLY, THEY ARE.
EUGENE'S RIGHT! THEY'RE OUR *FOSTER* PARENTS BY *LAW* AND WE SHOULD LISTEN TO WHAT THEY SAY.
YOU *NEVER* LISTEN TO WHAT THEY SAY, FREDDY.
NO, I NEVER LISTEN TO WHAT *YOU* SAY.
CAN WE PLEASE CHANGE THE CHANNEL? AMERICAN IDOL IS ON.
I AM *NOT* WATCHING AMERICAN IDOL, DARLA.
LOOK, WE'RE *NOT* GONNA CHANGE INTO *CAPTAIN THUNDER* UNLESS WE *ALL* SHOUT THE MAGIC WORD SO LET'S PUT IT TO A VOTE! AMERICAN IDOL OR GETTING OUR ASS KICKED BY WONDER WOMAN!
WELL, WHEN YOU PU IT *THAT* WAY FREDDY...
PIZZA.
UH, *WHAT?*
YOU WANT TO ORDER PIZZA, BILLY? THAT'S A *GREAT* IDEA! *REALLY* GREAT!
NO. EVERY FRIDAY NIGHT, WE ORDER PIZZA AND WE WATCH A MOVIE WITH MR. AND MRS. BECK. IT'S THE ONLY TIME WE *ACT* LIKE A FAMILY.
WHY SHOULDN'T IT BE? THE ONLY REAL FAMILY HERE IS YOU AND MARY, BILLY.
DO YOU EVEN REMEMBER WHAT THE WIZARD WAS TRYING TO TEACH US BY GIVING US THESE POWERS? FAMILY ISN'T ABOUT BLOOD, FREDDY. FAMILY'S ABOUT BOND.
JUST LIKE PIZZA NIGHT.
HAVE ANY OF YOU BESIDES MARY ACTUALLY *THOUGHT* ABOUT WHAT'S GOING TO HAPPEN IF AQUAMAN AND WONDER WOMAN *AREN'T* STOPPED?
NO MORE PIZZA?
NO MORE *ANYTHING.*

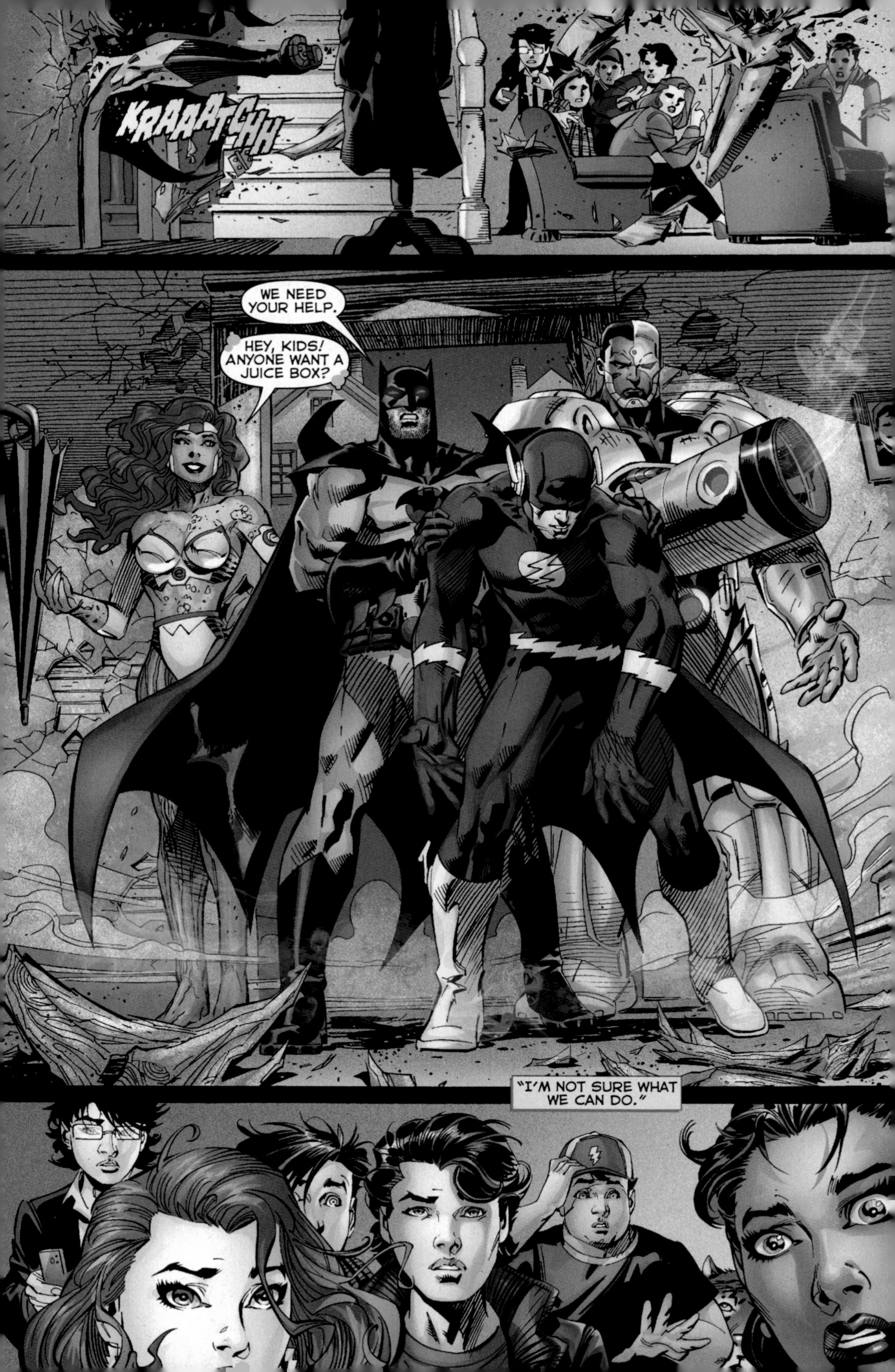
KRAAATCHH
WE NEED YOUR HELP.
HEY, KIDS! ANYONE WANT A JUICE BOX?
"I'M NOT SURE WHAT WE CAN DO."

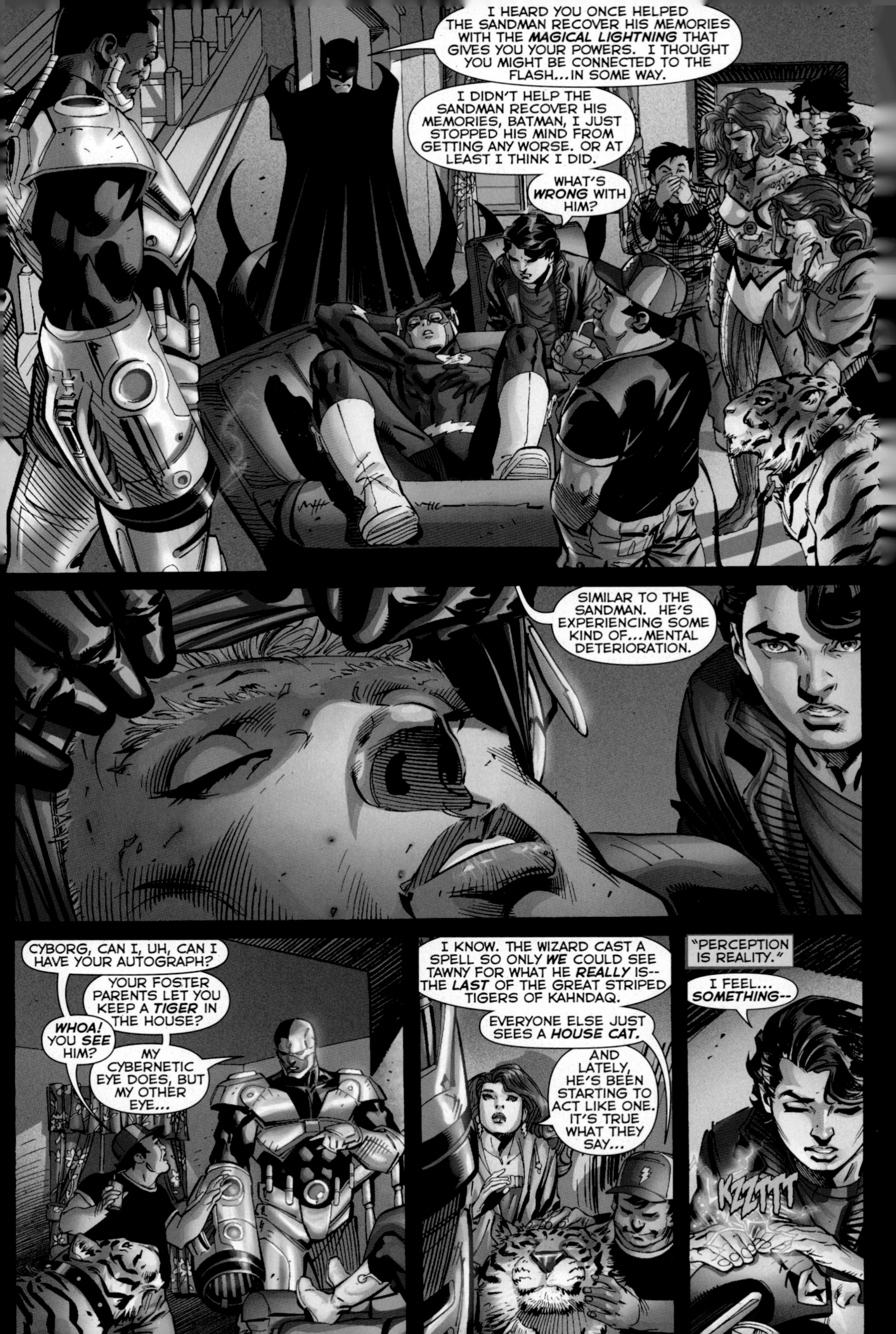
I HEARD YOU ONCE HELPED THE SANDMAN RECOVER HIS MEMORIES WITH THE MAGICAL LIGHTNING THAT GIVES YOU YOUR POWERS. I THOUGHT YOU MIGHT BE CONNECTED TO THE FLASH...IN SOME WAY.
I DIDN'T HELP THE SANDMAN RECOVER HIS MEMORIES, BATMAN, I JUST STOPPED HIS MIND FROM GETTING ANY WORSE. OR AT LEAST I THINK I DID.
WHAT'S WRONG WITH HIM?
SIMILAR TO THE SANDMAN. HE'S EXPERIENCING SOME KIND OF...MENTAL DETERIORATION.
CYBORG, CAN I, UH, CAN I HAVE YOUR AUTOGRAPH?
YOUR FOSTER PARENTS LET YOU KEEP A TIGER IN THE HOUSE?
WHOA! YOU SEE HIM?
MY CYBERNETIC EYE DOES, BUT MY OTHER EYE...
I KNOW. THE WIZARD CAST A SPELL SO ONLY WE COULD SEE TAWNY FOR WHAT HE REALLY IS-- THE LAST OF THE GREAT STRIPED TIGERS OF KAHNDAQ.
EVERYONE ELSE JUST SEES A HOUSE CAT.
AND LATELY, HE'S BEEN STARTING TO ACT LIKE ONE. IT'S TRUE WHAT THEY SAY...
"PERCEPTION IS REALITY."
I FEEL... SOMETHING--
KZZTTT

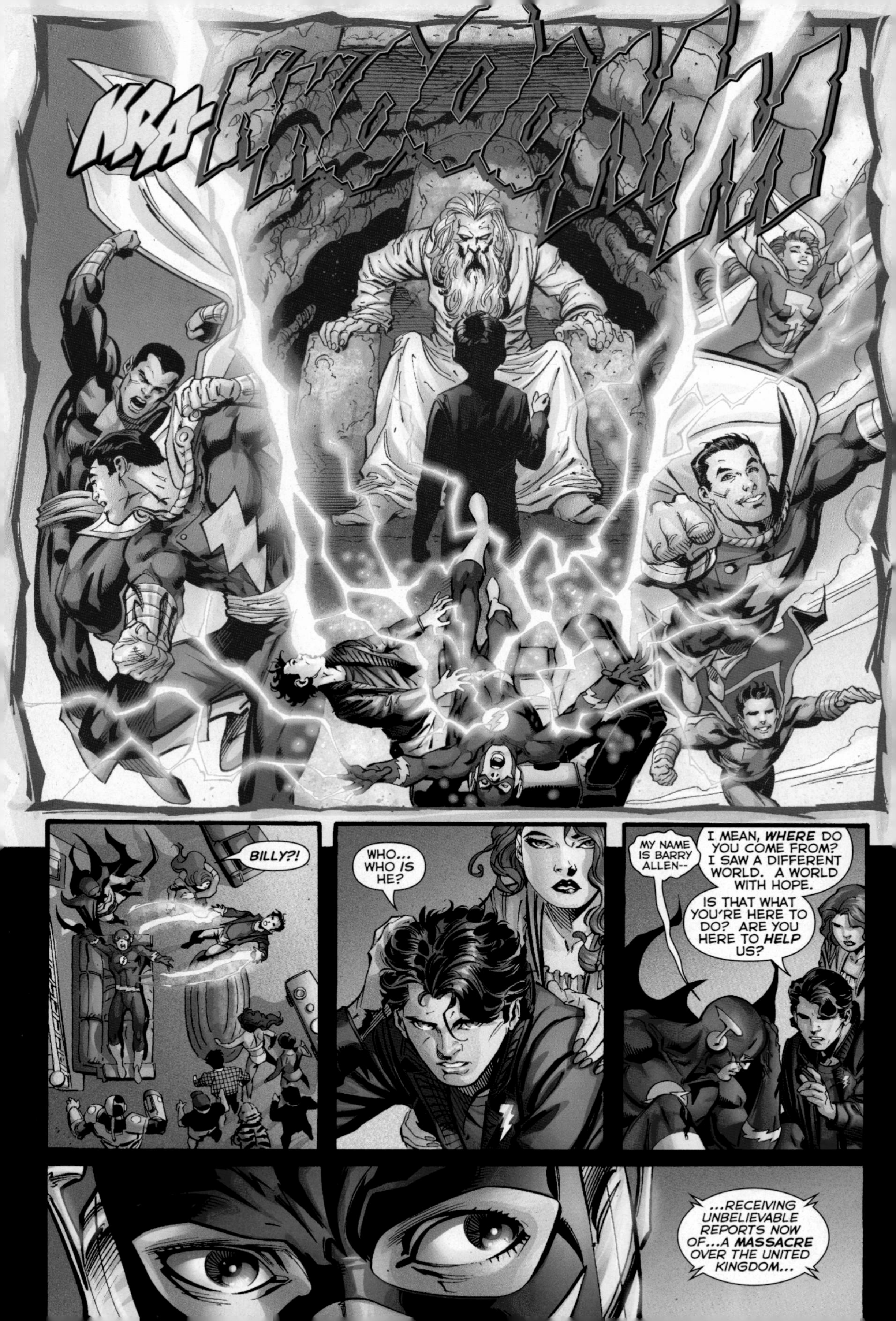

KRA-KKOOOOMM
BILLY?!
WHO... WHO IS HE?
MY NAME IS BARRY ALLEN--
I MEAN, WHERE DO YOU COME FROM? I SAW A DIFFERENT WORLD. A WORLD WITH HOPE.
IS THAT WHAT YOU'RE HERE TO DO? ARE YOU HERE TO HELP US?
...RECEIVING UNBELIEVABLE REPORTS NOW OF...A MASSACRE OVER THE UNITED KINGDOM...

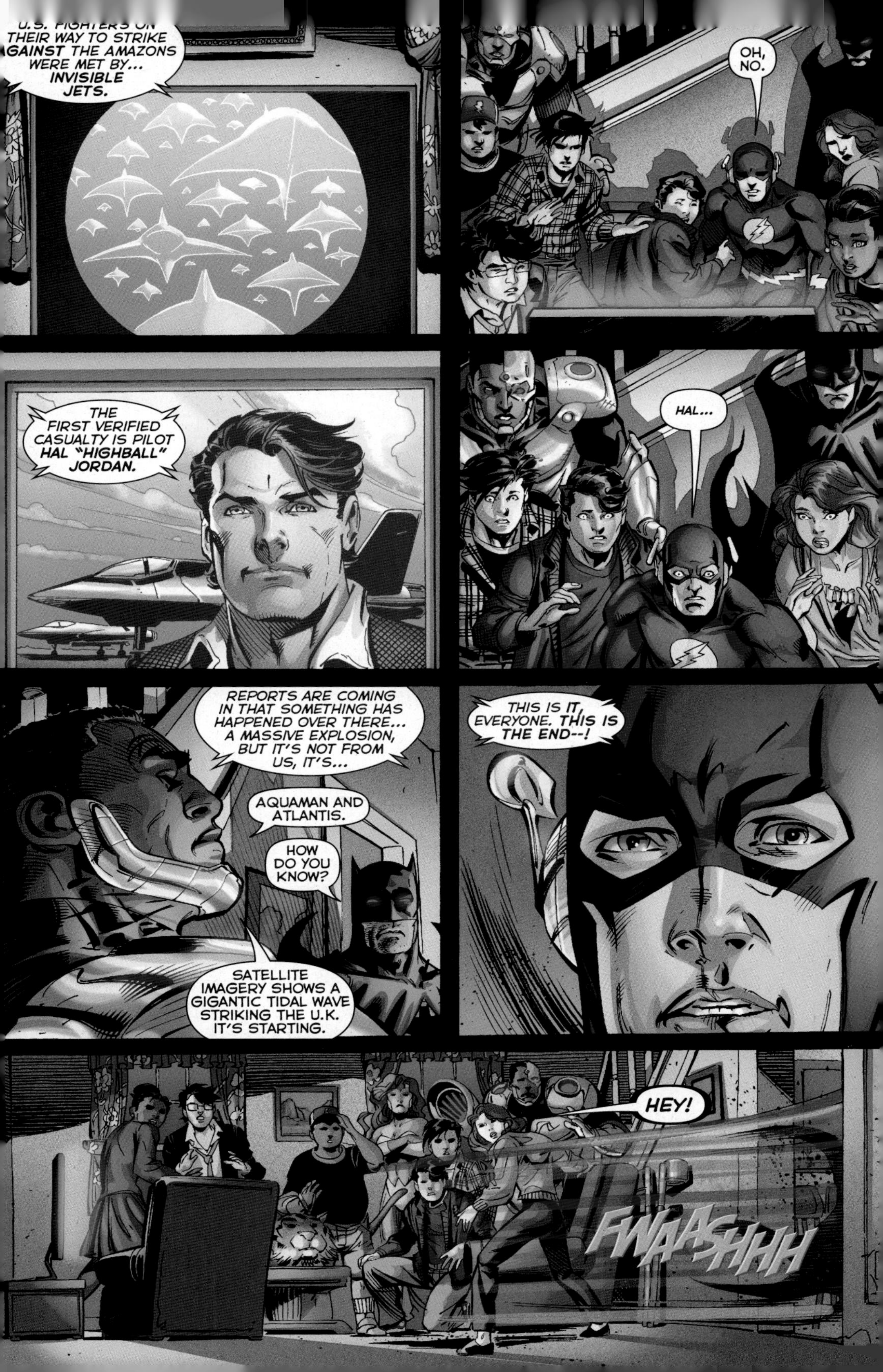
U.S. FIGHTERS ON THEIR WAY TO STRIKE AGAINST THE AMAZONS WERE MET BY... INVISIBLE JETS.
OH, NO.
THE FIRST VERIFIED CASUALTY IS PILOT HAL "HIGHBALL" JORDAN.
HAL...
REPORTS ARE COMING IN THAT SOMETHING HAS HAPPENED OVER THERE... A MASSIVE EXPLOSION, BUT IT'S NOT FROM US, IT'S...
AQUAMAN AND ATLANTIS.
HOW DO YOU KNOW?
SATELLITE IMAGERY SHOWS A GIGANTIC TIDAL WAVE STRIKING THE U.K. IT'S STARTING.
THIS IS IT, EVERYONE. THIS IS THE END--!
HEY!
FWAASHHH

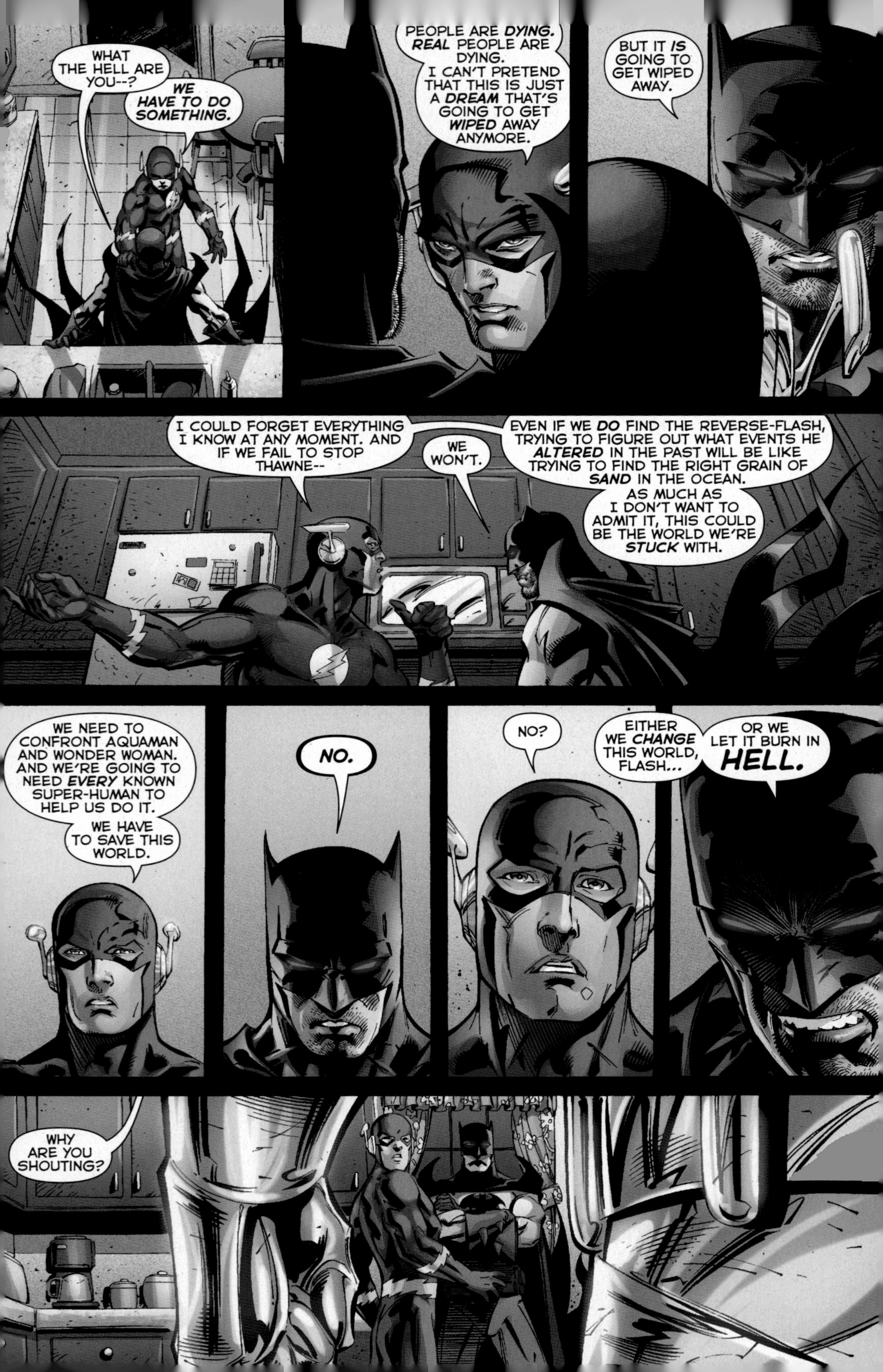

WHAT THE HELL ARE YOU--?
WE HAVE TO DO SOMETHING.
PEOPLE ARE DYING. REAL PEOPLE ARE DYING. I CAN'T PRETEND THAT THIS IS JUST A DREAM THAT'S GOING TO GET WIPED AWAY ANYMORE.
BUT IT IS GOING TO GET WIPED AWAY.
I COULD FORGET EVERYTHING I KNOW AT ANY MOMENT. AND IF WE FAIL TO STOP THAWNE--
WE WON'T.
EVEN IF WE DO FIND THE REVERSE-FLASH, TRYING TO FIGURE OUT WHAT EVENTS HE ALTERED IN THE PAST WILL BE LIKE TRYING TO FIND THE RIGHT GRAIN OF SAND IN THE OCEAN.
AS MUCH AS I DON'T WANT TO ADMIT IT, THIS COULD BE THE WORLD WE'RE STUCK WITH.
WE NEED TO CONFRONT AQUAMAN AND WONDER WOMAN. AND WE'RE GOING TO NEED EVERY KNOWN SUPER-HUMAN TO HELP US DO IT.
WE HAVE TO SAVE THIS WORLD.
NO.
NO?
EITHER WE CHANGE THIS WORLD, FLASH...
OR WE LET IT BURN IN HELL.
WHY ARE YOU SHOUTING?

WE HAVE SOME FRIGHTENED KIDS HERE.

WE'RE NOT *SCARED*, CYBORG, WE'RE *SMART*.

WHAT'RE YOU GUYS TALKING ABOUT? CAN WE TALK ABOUT IT TOO?!

YOU'RE IN COMMUNICATION WITH EVERYONE, RIGHT, VIC?

EVERYONE WHO?

EVERYONE WHO IS *REFUSING* TO HELP.

CALL THEM. TELL THEM WE'RE GOING TO PUT A STOP TO AQUAMAN AND WONDER WOMAN.

WHAT ARE YOU WAITING FOR?

THEY WON'T COME, FLASH. NOT UNLESS BATMAN DOES.

WHY *HIM*?

BECAUSE OF THE *URBAN LEGEND* BUILT UP AROUND *BATMAN* OVER THE *DECADES*.

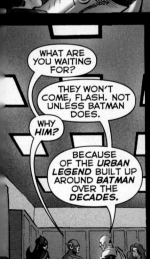

I KNOW HE'S A JUST A MAN IN A *COSTUME*, BUT EVERYONE ELSE SEES HIM AS SOMETHING *MORE.* THEY'VE HEARD THE STORIES AND BELIEVED THEM.

THEY THINK BATMAN'S *INVINCIBLE.*

NO ONE'S *INVINCIBLE.*

BUT THAT *FACT* SHOULDN'T BE HOLDING *ANYONE* BACK. WE *ALL* HAVE SOMETHING TO *OFFER.* WE *ALL* HAVE SOMETHING TO *LOSE.*

WE HAVE TO MOVE, AND WE HAVE TO MOVE *NOW.*

FLASH?

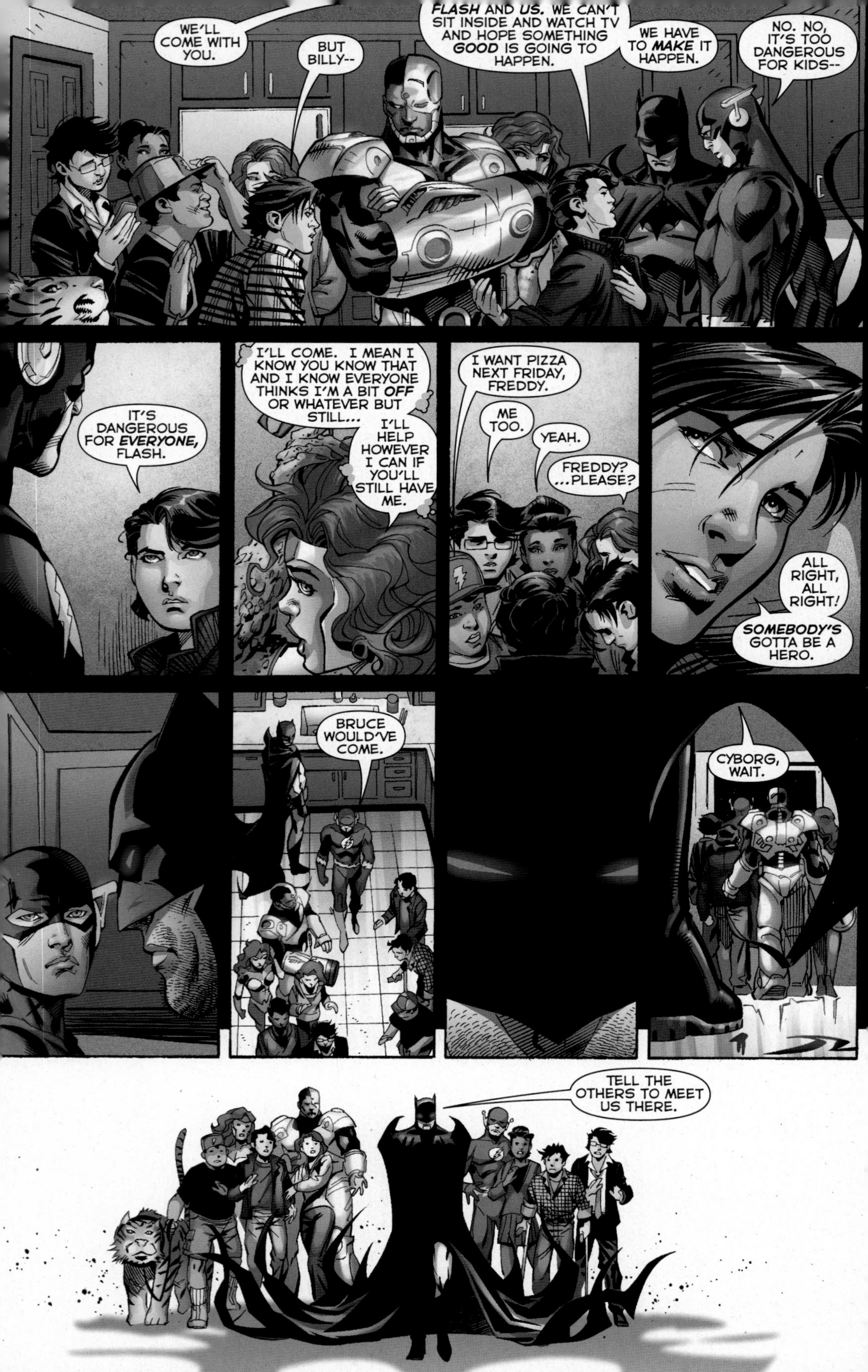
WE'LL COME WITH YOU.
BUT BILLY--
FLASH AND US. WE CAN'T SIT INSIDE AND WATCH TV AND HOPE SOMETHING GOOD IS GOING TO HAPPEN.
WE HAVE TO MAKE IT HAPPEN.
NO. NO, IT'S TOO DANGEROUS FOR KIDS--
IT'S DANGEROUS FOR EVERYONE, FLASH.
I'LL COME. I MEAN I KNOW YOU KNOW THAT AND I KNOW EVERYONE THINKS I'M A BIT OFF OR WHATEVER BUT STILL...
I'LL HELP HOWEVER I CAN IF YOU'LL STILL HAVE ME.
I WANT PIZZA NEXT FRIDAY, FREDDY.
ME TOO.
YEAH.
FREDDY? ...PLEASE?
ALL RIGHT, ALL RIGHT!
SOMEBODY'S GOTTA BE A HERO.
BRUCE WOULD'VE COME.
CYBORG, WAIT.
TELL THE OTHERS TO MEET US THERE.

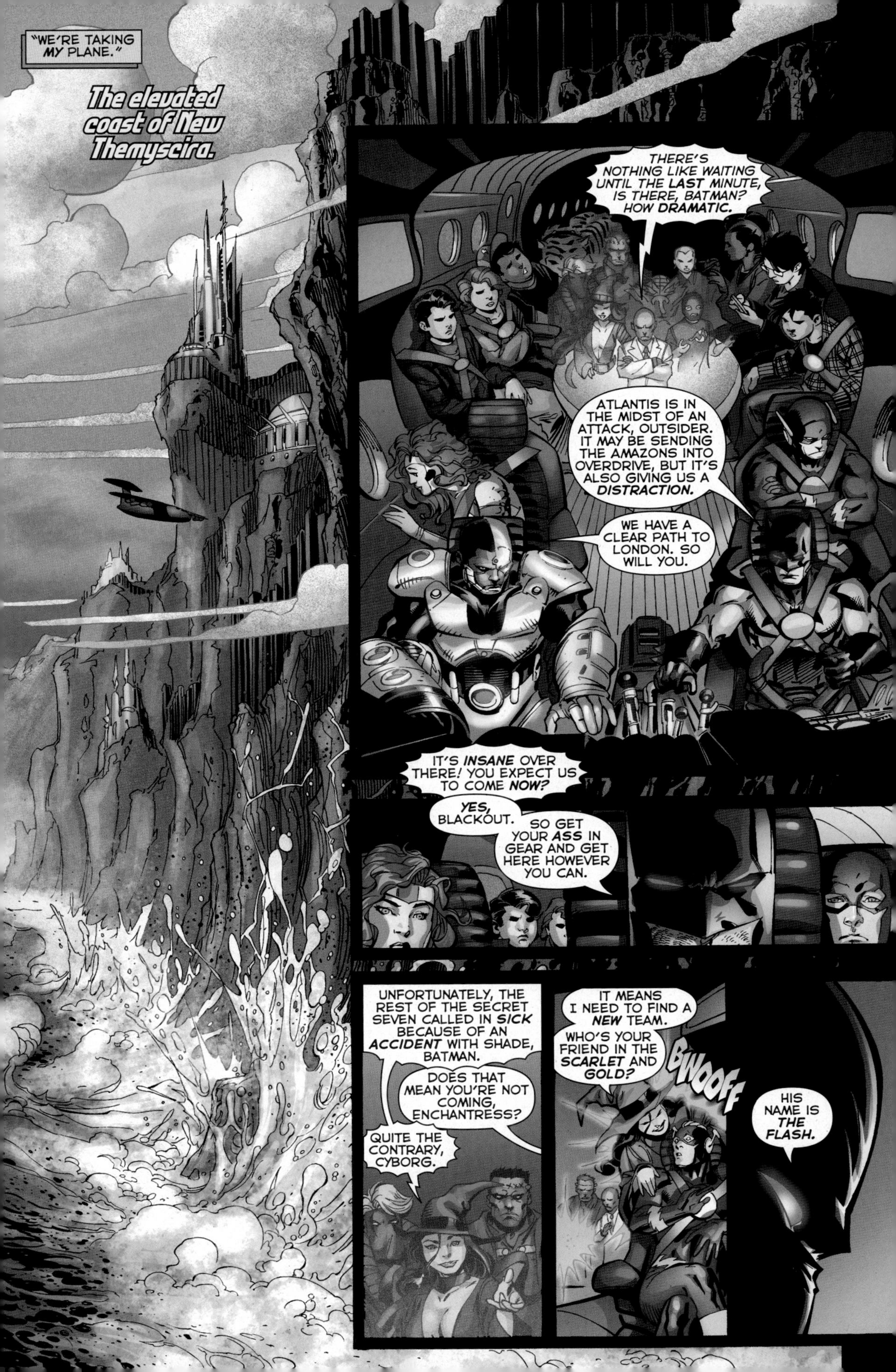

"WE'RE TAKING MY PLANE."
The elevated coast of New Themyscira.
THERE'S NOTHING LIKE WAITING UNTIL THE LAST MINUTE, IS THERE, BATMAN? HOW DRAMATIC.
ATLANTIS IS IN THE MIDST OF AN ATTACK, OUTSIDER. IT MAY BE SENDING THE AMAZONS INTO OVERDRIVE, BUT IT'S ALSO GIVING US A DISTRACTION.
WE HAVE A CLEAR PATH TO LONDON. SO WILL YOU.
IT'S INSANE OVER THERE! YOU EXPECT US TO COME NOW?
YES, BLACKOUT.
SO GET YOUR ASS IN GEAR AND GET HERE HOWEVER YOU CAN.
UNFORTUNATELY, THE REST OF THE SECRET SEVEN CALLED IN SICK BECAUSE OF AN ACCIDENT WITH SHADE, BATMAN.
DOES THAT MEAN YOU'RE NOT COMING, ENCHANTRESS?
QUITE THE CONTRARY, CYBORG.
IT MEANS I NEED TO FIND A NEW TEAM.
WHO'S YOUR FRIEND IN THE SCARLET AND GOLD?
BWOOFF
HIS NAME IS THE FLASH.

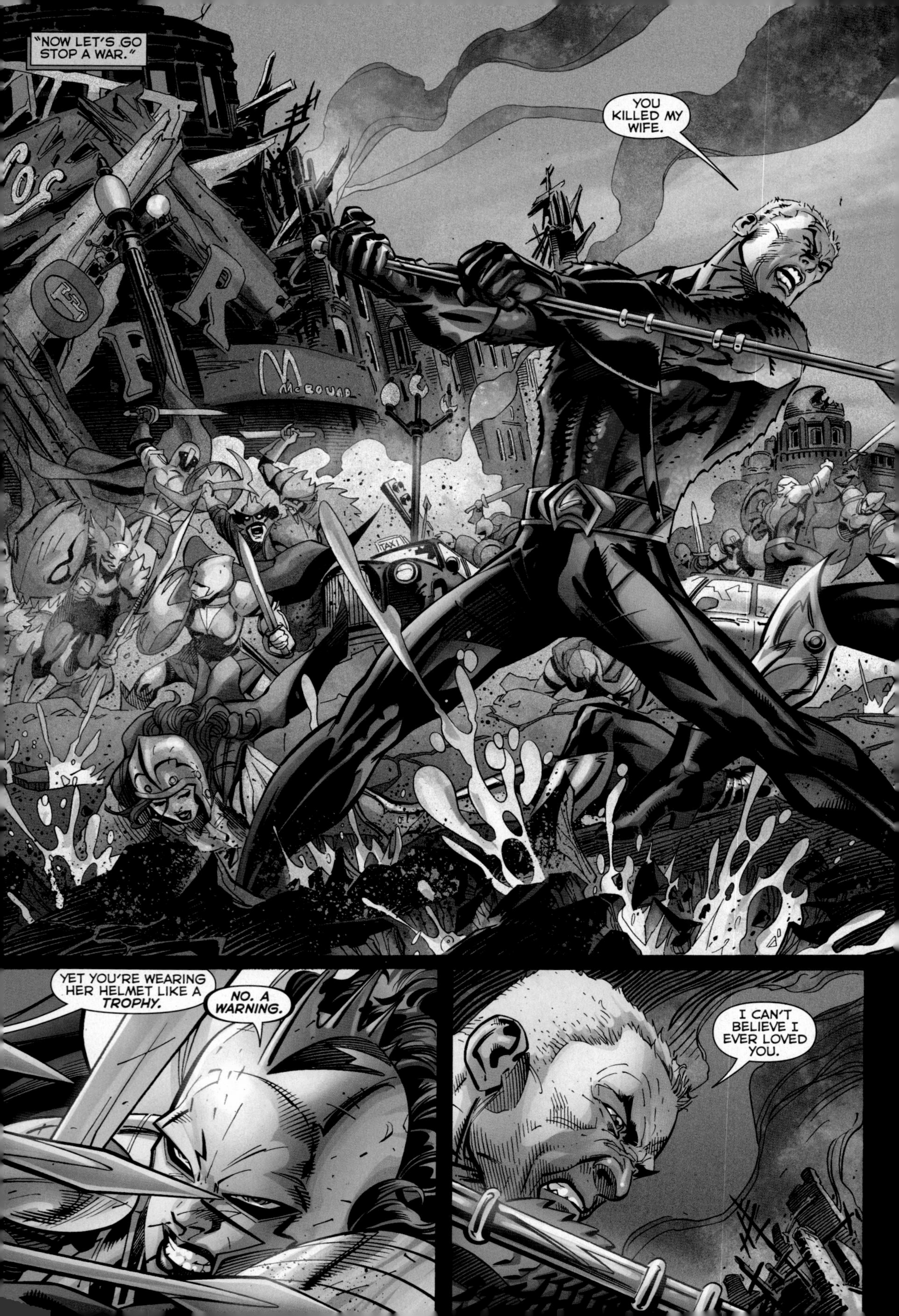
"NOW LET'S GO STOP A WAR."
YOU KILLED MY WIFE.
YET YOU'RE WEARING HER HELMET LIKE A TROPHY.
NO. A WARNING.
I CAN'T BELIEVE I EVER LOVED YOU.

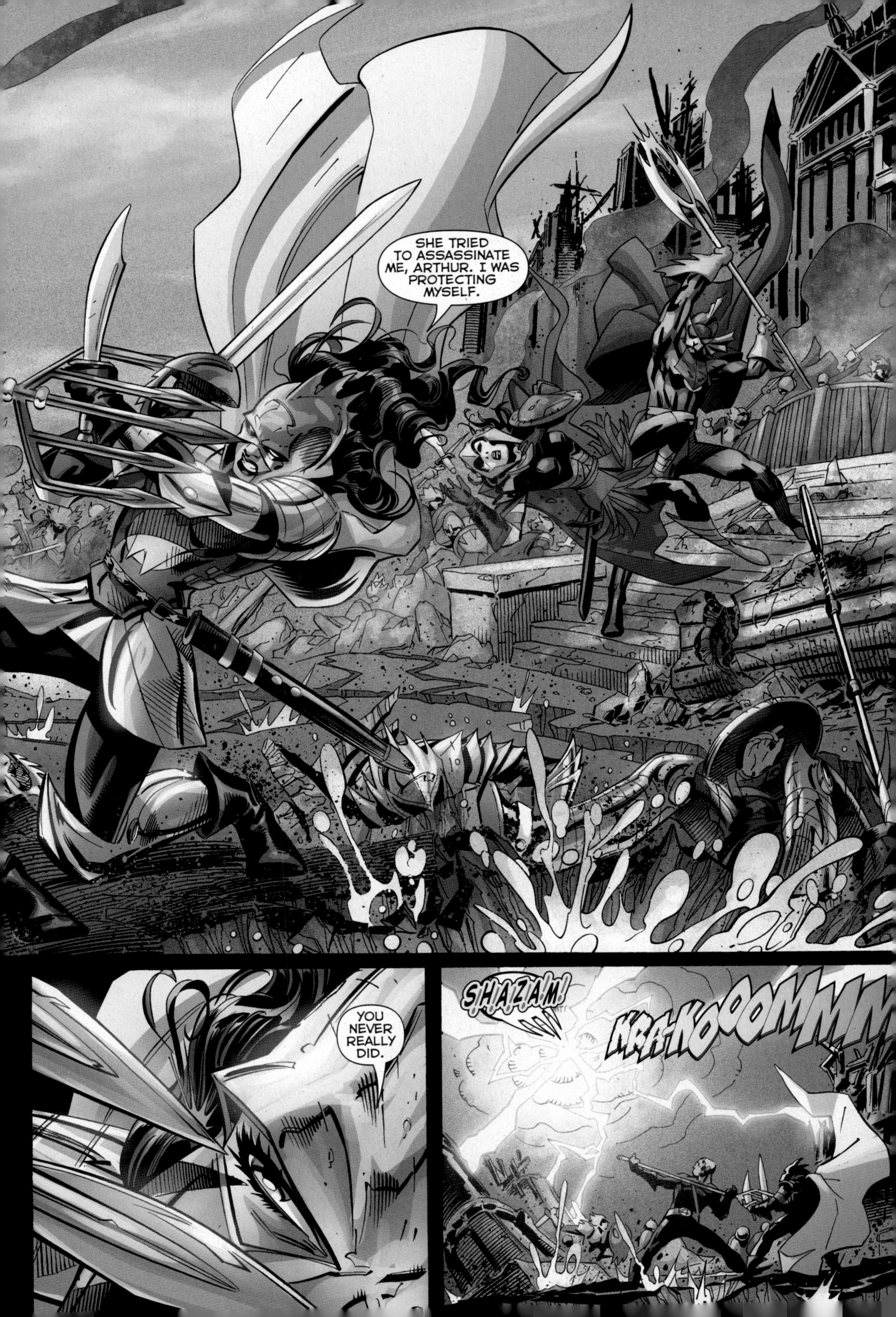
SHE TRIED TO ASSASSINATE ME, ARTHUR. I WAS PROTECTING MYSELF.
YOU NEVER REALLY DID.
SHAZAM!
KRA-KOOOMMMM

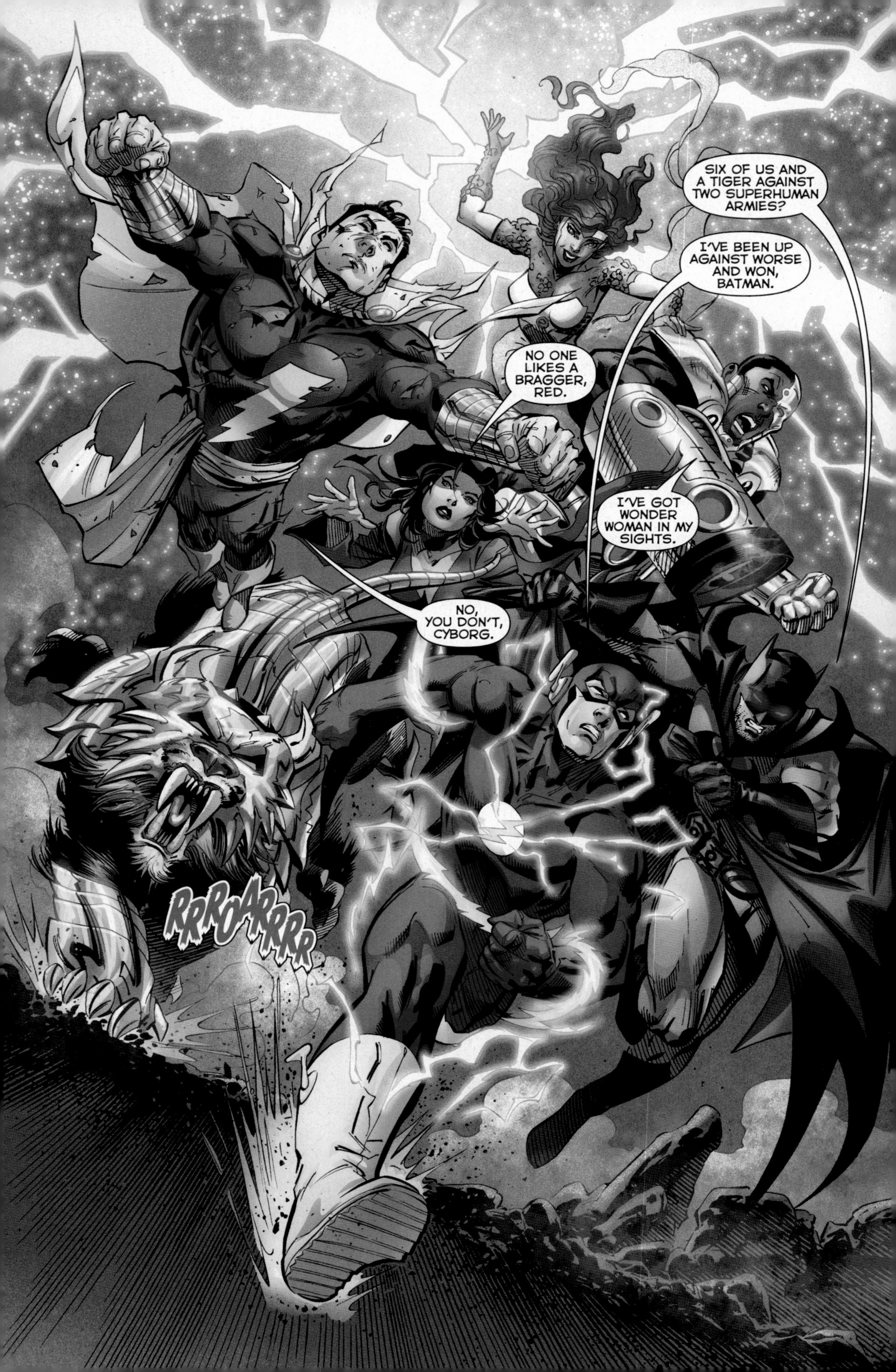
SIX OF US AND A TIGER AGAINST TWO SUPERHUMAN ARMIES?
I'VE BEEN UP AGAINST WORSE AND WON, BATMAN.
NO ONE LIKES A BRAGGER, RED.
I'VE GOT WONDER WOMAN IN MY SIGHTS.
NO, YOU DON'T, CYBORG.
RRROARRRR

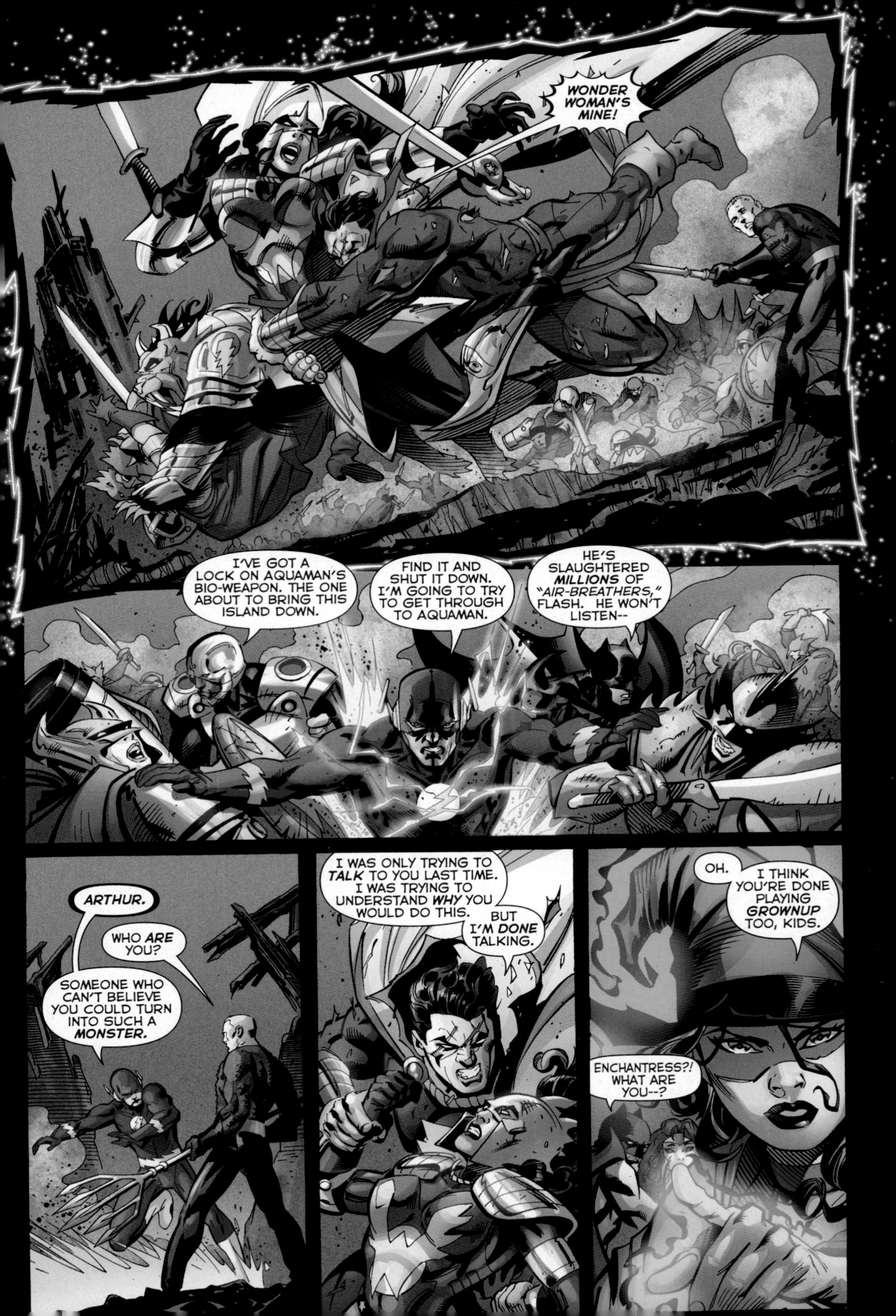
WONDER WOMAN'S MINE!
I'VE GOT A LOCK ON AQUAMAN'S BIO-WEAPON. THE ONE ABOUT TO BRING THIS ISLAND DOWN.
FIND IT AND SHUT IT DOWN. I'M GOING TO TRY TO GET THROUGH TO AQUAMAN.
HE'S SLAUGHTERED MILLIONS OF "AIR-BREATHERS," FLASH. HE WON'T LISTEN--
ARTHUR.
WHO ARE YOU?
SOMEONE WHO CAN'T BELIEVE YOU COULD TURN INTO SUCH A MONSTER.
I WAS ONLY TRYING TO TALK TO YOU LAST TIME. I WAS TRYING TO UNDERSTAND WHY YOU WOULD DO THIS.
BUT I'M DONE TALKING.
OH.
I THINK YOU'RE DONE PLAYING GROWNUP TOO, KIDS.
ENCHANTRESS?! WHAT ARE YOU--?

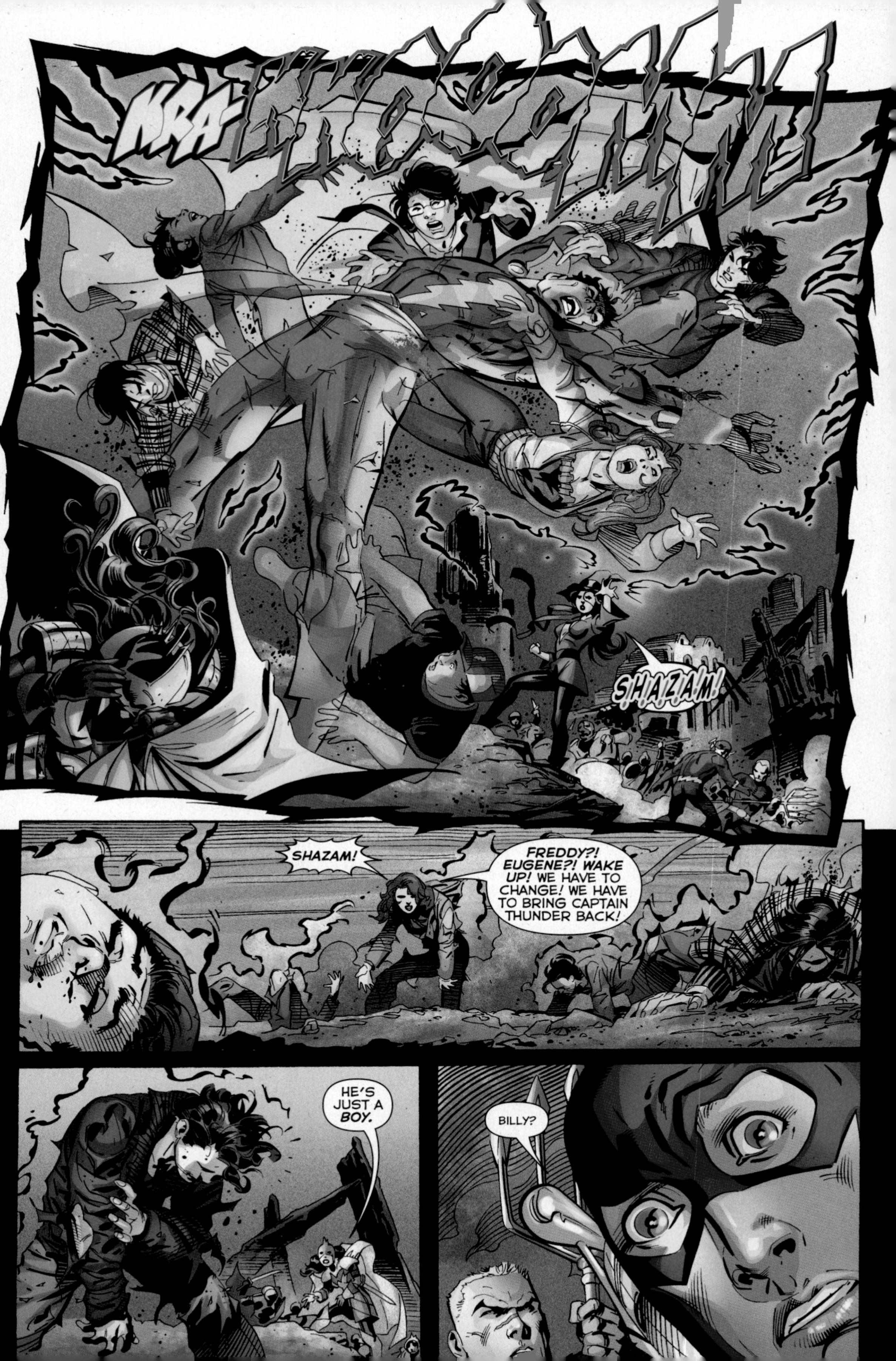
KRA-KROOOOOOM
SHAZAM!
SHAZAM!
FREDDY?! EUGENE?! WAKE UP! WE HAVE TO CHANGE! WE HAVE TO BRING CAPTAIN THUNDER BACK!
HE'S JUST A BOY.
BILLY?

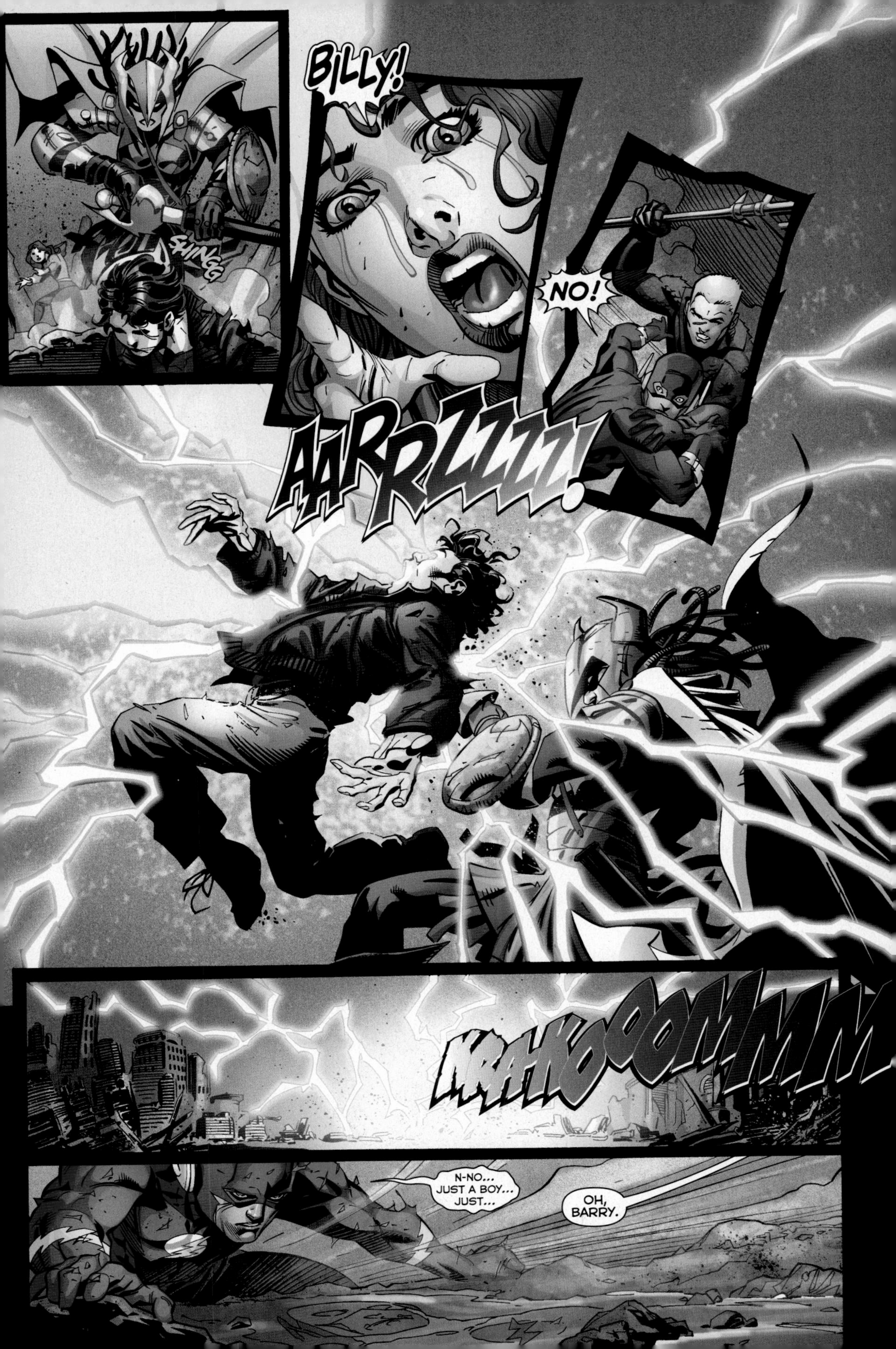
SHINGG
BILLY!
NO!
AARRZZZZZ!
KRAKOOOMMMM
N-NO... JUST A BOY... JUST...
OH, BARRY.

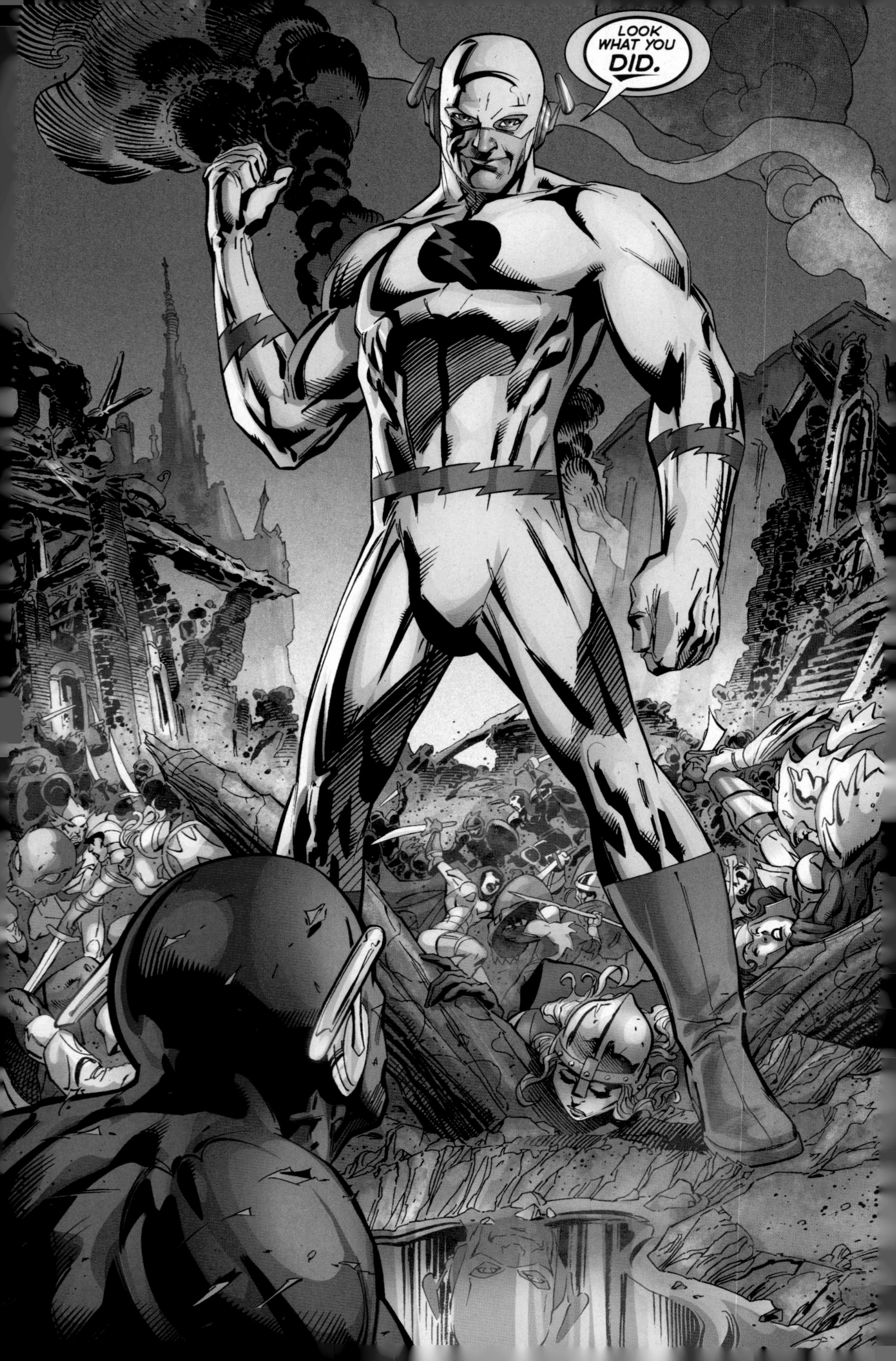
LOOK WHAT YOU DID.

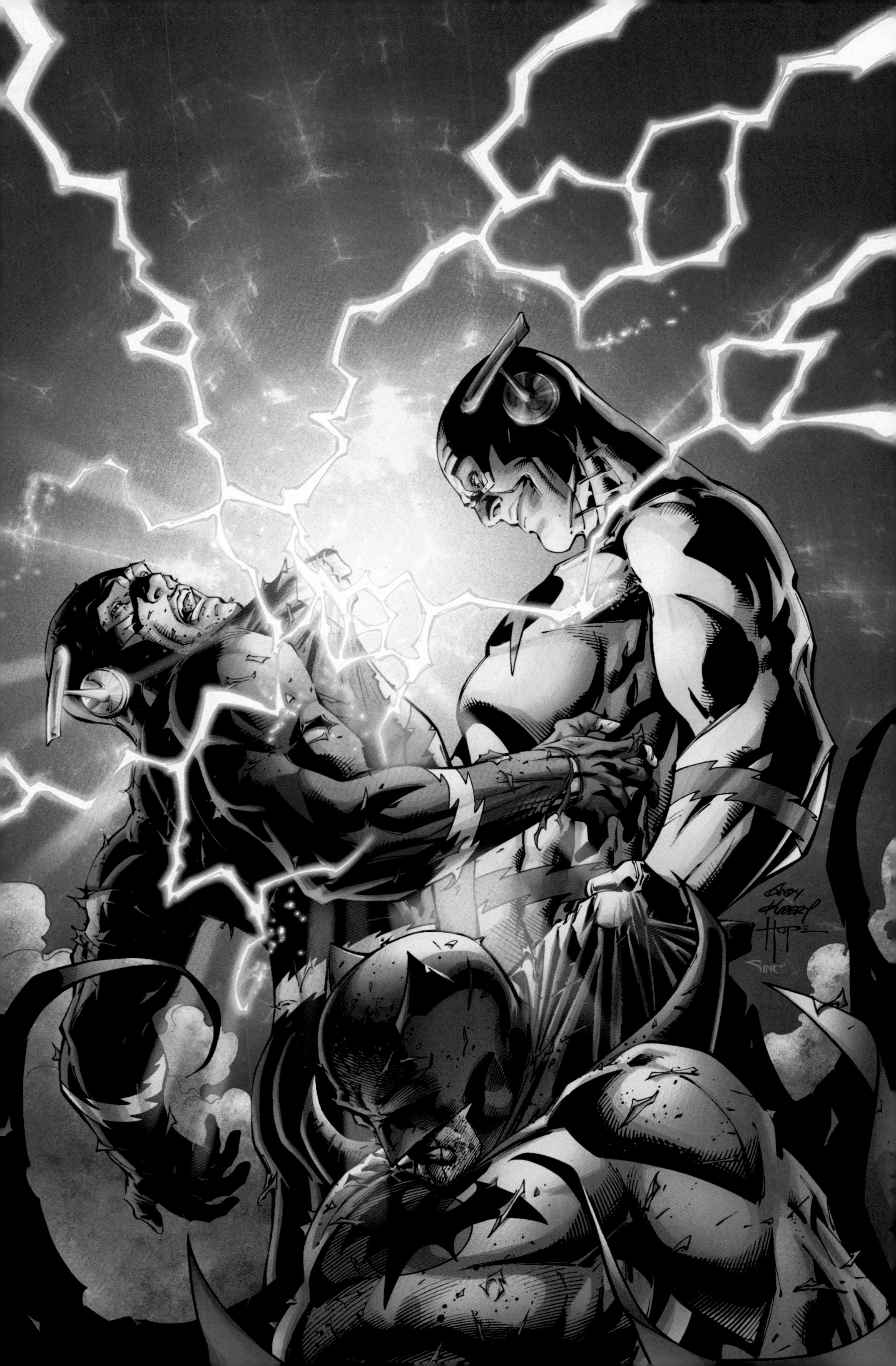

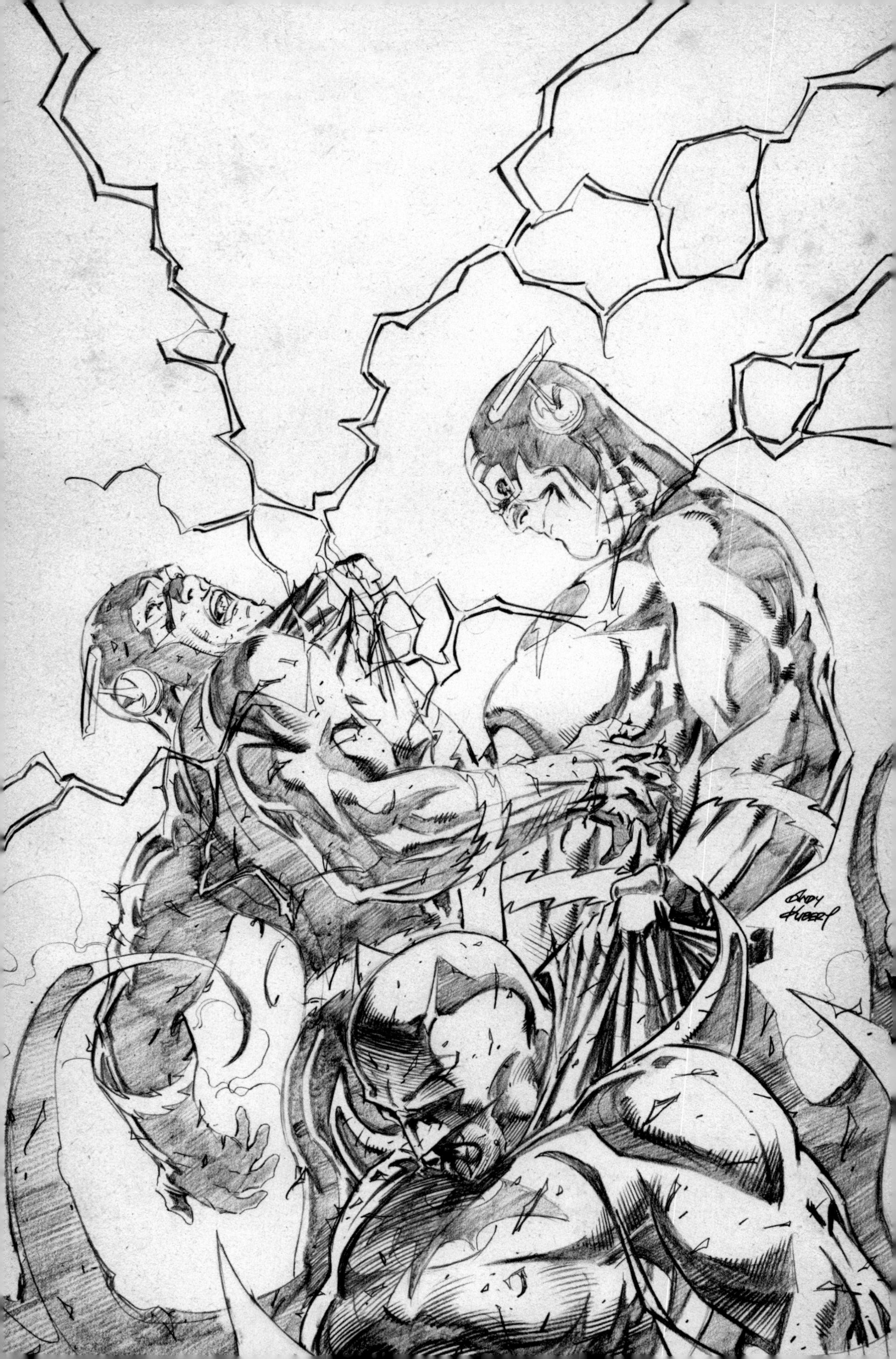
ANDY KUBERT

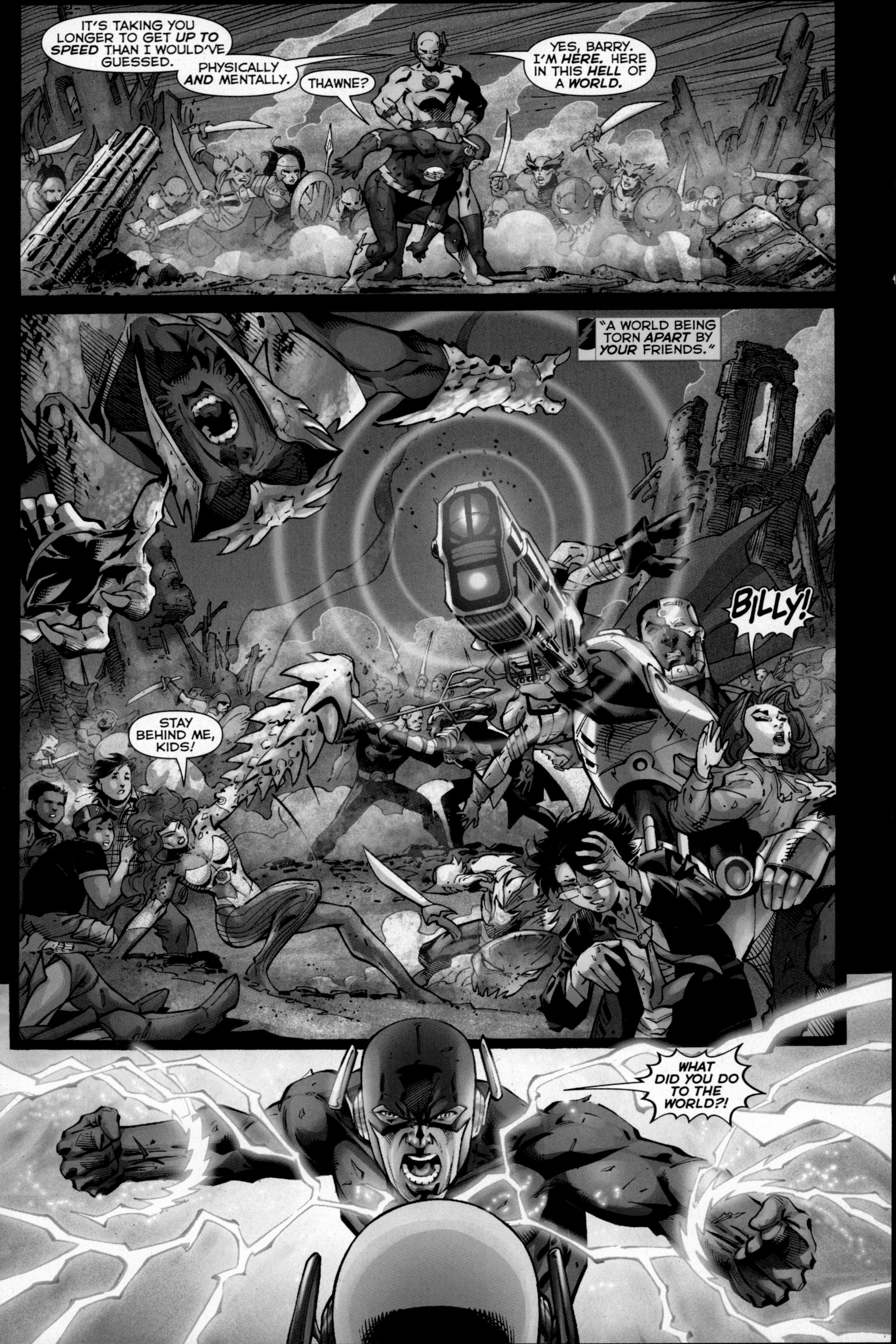

IT'S TAKING YOU LONGER TO GET UP TO SPEED THAN I WOULD'VE GUESSED.
PHYSICALLY AND MENTALLY.
THAWNE?
YES, BARRY. I'M HERE. HERE IN THIS HELL OF A WORLD.
"A WORLD BEING TORN APART BY YOUR FRIENDS."
BILLY!
STAY BEHIND ME, KIDS!
WHAT DID YOU DO TO THE WORLD?!

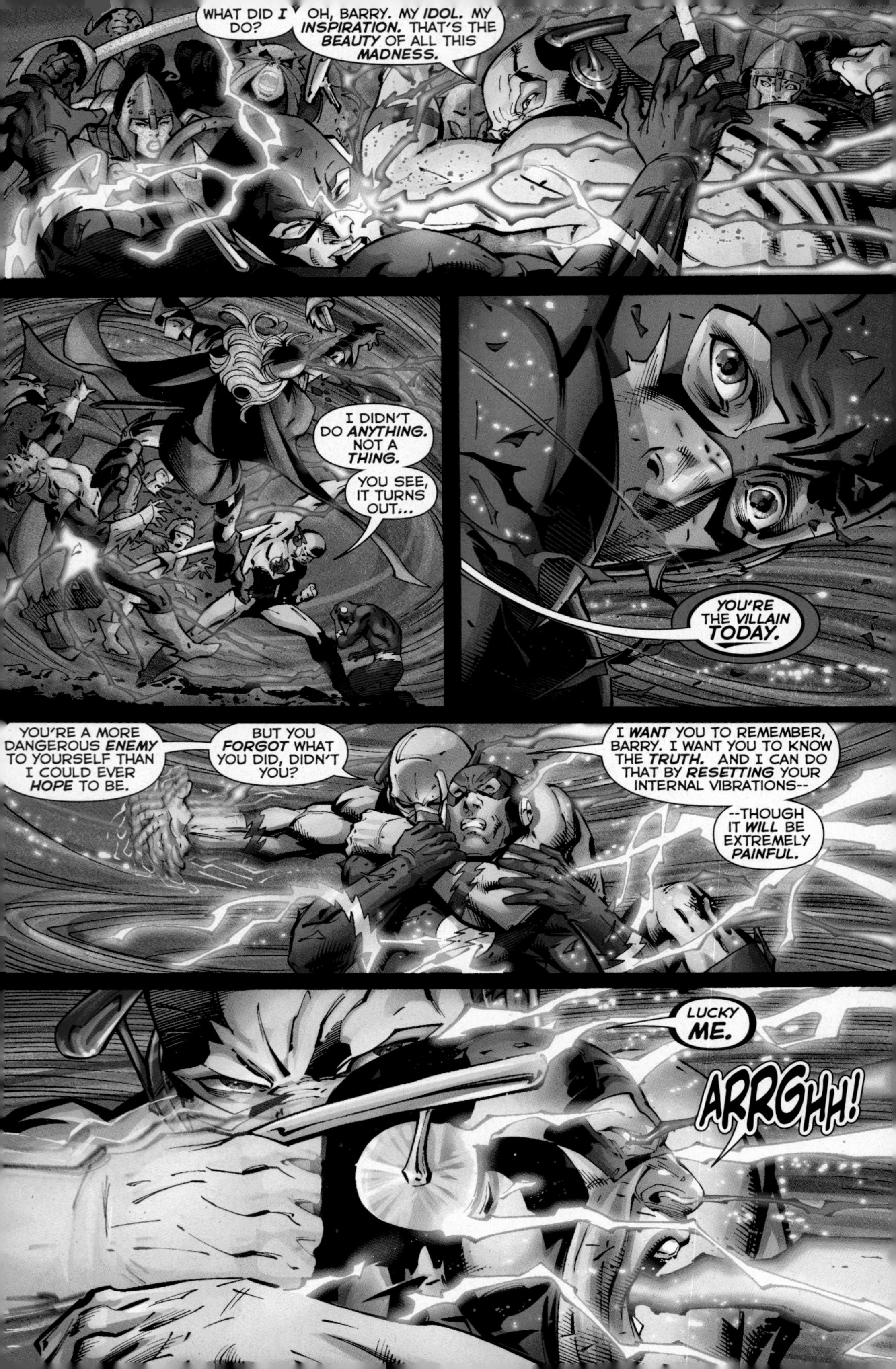
WHAT DID I DO?
OH, BARRY. MY IDOL. MY INSPIRATION. THAT'S THE BEAUTY OF ALL THIS MADNESS.
I DIDN'T DO ANYTHING. NOT A THING.
YOU SEE, IT TURNS OUT...
YOU'RE THE VILLAIN TODAY.
YOU'RE A MORE DANGEROUS ENEMY TO YOURSELF THAN I COULD EVER HOPE TO BE.
BUT YOU FORGOT WHAT YOU DID, DIDN'T YOU?
I WANT YOU TO REMEMBER, BARRY. I WANT YOU TO KNOW THE TRUTH. AND I CAN DO THAT BY RESETTING YOUR INTERNAL VIBRATIONS--
--THOUGH IT WILL BE EXTREMELY PAINFUL.
LUCKY ME.
ARRGHH!

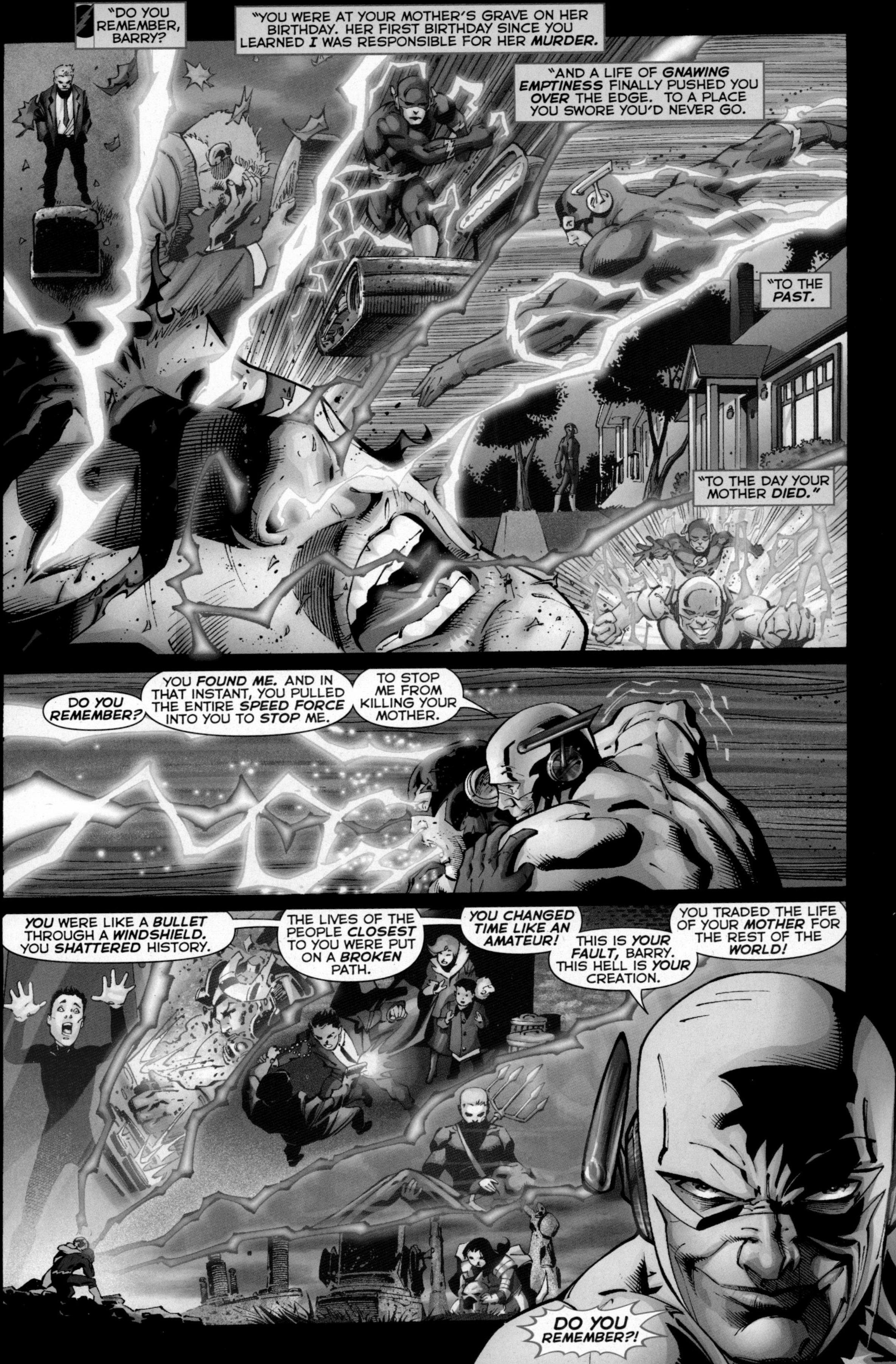
"DO YOU REMEMBER, BARRY?
"YOU WERE AT YOUR MOTHER'S GRAVE ON HER BIRTHDAY. HER FIRST BIRTHDAY SINCE YOU LEARNED I WAS RESPONSIBLE FOR HER MURDER.
"AND A LIFE OF GNAWING EMPTINESS FINALLY PUSHED YOU OVER THE EDGE. TO A PLACE YOU SWORE YOU'D NEVER GO.
"TO THE PAST.
"TO THE DAY YOUR MOTHER DIED."
DO YOU REMEMBER?
YOU FOUND ME. AND IN THAT INSTANT, YOU PULLED THE ENTIRE SPEED FORCE INTO YOU TO STOP ME.
TO STOP ME FROM KILLING YOUR MOTHER.
YOU WERE LIKE A BULLET THROUGH A WINDSHIELD. YOU SHATTERED HISTORY.
THE LIVES OF THE PEOPLE CLOSEST TO YOU WERE PUT ON A BROKEN PATH.
YOU CHANGED TIME LIKE AN AMATEUR!
THIS IS YOUR FAULT, BARRY. THIS HELL IS YOUR CREATION.
YOU TRADED THE LIFE OF YOUR MOTHER FOR THE REST OF THE WORLD!
DO YOU REMEMBER?!

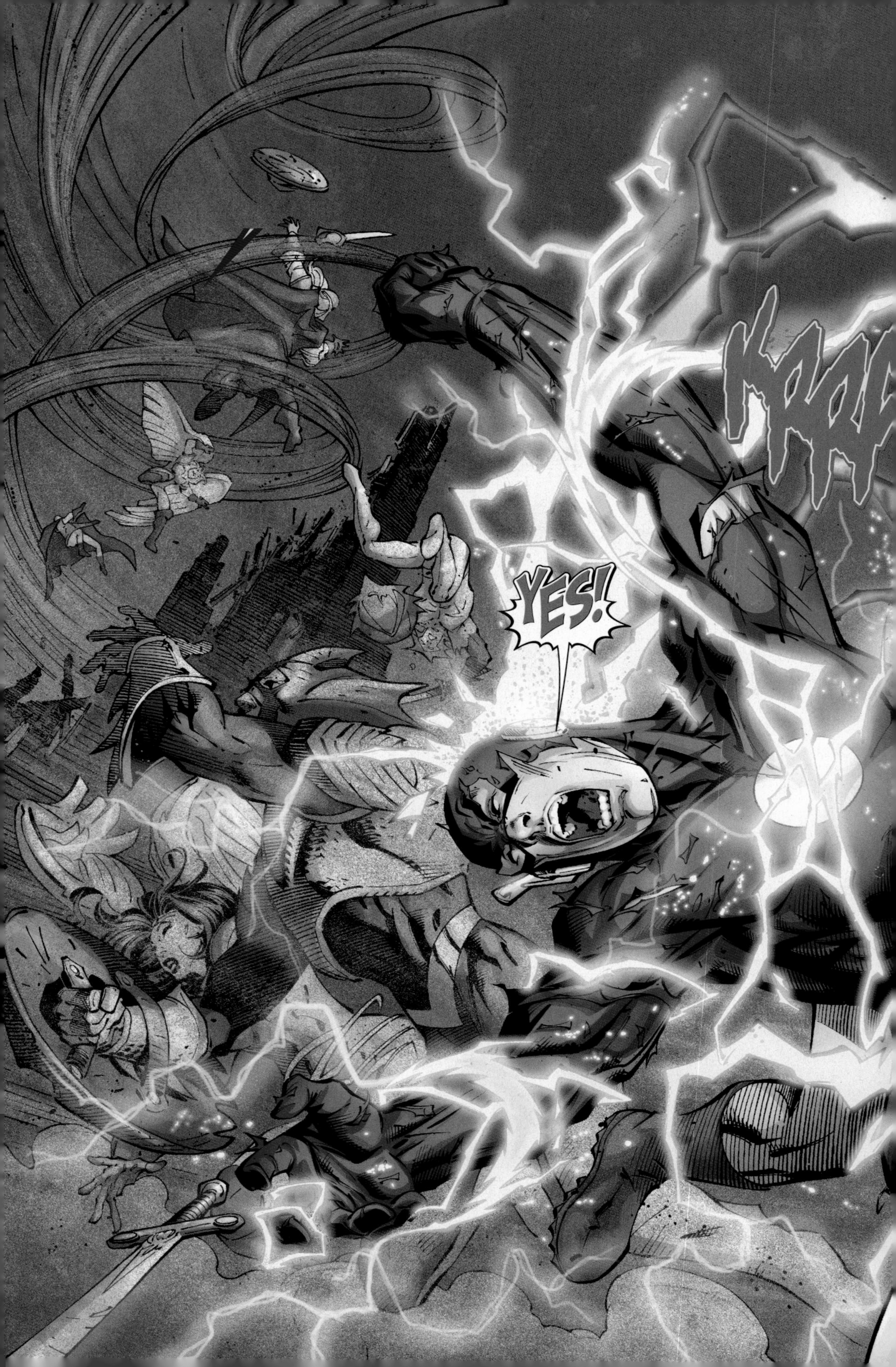
YES!

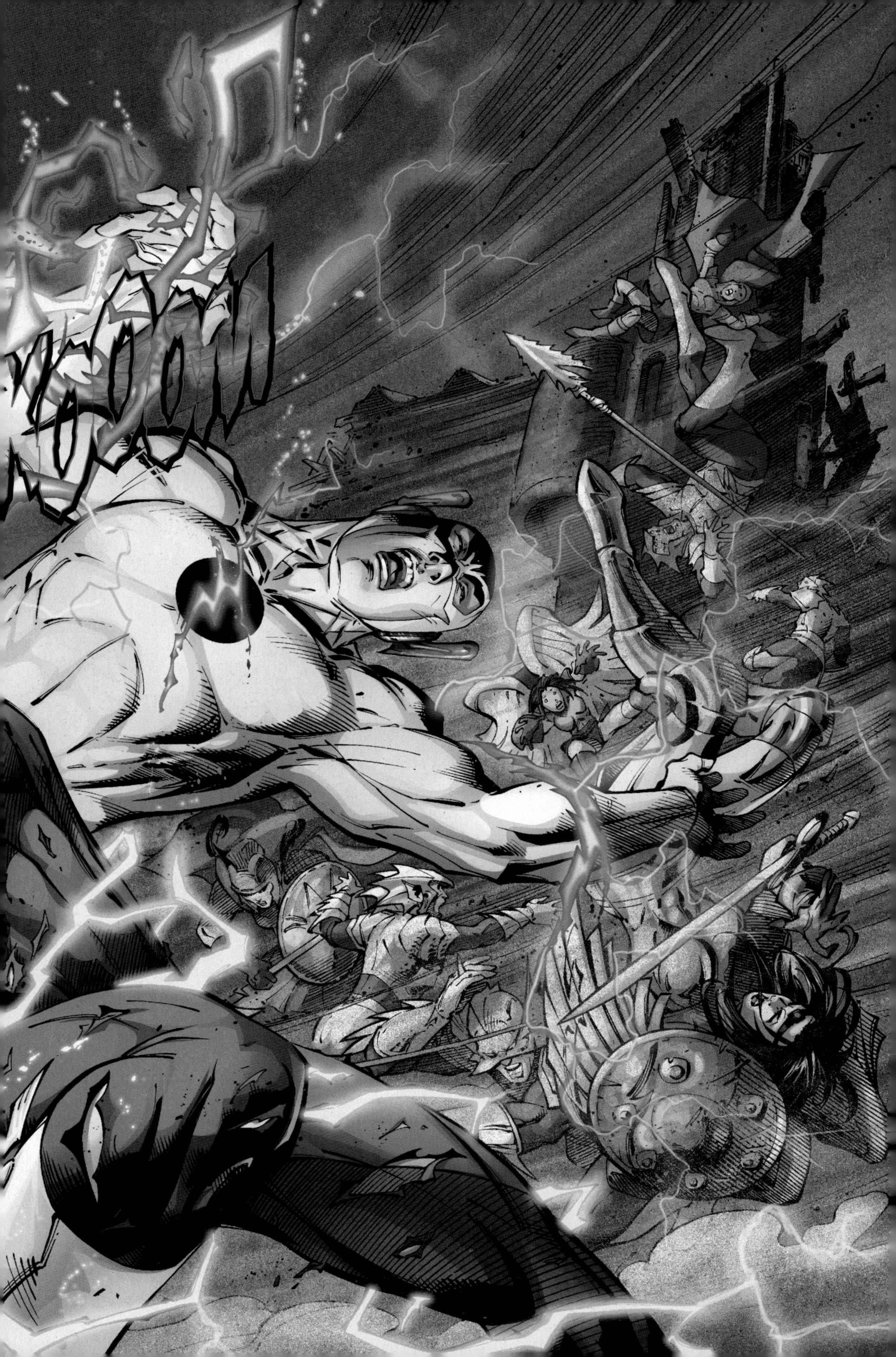

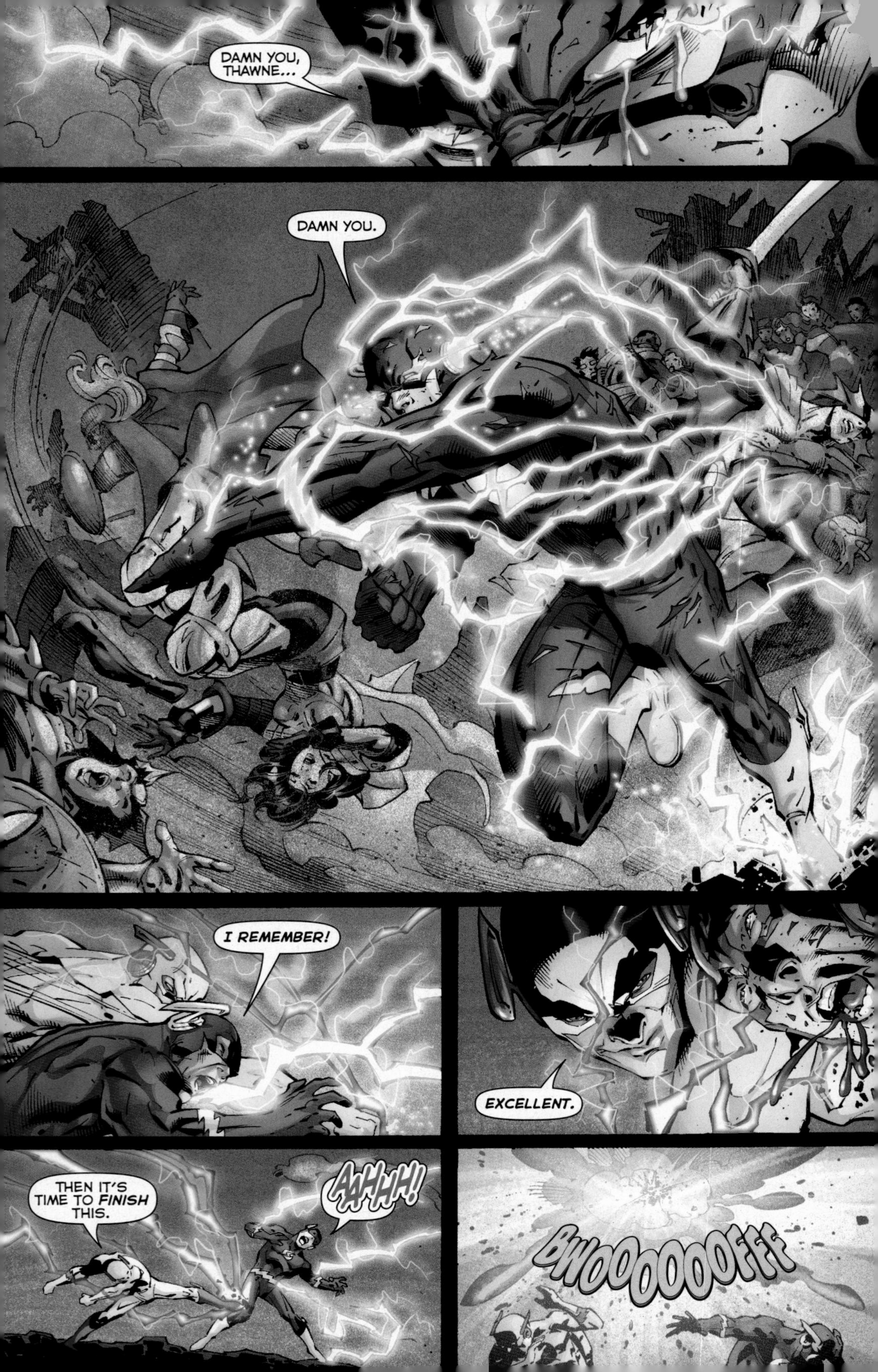
DAMN YOU, THAWNE...
DAMN YOU.
I REMEMBER!
EXCELLENT.
THEN IT'S TIME TO *FINISH* THIS.
AAHHH!
BWOOOOOOOFFF

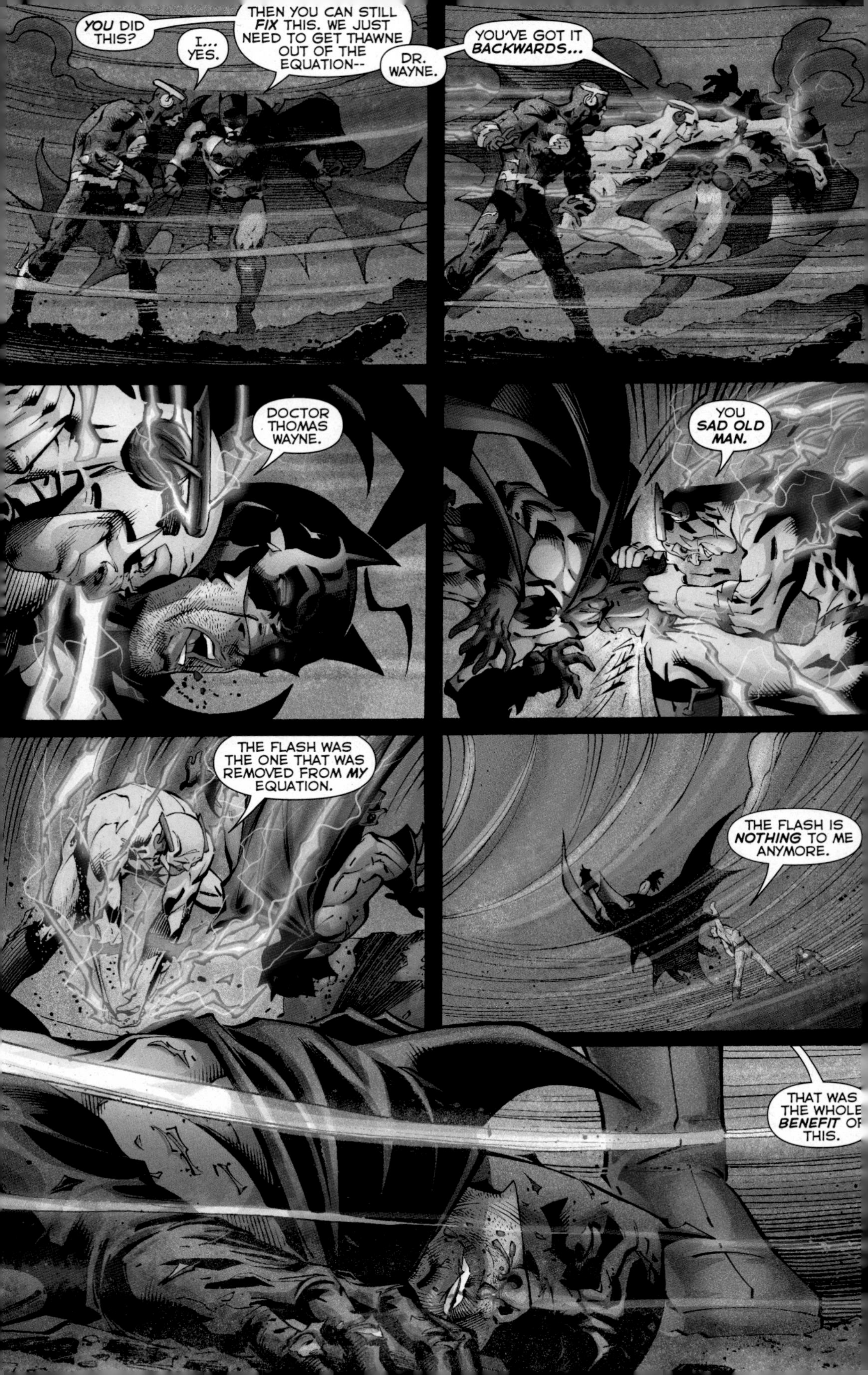
YOU DID THIS?
I... YES.
THEN YOU CAN STILL FIX THIS. WE JUST NEED TO GET THAWNE OUT OF THE EQUATION--
DR. WAYNE.
YOU'VE GOT IT BACKWARDS...
DOCTOR THOMAS WAYNE.
YOU SAD OLD MAN.
THE FLASH WAS THE ONE THAT WAS REMOVED FROM MY EQUATION.
THE FLASH IS NOTHING TO ME ANYMORE.
THAT WAS THE WHOLE BENEFIT OF THIS.

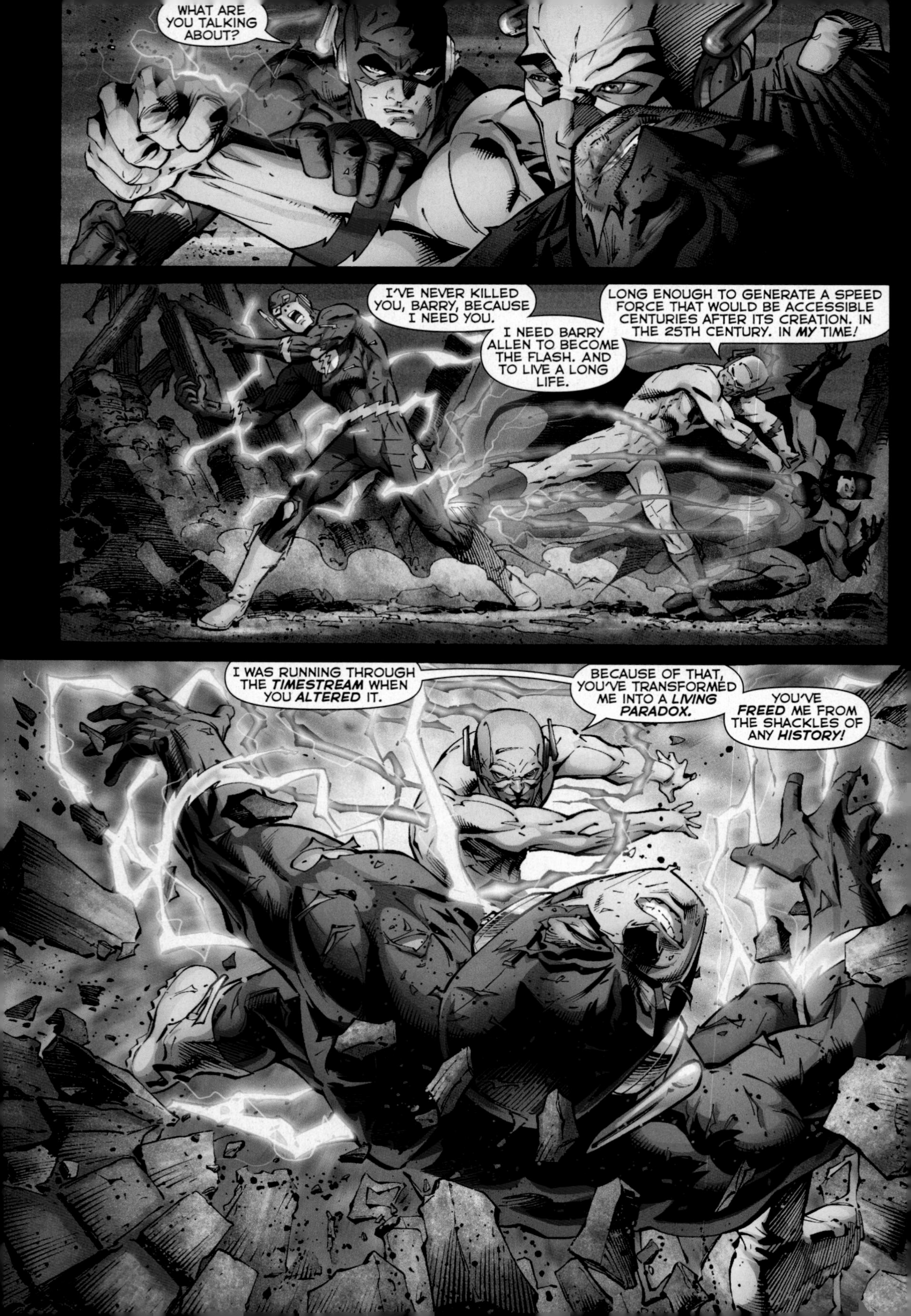

WHAT ARE YOU TALKING ABOUT?
I'VE NEVER KILLED YOU, BARRY, BECAUSE I NEED YOU.
I NEED BARRY ALLEN TO BECOME THE FLASH. AND TO LIVE A LONG LIFE.
LONG ENOUGH TO GENERATE A SPEED FORCE THAT WOULD BE ACCESSIBLE CENTURIES AFTER ITS CREATION. IN THE 25TH CENTURY. IN MY TIME!
I WAS RUNNING THROUGH THE TIMESTREAM WHEN YOU ALTERED IT.
BECAUSE OF THAT, YOU'VE TRANSFORMED ME INTO A LIVING PARADOX.
YOU'VE FREED ME FROM THE SHACKLES OF ANY HISTORY!

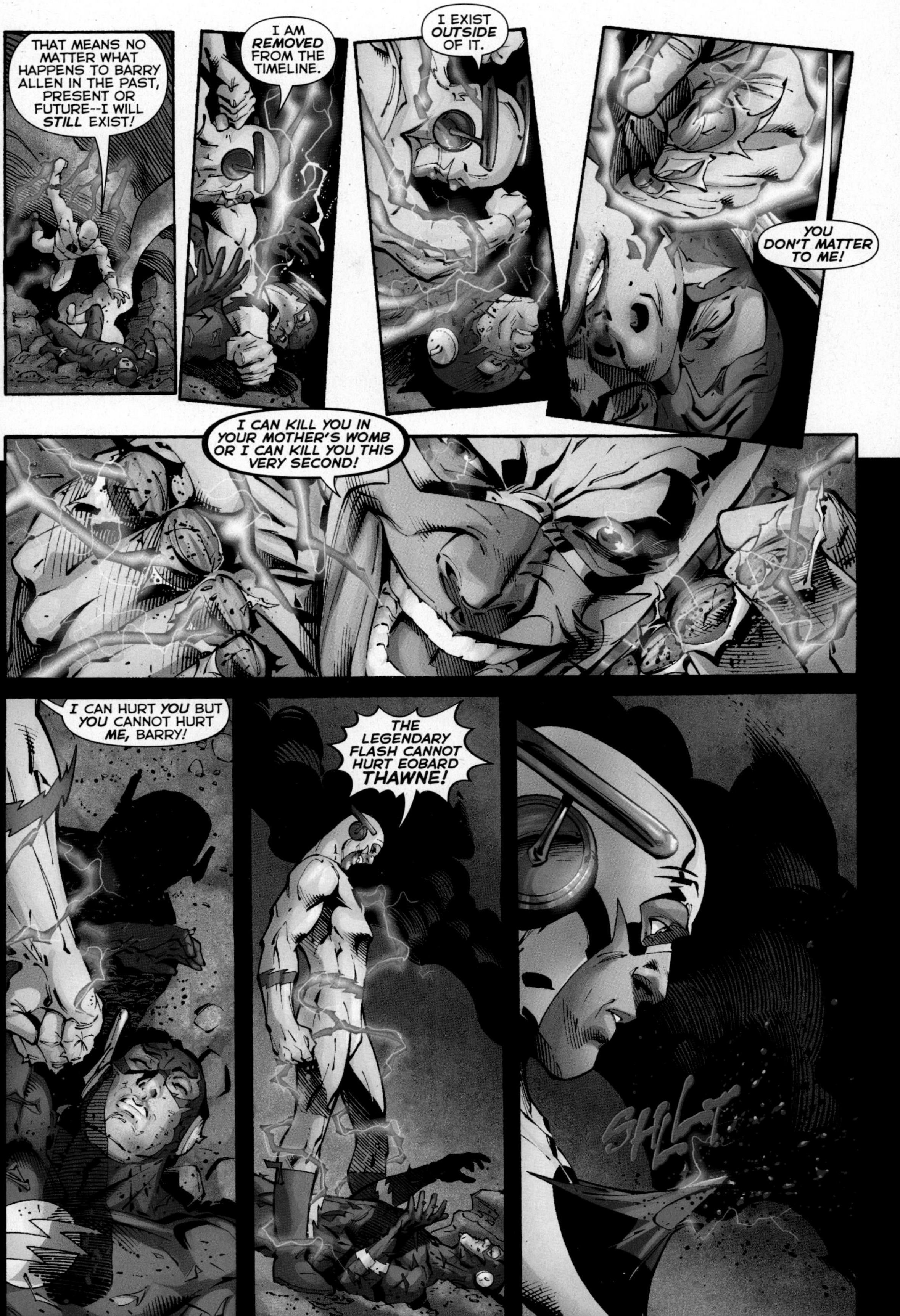
THAT MEANS NO MATTER WHAT HAPPENS TO BARRY ALLEN IN THE PAST, PRESENT OR FUTURE--I WILL STILL EXIST!
I AM REMOVED FROM THE TIMELINE.
I EXIST OUTSIDE OF IT.
YOU DON'T MATTER TO ME!
I CAN KILL YOU IN YOUR MOTHER'S WOMB OR I CAN KILL YOU THIS VERY SECOND!
I CAN HURT YOU BUT YOU CANNOT HURT ME, BARRY!
THE LEGENDARY FLASH CANNOT HURT EOBARD THAWNE!
SHLLT

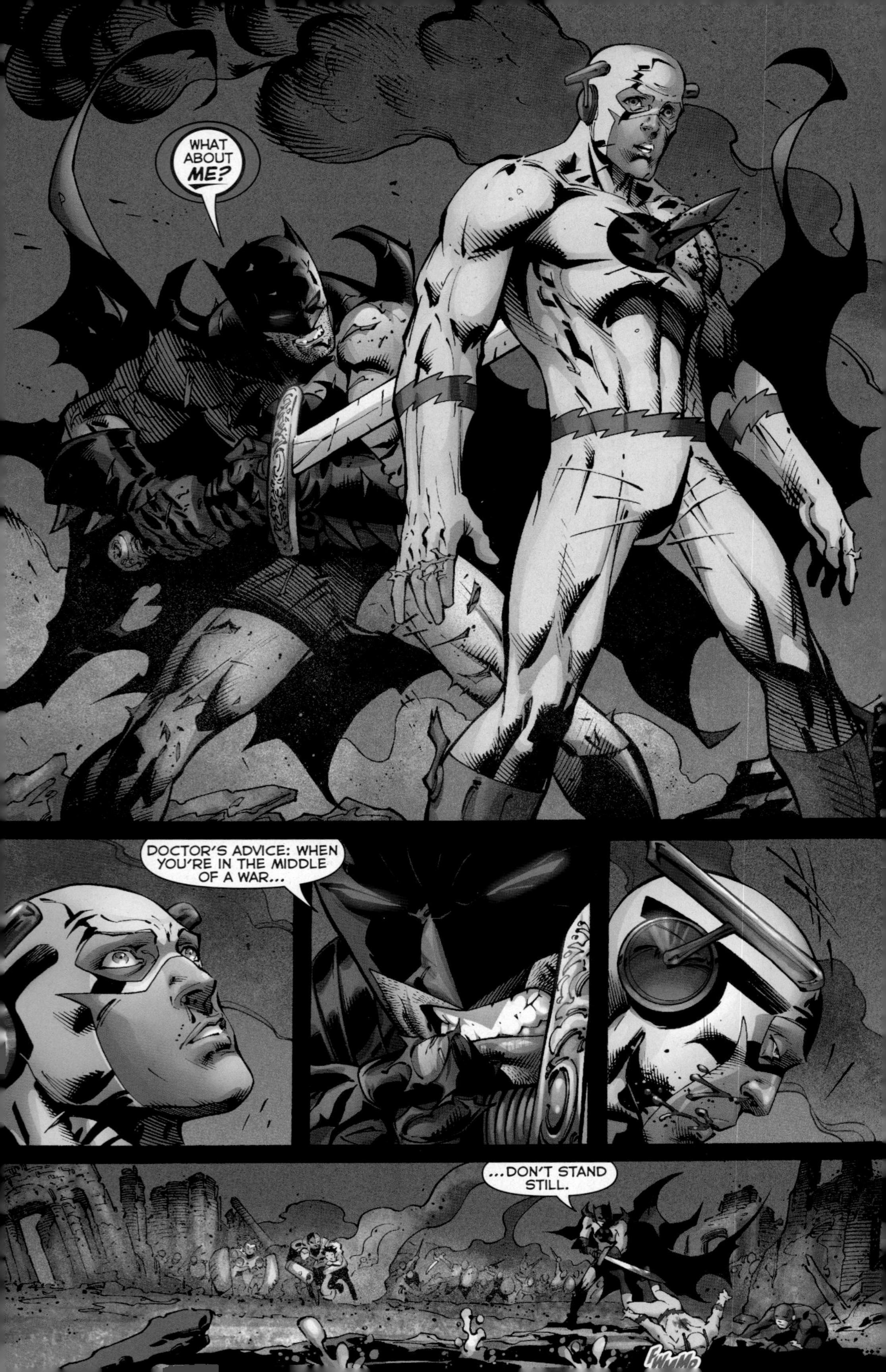
WHAT ABOUT ME?
DOCTOR'S ADVICE: WHEN YOU'RE IN THE MIDDLE OF A WAR...
...DON'T STAND STILL.

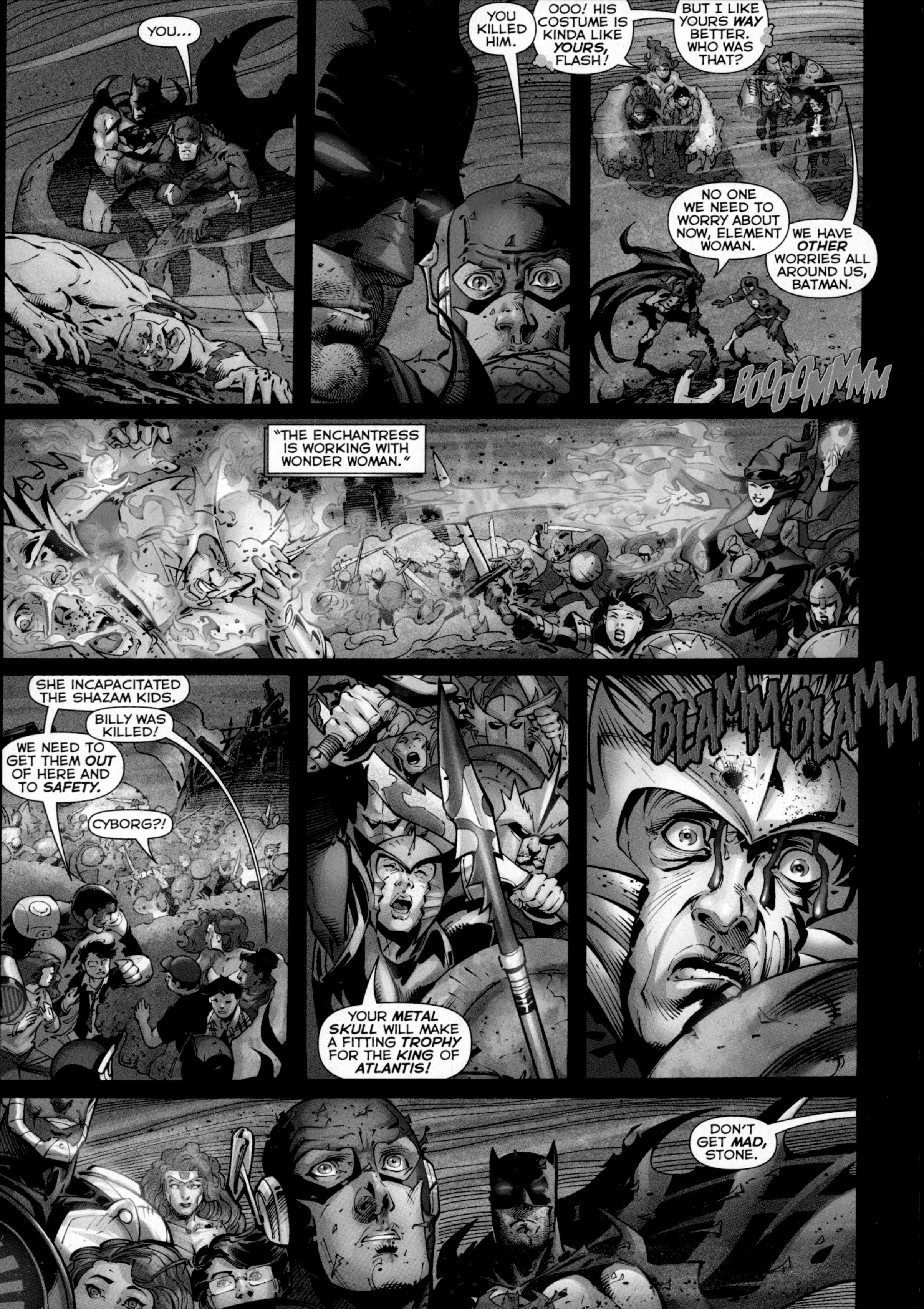
YOU...
YOU KILLED HIM.
OOO! HIS COSTUME IS KINDA LIKE *YOURS,* FLASH!
BUT I LIKE YOURS *WAY* BETTER. WHO WAS THAT?
NO ONE WE NEED TO WORRY ABOUT NOW, ELEMENT WOMAN.
WE HAVE *OTHER* WORRIES ALL AROUND US, BATMAN.
BOOOOMMMM
"THE ENCHANTRESS IS WORKING WITH WONDER WOMAN."
SHE INCAPACITATED THE SHAZAM KIDS.
BILLY WAS KILLED!
WE NEED TO GET THEM *OUT* OF HERE AND TO *SAFETY.*
CYBORG?!
YOUR *METAL SKULL* WILL MAKE A FITTING *TROPHY* FOR THE *KING* OF *ATLANTIS!*
BLAMM BLAMM
DON'T GET *MAD,* STONE.

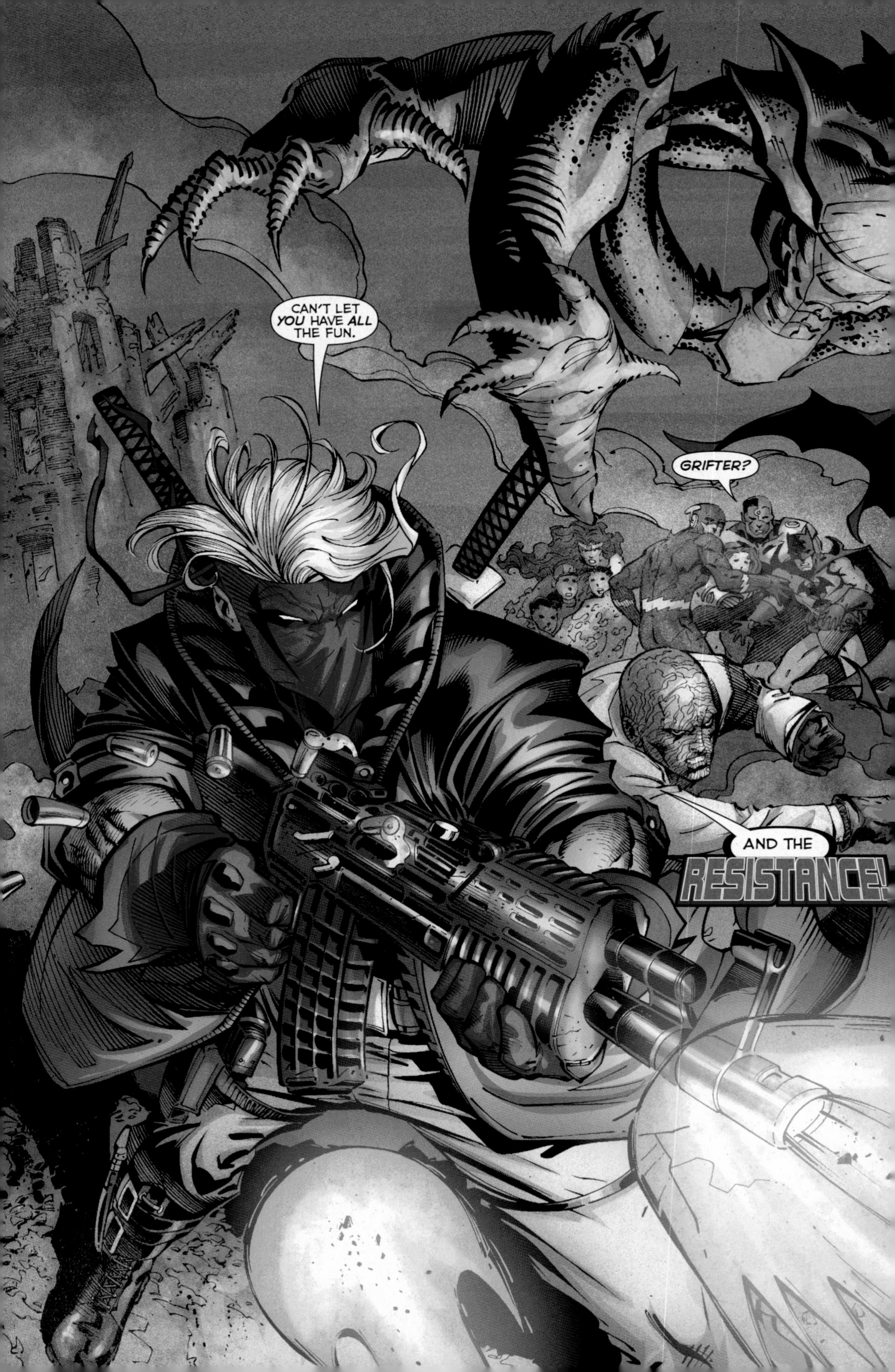
CAN'T LET YOU HAVE ALL THE FUN.
GRIFTER?
AND THE
RESISTANCE!

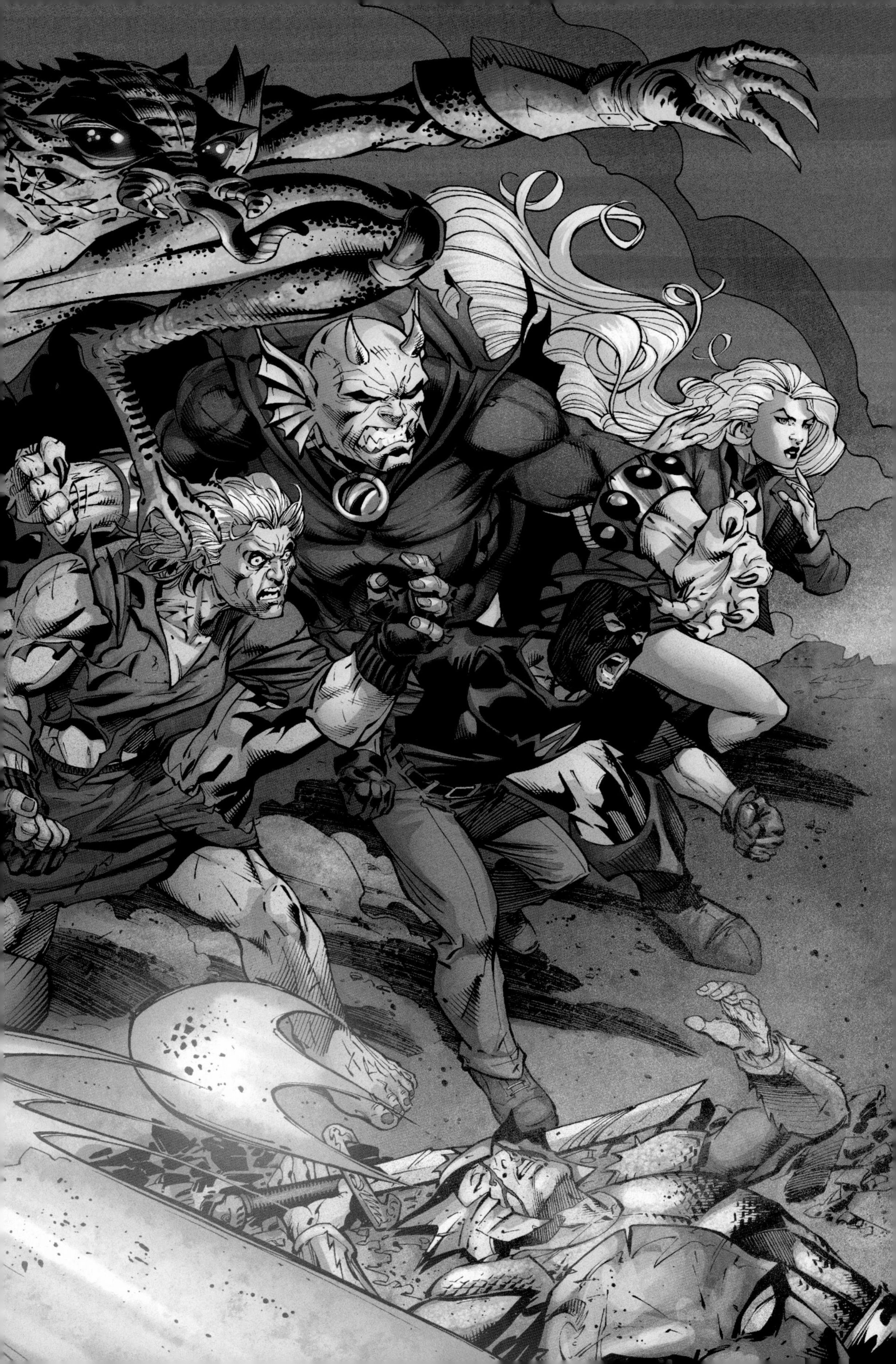

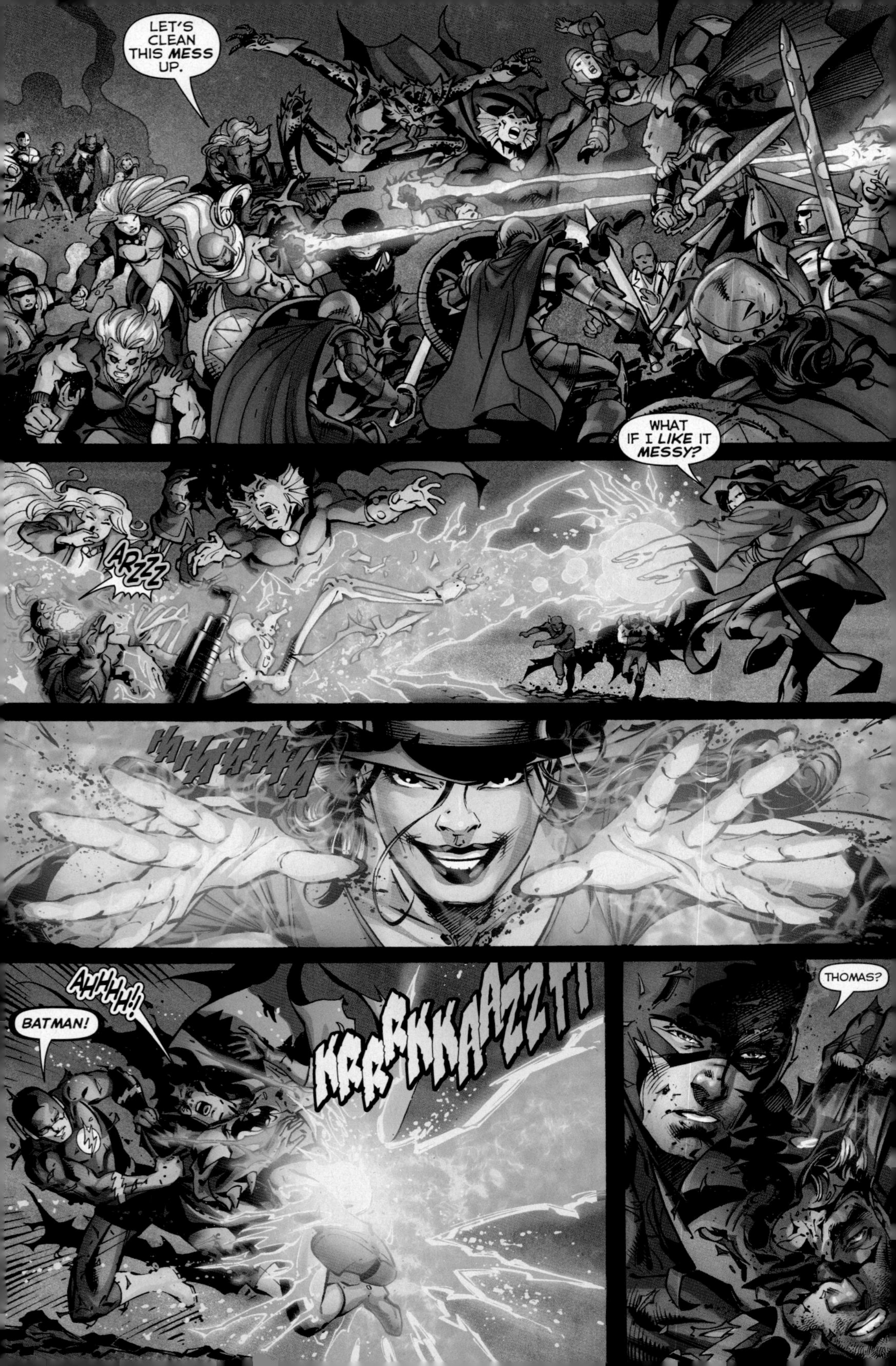
LET'S CLEAN THIS MESS UP.
WHAT IF I LIKE IT MESSY?
ARZZZ
HAHAHAHAHA
AHHHH!!
BATMAN!
KRRRKKAAZZZT!
THOMAS?

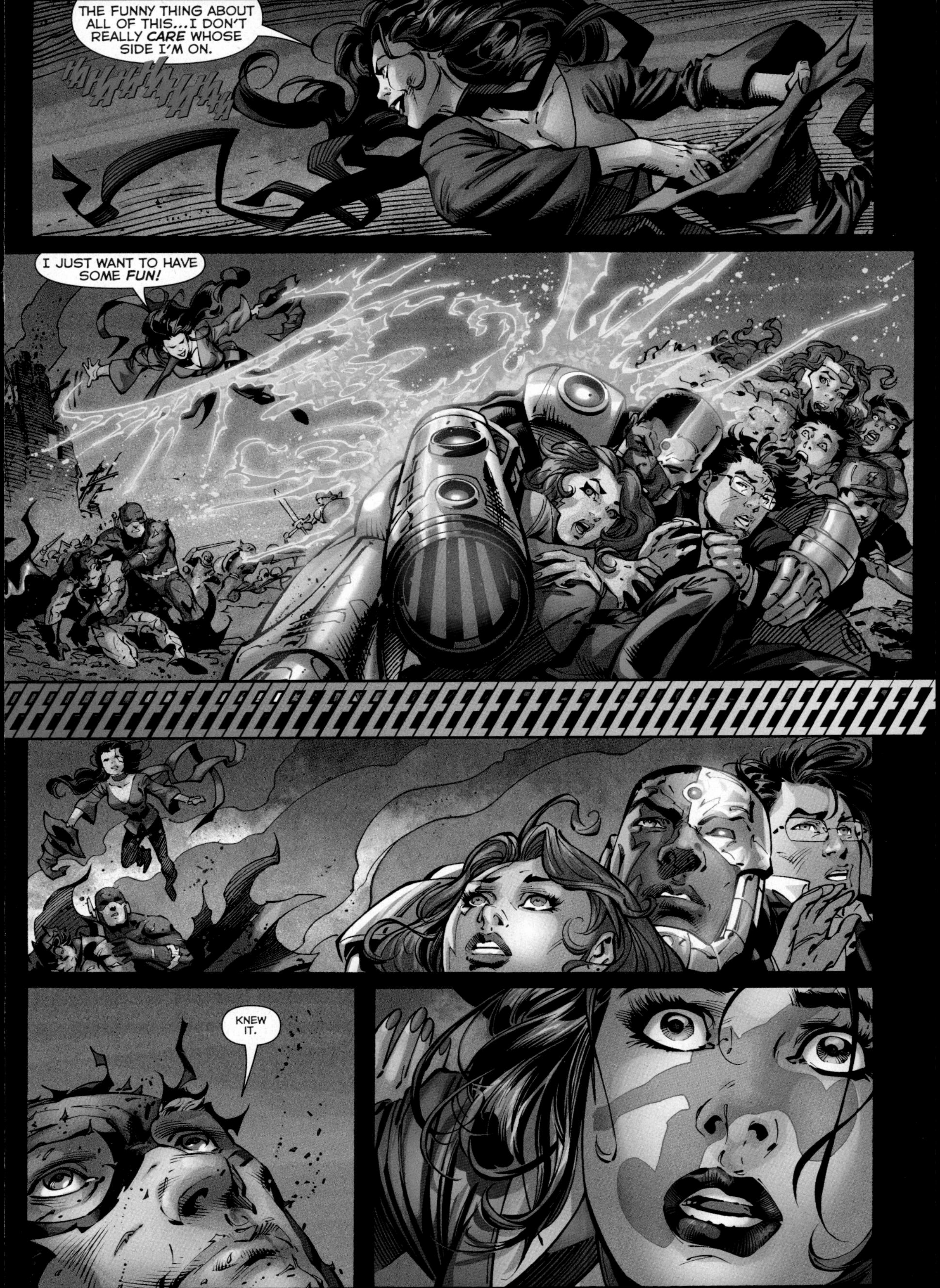
THE FUNNY THING ABOUT ALL OF THIS... I DON'T REALLY CARE WHOSE SIDE I'M ON.
I JUST WANT TO HAVE SOME FUN!
KNEW IT.

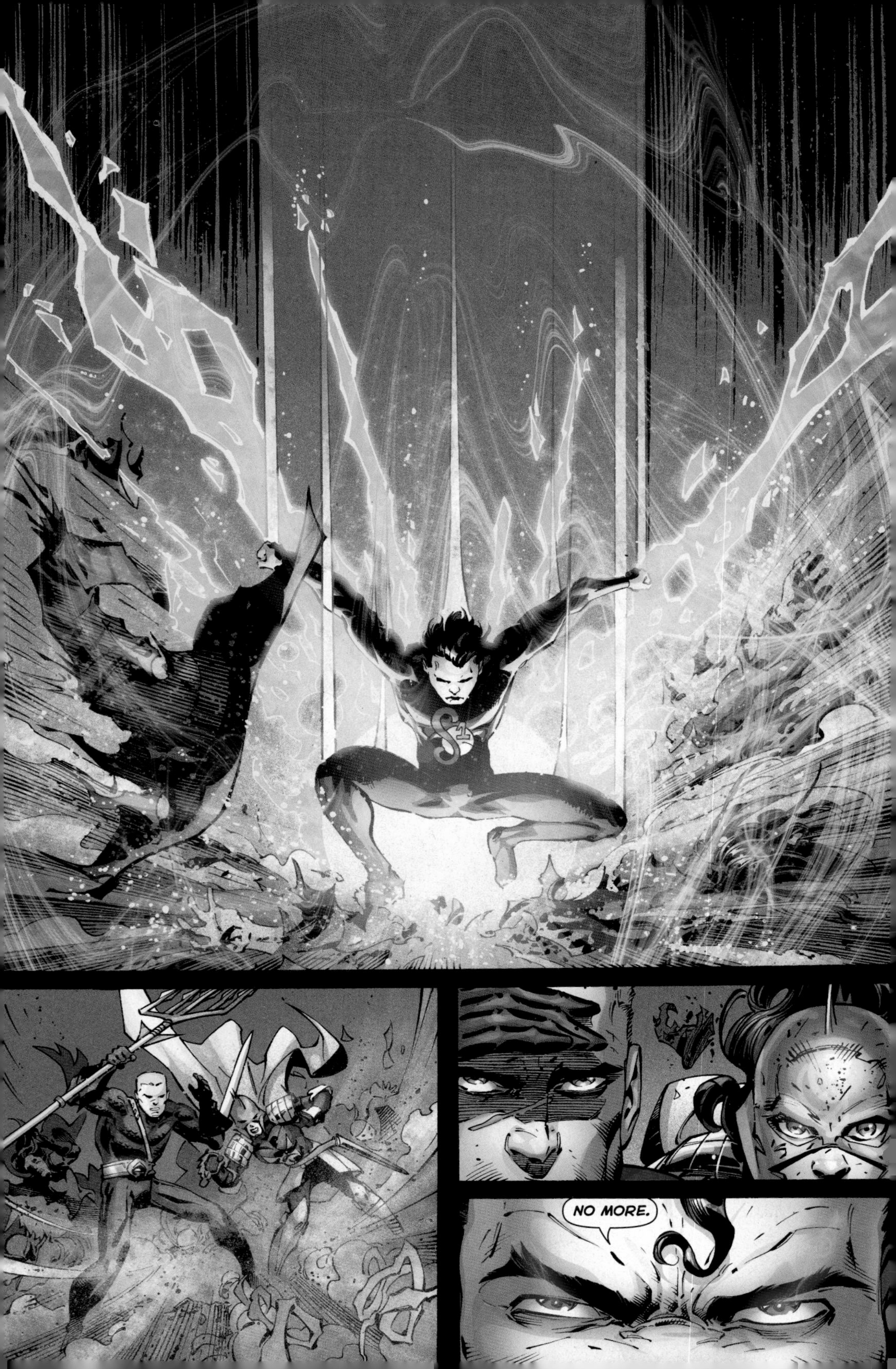
NO MORE.

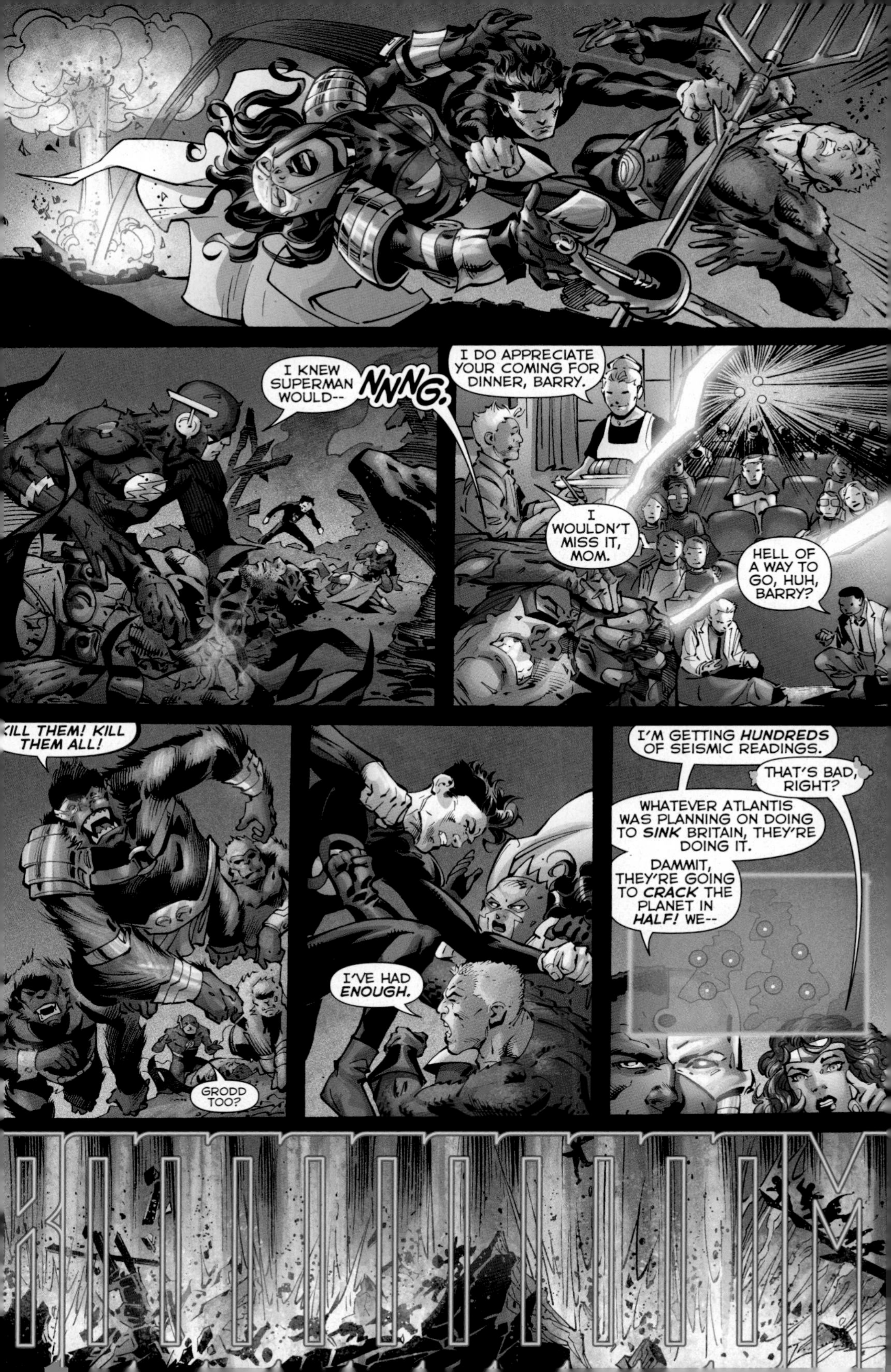
I KNEW SUPERMAN WOULD--
NNNG.
I DO APPRECIATE YOUR COMING FOR DINNER, BARRY.
I WOULDN'T MISS IT, MOM.
HELL OF A WAY TO GO, HUH, BARRY?
KILL THEM! KILL THEM ALL!
GRODD TOO?
I'VE HAD ENOUGH.
I'M GETTING HUNDREDS OF SEISMIC READINGS.
THAT'S BAD, RIGHT?
WHATEVER ATLANTIS WAS PLANNING ON DOING TO SINK BRITAIN, THEY'RE DOING IT.
DAMMIT, THEY'RE GOING TO CRACK THE PLANET IN HALF! WE--
BOOOOOOOOOM

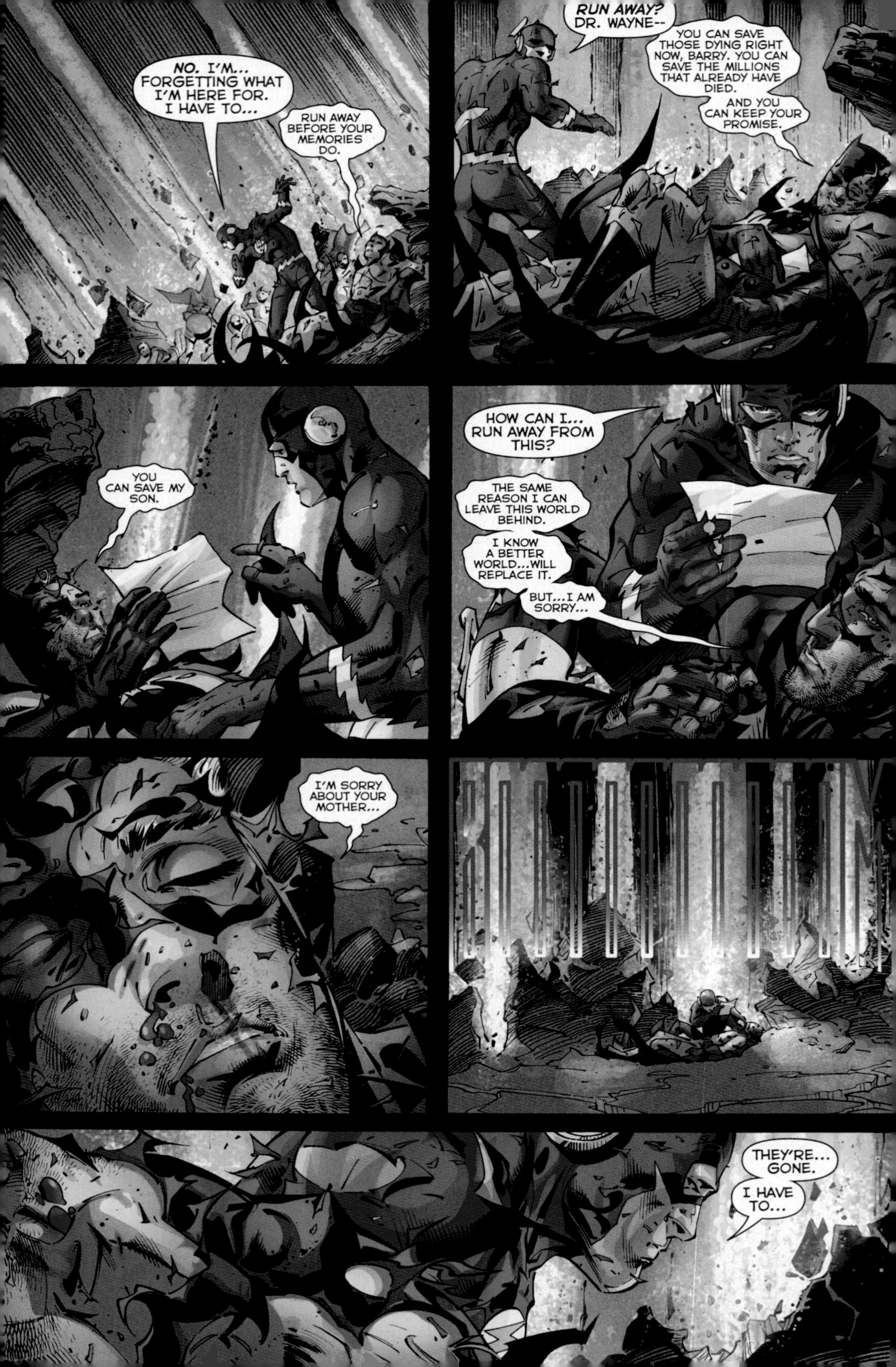
NO. I'M... FORGETTING WHAT I'M HERE FOR. I HAVE TO...
RUN AWAY BEFORE YOUR MEMORIES DO.
RUN AWAY? DR. WAYNE--
YOU CAN SAVE THOSE DYING RIGHT NOW, BARRY. YOU CAN SAVE THE MILLIONS THAT ALREADY HAVE DIED.
AND YOU CAN KEEP YOUR PROMISE.
YOU CAN SAVE MY SON.
HOW CAN I... RUN AWAY FROM THIS?
THE SAME REASON I CAN LEAVE THIS WORLD BEHIND.
I KNOW A BETTER WORLD...WILL REPLACE IT.
BUT...I AM SORRY...
I'M SORRY ABOUT YOUR MOTHER...
BOOOOOOOOM
THEY'RE... GONE.
I HAVE TO...

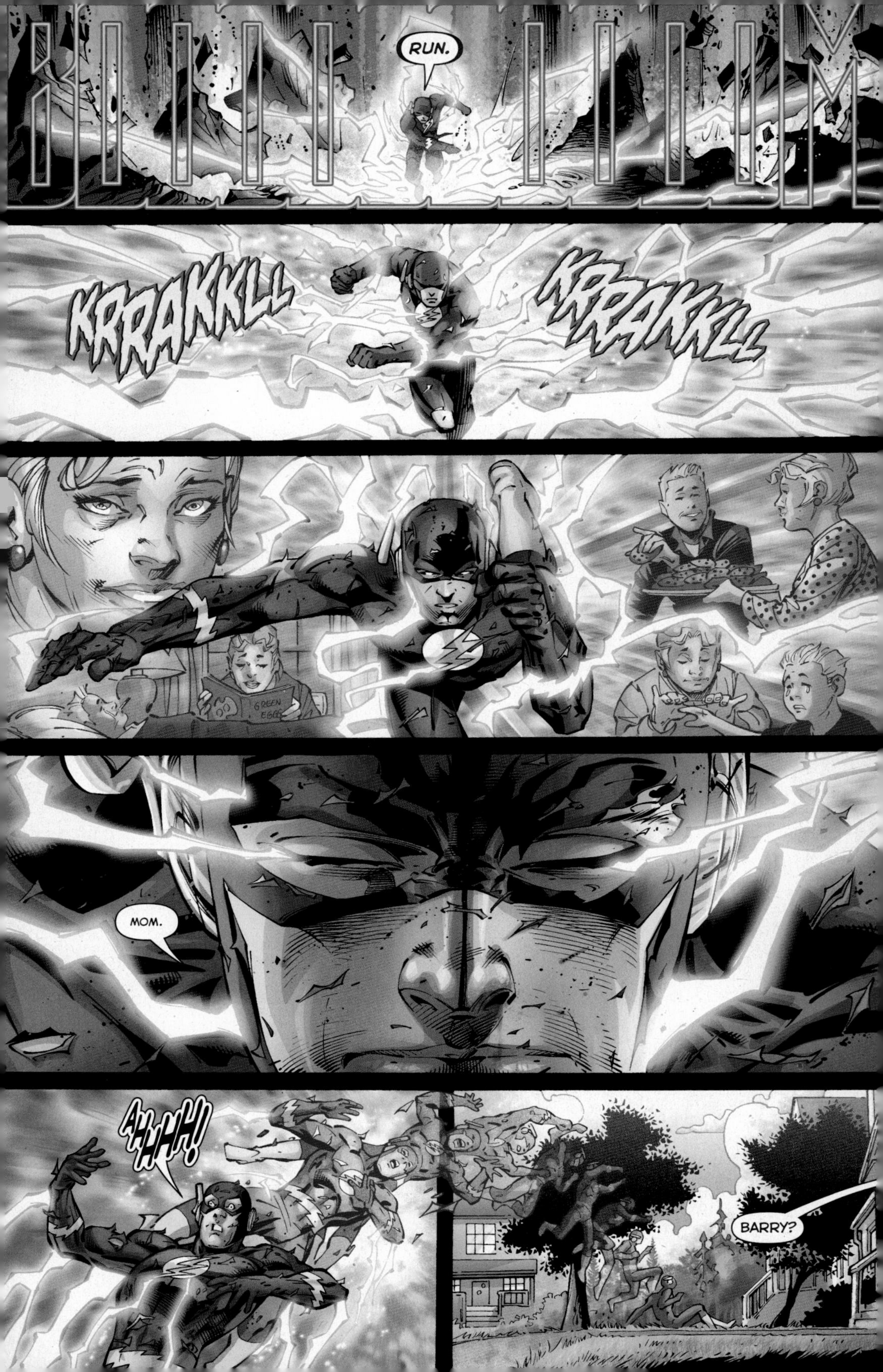
BOOOOOOM
RUN.
KRRAKKLL
KRRAKKLL
GREEN EGGS
MOM.
AHHHH!
BARRY?

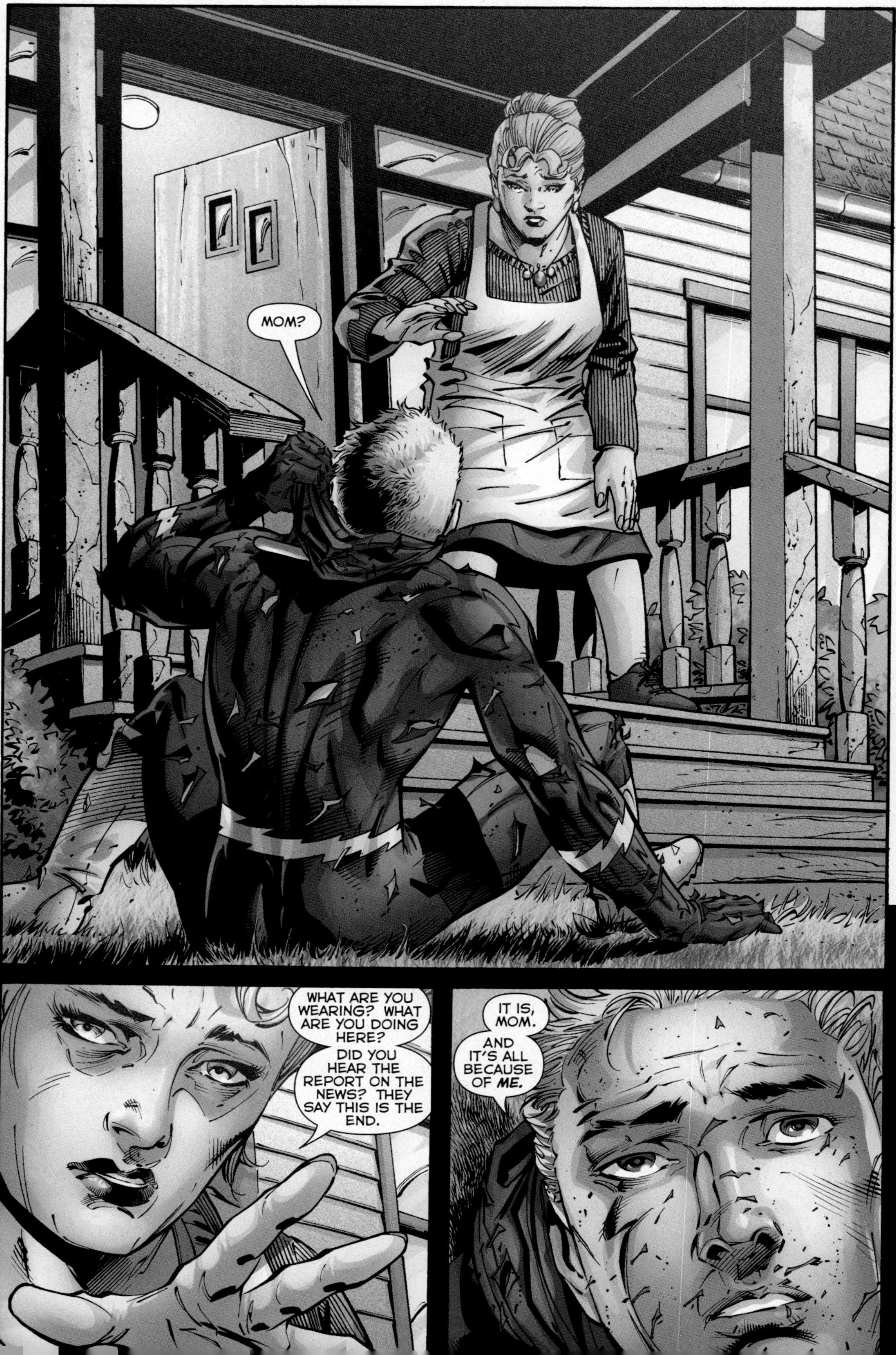
MOM?
WHAT ARE YOU WEARING? WHAT ARE YOU DOING HERE?
DID YOU HEAR THE REPORT ON THE NEWS? THEY SAY THIS IS THE END.
IT IS, MOM.
AND IT'S ALL BECAUSE OF *ME.*

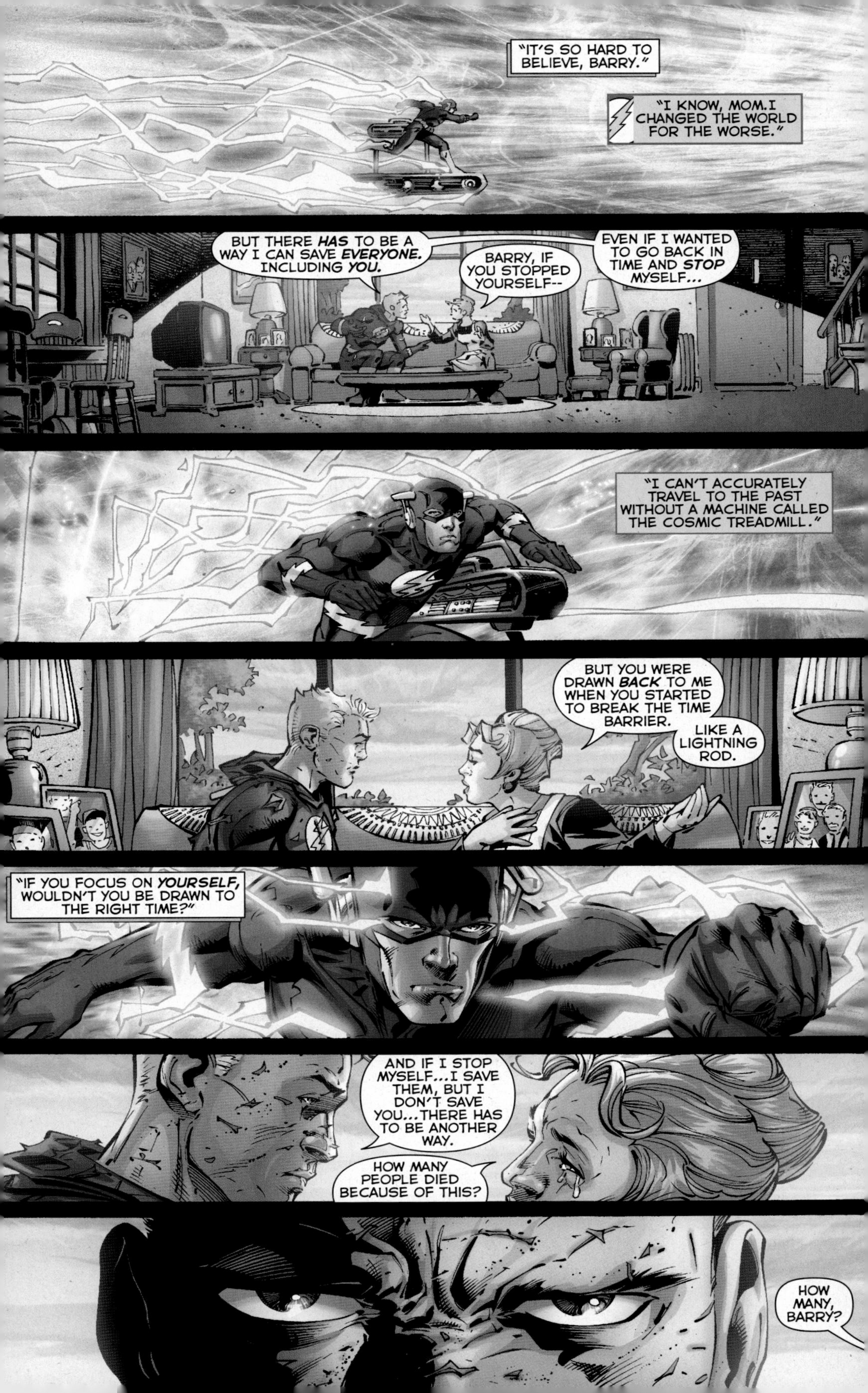
"IT'S SO HARD TO BELIEVE, BARRY."
"I KNOW, MOM. I CHANGED THE WORLD FOR THE WORSE."
BUT THERE HAS TO BE A WAY I CAN SAVE EVERYONE. INCLUDING YOU.
BARRY, IF YOU STOPPED YOURSELF--
EVEN IF I WANTED TO GO BACK IN TIME AND STOP MYSELF...
"I CAN'T ACCURATELY TRAVEL TO THE PAST WITHOUT A MACHINE CALLED THE COSMIC TREADMILL."
BUT YOU WERE DRAWN BACK TO ME WHEN YOU STARTED TO BREAK THE TIME BARRIER.
LIKE A LIGHTNING ROD.
"IF YOU FOCUS ON YOURSELF, WOULDN'T YOU BE DRAWN TO THE RIGHT TIME?"
AND IF I STOP MYSELF...I SAVE THEM, BUT I DON'T SAVE YOU...THERE HAS TO BE ANOTHER WAY.
HOW MANY PEOPLE DIED BECAUSE OF THIS?
HOW MANY, BARRY?

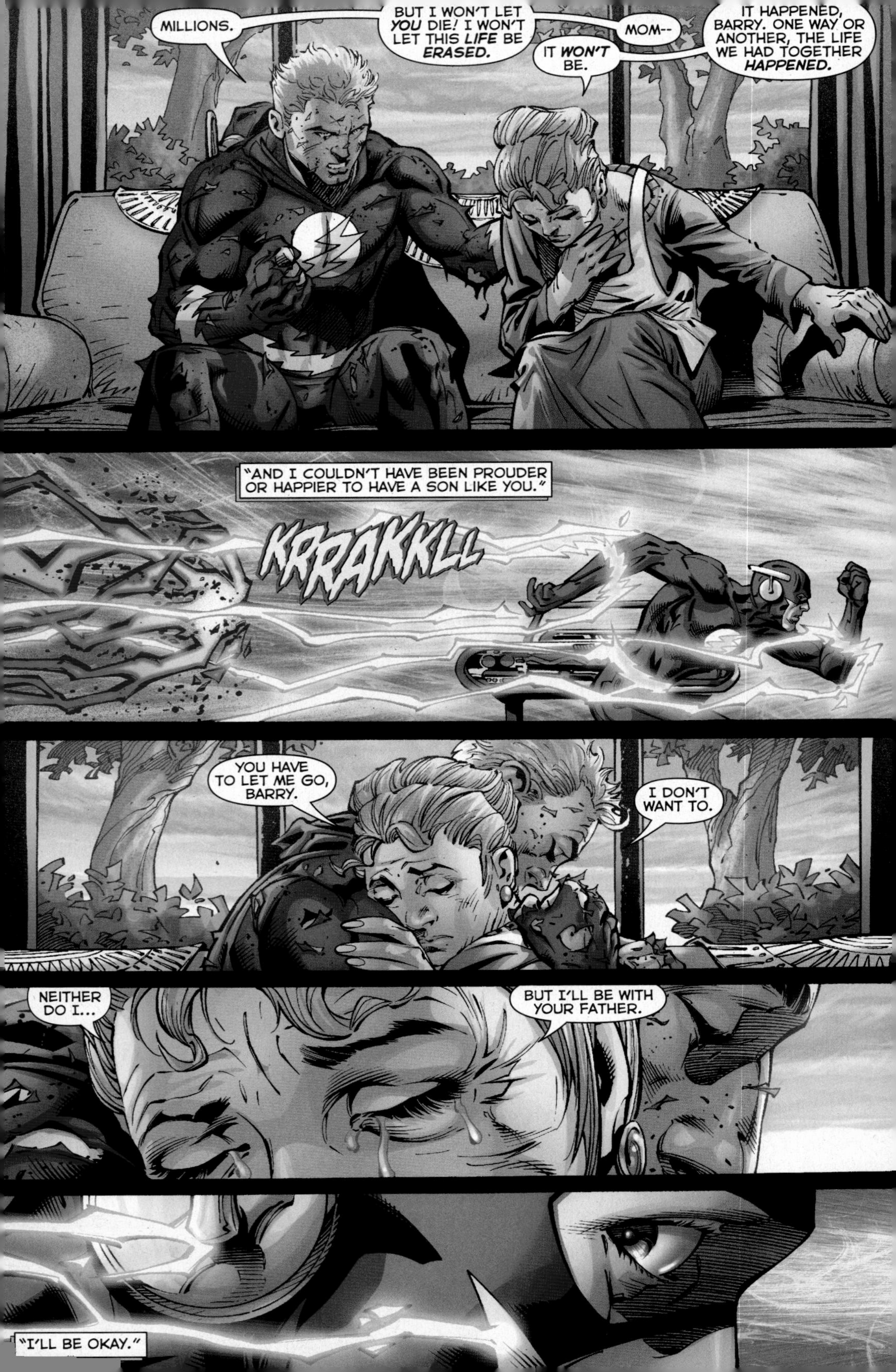
MILLIONS.
BUT I WON'T LET *YOU* DIE! I WON'T LET THIS *LIFE* BE *ERASED.*
MOM--
IT *WON'T* BE.
IT HAPPENED, BARRY. ONE WAY OR ANOTHER, THE LIFE WE HAD TOGETHER *HAPPENED.*
"AND I COULDN'T HAVE BEEN PROUDER OR HAPPIER TO HAVE A SON LIKE YOU."
KRRAKKLL
YOU HAVE TO LET ME GO, BARRY.
I DON'T WANT TO.
NEITHER DO I...
BUT I'LL BE WITH YOUR FATHER.
"I'LL BE OKAY."

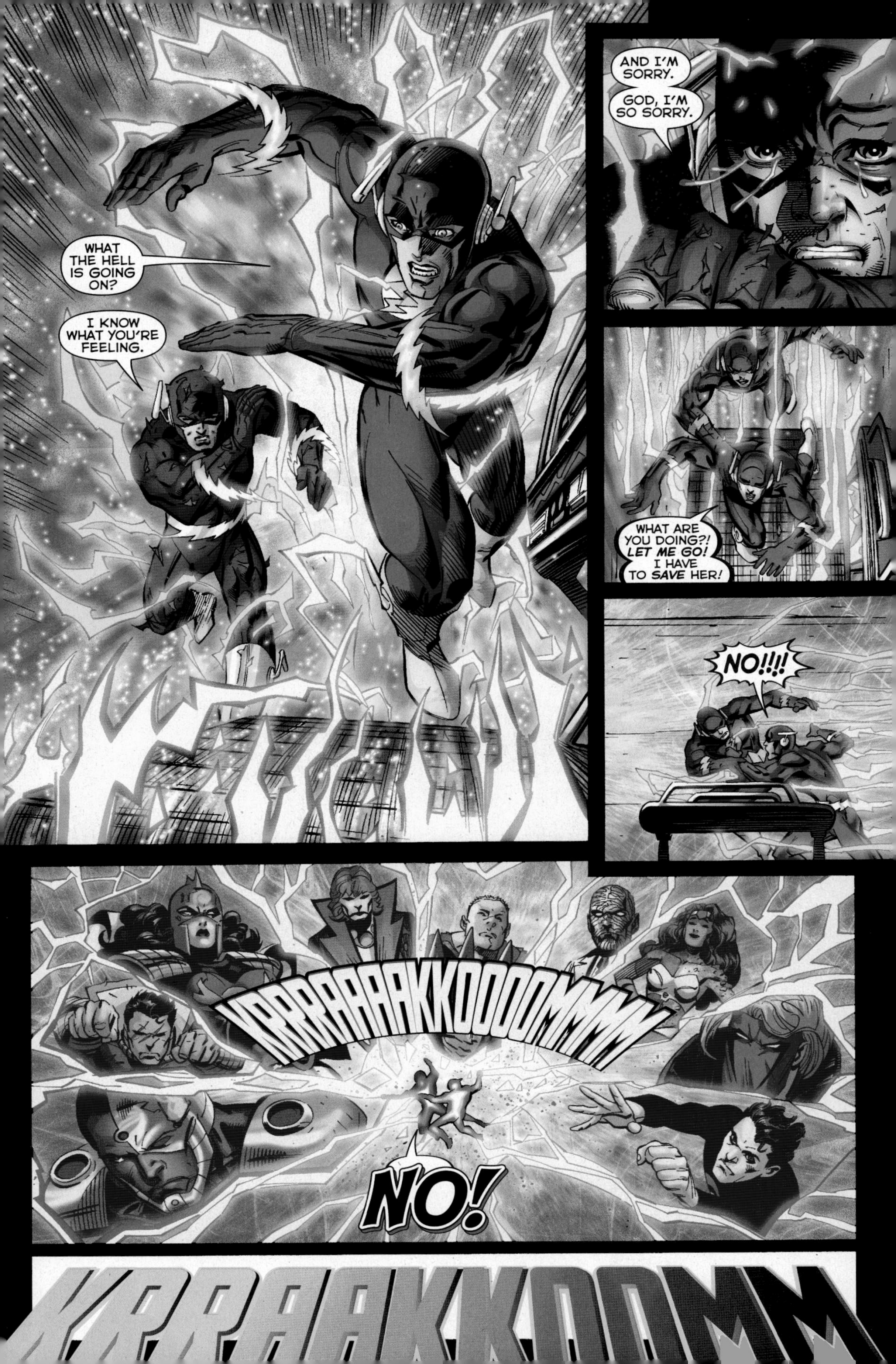

WHAT THE HELL IS GOING ON?
I KNOW WHAT YOU'RE FEELING.
AND I'M SORRY.
GOD, I'M SO SORRY.
WHAT ARE YOU DOING?! LET ME GO! I HAVE TO SAVE HER!
NO!!!!
KRRRAAAAKKOOOOMMMM
NO!
KRRAAKKOOMM

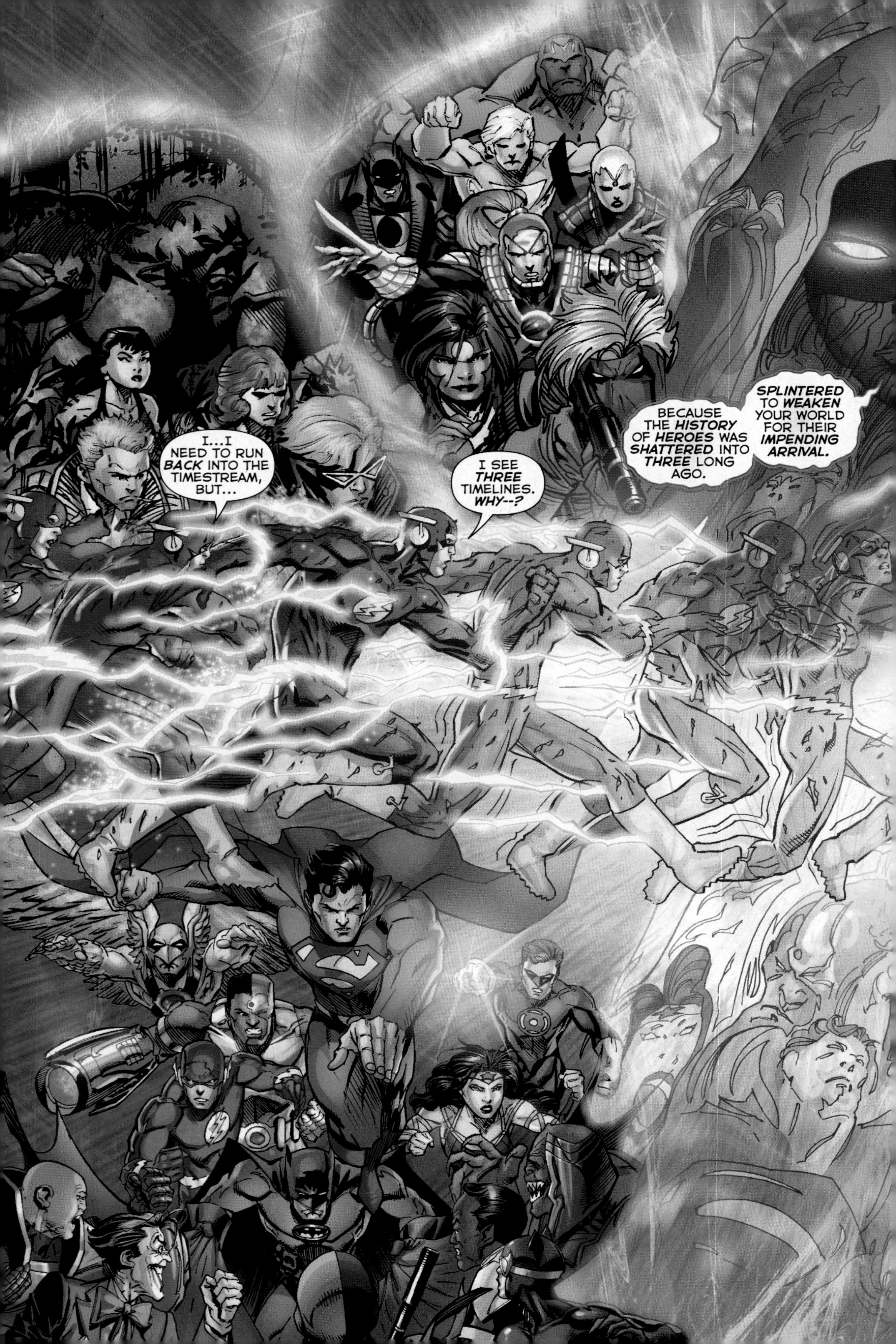
I...I NEED TO RUN BACK INTO THE TIMESTREAM, BUT...
I SEE THREE TIMELINES. WHY--?
BECAUSE THE HISTORY OF HEROES WAS SHATTERED INTO THREE LONG AGO.
SPLINTERED TO WEAKEN YOUR WORLD FOR THEIR IMPENDING ARRIVAL.

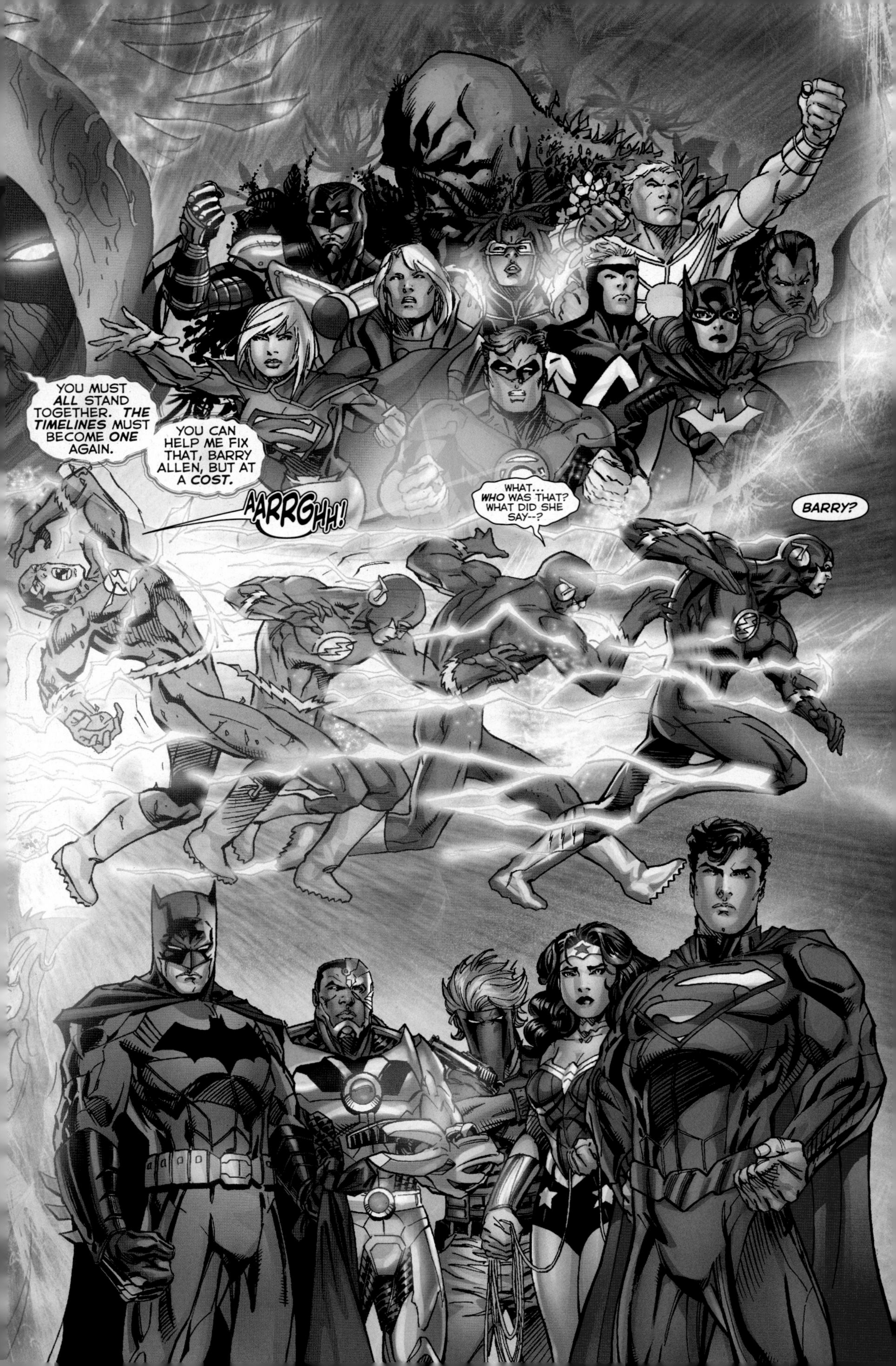
YOU MUST ALL STAND TOGETHER. THE TIMELINES MUST BECOME ONE AGAIN.
YOU CAN HELP ME FIX THAT, BARRY ALLEN, BUT AT A COST.
AARRGHH!
WHAT... WHO WAS THAT? WHAT DID SHE SAY--?
BARRY?

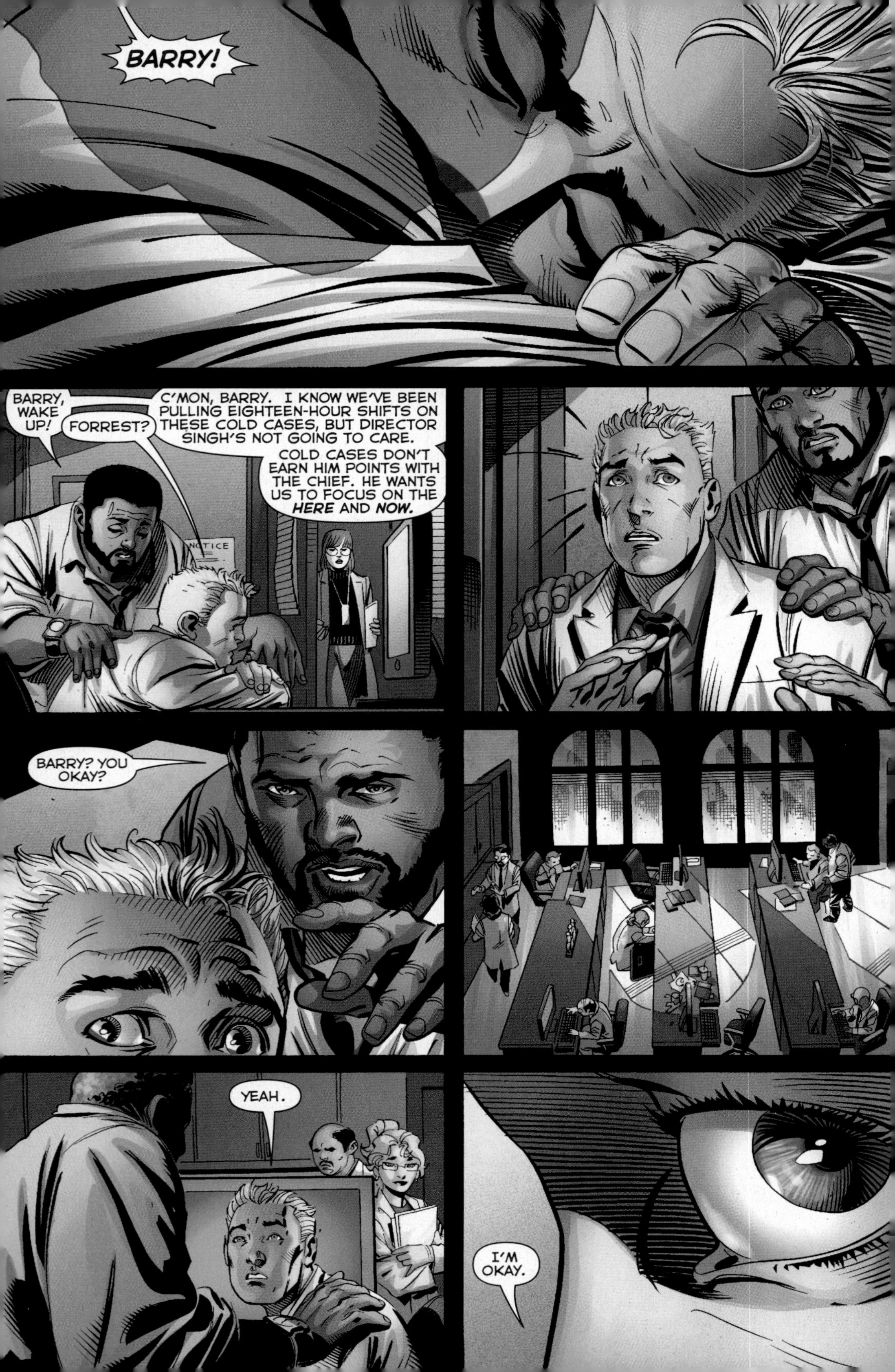
BARRY!
BARRY, WAKE UP!
FORREST?
C'MON, BARRY. I KNOW WE'VE BEEN PULLING EIGHTEEN-HOUR SHIFTS ON THESE COLD CASES, BUT DIRECTOR SINGH'S NOT GOING TO CARE.
COLD CASES DON'T EARN HIM POINTS WITH THE CHIEF. HE WANTS US TO FOCUS ON THE *HERE* AND *NOW.*
NOTICE
BARRY? YOU OKAY?
YEAH.
I'M OKAY.

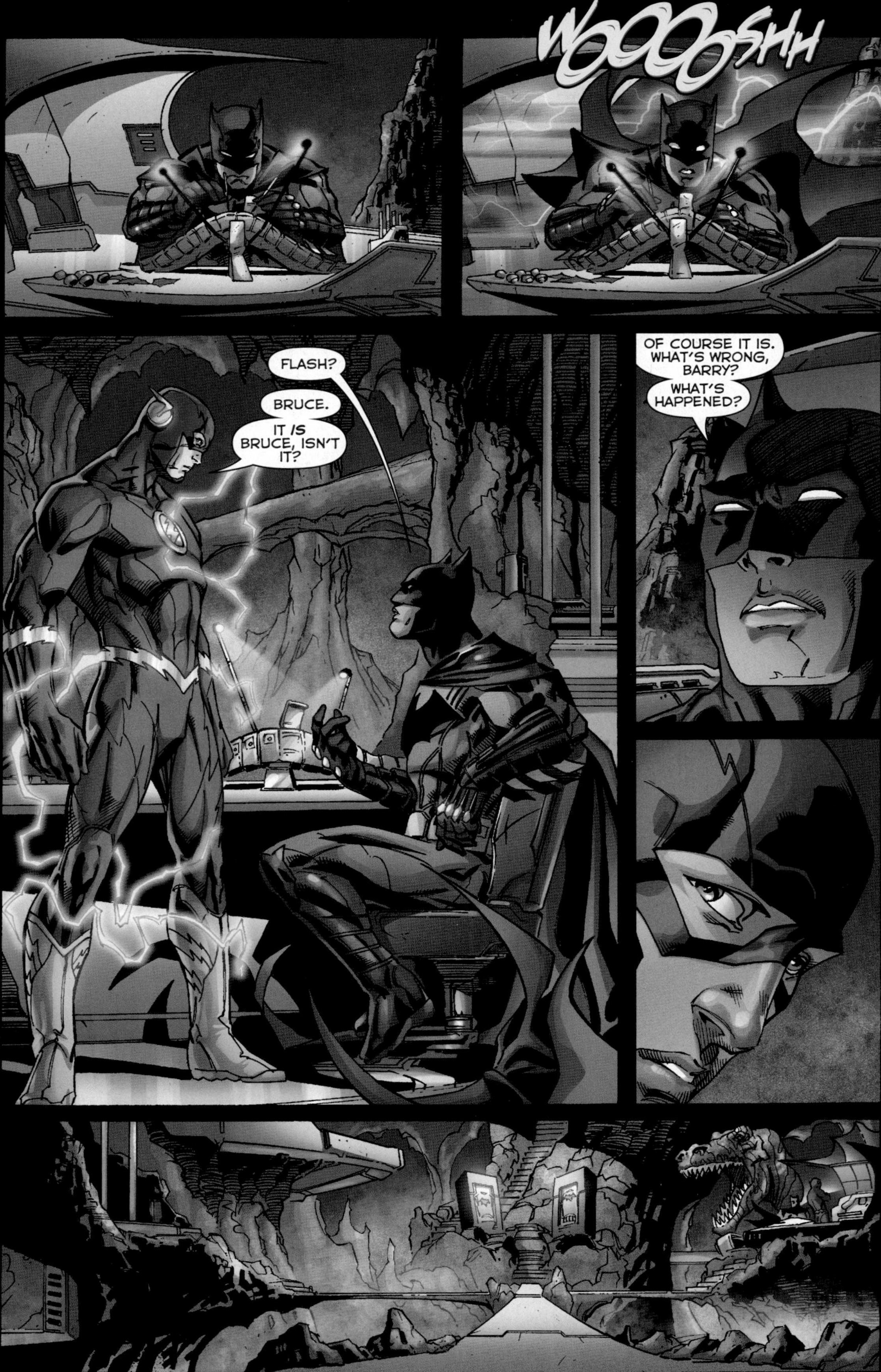
WOOOOSHH
FLASH?
BRUCE.
IT *IS* BRUCE, ISN'T IT?
OF COURSE IT IS. WHAT'S WRONG, BARRY?
WHAT'S HAPPENED?

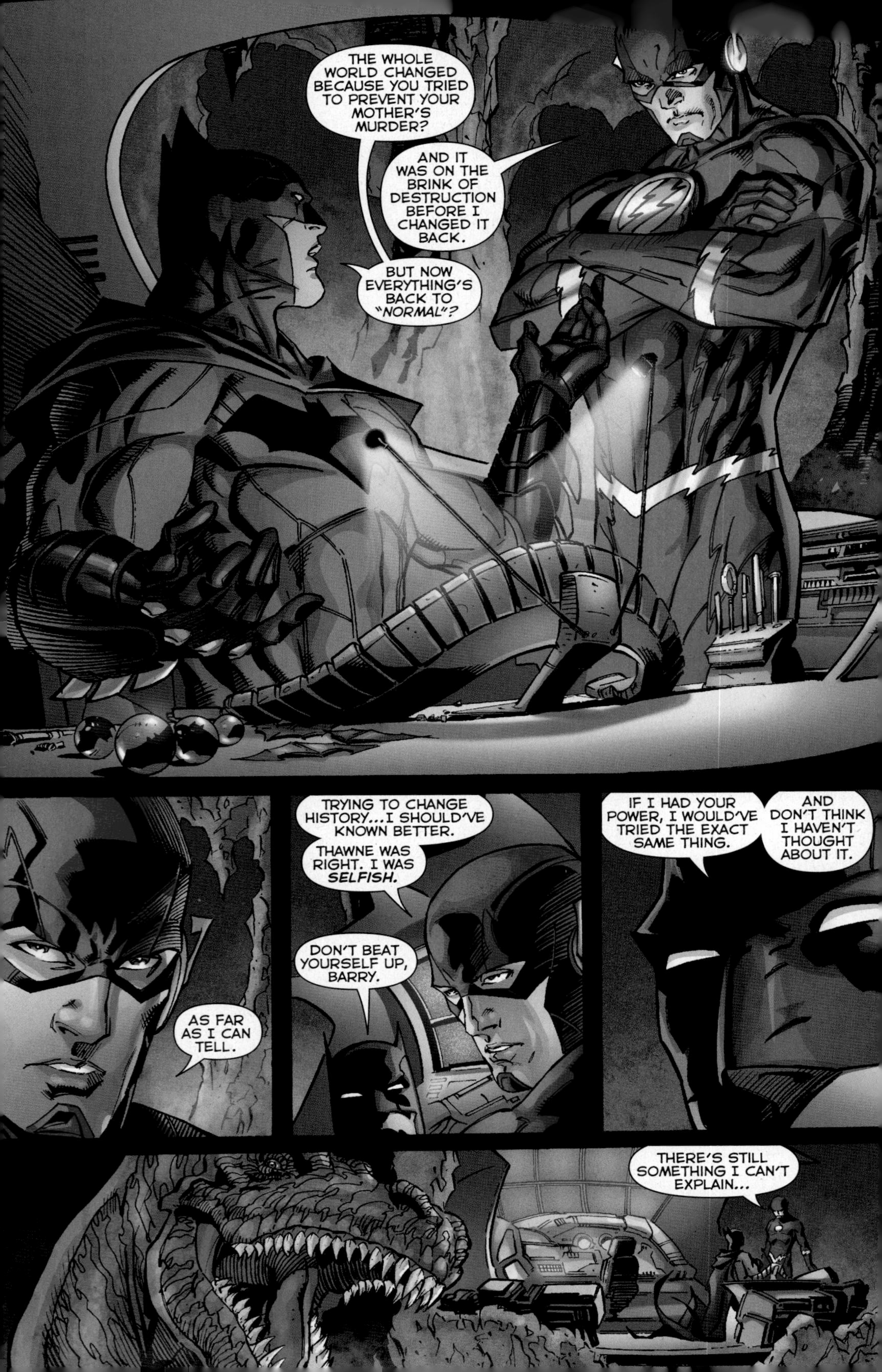
THE WHOLE WORLD CHANGED BECAUSE YOU TRIED TO PREVENT YOUR MOTHER'S MURDER?
AND IT WAS ON THE BRINK OF DESTRUCTION BEFORE I CHANGED IT BACK.
BUT NOW EVERYTHING'S BACK TO "NORMAL"?
AS FAR AS I CAN TELL.
TRYING TO CHANGE HISTORY...I SHOULD'VE KNOWN BETTER.
THAWNE WAS RIGHT. I WAS SELFISH.
DON'T BEAT YOURSELF UP, BARRY.
IF I HAD YOUR POWER, I WOULD'VE TRIED THE EXACT SAME THING.
AND DON'T THINK I HAVEN'T THOUGHT ABOUT IT.
THERE'S STILL SOMETHING I CAN'T EXPLAIN...

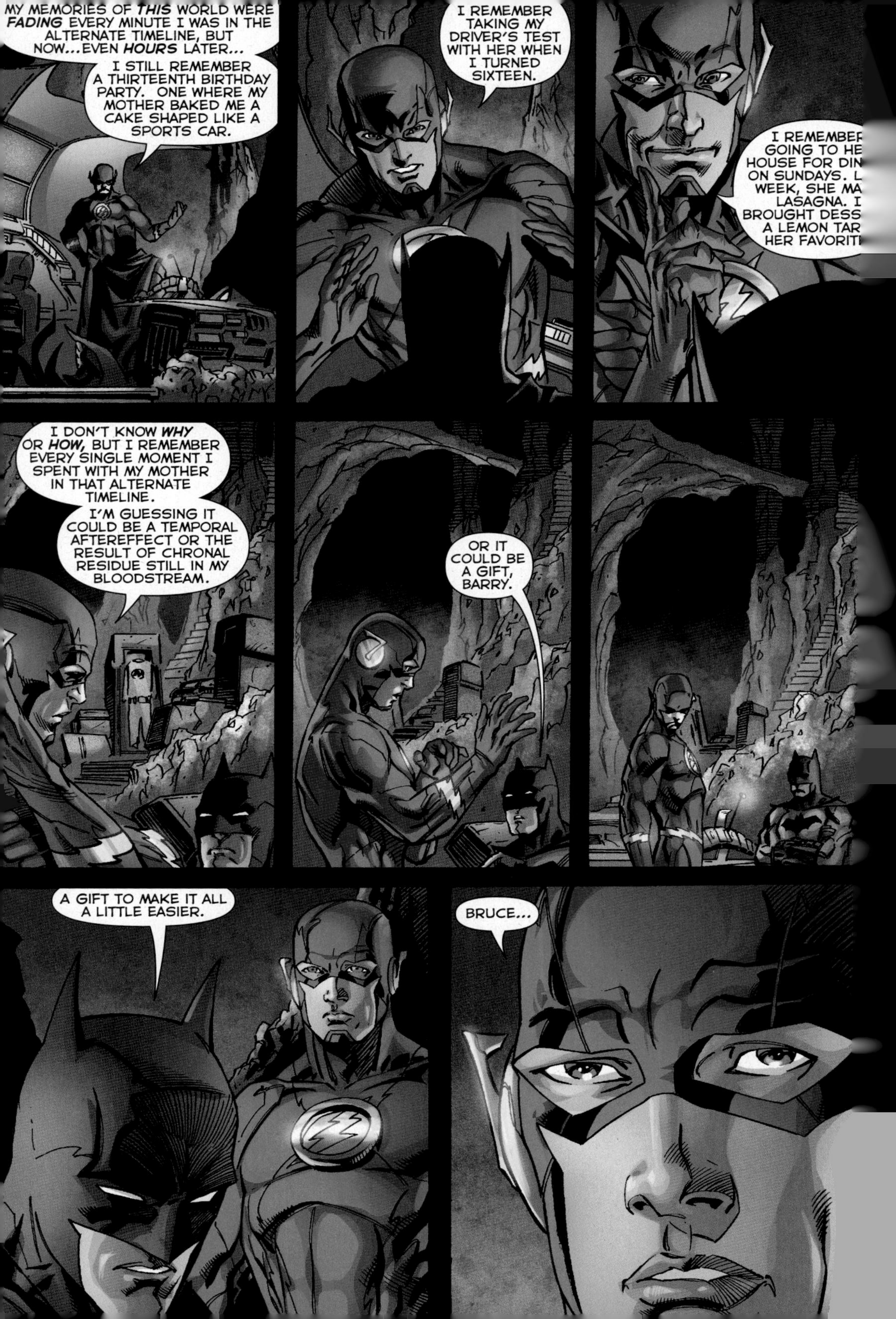
MY MEMORIES OF *THIS* WORLD WERE *FADING* EVERY MINUTE I WAS IN THE ALTERNATE TIMELINE, BUT NOW... EVEN *HOURS* LATER...
I STILL REMEMBER A THIRTEENTH BIRTHDAY PARTY. ONE WHERE MY MOTHER BAKED ME A CAKE SHAPED LIKE A SPORTS CAR.
I REMEMBER TAKING MY DRIVER'S TEST WITH HER WHEN I TURNED SIXTEEN.
I REMEMBER GOING TO HE HOUSE FOR DIN ON SUNDAYS. L WEEK, SHE MA LASAGNA. I BROUGHT DESS A LEMON TAR HER FAVORIT
I DON'T KNOW *WHY* OR *HOW,* BUT I REMEMBER EVERY SINGLE MOMENT I SPENT WITH MY MOTHER IN THAT ALTERNATE TIMELINE.
I'M GUESSING IT COULD BE A TEMPORAL AFTEREFFECT OR THE RESULT OF CHRONAL RESIDUE STILL IN MY BLOODSTREAM.
OR IT COULD BE A GIFT, BARRY.
A GIFT TO MAKE IT ALL A LITTLE EASIER.
BRUCE...

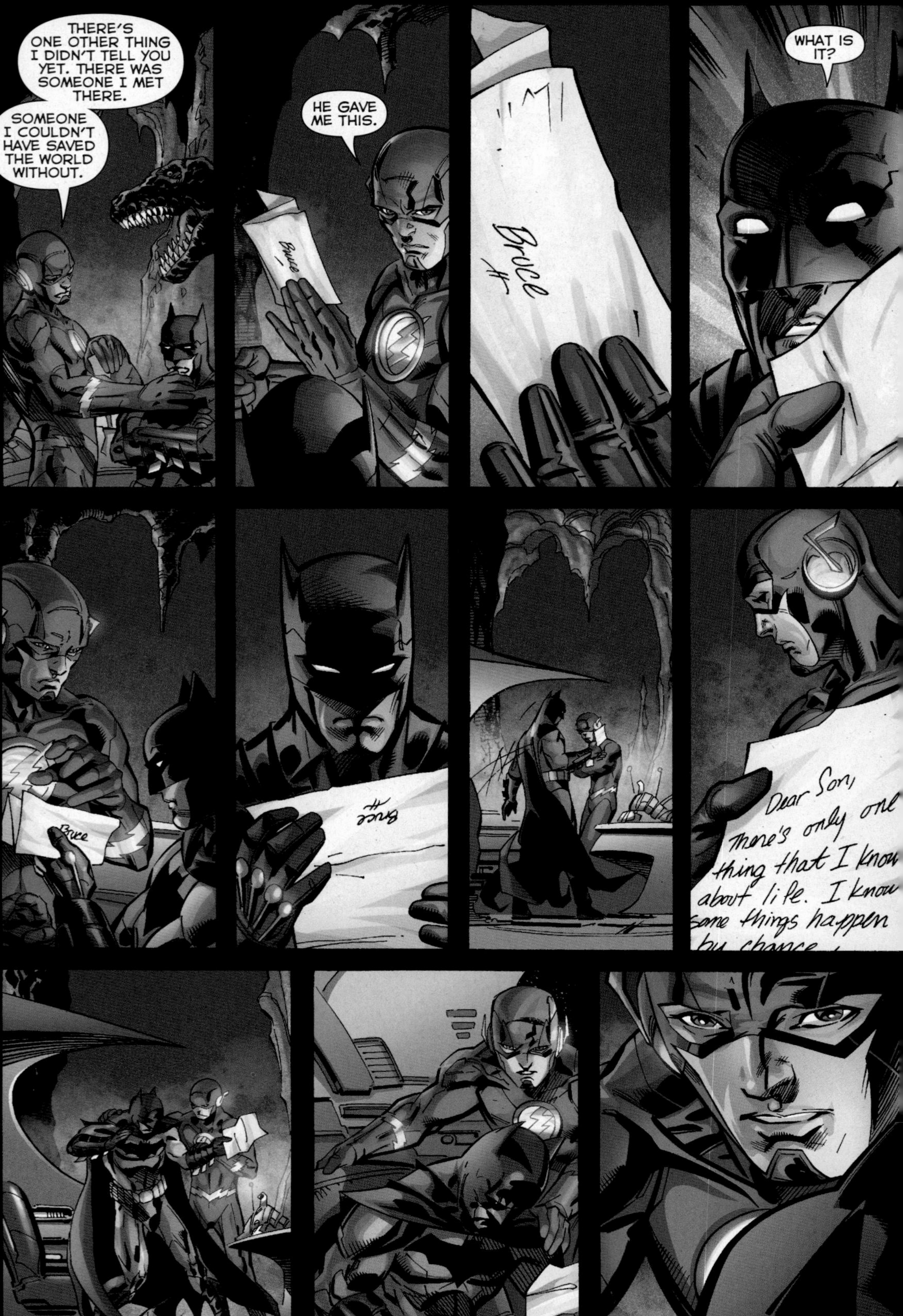
THERE'S ONE OTHER THING I DIDN'T TELL YOU YET. THERE WAS SOMEONE I MET THERE.
SOMEONE I COULDN'T HAVE SAVED THE WORLD WITHOUT.
HE GAVE ME THIS.
Bruce
WHAT IS IT?
Dear Son,
There's only one
thing that I know
about life. I know
some things happen

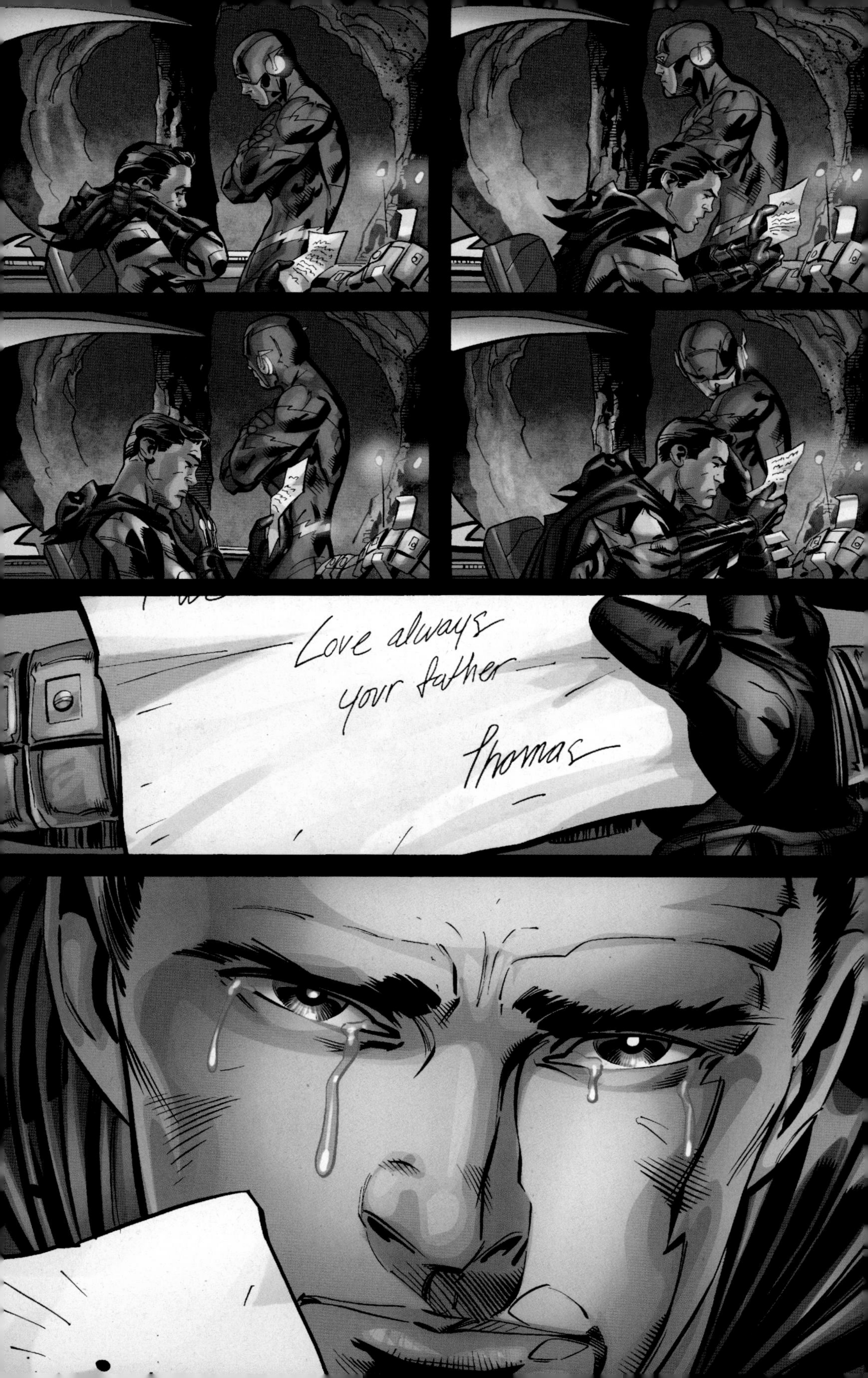
Love always
your father
Thomas

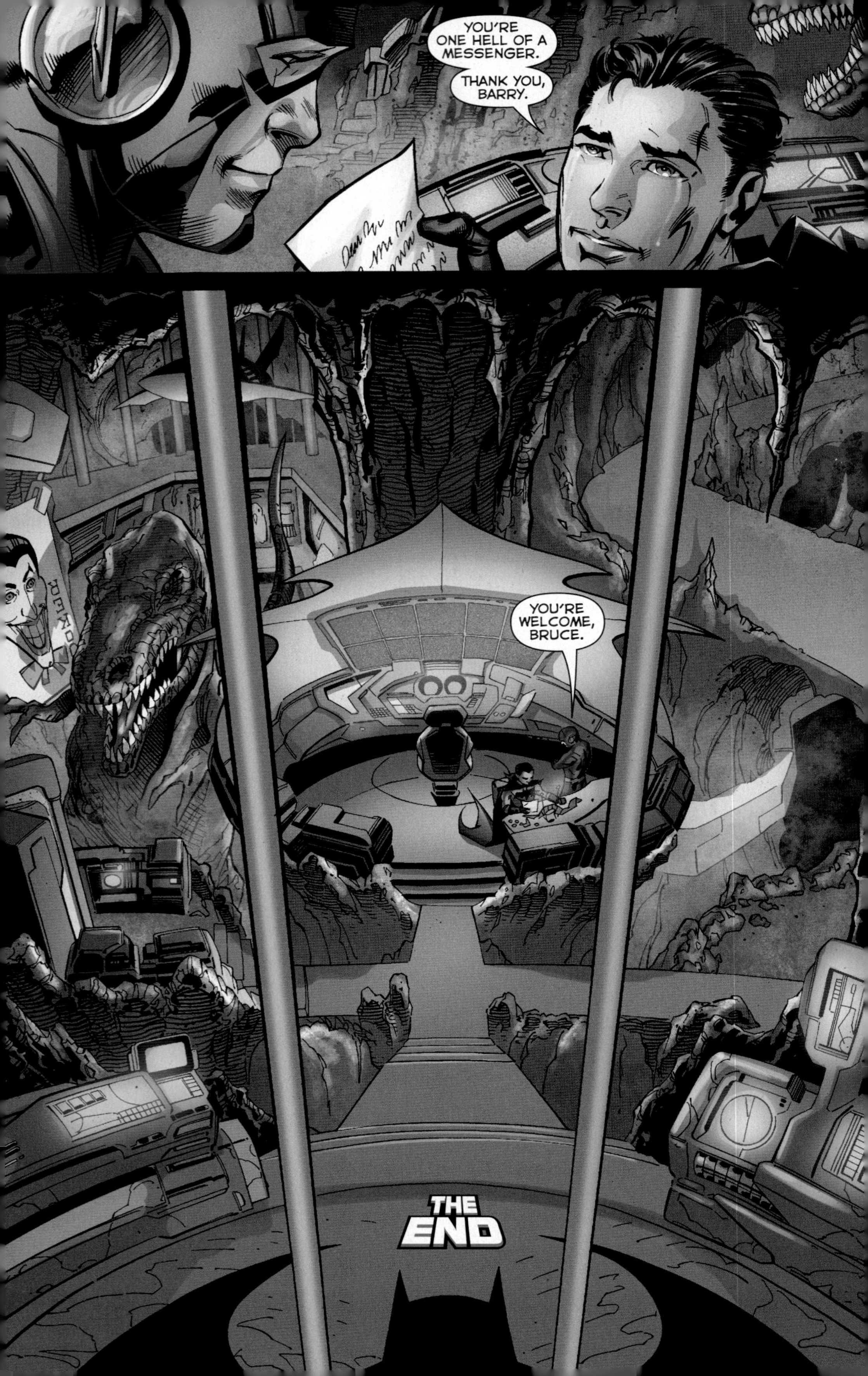
YOU'RE ONE HELL OF A MESSENGER.
THANK YOU, BARRY.
YOU'RE WELCOME, BRUCE.
THE END

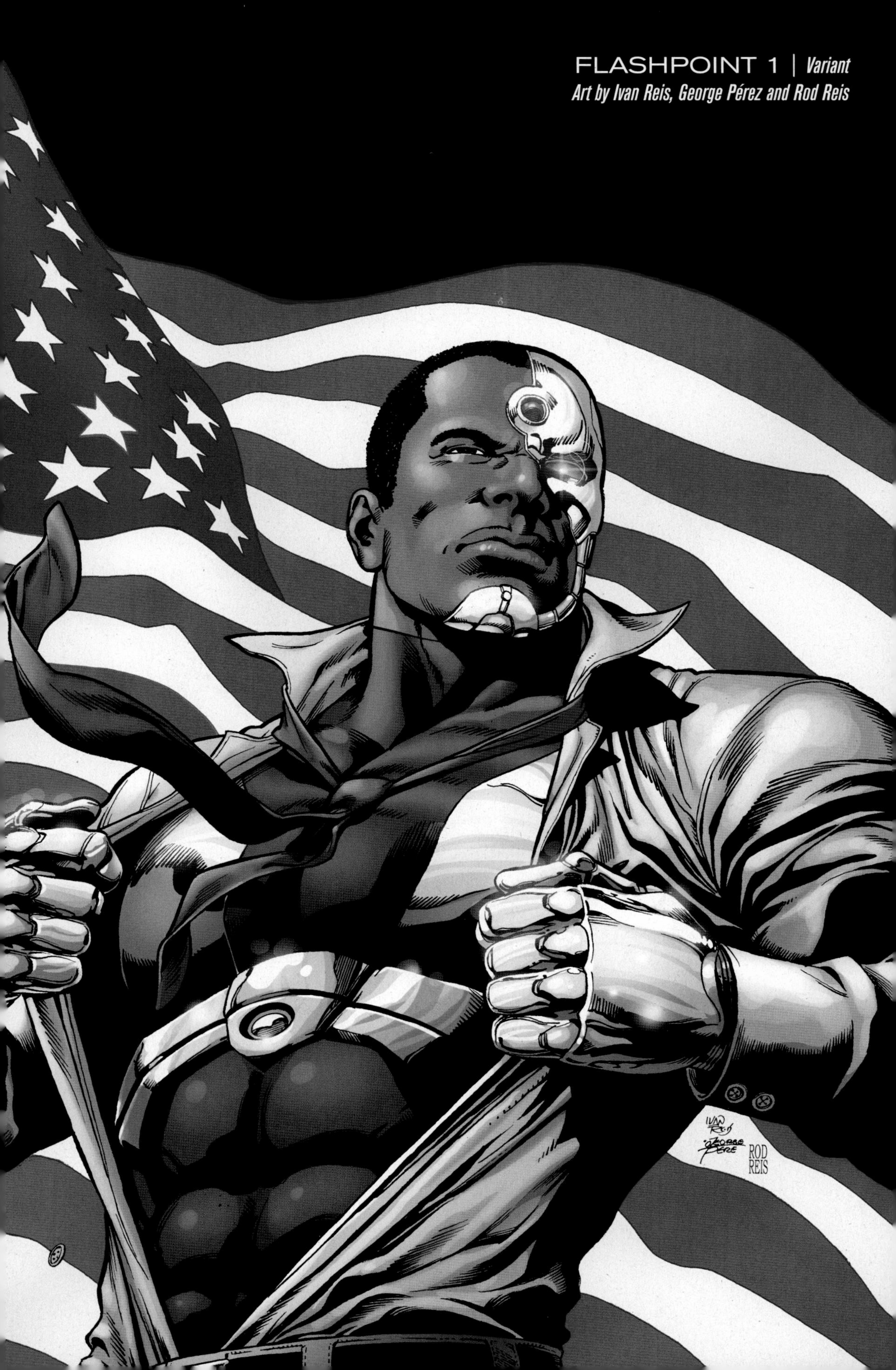
ROD
REIS

FLASHPOINT 1 | *Variant*

Art by Ivan Reis, George Pérez and Rod Reis

FLASHPOINT 1 |

Promotional Variant by Andy Kubert, Sandra Hope & Alex Sinclair

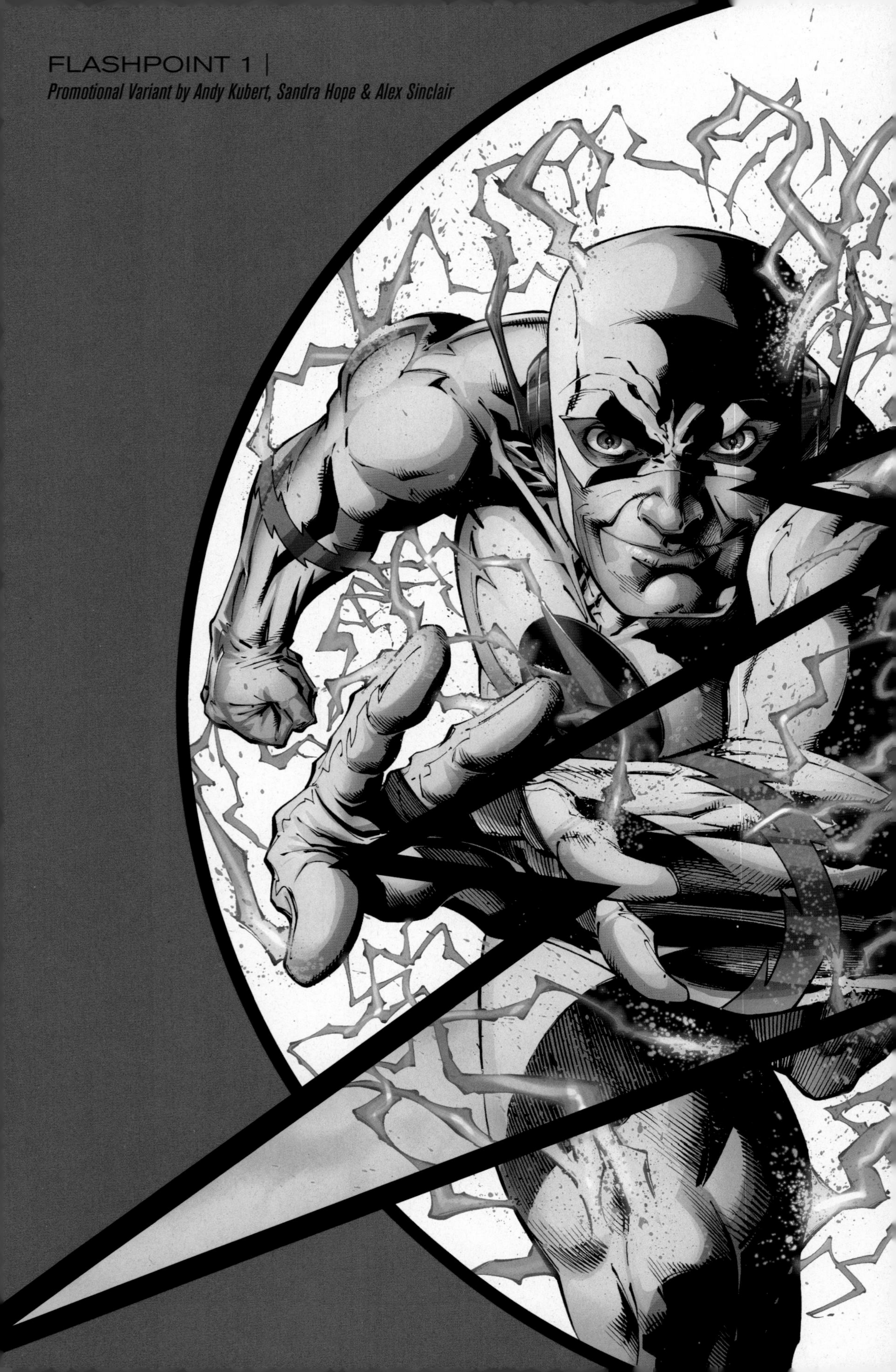

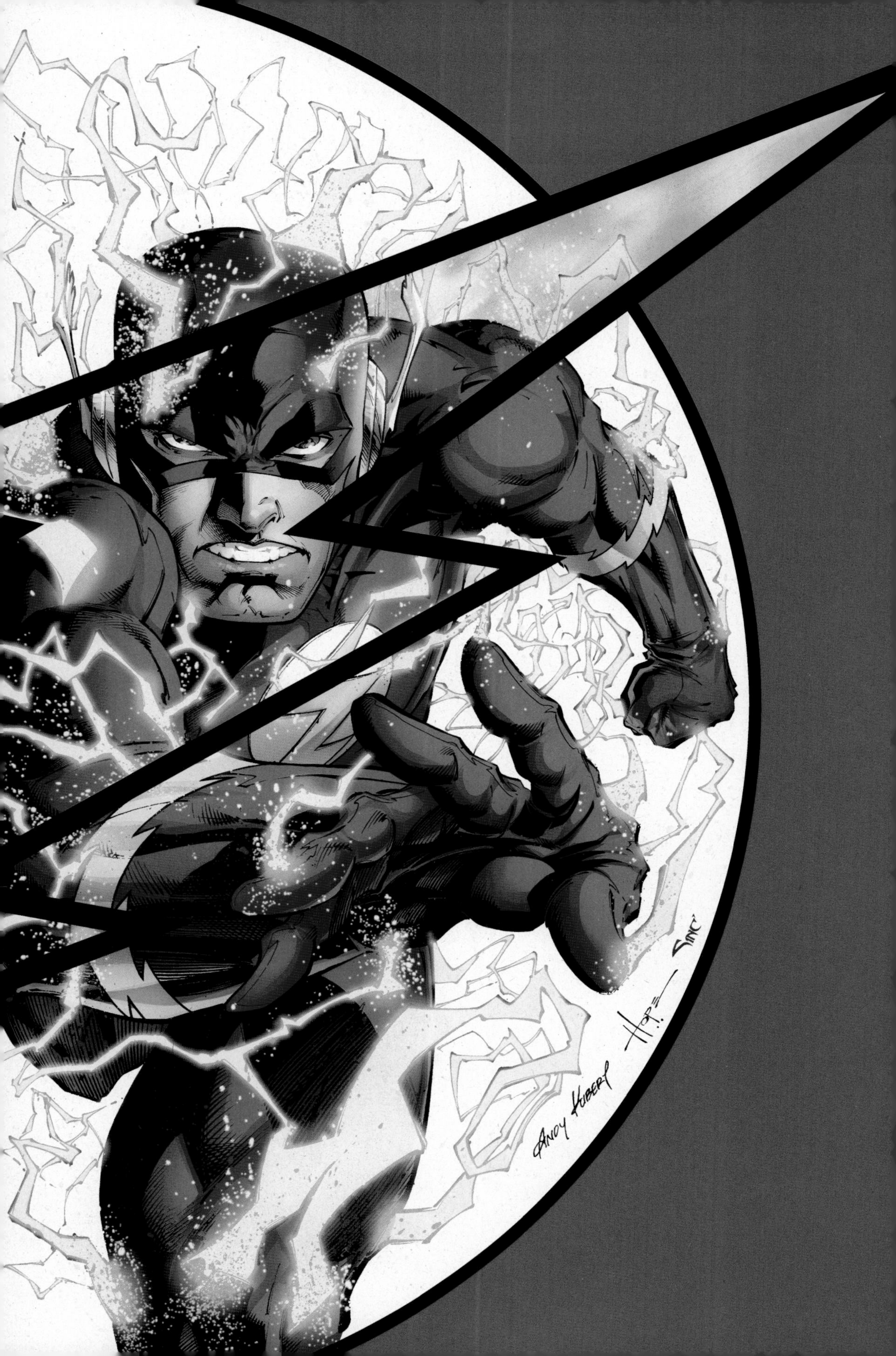
ANDY KUBERT

FLASHPOINT 2 | *Variant*
Art by Ivan Reis, George Pérez and Rod Reis

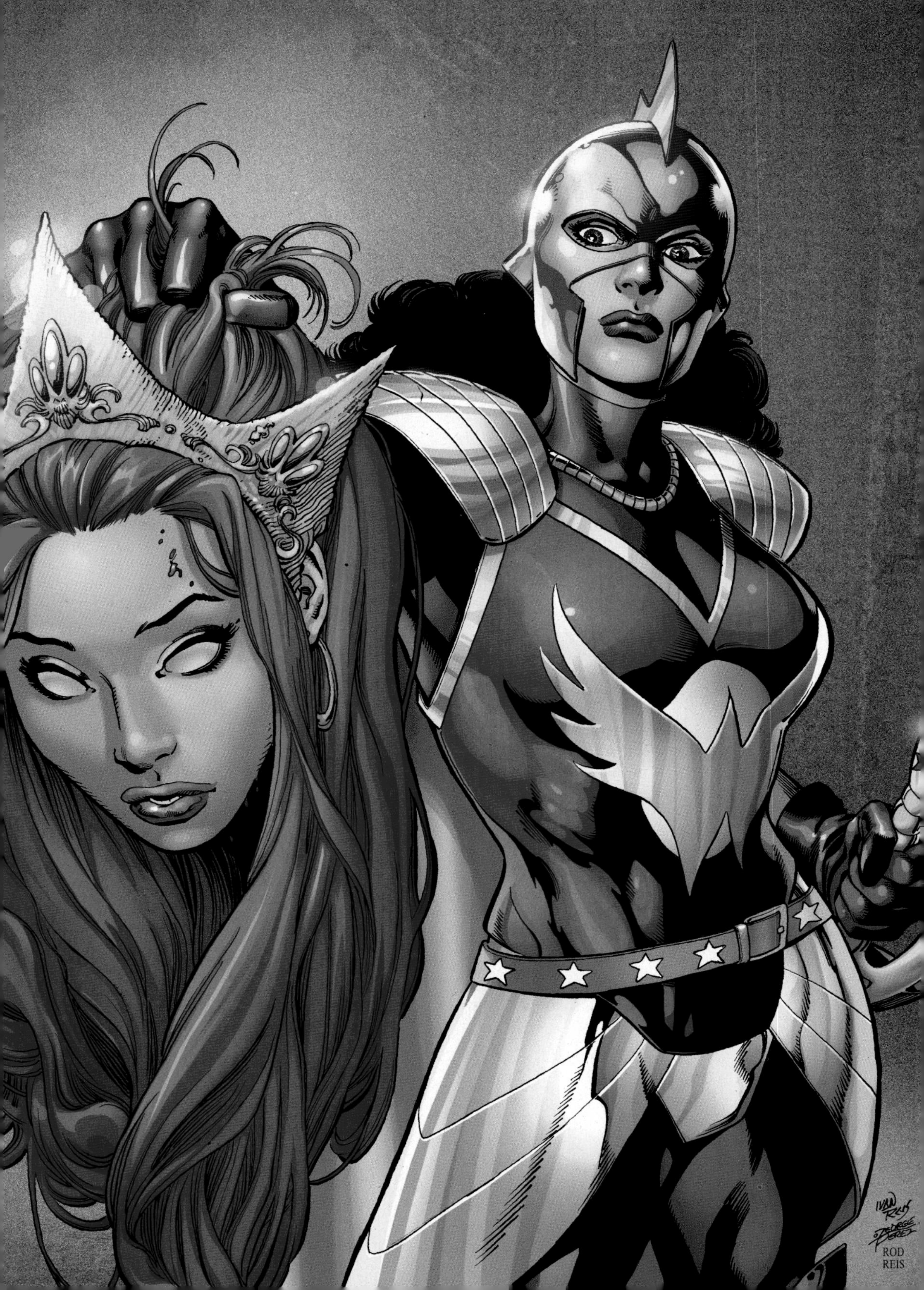
ROD
REIS

FLASHPOINT 3 | *Variant*

Art by Ivan Reis, George Pérez and Rod Reis

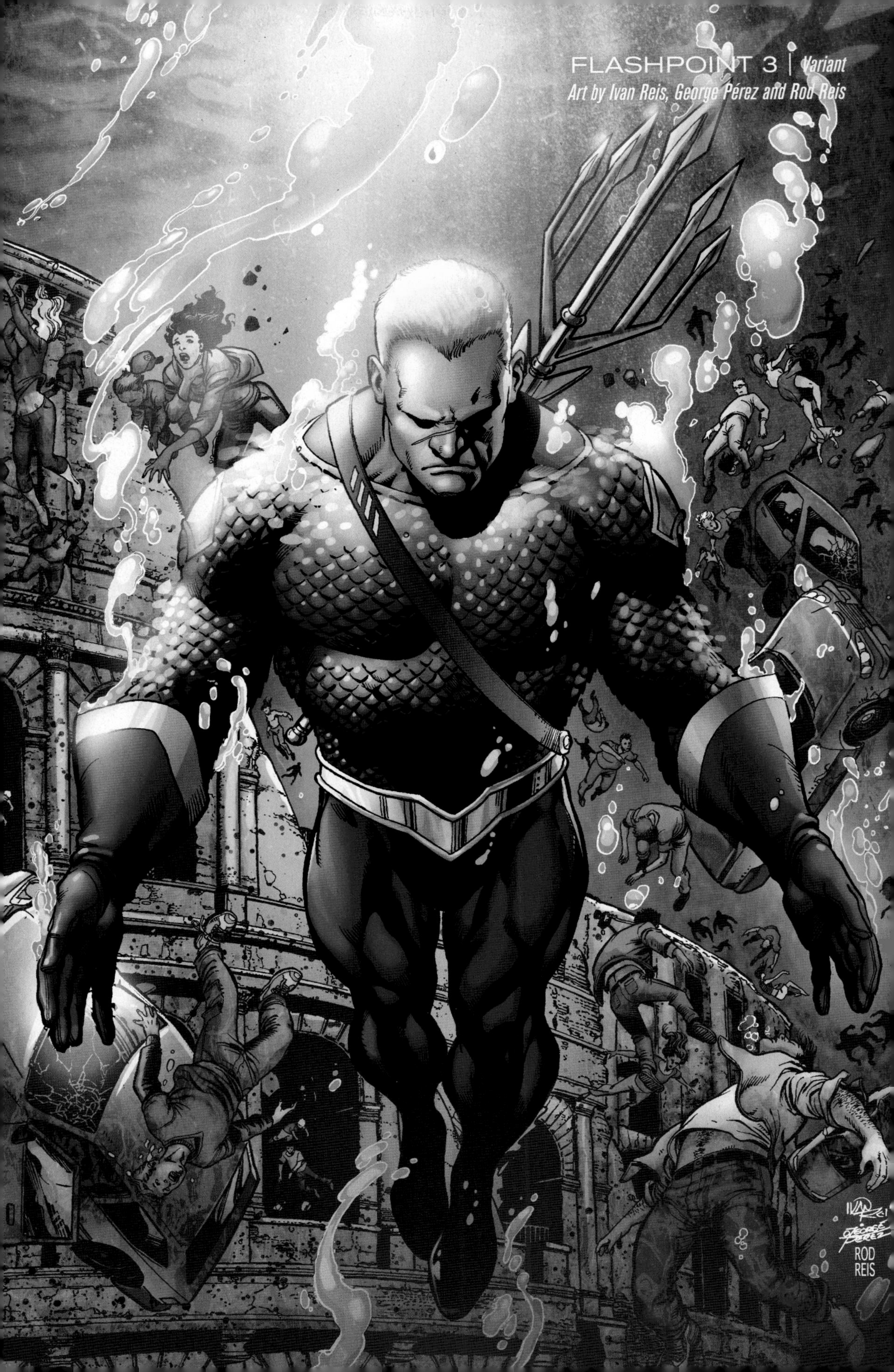
ROD
REIS

FLASHPOINT 4 | *Variant*

Art by Rags Morales and Nei Ruffino

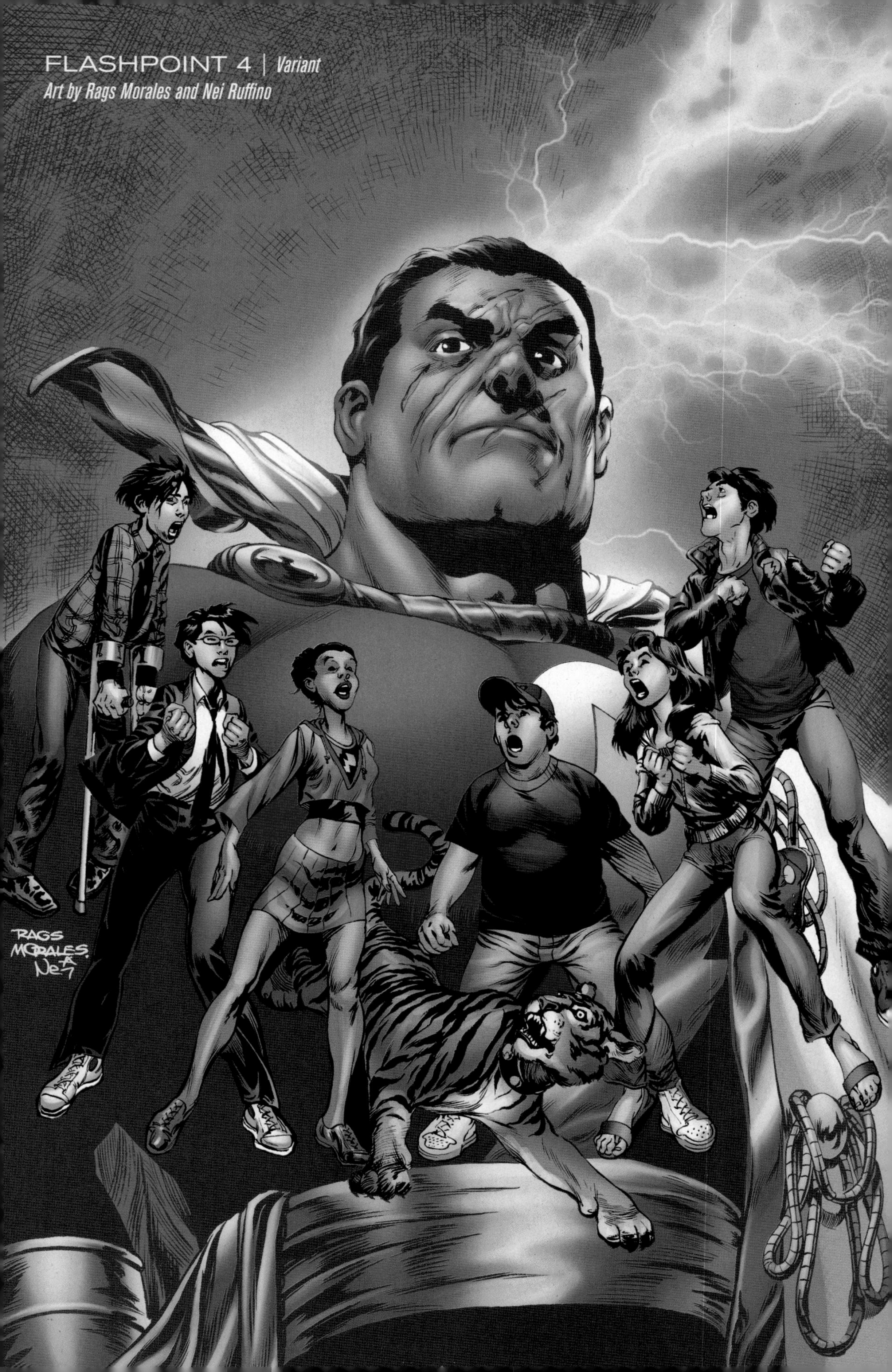
RAGS MORALES.

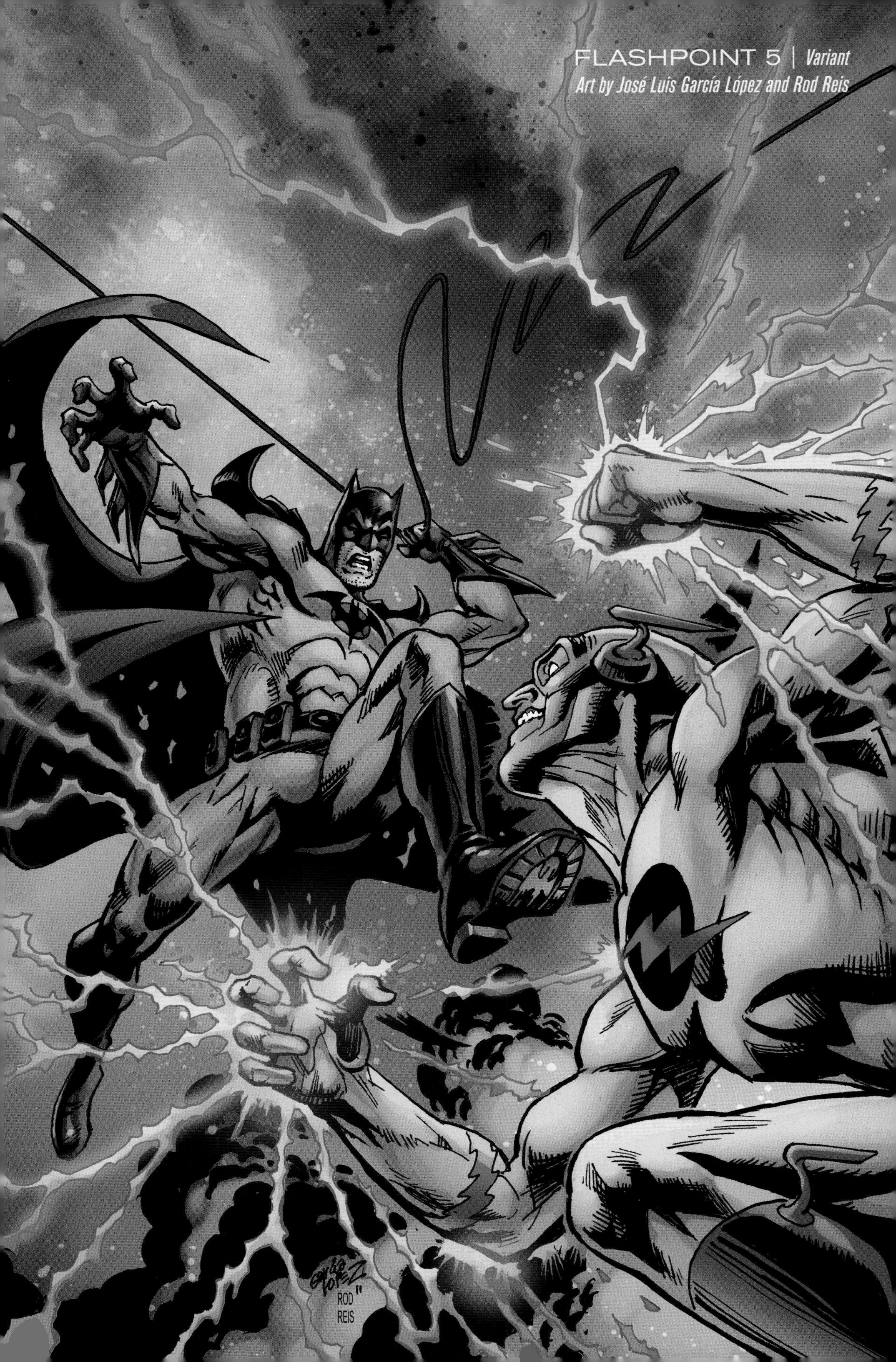
ROD
REIS

FLASHPOINT 5 | *Variant*

Art by José Luis García López and Rod Reis

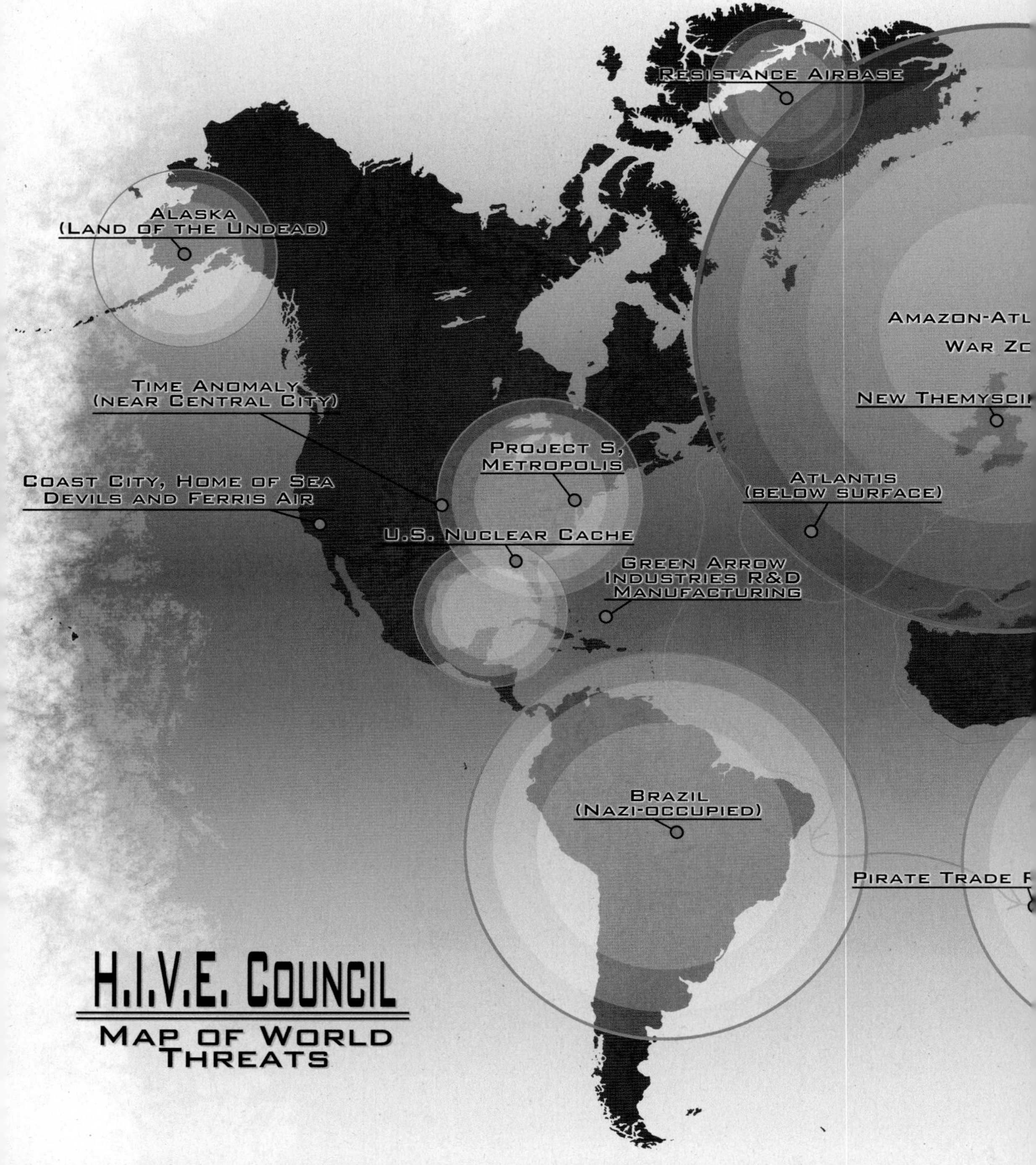
Resistance Airbase
Alaska (Land of the Undead)
Amazon-Atl
War Zo
Time Anomaly (near Central City)
New Themysci
Project S, Metropolis
Coast City, Home of Sea Devils and Ferris Air
Atlantis (below surface)
U.S. Nuclear Cache
Green Arrow Industries R&D Manufacturing
Brazil (Nazi-occupied)
Pirate Trade
H.I.V.E. Council
Map of World Threats

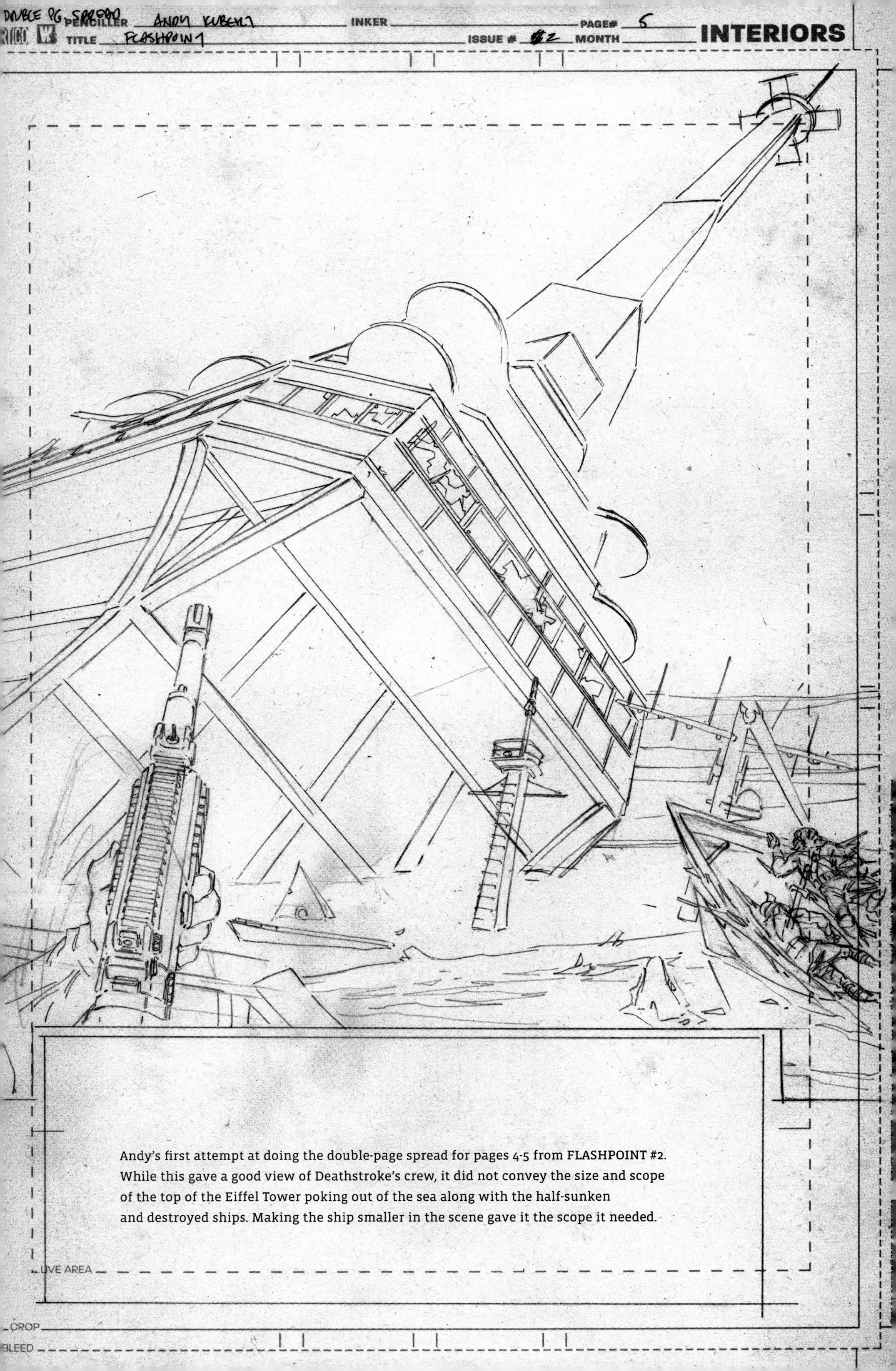
DOUBLE PG SPREAD
PENCILLER ANDY KUBERT
INKER
PAGE# 5
TITLE FLASHPOINT
ISSUE # #2
MONTH
INTERIORS

Andy's first attempt at doing the double-page spread for pages 4-5 from **FLASHPOINT #2**. While this gave a good view of Deathstroke's crew, it did not convey the size and scope of the top of the Eiffel Tower poking out of the sea along with the half-sunken and destroyed ships. Making the ship smaller in the scene gave it the scope it needed.

FLASH

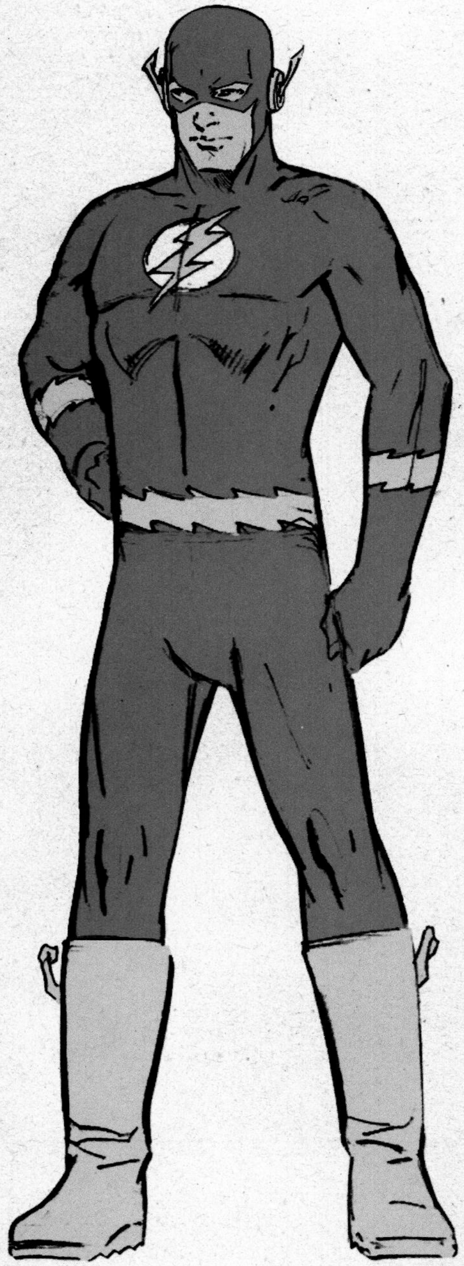

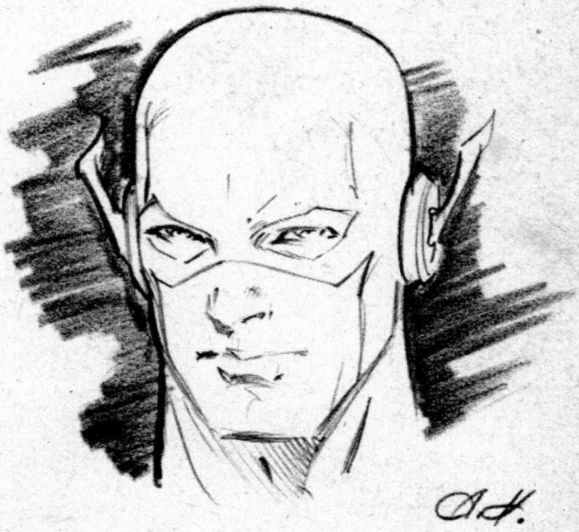

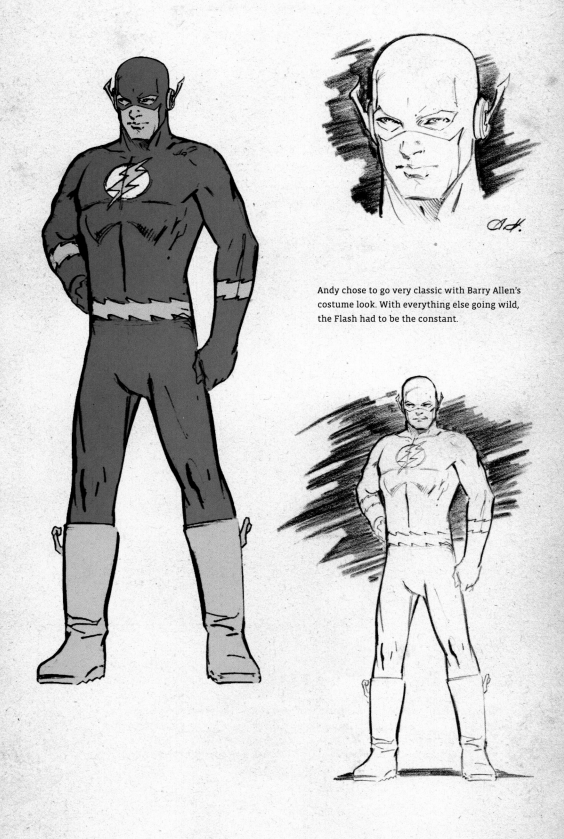

Andy chose to go very classic with Barry Allen's costume look. With everything else going wild, the Flash had to be the constant.

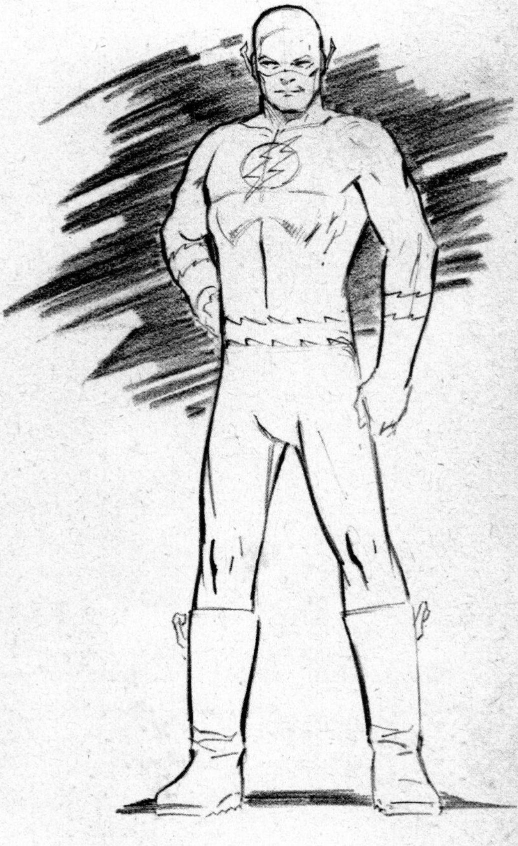

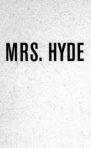

MRS. HYDE

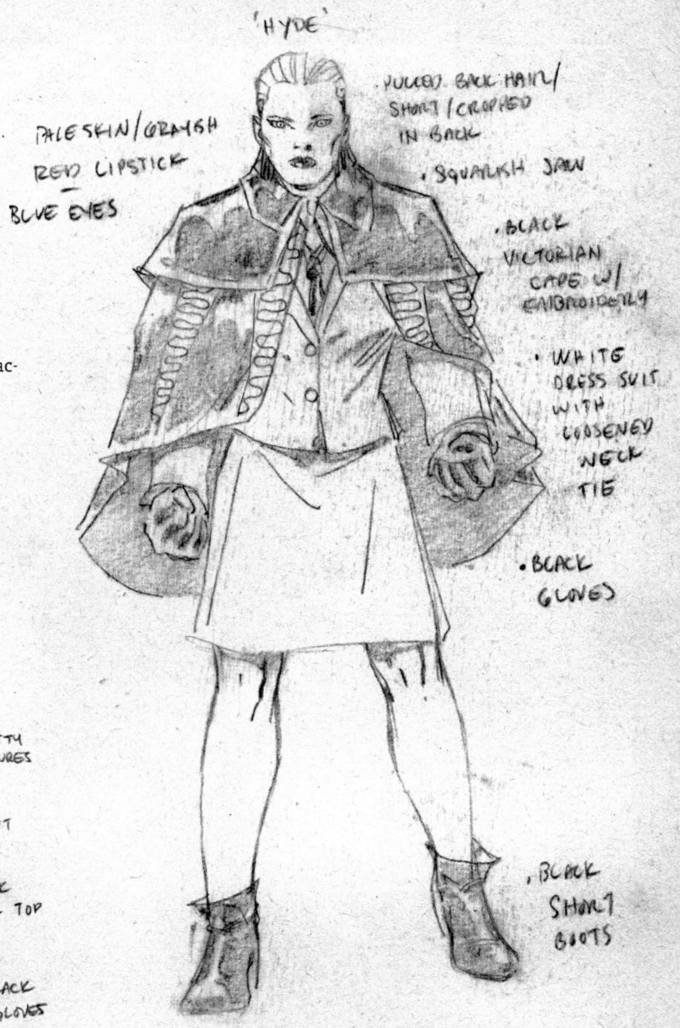
'HYDE'
PULLED BACK HAIR/ SHORT/CROPPED IN BACK
PALE SKIN/GRAYISH
RED LIPSTICK
BLUE EYES
SQUARISH JAW
BLACK VICTORIAN CAPE W/ EMBROIDERY
WHITE DRESS SUIT WITH LOOSENED NECK TIE
BLACK GLOVES
BLACK SHORT BOOTS

Two looks for Mrs. Hyde. Originally, the artist envisioned a more militaristic take on the character, but writer Geoff Johns wanted a more Victorian quality.

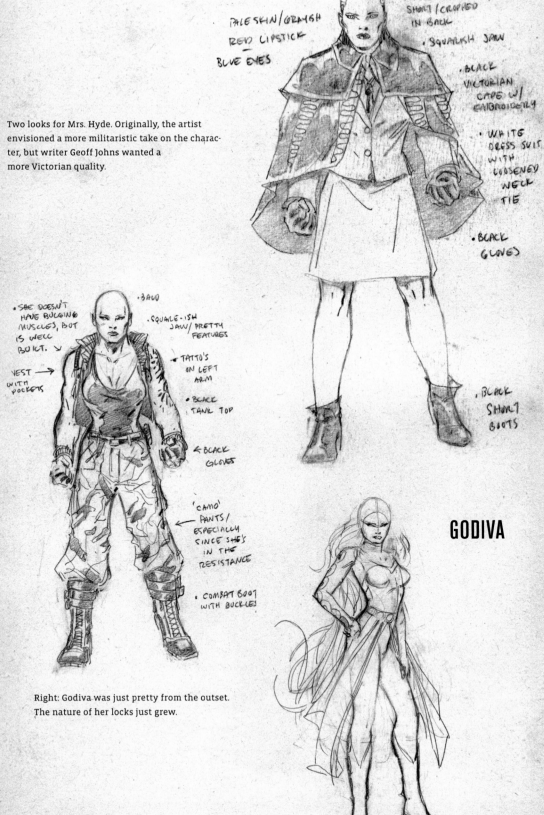

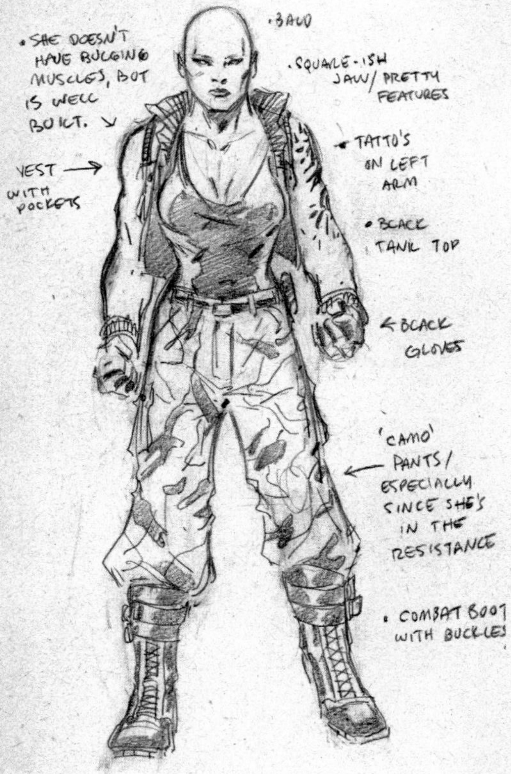
SHE DOESN'T HAVE BULGING MUSCLES, BUT IS WELL BUILT.
VEST WITH POCKETS
BALD
SQUARE-ISH JAW/ PRETTY FEATURES
TATTO'S ON LEFT ARM
BLACK TANK TOP
BLACK GLOVES
'CAMO' PANTS/ ESPECIALLY SINCE SHE'S IN THE RESISTANCE
COMBAT BOOT WITH BUCKLES

GODIVA

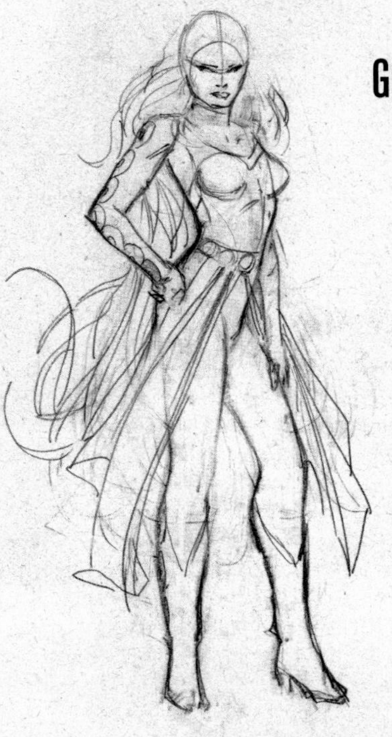

Right: Godiva was just pretty from the outset. The nature of her locks just grew.

AQUAMAN

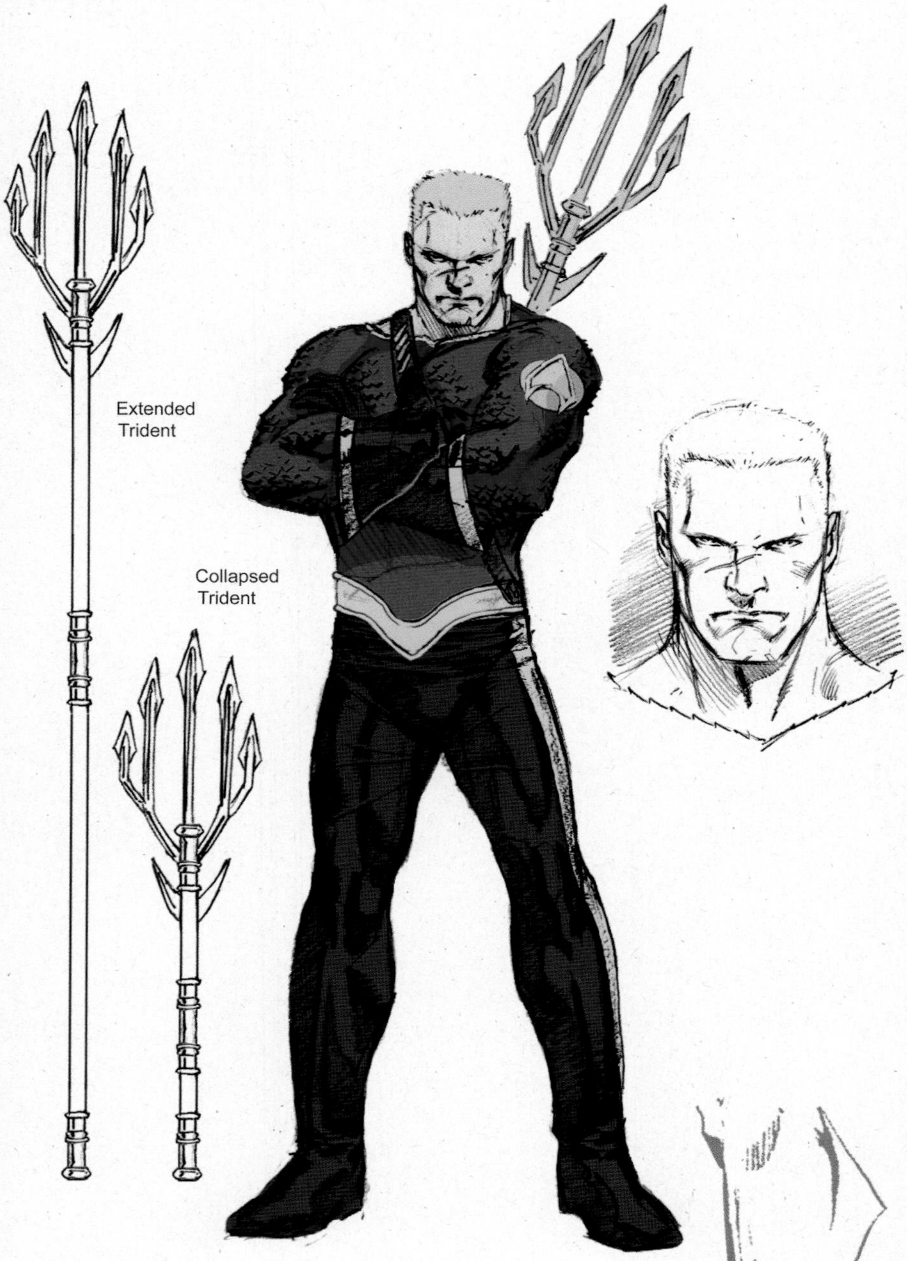
Extended
Trident
Collapsed
Trident

From the outset it was decided that this Arthur Curry would be a harsher Aquaman. Having no real interaction with the surface world or the Justice League would change his worldview. While his costume remained mostly intact, the marking on his tunic and stripe down his pants, coupled with a more severe hair cut and scar, gave him a more militaristic look. The red and black were a subtle reference to the original Aqualad character not seen in the series.

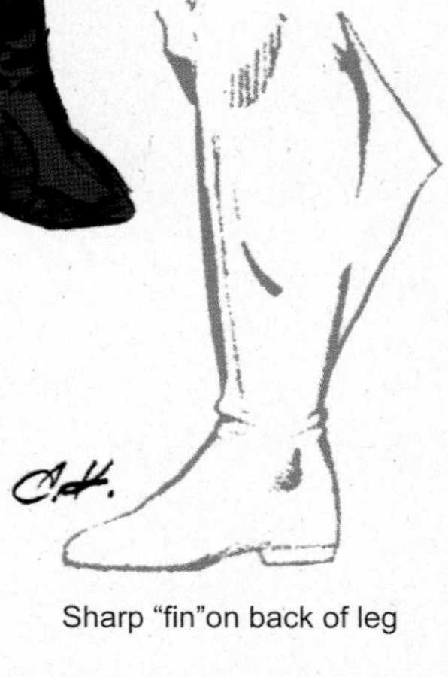

Sharp “fin”on back of leg

S!H!A!Z!A!M!

The SHAZAM kids gave Andy a chance to re-imagine a whole new Marvel family with new and familiar faces.

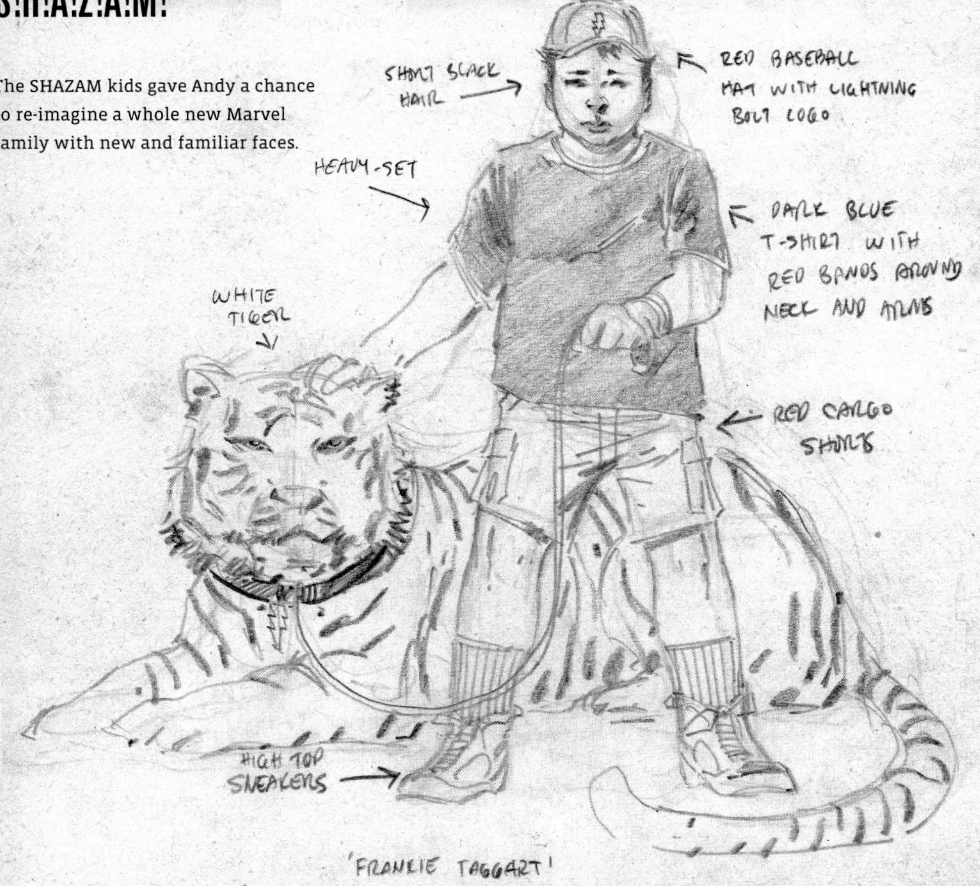

SHORT BLACK HAIR
RED BASEBALL HAT WITH LIGHTNING BOLT LOGO
HEAVY-SET
DARK BLUE T-SHIRT WITH RED BANDS AROUND NECK AND ARMS
WHITE TIGER
RED CARGO SHORTS
HIGH TOP SNEAKERS
'FRANKIE TAGGART'

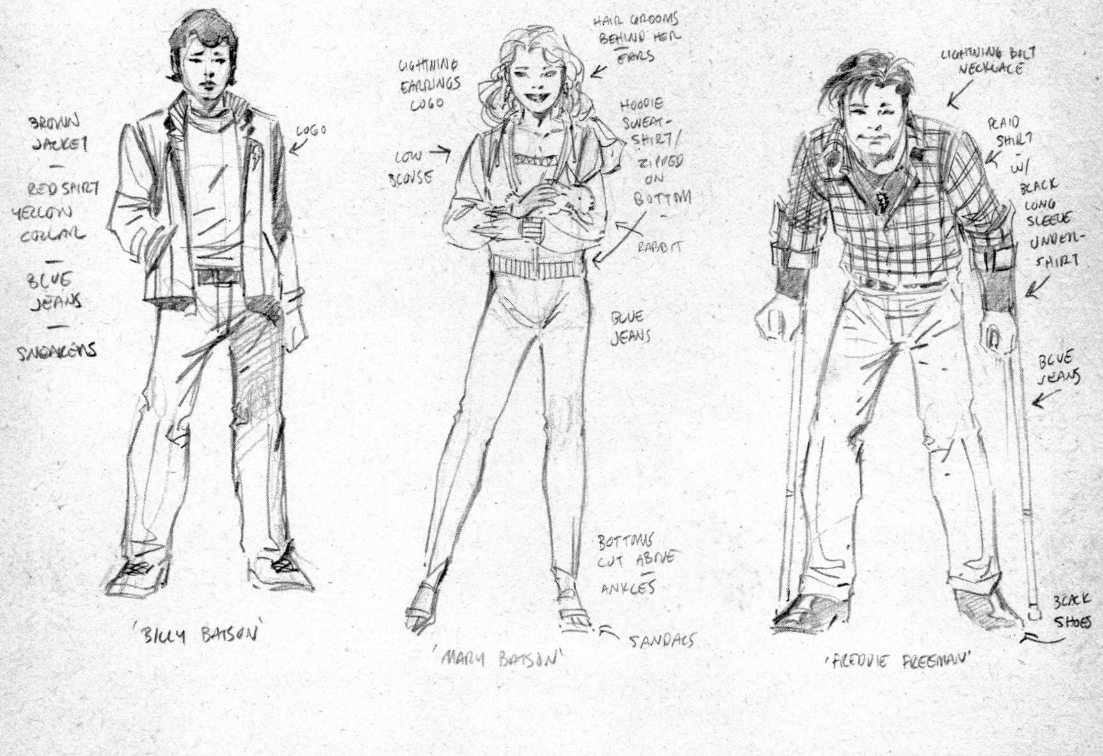

BROWN JACKET
RED SHIRT YELLOW COLLAR
BLUE JEANS
SNEAKERS
LOGO
'BILLY BATSON'
LIGHTNING EARRINGS LOGO
HAIR GROOMS BEHIND HER EARS
LOW BLOUSE
HOODIE SWEAT-SHIRT/ ZIPPED ON BOTTOM
RABBIT
BLUE JEANS
BOTTOMS CUT ABOVE ANKLES
SANDALS
'MARY BATSON'
LIGHTNING BOLT NECKLACE
PLAID SHIRT W/ BLACK LONG SLEEVE UNDER-SHIRT
BLUE JEANS
BLACK SHOES
'FREDDIE FREEMAN'

WONDER WOMAN

Wonder Woman represented an elegance coupled with razor-sharp deadliness. During her design the wicked idea came up that her helmet once belonged to Mera. How she got it would be one of the driving forces between her and Aquaman.

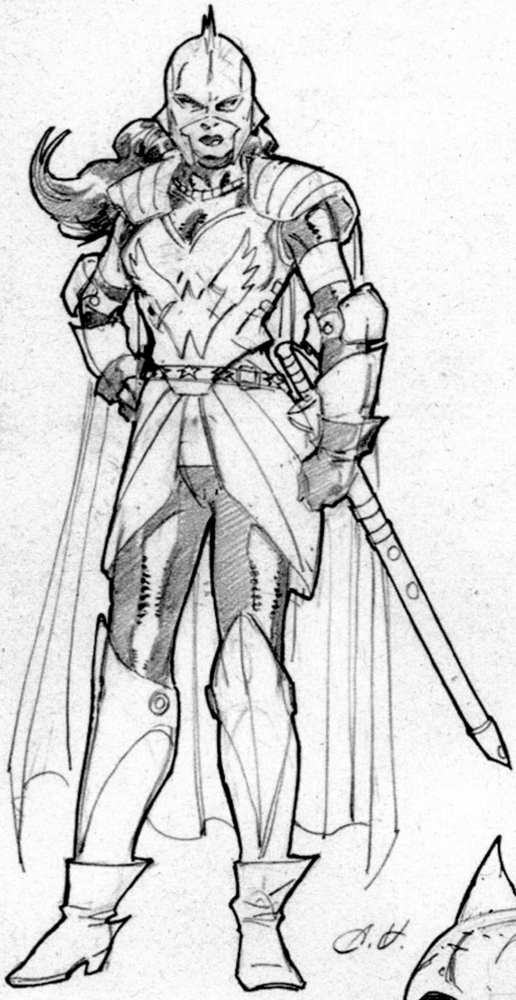

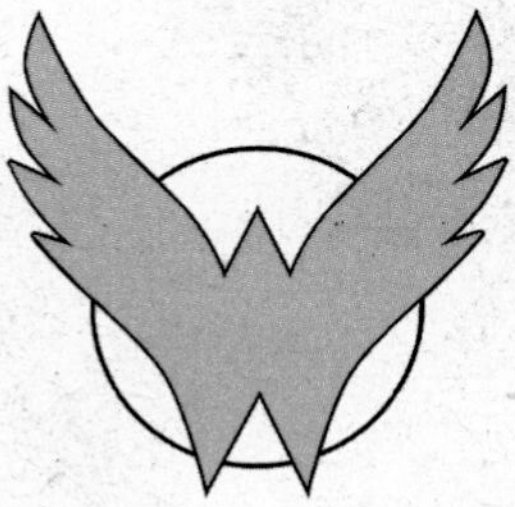

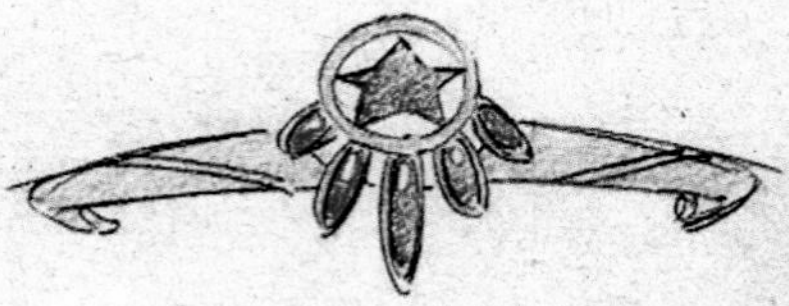

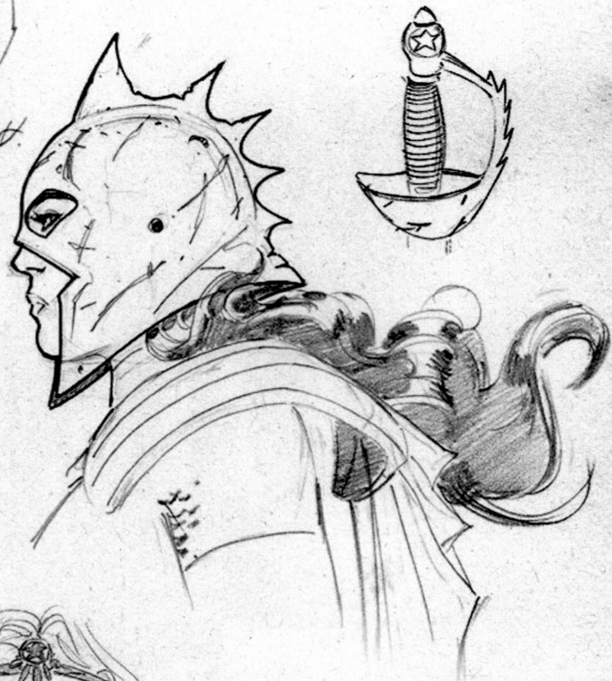

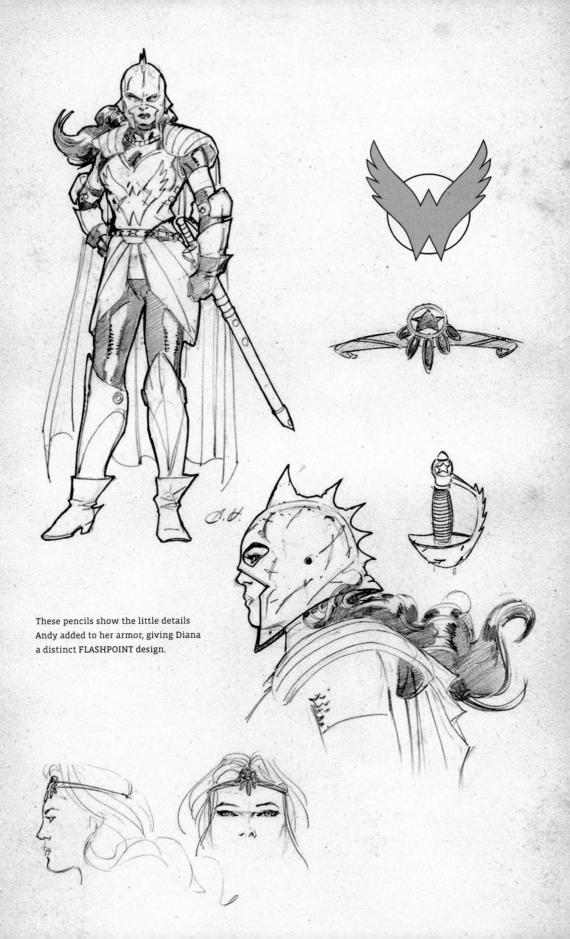

These pencils show the little details Andy added to her armor, giving Diana a distinct FLASHPOINT design.

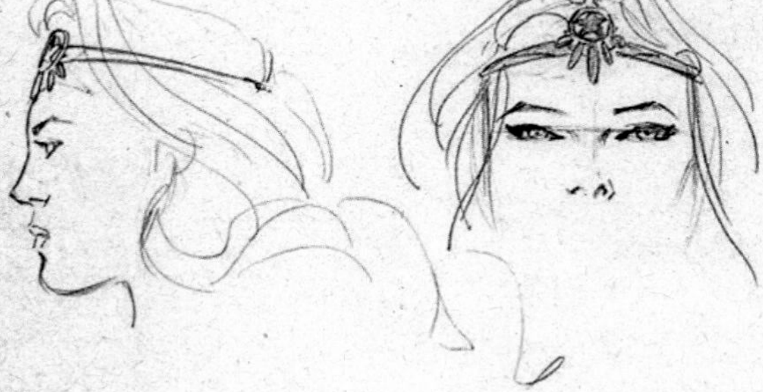

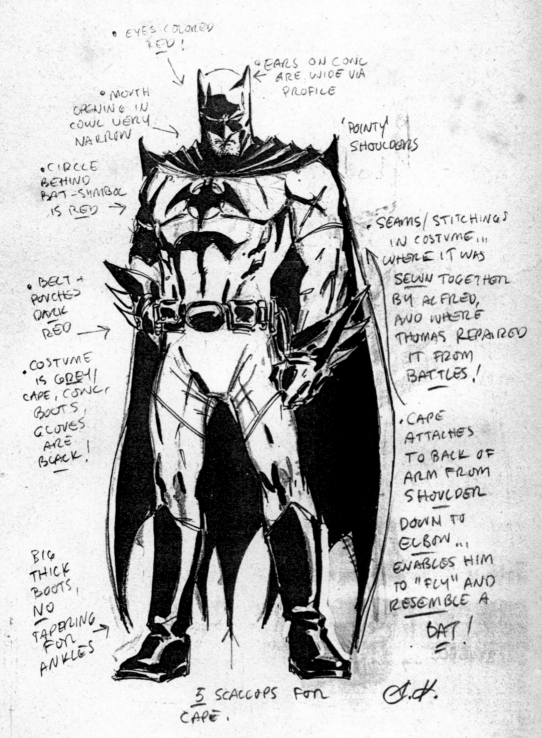

FLASHPOINT BATMAN

- EYES COLORED RED!

- EARS ON COWL ARE WIDE VIA PROFILE

- MOUTH OPENING IN COWL VERY NARROW

'POINTY' SHOULDERS

- CIRCLE BEHIND BAT-SYMBOL IS RED →

- SEAMS/ STITCHINGS IN COSTUME... WHERE IT WAS SEWN TOGETHER BY ALFRED, AND WHERE THOMAS REPAIRED IT FROM BATTLES!

- BELT + POUCHES DARK RED →

- COSTUME IS GREY! CAPE, COWL, BOOTS, GLOVES ARE BLACK!

- CAPE ATTACHES TO BACK OF ARM FROM SHOULDER DOWN TO ELBOW... ENABLES HIM TO "FLY" AND RESEMBLE A BAT!

BIG THICK BOOTS, NO TAPERING FOR ANKLES →

5 SCALLOPS FOR CAPE.

A.K.

On this page and the next we see how Andy evolved the concept of a classic 1940s original Batman into the look that Thomas Wayne would adopt as his own. In all our minds, this was Clint Eastwood as the Dark Knight.

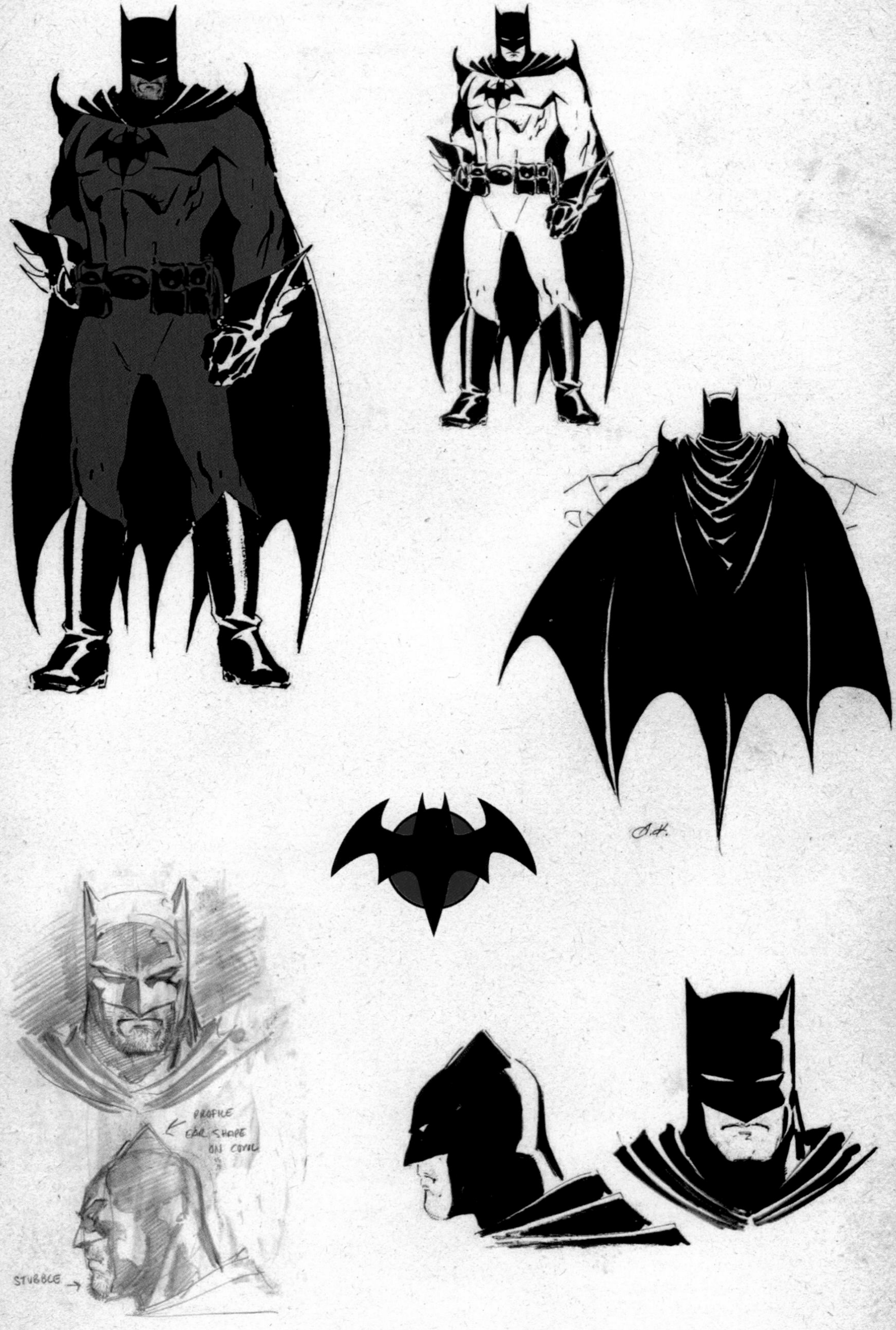

PROFILE EAR SHAPE ON COWL
STUBBLE

SUPERMAN

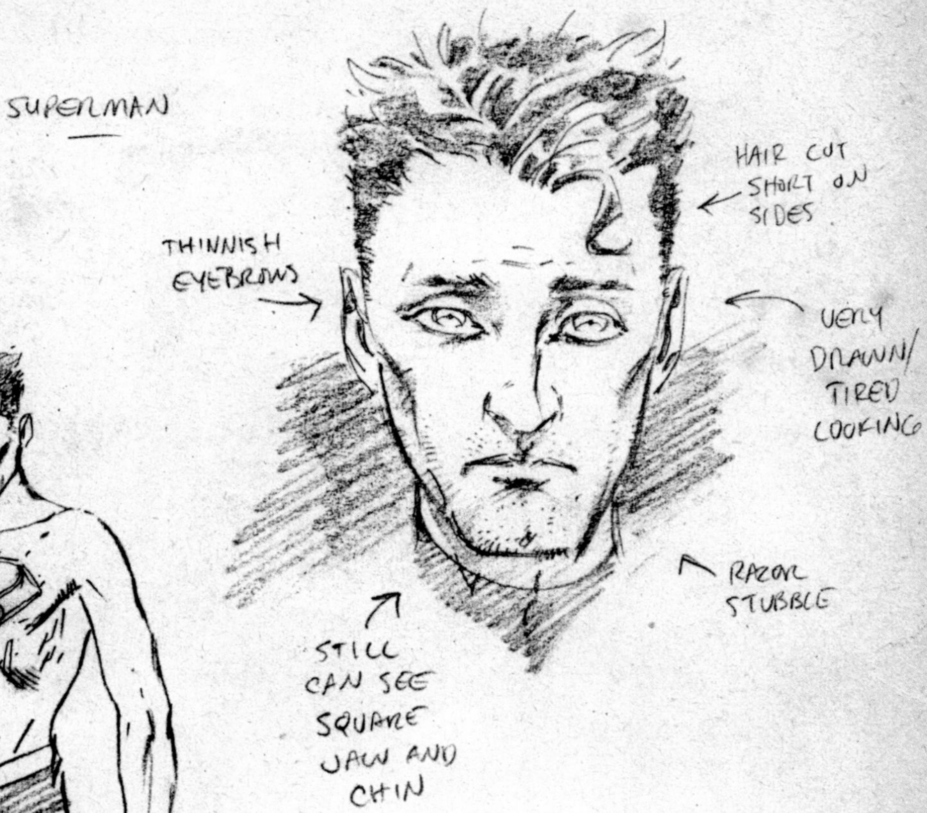
SUPERMAN
HAIR CUT SHORT ON SIDES
THINNISH EYEBROWS
VERY DRAWN/ TIRED LOOKING
RAZOR STUBBLE
STILL CAN SEE SQUARE JAW AND CHIN

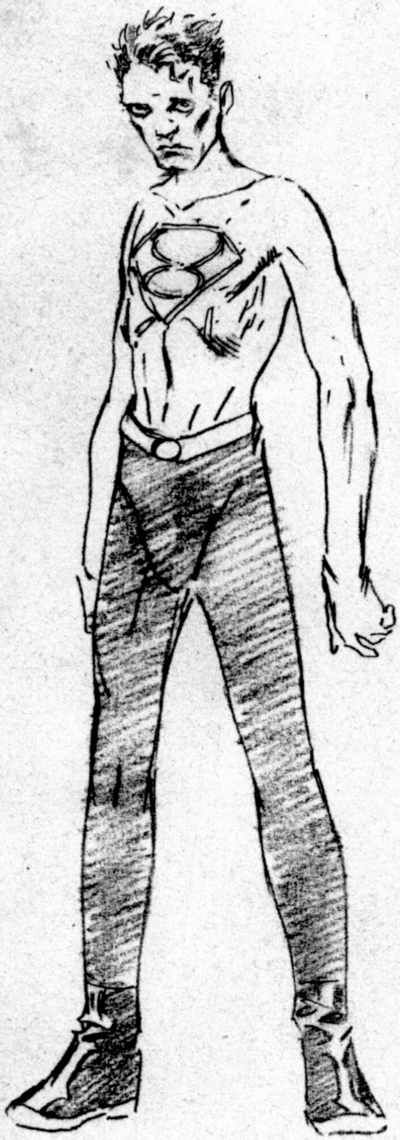

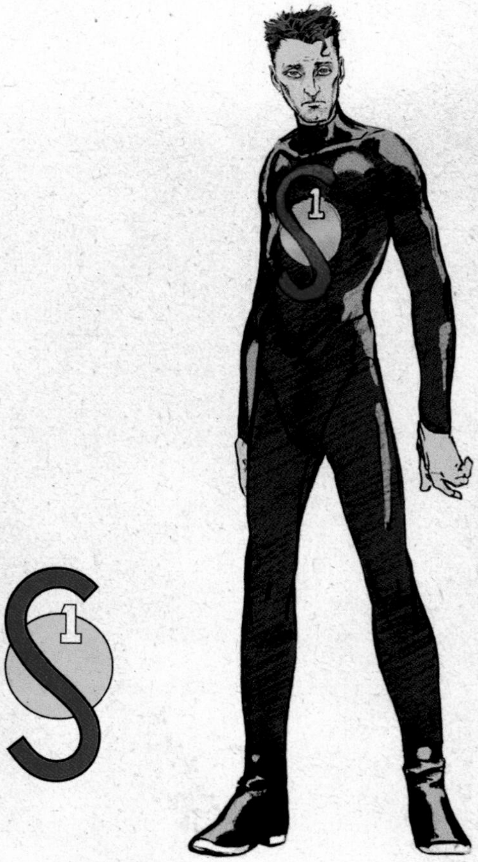
1

When it came to Superman, you could not have gone more different. Writer Geoff Johns really had an isolated and meek Kryptonian imprisoned on Earth and Andy masterfully realized it. Kal's eyes say it all.

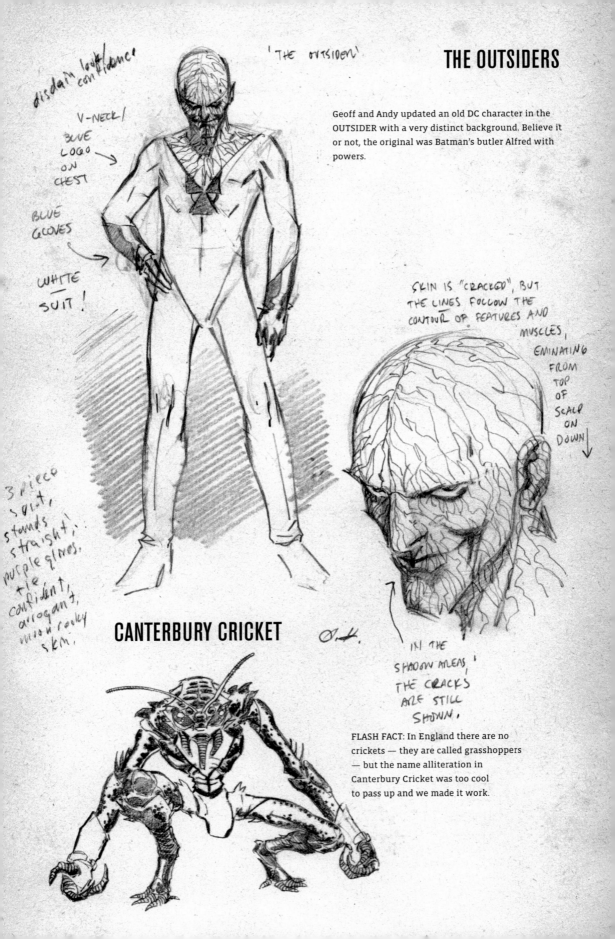

THE OUTSIDERS

Geoff and Andy updated an old DC character in the OUTSIDER with a very distinct background. Believe it or not, the original was Batman's butler Alfred with powers.

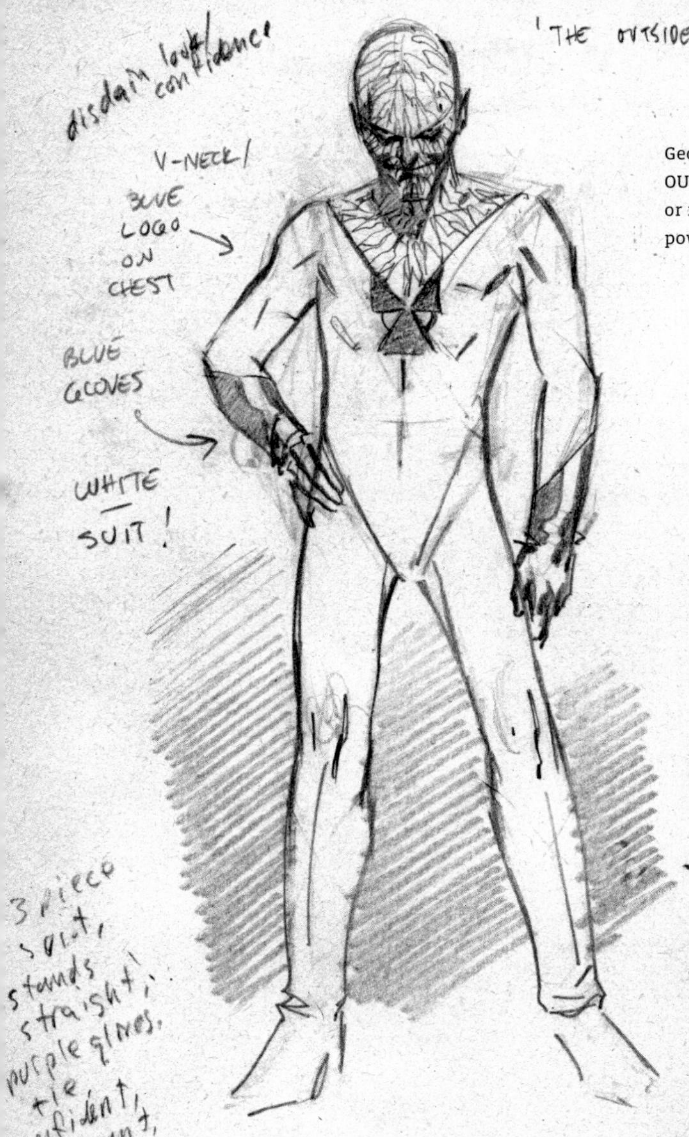
'THE OUTSIDER'
disdain look/confidence
V-NECK/
BLUE LOGO ON CHEST
BLUE GLOVES
WHITE SUIT!
3 piece suit, stands straight, purple gloves, tie
confident, arrogant,

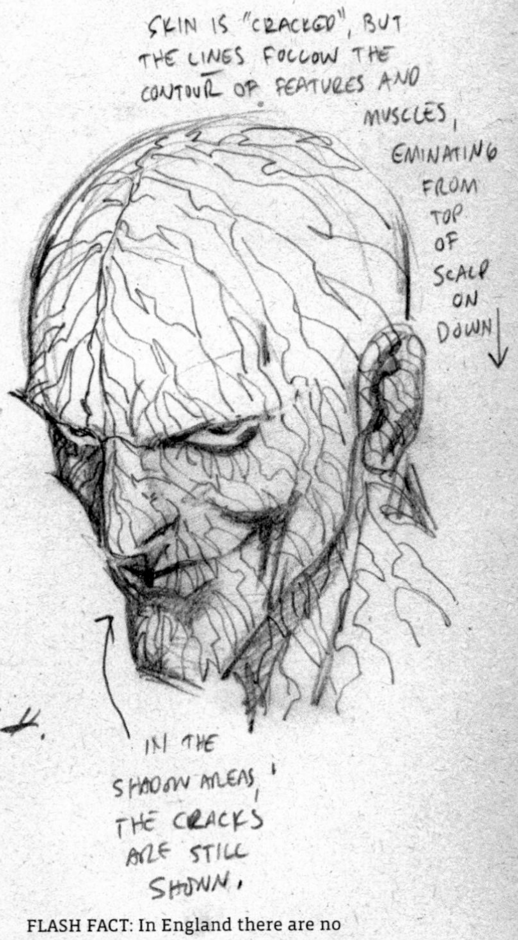
SKIN IS "CRACKED", BUT THE LINES FOLLOW THE CONTOUR OF FEATURES AND MUSCLES, EMINATING FROM TOP OF SCALP ON DOWN
IN THE SHADOW AREAS, THE CRACKS ARE STILL SHOWN.

CANTERBURY CRICKET

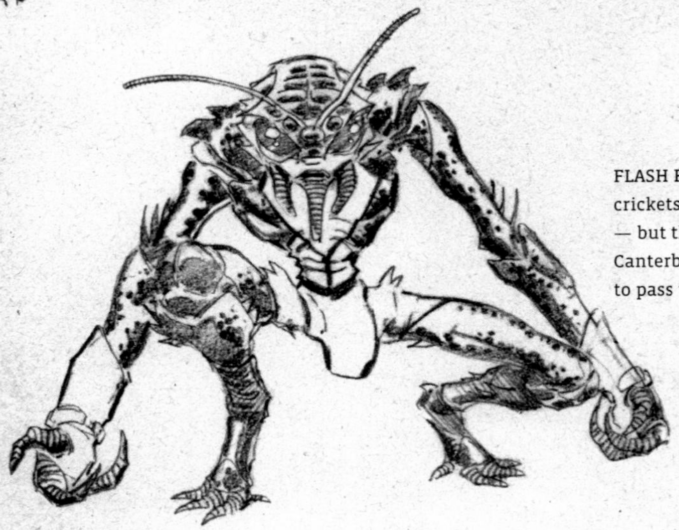

FLASH FACT: In England there are no crickets — they are called grasshoppers — but the name alliteration in Canterbury Cricket was too cool to pass up and we made it work.

CYBORG

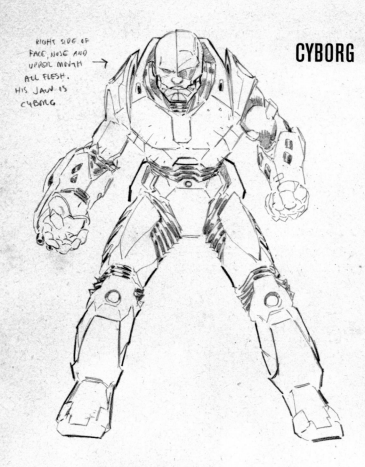

RIGHT SIDE OF FACE, NOSE AND UPPER MOUTH ALL FLESH. HIS JAW IS CYBORG

CYBORG SYMBOL

Coming out of FLASHPOINT, Geoff really wanted to raise the profile of long-time Titan Cyborg. Andy tried variations on his armor to keep in mind Geoff's notion that he is a walking tank. We toyed with the idea of giving him an emblem but eventually abandoned it.

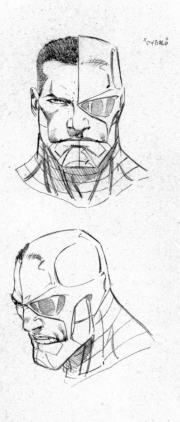

"CYBORG"

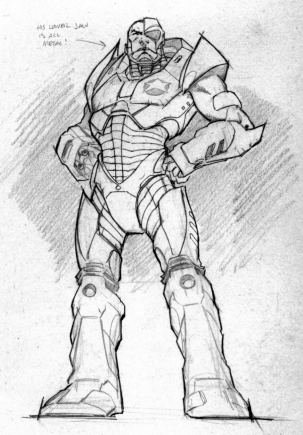

HIS LOWER JAW IS ALL METAL!

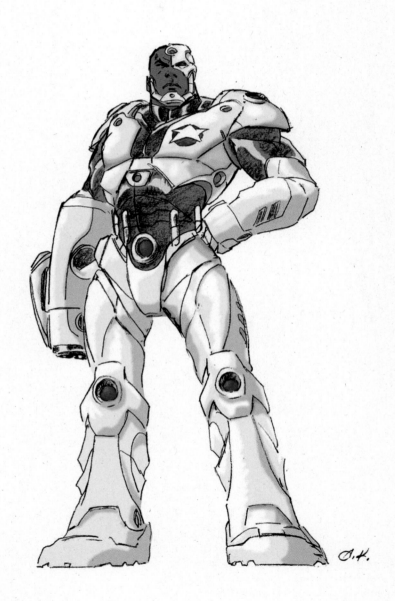

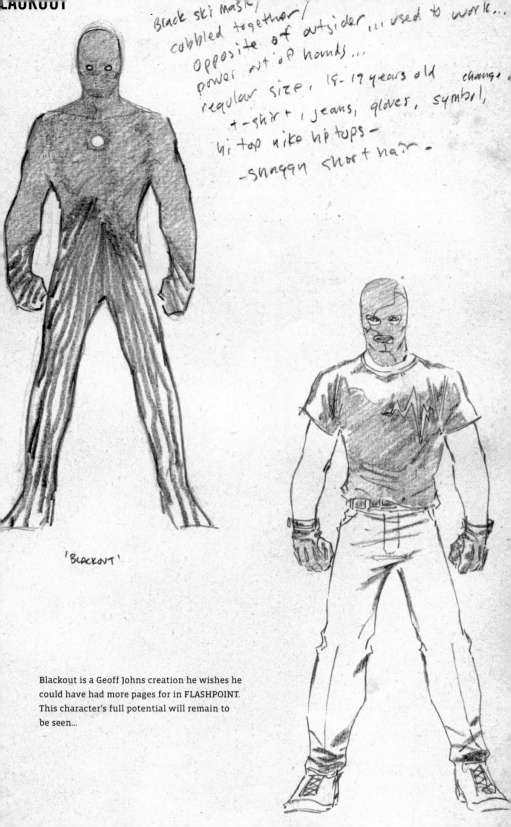

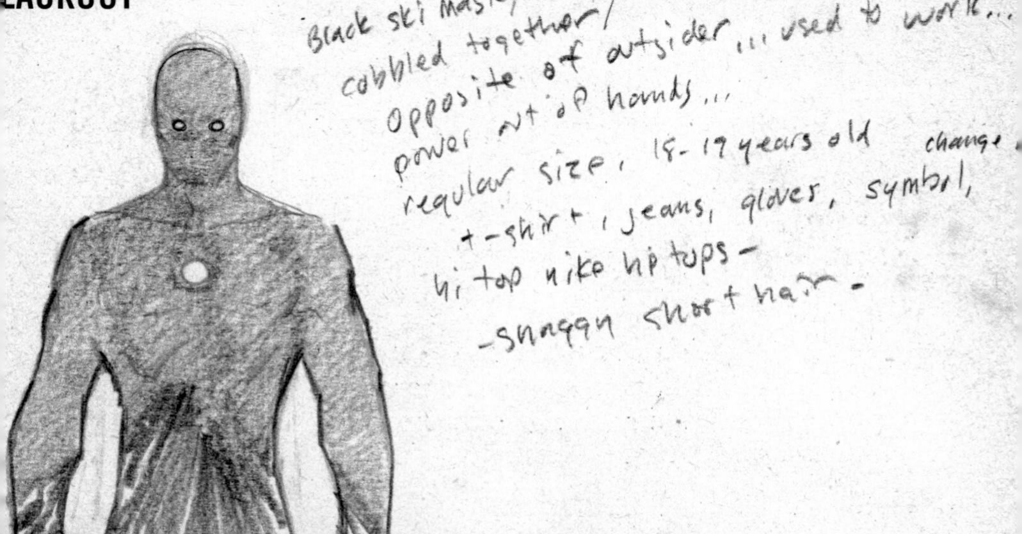
Black ski mask/
cobbled together/
opposite of outsider ... used to work...
power out of hands...
regular size, 18-19 years old change,
t-shirt, jeans, gloves, symbol,
hi top nike hi tops -
-shaggy short hair -
'BLACKOUT'

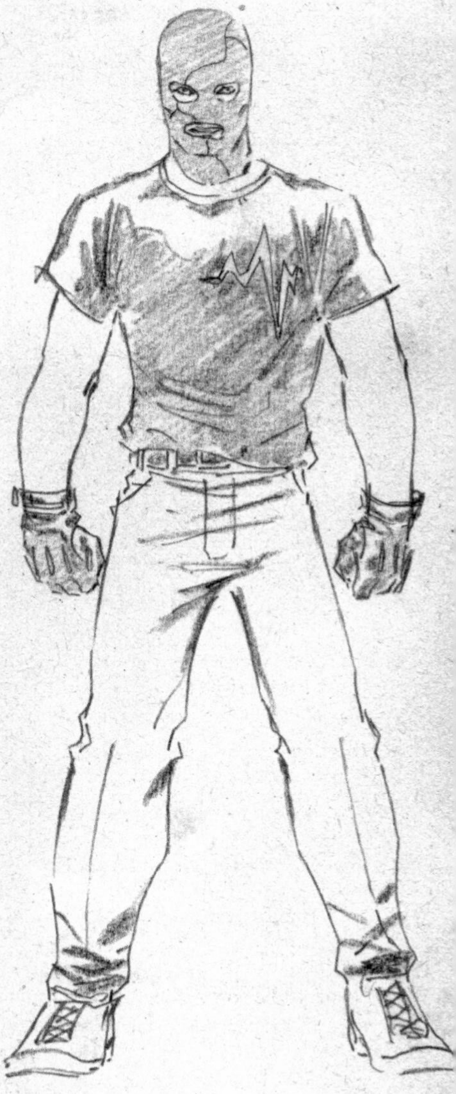

Blackout is a Geoff Johns creation he wishes he could have had more pages for in FLASHPOINT. This character's full potential will remain to be seen...

SANDMAN

Sandman is not a well man, having seen or dreamt that all his friends died. He is encased in a walking life-support suit.

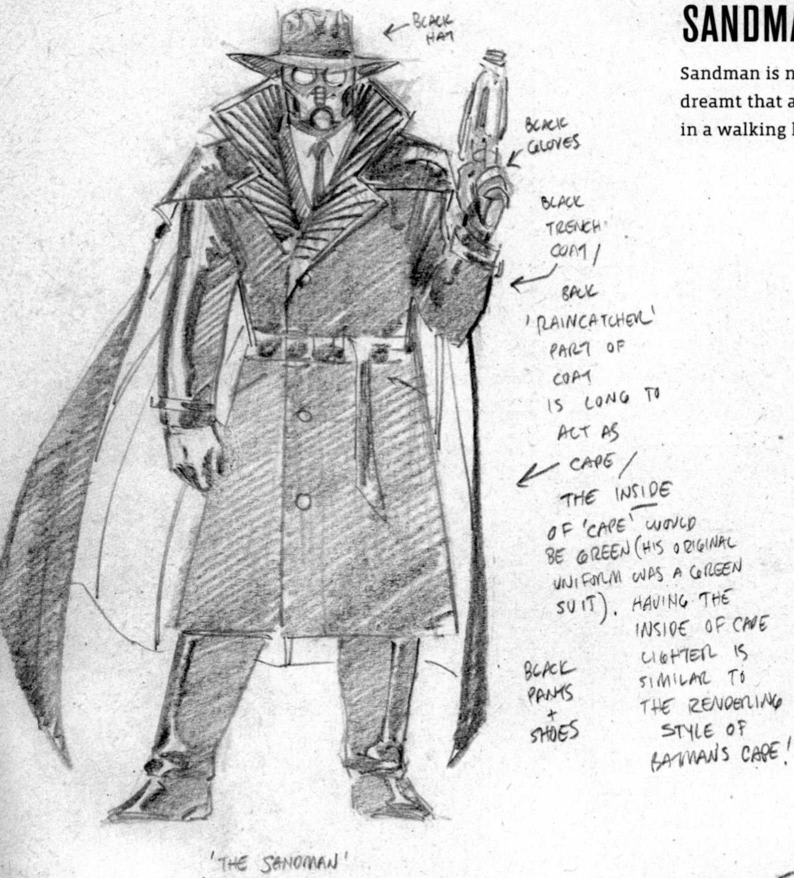
BLACK HAT
BLACK GLOVES
BLACK TRENCH COAT / BACK 'RAINCATCHER' PART OF COAT IS LONG TO ACT AS CAPE / THE INSIDE OF 'CAPE' WOULD BE GREEN (HIS ORIGINAL UNIFORM WAS A GREEN SUIT). HAVING THE INSIDE OF CAPE LIGHTER IS SIMILAR TO THE RENDERING STYLE OF BATMAN'S CAPE!
BLACK PANTS + SHOES
'THE SANDMAN'

GODIVA

Yet another more refined view of Godiva.

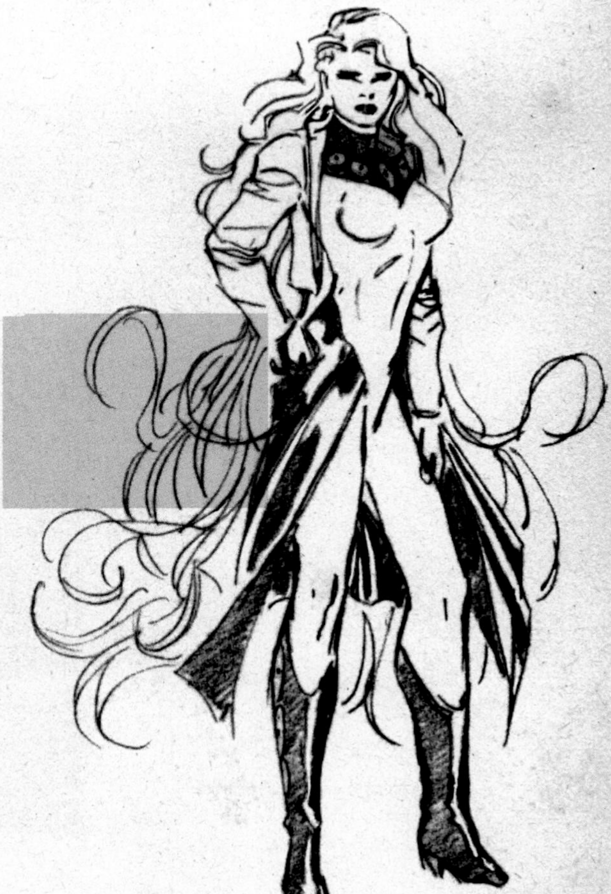

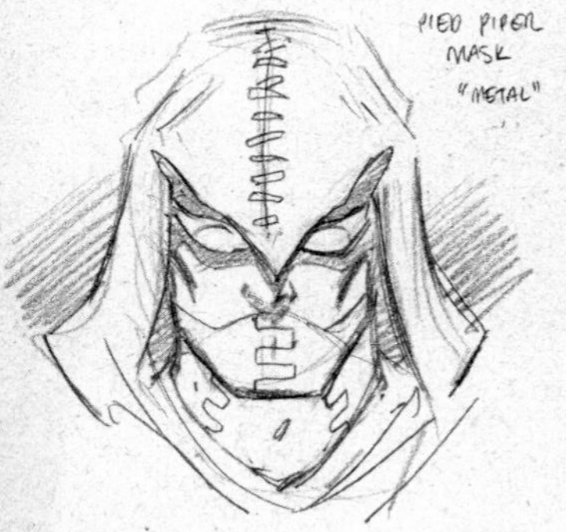
PIED PIPER MASK "METAL"

PIED PIPER

Pied Piper's new look resulted in a rivalry between he and Central City's "hero," Citizen Cold.

FLASH
LYING
IN
RUBBLE,
TORN,
BEATEN,
ABOUT
TO
BE
DEALT
FINAL
BLOW
BY
AQUAMAN
+
WONDER
WOMAN

ELECTRICITY COMING FROM FLASH + HIS SYMBOL !!

A sketch of the fourth cover by Andy.

FLASHPOINT #5

REVERSE
FLASH
CRUSHING
FLASH'S
SYMBOL/
ELECTRICITY
COMING
OUT
OF
IT.

A sketch of the fifth cover by Andy.
Throughout all of the covers, lightning
is the consistent motif unifying them.